Five Empresses

Court Life in Eighteenth-Century Russia

Evgenii V. Anisimov

Translated by Kathleen Carroll

Westport, Connecticut
London

Library of Congress Cataloging-in-Publication Data

Anisimov, E. V. (Evgenii Viktorovich)
  [Zhenshchiny na rossiiskom prestole. English]
  Five empresses: court life in eighteenth-century Russia / Evgenii V. Anisimov ;
translated by Kathleen Carroll.
     p. cm.
  Includes bibliographical references and index.
  ISBN 0-275-98464-8 (alk. paper)
    1. Empresses—Russia—Biography. 2. Women—Russia—Biography. 3. Russia—
History—18th century. I. Title: 5 empresses. II. Title.
DK127.4.A5513 2004
947'06'092—dc22
  [B]   2004050588

British Library Cataloguing in Publication Data is available.

Copyright © 2004 by Bronze Horseman Literary Agency

Library of Congress Catalog Card Number: 2004050588
ISBN: 0-275-98464-8

First published in 2004

Praeger Publishers, 88 Post Road West, Westport, CT 06881
An imprint of Greenwood Publishing Group, Inc.
www.praeger.com

Printed in the United States of America

The paper used in this book complies with the
Permanent Paper Standard issued by the National
Information Standards Organization (Z39.48–1984).

10 9 8 7 6 5 4 3 2 1

Contents

Acknowledgments

The author wishes to express his gratitude to those who worked on the English edition of his book. Kathleen Carroll, the primary translator of the Russian, had the sensitivity and skill to keep the lively style of the original. She benefited from the assistance of a native speaker Nikolai Konstantinovich Sergeev to get the gist of the often colloquial and idiomatic Russian style of the original. The editor and manager of the project, Iurii Sergeevich Pamfilov, ensured the accuracy and literary quality of the translation. Clarifying with the author the most knotty questions, he showed real linguistic intuition. Rachel Williams of the Binghamton University Center for Research in Translation translated many quotations from eighteenth-century French into good modern English. With patience and precision Irina Dekopova corrected on the computer a translation that went through several stages of editing and revision. Natalia Zheleznaia expertly transferred to computer printed illustrations from nineteenth-century editions, so that we could publish images of some of the places and the people appearing in our history. The translation and literary agency (Bronze Horseman) stinted neither time nor resources to produce a first-rate translation. Heather Ruland Staines, history editor at Praeger-Greenwood Publishers, recognized the general and scholarly interest of the work, and arranged courteously and efficiently for its publication. House of Equations, Inc. skillfully turned the manuscript into book form, solving problems with alacrity and meeting a difficult schedule.

CHAPTER 1

The Cinderella from Livland

(Catherine I)

Emperor Peter the Great died in the early morning of January 28, 1725, in his small bedroom-study on the second floor of the Winter Palace. His death did not come easy. Excruciating pain wracked his body; the best efforts of experienced doctors brought no relief, and death was to him a deliverance from unbearable suffering.[1]

But the first Russian emperor, like almost anyone else, did not want to die. More than once he had looked death straight in the eye on battlefields and stormy seas; yet now he was clinging desperately to life and, according to one contemporary, "grew very fainthearted and even displayed a petty fear of death."[2] He prayed fervently and frenziedly, confessing and taking communion several times. Attending priests did not leave his bedside; he wept and clutched their hands. It seemed as if he were using the Orthodox priests' brocade chasubles, gleaming in the faint candlelight, as a screen against death, which stared at him steadily from the darkness of night.

The tsar, always merciless toward any violators of his strict laws, gave the order to release criminals from jails and to forgive government officials their debts and fines, an act that, according to Russian custom, was supposed to save his soul. Until the very end he had hope in God's mercy as well as in his own vitality, for he was only fifty-two years old and there were so many ideas and plans for the future ahead . . .

The teary-eyed empress Catherine Alekseevna, a stout, comely woman, did not leave the bedside of the dying tsar in the crowded study (big as a giant, the tsar was fond of small cozy rooms with low ceilings). She tried to comfort him, but he hardly looked in her direction. It can be said with certainty that, during the last hours of his life, agonizing contemplation of Russia's future tormented the great reformer no less than his physical anguish. It was for her sake he had toiled so in merciless disregard of his own strength and health; in her name he had forced his subjects to study, build, sail the seas, die in battles and in grueling labor. Peter had created a great empire and now, leaving life, he was in despair. He did not know to whom to bequeath this great heritage: the ancestral throne of the Muscovite tsars exalted by him with the imperial crown in 1721; the young capital of the empire, St. Petersburg; a victorious two hundred thousand–man army; a

Peter the Great. From A. V. Morozov, *Katalog moego sobraniia russkikh gravirovannykh i litografirovannykh portretov* (Catalogue of My Collection of Engraved and Lithographed Portraits), vol. 3 (Moscow, 1913), folio CCCXXXIX.

formidable navy; a country so vast it stretched from the Baltic Sea to the Pacific Ocean. And there was no one in the world who could alleviate either the corporal or the spiritual agony of the great tsar. Relatives, associates, and old friends crowded around him. But in his hour of death there was no one there for him to rely on, no one on whom his gaze could rest hopefully.

Legend has it that Peter tried to write a will just before his death, but succeeded in scratching only two words on the paper: "Leave everything . . ." and then he lost control of his hand. Facts dispute this legend's authenticity. The last word that Archbishop Feofan Prokopovich heard the emperor utter was the word "later," which was accompanied by one last impatient and abrupt gesture, as if to say: "Go away everybody, leave me alone; I will make my decision later." That is probably what he wanted to tell the people who stood over him.

But "later" never came. The tsar who had ruled Russia for more than thirty years died at 5:15 A.M. on January 28. It was the end of a great era, and new, troubled times lay ahead.

* * *

Actually, those times had arrived several hours before Peter's death. Beyond the walls of the study where he lay dying, confusion and alarm prevailed. The absence of a will by Peter the Great created a dramatic situation. The fate of the imperial throne would have to be decided in a clash of court factions, small groups of nobility, high-ranking government officials, and generals. There were two rival factions. One comprised the tsar-reformer's closest associates, statesmen who came to power thanks to their abilities and Peter's particular favor. He surrounded himself with only the most loyal and energetic people, regardless of their birth.

Considered first among Peter's associates was His Most Serene Prince Aleksandr Menshikov. About the same age as Peter, he was for many years the tsar's favorite. The illiterate son of a court stableman, he started out as a batman, and later rose to field marshal general, and in another sphere a member of the British Royal Society. Apparently, the president of the society, the great Isaac Newton, could not refuse the persistent and impudent petitioner from St. Petersburg without offending his sovereign, Peter the Great.

Menshikov's allies were very influential people: the chancellor of the empire, Count Gavriil Golovkin; Archbishop Feofan Prokopovich, who administered the Russian Orthodox Church; the chief of the Secret Chancery, Count Peter Tolstoi; the procurator-general of the Senate, Count Pavel Iaguzhinskii; and Aleksei Makarov, Peter the Great's personal secretary. These were "new" persons whose power and influence could come to an end with Peter's death. So in spite of some internal animosity they immediately rallied in unison behind Empress Catherine, Peter's wife, who was made of the same stuff as they. Like them she was not of noble birth, owed her position to Peter's graces, and was full of initiative and determination.

On one of the rare occasions when Catherine left her dying husband's bedroom, these dignitaries held a meeting; several Guards' officers were also present. Catherine's sad expression, the moving and affectionate words she used when addressing them—forsaken fledglings of Peter's nest—and, finally, generous promises, all had an effect, and the Guards pledged to help Catherine ascend the throne by thwarting Grand Duke Peter Alekseevich, the candidate from the other faction.

The grand duke was Peter the Great's grandson and the son of the late tsarevich Aleksei Petrovich. Though he was only nine years old, he constituted a menace to the new people. On his side was the tradition of succession to the throne through the direct male line of descent, in this case from grandfather to grandson; he was also supported by the high-born nobility—the Dolgorukii and Golitsyn princes, and others who were discontented with Peter's reforms. Also on the side of Peter's grandson were all those who sought an easing of the rigid policies of the regime and hoped for a respite from the furious pace of reform that Peter the Great had started in Russia.

Both court factions were prepared to fight for power, but everyone was waiting for Peter's eyes to close forever. This is how Count Henning Frederick Bassewitz from Holstein, a participant and witness of the events that occurred in the dramatic early morning hours of the 28th of January, described the situation: "We awaited the moment when the monarch would breathe his last so that we could set to work. As long as there was still a sign of life in him nobody dared to do anything: so deep were the respect and fear which this hero evoked in the people."[3] This is accurate, for the magic force of Peter the Great was strong. Reason also called for waiting—it had happened in history so many times before that a dying ruler suddenly recovered, and woe to those who had thought that his last hour had come.

Then the clock struck five and shortly thereafter doctors announced an end to the agony—Peter the Great no longer belonged to the people: he now belonged to God and to history. The final act of the political drama began. Both actors and spectators gathered in a brightly illuminated hall of the Winter Palace: senators, presidents of colleges (government departments), church hierarchs, generals, and senior officers. The crowd murmured excitedly. Suddenly all fell silent—the doors opened and into the room hurried Menshikov, Golovkin, and Makarov, followed by the empress herself. Her voice choked with grief, Catherine broke the anticipated but startling news that their sovereign, her beloved husband, "has passed to his eternal rest," leaving behind his orphaned subjects. Then she composed herself, as she had done so often, and spoke courageously and resolutely. At the end of her short speech she made it known that she would competently continue the policies of the late emperor, be attendant to her subjects, and promote the welfare of the empire, whose throne Peter the Great had shared with her.

Having done everything she could do in that situation, supported by courtiers and in tears, Catherine left the room. Then Menshikov stepped forward and successfully conducted the night meeting. When it became known that the dying Peter had neither written nor said anything regarding his successor, everybody was anxious. In such cases, following the old Russian tradition, the new autocrat was to be appointed by a "state" general assembly, implying a council of the highest civil and ecclesiastical dignitaries. However, this type of collective decision would be a grave disadvantage to Catherine's faction, since the majority would probably speak for transfer of the throne to Grand Duke Peter. Therefore, Menshikov and his supporters began to persuade all those present that the throne belonged to Catherine, the emperor's widow, who had already received the imperial crown from Peter the Great in the spring of 1724.

He failed, however, to convince the opponents of the humbly born empress. Seeing that many were vacillating, the grand duke's faction began to

Empress Catherine I. From the journal *Russkaia starina* (Russia of Old) (St. Petersburg, 1890), tip-in plate.

persuade those assembled in the hall to swear allegiance to Peter Alekseevich, for there could be no doubt of his right to occupy the throne. Tempers flared; it seemed that no compromise could be reached. And then Menshikov's faction resorted to their secret weapon—the Most Serene Prince had summoned the Preobrazhenskii and Semenovskii Guards Regiments. The roll of regimental drums was suddenly heard in the street outside the Winter Palace. Everybody rushed to the windows and saw through the windowpanes covered with frost the Guards in full-dress uniform. Prince Nikita Repnin, president of the College of War and supporter of Grand Duke Peter, tried to find out who dared to summon the Guards without his order, but he was rudely cut off, and the excited soldiers filled the hall. The proposals made by the grand duke's faction could not be heard, for the Guards shouted triumphantly in favor of their "Mother-tsarina" and threatened impudently to "break the heads of boyars" should they not obey Catherine.

Seizing an opportune moment, Menshikov's voice rose above the crowd: "Long live our most august sovereign Empress Catherine!" "Viva Empress Catherine," cried the Guards. As Bassewitz writes in his book, "these last words were immediately resounded by all those present, each wanting to appear to the rest as if he were joining in of his own free will, and not merely imitating the example of others."[4] It all ended quietly and without bloodshed. Catherine I succeeded to the throne, and by 8 A.M. a manifesto had been issued proclaiming her succession, and the Guards were given vodka.

Thus it was that on January 28, 1725, the Guards played a political role for the first time in the drama of Russian history. Peter the Great created the first two Guards regiments in 1692 in opposition to the *strel'tsy,* the privileged infantry regiments of the Muscovite tsars, who by the end of the seventeenth century had begun to interfere in politics. Peter referred to the strel'tsy scornfully as janissaries. He did have reason to hate them—all his life he remembered one terrible May morning in 1682 when he was ten years old—obeying the order of Peter's elder half sister and rival Sophia, the strel'tsy, intoxicated with blood and a sense of impunity, hurled Peter's closest relatives and faithful servants down from the high Kremlin porch onto the spears of their bloodthirsty comrades crowded below.

But no sooner had Peter, the founder and first colonel of the Preobrazhenskii Guards Regiment, passed on than his favorites in green full-dress uniforms turned into the new janissaries. The history of the Russian Guards of the eighteenth century is full of contradictions. Well-equipped, expertly trained, and armed with the latest weapons, the Guards became the pride of the Russian throne and its source of support throughout the century. The outcome of battles, campaigns, and entire wars had often been decided in Russia's favor thanks to the courage, steadfastness, and selflessness of the Guards. Many a generation of Russians felt deep patriotic pride when they saw the severe splendor of the Guards regiments as they marched

Aleksandr D. Menshikov. From A. V. Morozov,
*Katalog moego sobraniia russkikh gravirovannykh
i litografirovannykh portretov* (Catalogue of My
Collection of Engraved and Lithographed Portraits),
vol. 3 (Moscow, 1913), folio CCLXII.

across the Field of Mars, the main venue of military celebrations in St. Petersburg in the eighteenth and nineteenth centuries.

Yet there exists another, less heroic page in the chronicles of the Imperial Guards. The Guards—handsome blades, duelists, and dandies, spoiled by the attention of urban and provincial ladies—constituted an especially privileged military group within the Russian army, which had its own traditions, customs, and mentality. The Guards' primary responsibility was to maintain the peace and security of the court and royal family. Posted outside and inside the tsar's palace, the Guards saw the seamy side of court life, which appeared magical to millions of simple subjects. They saw the favorites stealing by into the royal bedroom suites; they heard the gossip and outrageous quarrels that were an inherent part of life at court. The Guards did not tremble in reverence before the dazzling courtiers and all their gold and diamonds. Having grown accustomed to all this, splendid ceremonies bored them, and they had their own opinion about everything.

Also of note was the Guards' exaggerated idea of their role in life at court, in the capital, and in the fate of Russia. Meanwhile, it became known that the "fierce Russian janissaries" could be controlled through flattery, promises, and bribes. Smart weavers of court intrigue and adventure sparked the Guards' passions and directed them so skillfully that the handsome men with mustaches did not have the slightest suspicion of their pitiful role as puppets.

The Guards were equally dangerous to those who made use of their services. Quite often the power of emperors and their top dignitaries was taken hostage by this uncontrollable and capricious crowd of Guards. The ominous role that the Guards were to play in Russian history was well understood by the penetrating Jean-Jacques Campredon, the French envoy in Petersburg, who wrote to his ruler, Louis XV, immediately following Catherine I's succession: "The decision of the Guards is law here."[5] And that was the truth. The eighteenth century went down in Russian history as the century of palace coups. The Guards carried out the overthrows, as the reader will see while reading the stories of the heroines in this book. And this dubious tradition began on that dark January night in 1725.

The day of January 28, 1725, saw St. Petersburg under the rule of a new sovereign. Who was she, this Empress Catherine I?

"Catherine is Swedish!" asserted the historian Natalia Belozerskaia.[6] In her opinion, the future empress of Russia was born in Sweden into the family of an army quartermaster, Johann Rabe. When she was baptized into the Lutheran faith, she was christened Martha. After Rabe's death, the family moved to Livland, a Swedish province at that time, and settled in Riga. Martha's mother soon died, and she was placed in an orphanage. Later she was taken in by Pastor Glück, a person well known in the small Livland town of Marienburg (now Aluksne, located on the road between Riga and Pskov).

There are several facts which support Belozerskaia's opinion. In one of Peter's letters to his wife, while congratulating her on the anniversary of the taking of the first Swedish fortress in the Northern War, Nöteborg on the Neva River, in 1702, he writes jokingly that with the capture of the fortress "the Russians have gained a foothold in *your* lands."[7] In 1725, during a conversation with Campredon, Catherine, not wanting those nearby to understand the subject of their conversation, abruptly switched over to the Swedish language, in which the French diplomat was fluent.

The opponents of Catherine's Swedish origin argue with reason that there is nothing necessarily of Swedish nationality in the above facts: Livland had been a Swedish province for about 100 years, the Swedish language being the official language on its territory; and Martha-Catherine was technically a subject of the king of Sweden. This explains both Peter's joke and Catherine's knowledge of the Swedish language. Most historians are now convinced that Catherine's name was Martha Skavronskaia and that she was born on April 5, 1684, in Livland, a region inhabited by the Latvians, and descended from Latvian peasants. When she became an orphan she was taken into Pastor Glück's home.

We do not know much about Martha's early life. We do not know how she was brought up and what education she was given in her childhood and youth. She probably had only a rudimentary knowledge of reading, writing, and arithmetic. Catherine's literacy is open to question—she learned only to speak Russian, not to write it. Her letters to Peter, even the most intimate ones, are all written by the hand of a court scribe. One thing is clear, though: the orphaned girl was a maid in Pastor Glück's house; she worked in the kitchen and at the laundry. Nature had endowed her with physical stamina, and by the age of eighteen she looked healthy and beautiful, attracting the attention of young men aspiring to take her hand in marriage.

In fact, Martha's youth coincided with a sad epoch in the history of Livland. In 1700, the Northern War broke out; Russia set out against Sweden, and in 1701, the Russian army, under the command of Field Marshal Boris Sheremetev, moved like a thundercloud across southern Livland. Peter had no thoughts of annexing the Swedish provinces at that time. Therefore, the objective of the Russian army in 1701–1702 was to destroy this traditional breadbasket of the Swedish kingdom. Refugees from the Russian-Swedish border brought bad news to Marienburg: the Russians had destroyed everything in their path—farmsteads, buildings, crops. They took cattle and people to Russia. The principal forces of Charles XII, the king of Sweden, were concentrated in Poland, which turned into the main theater of war; the weak corps of General Schlippenbach defending Livland was unable to protect its inhabitants from the invasion of a large and cruel enemy army.

Yet despite the dangers of invasion, life went on. In the summer of 1702, Martha married a Swedish soldier, a trumpeter. They were not destined to partake in familial happiness. In August, when Martha's husband was on a mission in Riga, Sheremetev's forces approached Marienburg intending to besiege it, and the war, which was to change Martha's life, was now right on the threshold of her home.

Before the Russian forces had time to besiege Marienburg, Major Til, the commandant of this old, weakly defended fortress, having appraised his unenviable position, decided to surrender, appealing to the mercies of his conqueror and stipulating honorable conditions of capitulation, namely, free withdrawal for the garrison and the town's people. Sheremetev accepted these terms. Til came out of the fortress and signed a treaty of surrender. The Russian forces began entering the town just as the citizens were leaving their homes. Everything was going well, quietly and peacefully, until an unforeseen event occurred, which changed drastically the fate of thousands of people, including Martha.

Let us take a look at Peter the Great's journals or daily notes, which contain entries about even the most minor events of the Northern War of 1700–1721: "The Commandant, Major Til, accompanied by two captains, came out to our supply train to surrender the town, under an agreement according to which the citizens started to leave. Meanwhile, Artillery Captain Wolf and a lance-cadet entered the fortress powder-magazine (the cadet had also forced his wife to accompany him), where they set fire to the gunpowder and blew themselves up. Many people from both sides were killed by the explosion, and as a punishment for this, the garrison and the citizens were not released under the treaty but taken prisoner instead."[8]

The deafening explosion shook the earth, and sent fragments of the fortress structures hurling onto the heads of the Russian soldiers. Sheremetev tore up the treaty of voluntary surrender of the fortress. This meant that henceforth Marienburg was considered a town taken by storm and thus given to the conquering soldiers for plunder. The citizens and the garrison, one and all, were considered war prisoners. Russian soldiers rushed into the town. Cries and shooting were heard here and there. The soldiers pillaged the houses, seizing all their inhabitants—men, women, and children. They took the stolen goods back to camp, and the prisoners as well. Brisk trade and interchange of captured spoils took place immediately.

The fate of war prisoners in Russia in those days was a sad one. According to an old custom they became the slaves of those who captured them. Here is an account written in Moscow by de Bruin, a foreign traveler and diplomat, when the Livland campaign ended: "About eight hundred Swedish prisoners, men, women, and children, were brought to Moscow on September 14. First they were sold for three and four guldens per head, but in a few days the price was raised to twenty and even thirty guldens. With prices so cheap, foreigners gladly bought the prisoners, the latter being very pleased with this, for foreigners bought them to make use of their services only during the war period; after that the prisoners would be set free. Russians also bought a lot of these prisoners, but the most unfortunate were those who fell into the hands of the Tartars, for the latter would take and hold them in servitude—a miserable state indeed."[9]

Martha found herself among the Livland captives. But she was not among those who were taken to Moscow as live goods to be sold dirt-cheap to Tartars. Another destiny awaited her . . .

* * *

"Catherine is not Russian," Vasilii Kobylin, a retired corporal of the Ingermanland Regiment, told his friends (among whom there was naturally an informer) in 1724. "And we know how she was taken into captivity and brought under a flag with nothing on but a shirt, and put under guard, and our sentry officer dressed her in a caftan. Together with Prince Menshikov she must have used magic roots to bewitch His Majesty [Peter]."[10] Such remarks were quite typical and often repeated among the simple people. As often happens with any rumor circulating in a crowd, there was some truth to it.

Martha, together with other prisoners, was brought to the center of the regiment camp. Here, near the regimental banner, with the guard on duty, the booty was being piled up, and the spoils from the captured fortress were being exchanged and sold. The soldiers who had no *pomest'ia* (service estates) hurried to get rid of their captives, selling them for almost nothing to their well-to-do comrades and officers. One contemporary, relating the words of an eyewitness, states that a certain Captain Bauer got Martha as a present from a brownnosing soldier who figured that in doing so he would be promoted. Thereupon the captain himself, for the same reason, presented the beautiful girl to Field Marshal Sheremetev. We do not know how Martha felt about it, being not so very long ago a free person, but we can presume her plight was not very pleasant.

Martha spent about six months in the household of Boris Sheremetev, who was fifty years old, an aged man in those days. She was registered as a laundress, but actually she served as a concubine. In late 1702 or early 1703 she ended up with Aleksandr Menshikov. We do not know how Peter's bold and bright favorite obtained Martha; but it is quite likely that he simply took away the attractive girl from the field marshal, and probably even put the old man to shame for such indecent voluptuousness at his venerable age. Menshikov rarely wasted time with explanations to his sovereign's subjects; he was known for his curtness and impudence.

Martha did not stay long at Menshikov's. By that time the Most Serene Prince had decided to settle down, and had chosen a bride, Dar'ia Arsen'eva, from a respectable noble family. Any connection with a Livland concubine might do harm to Menshikov, who had set his mind on a respectable future. In short, Peter, a regular visitor to his favorite's home, was introduced to Martha; their eyes met, and Russian history took an entirely new direction.

Let us once again digress for a moment and ponder the vicissitudes of life and fate. The reader cannot yet have forgotten the crazed Captain Wolf, who had blown up the powder-magazine in the fortress of Marienburg. This unconscionable act cut short the lives of many people, but it also had a direct effect on the fate of Russia. We must always remember and keep in mind that every moment of history is latent with several possible versions of its continuation, and our choice of paths often depends on mere chance, on favorable or unfavorable coincidence. There is, of course, a strong and stable "wind of history" that blows in a certain set and often even predictable direction. But still much depends on chance. Indeed, if Wolf had changed his mind at the last moment or had not found the keys to the powder-magazine, then the citizens and the garrison would have peacefully left the fortress and moved, in a crowd, along the dusty road toward Riga to reach it in two or three days' time. Here Martha would have found her husband and in 1710, when the Russian forces approached the walls of the Livland capital, she would probably have moved together with hundreds of other refugees from Riga to Sweden or elsewhere, and her ordinary fate would have been dissolved in thousands of similar fates of soldiers' wives and widows. However, either by accident or by the will of God, things turned out differently: Wolf performed his senseless act; Martha became the prisoner of the Russians and later their empress.

Corporal Kobylin suggests that Catherine charmed the tsar with the help of Menshikov and witchcraft. Of course, there was no love-potion whatsoever, yet there are two facts that deserve our particular attention. First, Catherine and Menshikov remained close friends throughout their lives. Later on, when Catherine joined the tsar on his campaigns, she left that which she treasured most of all, her children, daughters Anna, Elizaveta, Natalia, and son Peter, under the charge of the Most Serene Prince and his family. And she did not have to worry about them, for reliable Menshikov had never let her down: in his rich and comfortable palace, in the company of his daughters and a son, under the supervision of his wife Dar'ia and her sister Varvara, Catherine's children felt at home; they were surrounded with good care and attention. Each time she opened a letter from St. Petersburg, Catherine learned that her children "are in good health." The empress never forgot Aleksandr Menshikov. She wrote joking letters to him and gave him presents. One time when she was with the tsar abroad she sent Menshikov a present, a camisole, and in the accompanying letter wrote: "I am sending to Your Worship a camisole of the latest fashion that has appeared here. Only four persons have such camisoles in their possession; they are: His Majesty the tsar; the Austrian King Charles VI; the King of England; and you yourself." This old friend of a stableman's son knew how to flatter ambitious Aleksandr, who dreamt of a small and modest but real ducal crown.

When the light-fingered Menshikov was caught in an act of theft from the state treasury, and the gallows were already looming over him, the empress came to his aid and dissuaded the tsar from punishing the majestic embezzler of public funds. And Menshikov repaid Catherine in kind, bowing his head before the tsaritsa, and executing her imperial will attentively and with due respect. She always had his reliable shoulder to lean on.

Their bond was not based on hidden romance, nor on fond recollections of a past romance. What united Menshikov and Catherine was their similar fate. Both of common birth, they were despised and condemned by the envious nobility, and survived only by helping one another.

As for Menshikov, so for Martha-Catherine the tsar's affection was abiding. According to Corporal Kobylin's account, Peter had such a fervid and lasting love that many contemporaries believed it to be the effect of some love-potion. How could it be otherwise? How else could a Livland prisoner lure the formidable tsar, who later jokingly wrote to this effect in a letter to his wife: "That's what you, Eve's daughters, do to old men!" However, for everything there is a non-supernatural explanation, and this explanation is found in the life Peter had led up to that very day when he met Martha at Menshikov's.

Peter's family life had been a total failure. In 1689, at the age of seventeen, he was married, without being asked his wishes, to Evdokia (Eudoxia) Lopukhina, who was then twenty years old. It was a marriage of convenience arranged by the court advisers serving Peter's mother, the widowed Tsaritsa Natalia. Tsaritsa Natalia was at that moment engaged in intrigue against the party of the current ruler Tsarevna Sophia, who sought to block Peter and his side of the family from power. From the onset, the newly married couple became puppets in the hands of court intrigues and naturally nobody gave much heed to their feelings.

Peter and Dunia (this was the Tsaritsa Evdokia Fedorovna's diminutive name) lived together for about ten years. Dunia gave birth to three sons, of which only one, the Tsarevich Aleksei, grew to adulthood (to his own misfortune). Peter and Dunia's marriage was not a happy one. It was obvious that Dunia was not a suitable match for Peter; they seemed to be living in different times, in different epochs: Peter lived in eighteenth-century Europe, characterized by its freedom, openness, and pragmatism, while Dunia was brought up in the traditions of a patriarchal Orthodox family and remained in seventeenth-century Russia, where God-fearing women meekly adhered to the traditions and commands of the Domostroi.

Peter and Dunia's family drama reflected the social and moral rupture resulting from radical reform and revolution. Like an earthquake, this breakup cleft every class of society in Russia, even splitting the very souls of the Russian people, filling them with mounting uneasiness, anxiety, and fear of the future. Russian families, including that of the tsar himself, were rent. The values inherent in Dunia's world view clashed with her husband's changing values.

The spouses' personalities did not match up, either. Peter's impetuous, unceremonious, and self-centered nature collided with the stubbornness and resentfulness of the arrogant, obstinate, and strong-willed person that Dunia was. Peter left the palace more and more frequently, visiting shipyards, participating in battle drills, setting out on long journeys, while Dunia, unwilling to change the centuries-old lifestyle of a Russian tsaritsa, stayed behind in Moscow waiting for her husband's return. As the years passed, the gulf separating Peter and his wife grew wider and wider. Taking into account Peter's interests and tastes, he could only be happy with a different type of woman, one who dressed fashionably (by European standards) and was a lively dance partner and a courageous companion during exhausting campaigns, as well as a helpmate in his incessant toils to change Russia. Dunia could not fulfill this role, and in fact was not the least interested in trying to do so.

They broke off their relations in 1698. Returning from his European travels, the tsar gave orders that the wearisome Dunia be sent to a monastery and never again set foot in Moscow. The patriarch and several of Peter's closest associates were to carry out this tough mission. With great difficulty, practically by force, Dunia was transported to Suzdal' and confined in the Pokrovskii Monastery there.

Twenty-nine years old and full of strength, Dunia desperately resisted being buried alive in the crypt of a monastery cell. She wanted to live. Every day for two and a half months a special envoy from Peter visited Dunia, trying to persuade her to take the veil. At last, with extreme reluctance, she agreed and became the nun Elena. However, she did not resign herself fully to this fate and almost immediately refused to wear monastic clothing and to lead the life of a nun.

In 1710, she began a love affair with Major Stepan Glebov, who was assigned for a time to Suzdal'. Later on, the authorities intercepted Dunia's love-letters, full of flaming passion and melancholy, which testify to her energetic, ardent, lively, and sensitive nature: "Have you forgotten me so soon? Have I failed to please you? Did I not shed enough tears on your face, your arms, and every part of your body, your wrists and ankles . . . You are my light, my soul, my joy! The cursed hour of our parting must be near. I wish my soul would leave my body! Oh, my light! How can I live on this Earth without you? How to stay alive? God alone knows how much I care for you. Wear my ring, my darling, love me, I'll have another just like it made for myself . . . I shall not leave you till the end of my days."[11] This affair did not last long: Glebov left Suzdal' and forgot Dunia. However, in 1718, when Peter learned of this secret love, he punished them most cruelly: following excruciating torture at the tsar's decree, Glebov was impaled. The former tsaritsa was transferred to a monastic cell in Ladoga, a small town near Lake Ladoga.

The tsaritsa's dramatic story, banished, disgraced, and placed in a monastery, had left an impression in people's memory. The political police had arrested many people who had expressed sympathy for Evdokia, declaring that she was the one legitimate wife of the Russian tsar and that the time of her liberation would eventually come. Among the Secret Chancery records there is a song about Evdokia, which people sang at the risk of being sent into exile to Siberia, having their tongues cut out, or being executed. Here are some words from the song: "A young maid I am and sitting near my love/My dear friend's scolding me, reproving me/He's ordering me to join a monastery." The song ends with the young nun's words in answer to the question asked by noble travelers who have come to the monastery: "I have been made a nun by the tsar himself/Forced to take the veil by Peter the First/Through his fierce snake."

"The fierce snake" lived in Kokui, the Foreign Settlement in Moscow. She was beautiful and convivial. Her name was Anna Mons, or Anchen. She was the daughter of a wine merchant, and Peter had long been having an affair with her. She was the one Peter began visiting openly after his return from abroad. Anna had been introduced to Peter one day by his closest friend, Francis Lefort from Switzerland, a jovial, kind, and gregarious man. When Peter no longer considered it necessary to conceal his liaison with Anna, he got rid of Dunia.

Life with Anchen, however, failed to bring Peter happiness. A charming, fair-haired beauty, only her appearance matched Peter's ideal of a woman whom he could love. And although she could sing German songs merrily and dance the minuet gracefully, she lived essentially in another world, one that was far away from that of Peter.

Anchen was a rather uncultured burgher who sought a well-off, prosaic, and quiet life in a comfortable home. She probably dreamed of growing beautiful flowers in window boxes, of looking after the children, of running an efficient household (the traits of a practical housewife can be seen in her letters to Peter). Her goal seemed to be to sit by the fireplace knitting and waiting for a Michael or Klaus to come home from work or the pub.

I want the reader to believe me: I am far from being ironical or condemnatory of Anchen's choice. Each is free to choose his own fate. Admittedly, Anchen was a remarkable woman. She was clever enough to understand that Peter's love would open for her the way to fame, wealth, and honor. She could even become the Russian tsaritsa! Peter did have serious intentions. In 1707, several years after breaking up with her, Peter confessed disappointedly to the Prussian envoy Keiserling, who was asking the tsar's permission to marry Anchen, that he "had been bringing Miss Mons up for himself with the sincere intention of marrying her."[12] And this is credible, for he did actually marry the ignoble Catherine, making her, a former laundress, tsaritsa. In short, the liaison with the tsar was a fantastic chance for Anchen, but she did not take advantage of it.

I believe the secret is simple: Anchen did not love Peter, and she could not accept his rather wild habits and difficult nature. She did not want to share with the tsar the wild, restless, often drunken and dangerous life of an eternal wanderer in his own country. For a long time Peter refused to understand this. In 1702, the Saxonian envoy to Russia, Königseck, drowned, and among his papers were found love-letters from Anchen. The tsar was beside himself with bitterness and vexation. On his orders, Anchen and her relatives were placed under house arrest for several years.

After 1702 Peter no longer paid visits to Anchen, but we know for sure that it took Peter a long time to get over his first love. Martha-Catherine had become part of Peter's life with the help of her patron Menshikov, who did everything he could to prevent rumors about Anchen's new flames from reaching the tsar so as not to reopen old wounds and create vain illusions. Menshikov's efforts had even caused a great diplomatic scandal when the prince physically threw Keiserling out when the latter came to see the tsar about his marriage, the servants roared with laughter at the sight. The reason for Menshikov's uneasiness is clear: Martha, who by that time had received the Orthodox name of "Catherine," was still a newcomer in Peter's heart, and her position was therefore still unstable.

Catherine had nothing in common with Dunia and Anchen. Being uprooted all too early from the land to which she was accustomed, having experienced both good and evil, she possessed the rare ability of adapting herself to life. She could just as easily have remained the faithful wife of a Swedish trumpeter, the uncomplaining laundress of an old field marshal, or Menshikov's lover. With the same calmness she accepted her predestination to become tsaritsa. Everything in her life had depended on circumstances. Her humble tree of life grew by submitting to the contours of life, putting forth in any poor soil her strong roots, and eventually coming to bloom.

Adaptability to life's circumstances is an important character trait, but obviously this was not enough to win Peter's heart as Martha-Catherine did. The tsar had never been a gloomy misogynist. He was always surrounded by plenty of those who, in Petrine Russia, were called *metressy,* that is, mistresses. He took them with him on his travels and enjoyed their company in his leisure. Many of these undemanding women would probably have gladly adapted themselves to the manners and habits of their austere ruler, but it was not that easy.

The history of Anna Mons reveals that the great tsar, a cruel and awe-inspiring man, was in many respects helpless and vulnerable. A man of sincere, simple, and deep feelings, he was at the same time austere and distrustful, paying no heed to others' words and deeds. In order to penetrate his iron soul, to win his trust, it was not enough to put on airs, be obsequiously accommodating, and undress obligingly. Martha intuitively had found the one true way to Peter's heart, and starting out as one of his mistresses, she slowly but surely allayed his distrust and fear of making another mistake, and ultimately did achieve her goal.

The first mention of Catherine's name occurs in a letter which Menshikov wrote in the spring of 1705 during his stay with Peter in Kovno (Kaunas), Lithuania. War was raging. In that letter sent to Moscow and addressed to his fiancée, Dar'ia Arsen'eva, Menshikov conveyed Peter's order to send to Kovno "Katerina Trubachova and two other girls immediately" so that they could put the tsar's modest wardrobe in order, and to "wash and mend" some of his clothes.[13] As we see, Catherine, whose surname was derived from her first husband's military profession (he was a trumpeter, and the word *Trubachova* means "trumpeter's"), is mentioned among others. But noteworthy is the fact that girls for mending and washing were to be sent from Moscow. Apparently, either girls were not available any nearer, or these girls were better at washing and mending. That Catherine was Peter's former servant is clear from one of the empress's jokes in a letter written many years later hinting at the tsar's new mistresses, wherein she wrote that she, an "old washwoman," might be useful to him one day as well.

Around 1705, Catherine's position began to change. Peter—and this needs to be emphasized—officially recognized the children she had borne. In March 1705, the tsar wrote to Dar'ia Arsen'eva and her sister Varvara, Catherine's girlfriends: "Be so kind as to look after my Petrushka; see to it that *my* son receives clothing, drink and food."[14] In the fall of that same year, Catherine gave birth to a second son, Pavel; in one of her letters she ordered the following signature to be put: "Along with two others" (*Sam-tret'*), which meant she and the two children. This was an allusion to the ancient Russian saying at harvest time: you plant one seed and reap three. Peter and Pavel died in infancy from children's diseases that, in those days, mowed down children like soft grass all over the world. These losses, however, had no ill effect on relations between the tsar and his Livland captive. His affection for her grew ever stronger and he always found time to send her a small present or a short note about his life. He addressed his letters to Preobrazhenskoe, a Moscow suburb, where Catherine spent her first several years in the royal palace.

Preobrazhenskoe was Peter's paternal home. He had spent his childhood and youth in the Kremlin, from which Tsarevna Sophia ousted him. His mother, Tsaritsa Natalia, lived in Preobrazhenskoe until her death in 1694. His rise to power and glory had started there. In the early years of the Northern War, Preobrazhenskoe became home for Peter's sister, Natalia, the person he felt closest to after his mother's death. Born in 1673, Natalia was one year younger than her brother, and had nothing in common with her sister-in-law, Tsaritsa Evdokia. Natalia was the first of the vast Romanov family to accept not only without resistance but with obvious pleasure all that Peter's reforms offered—European clothes, finery, fancy hair, unusual customs, and entertainment. Tsarevna Natalia did not lock herself in her chamber and she did not enter a monastery, as was usual for unmarried tsars' daughters in the seventeenth century. Instead, she lived freely in Preobrazhenskoe in "an open house," an expression used at that time for one that received guests and foreign visitors. Contemporaries viewed Preobrazhenskoe as an island of new European lifestyle and genteel manners. Everyone in Moscow knew about the court theater in Preobrazhenskoe, a rare and unusual thing in those days. Its creator and director was Peter's sister.

There is a portrait of Tsarevna Natalia Alekseevna painted after her early death in 1716. In it, we see a stately, fair-haired, dark-eyed woman with a large nose, round chin, and high hairdo fashionable in those days. She was not beautiful, but she was intelligent, a quality that Peter admired in his younger sister.

The old Preobrazhenskii palace had a cozy and lived-in atmosphere, and life there was quiet and calm. The thunder of the Northern War did not reach the peaceful gardens and meadows where Natalia and her chamber-maids used to stroll. Peter's gregarious and benevolent sister united around herself a group of young women with similar attitudes and interests. Among them were Anna Tolstaia and the two Arsen'ev sisters, Dar'ia Arsen'eva being Aleksandr Menshikov's fiancée. Menshikov's two sisters were there as well.

It was no coincidence that Peter sent his Livland captive Martha to Preobrazhenskoe to stay with his sister and the other women in her circle. In the calm and friendly company of new friends, and under the protection of the tsar's sister, Martha received instruction in Russian customs and in the language in which she was finally able to say the ritual words pronounced in Russian during the Orthodox rite of baptism. At baptism she received the name Catherine Alekseevna. The second part of the full name, the patronymic, that is, the father's first name, she received from the person playing the role of godfather during the baptism ceremony. This was the tsarevich Aleksei Petrovich, the son of Peter and Tsaritsa Evdokia.

At first Peter did not write to Catherine personally. Instead, he asked Natalia, Anysia, or the Arsen'ev sisters to convey his regards "to those who carry weapons and to those who ply the needle." Catherine was implied in the latter group. Everybody could clearly see who lured the tsar to Preobrazhenskoe, where he hurried upon return from his long campaigns. Catherine's life at Preobrazhenskoe was a sort of probation period, and she passed the test. Her sweet and delicate nature, unpretentiousness, and liking for hard work pleased all around her, and eventually one of the tsar's close relatives advised him to give up his wanderings and marry Catherine.

In fact, they should have wed much sooner. Peter and Catherine were practically married already. Only theirs was not a church-sanctioned union, and, as such, was considered illegal and sinful in the eyes of the Orthodox Church. On the other hand, it did appear that it was a real and lasting bond. In January 1707, while away on a campaign, Peter received news of the birth of a third child, a daughter, Catherine. In her letter, Catherine senior wrote jokingly that the birth of a daughter was a good omen—a sign of peace. The Northern War was then entering its most difficult period; the Swedes had driven the Russian army from the Polish lands they had occupied, and Charles XII was about to invade Russia. The situation was critical. Peter sought peace but Charles, bellicose and sanguinary, ignored Peter's outstretched hand. The tsar responded to Catherine's joke: "If that's how things are, then I will probably be more happy to have a daughter than two sons."[15] Keeping in mind that a male monarch always dreams of having male heirs, we can only assume that Peter was grateful to Catherine for her opportune jest, for a gentle and keen understanding of his problem.

But the peace for which he so longed seemed no closer in January 1707 than at any other time since the beginning of the war in 1700. The tsar could not know then that the war would last another fourteen years. In January 1708, when Charles launched an all-out offensive, the situation looked desperate—Peter fled Grodno a mere two hours before the Swedes seized the town. It must have been then that the tsar hastily wrote the following note, which sounds as if it were meant as a last will and testament: "Should something, by the will of God, happen to me, then give the three thousand rubles that are now at Prince Menshikov's house to Catherine . . . and the little girl."[16] That was all that he, a soldier preparing for mortal combat, could do for the woman dearest to him.

In those troubled years their letters resembled the hasty notes of two lovers fixing dates they have to continuously postpone or cancel; telling how much they miss one another; expressing their worries when the other neglects to write for a long time; catching traces of vague rumors, and rereading time and again the short, fragmentary lines sent by chance couriers whenever the opportunity arose. There's no time for meetings, and if they do meet, it's at odd moments, for the war, like a hot flame, devours all of his time and strength. In a letter dated 1712 to Catherine, Peter wrote: "You know very well—in one hand I hold both a sword and a pen, and I have no helpers." Neither could Catherine help him. All she could do was to sympathize with him and support him: "My darling, my joy, and my hope! I wish you health for many years to come. I thank you for your kindness in sending me a letter which I was very glad to receive and which caused me to weep plenty while I was reading it. I had the feeling I had just met with you in person. In the future, my hope, do not trouble to write to me anymore—you have enough work to do. Now I, your milk cow, humbly implore you not to delay your return home, for all is better with you here."[17]

Then came the year 1709, the year of the illustrious victory of the Russian forces over the Swedes near the Ukrainian city of Poltava, where Charles XII met total and irrevocable defeat. The wheels of war were now rolling westward from the east; everything changed at one go. Peter, the victor over the Viking-King, regains confidence and composure. The tsar worries no more about his young city and future capital of St. Petersburg, which he founded in 1703. He decides to settle there permanently; he transfers state offices to the new city, carries out intensive construction, and fortifies the naval fortress Kronstadt on the mouth of the Neva River. Here, in St. Petersburg, his favorite place, far away from his foes and envious people in Moscow, he sets out to build the home, the eagle's nest, which he, the ruler of so vast a country, has never had. He moves to St. Petersburg members of the Romanov family, but only those whom he considers to be close relatives, among them his sister Natalia; Praskovia Fedorovna, his sister-in-law and the widow of his elder brother the tsar Ivan V, who died in 1696; and Ivan V's three daughters, Anna (the future empress, whose life is described in the next chapter), Praskovia, and Catherine. And the tsar brings his own Catherine to St. Petersburg. She is seen more and more often with him.

Still, they have only bad luck with children who die one after the other in infancy. The parents react calmly, as it was a common thing in those days: "God giveth and God taketh away." New children will come, the tsar reassures Catherine in one of his letters. There was every reason to be optimistic: in 1708 Anna was born, and on December 18, 1709—Elizabeth. Six months later, on May 1, 1710, when Peter was sailing the Finland skerries aboard a new ship, the *Lizetta,* named after his daughter, he wrote a letter to Catherine conveying his regards to his large family, such a drastic turnaround in the former bachelor's life of the tsar: "Bow for me to my sister, sister-in-law, nieces, and other people at home. Kiss the little ones, and give my special regards to the four-legged darling."[18] That was what he called his youngest and favorite daughter, Elizabeth, who had just started to crawl.

One more year passed, and in the spring of 1711 the hearts of Peter and Catherine were again filled with anxiety. War had broken out with Turkey, Russia's powerful southern neighbor. It was a hard war for Russia, for to fight on two fronts—with the Swedes and the Turks—was a dangerous undertaking. So Peter concentrated his efforts in the south in order to keep the war with the Turks away from the Ukraine and Poland, which were the principal theater of operations in the Northern War.

Ominous forebodings troubled the tsar when he embarked on this campaign, "the outcome of which is known only to God," he wrote to Menshikov, who remained behind, in St. Petersburg. Just prior to his departure—and he took Catherine with him—he did what he had been preparing to do for a long time: he declared his engagement to her, and, already in transit, he requested faithful Aleksandr Menshikov, in whose charge he had left his daughters Annushka and Lizan'ka, to take care of the girls should they happen to become orphans. Yet if God is merciful and grants victory or at least a safe return home, then they will have a chance to celebrate the wedding of Peter and Catherine in "Paradise"; that is what the tsar called his St. Petersburg, at that time still a modest little city on the shores of the Neva River. Peter's intuition did not mislead him. In early July 1711, the Turks managed to surround the Russian army on the Pruth River in Moldavia. The Turks' numerical superiority and continuous dense fire, the Russians' lack of ammunition and inadequate food and water supply, and the broiling Moldavian sun had turned a few days of siege into an absolute hell for the victors of Poltava, who had counted on an easy victory here. The night of July 10 was the most dramatic of all. After long negotiations and correspondence, when Peter had despaired of concluding an acceptable peace treaty with the Turks, he interrupted the long meeting of the War Council and ordered the generals to get ready to make a breakthrough the next morning. It was a mortally dangerous plan; an attempt by the weakened Russian army to break through the positions of the Turks might end in catastrophe with the destruction of the best forces, the death or capture of the tsar himself, and the ruin of that which had been achieved by the new Russia as well as all hopes for its future. A stray bullet or cannonball might just as stupidly and ruthlessly alter the course of history as had Captain Wolf from the Marienburg garrison.

And at this critical moment Catherine displayed courage, will, and resourcefulness. While Peter was having a rest before the morning attack, she reconvened the War Council and reassessed the extreme danger of the planned breakthrough. Then she woke Peter and persuaded him to write one more, final, letter to the Vizier Baltaa Mehmet-Pasha, commander in chief of the Turkish forces. As legend has it, with this letter Catherine sent, without the tsar's knowledge, all her jewelry: memorable heirlooms, presents from Peter. It's possible that this helped to solve the problem, for in the morning the Vizier gave consent to enter negotiations and signed a peace treaty with the Russians. For the Russians the Pruth nightmare had ended.

On November 24, 1714, when rewarding his wife with the new Order of St. Catherine, Peter announced that this order "has been instituted to commemorate Her Majesty's participation in the battle with the Turks on the Pruth River, where, in such dangerous circumstances she had proven herself to everyone not as a weak woman, but as a brave man."[19] Later, in his 1723 decree regarding Catherine's coronation, Peter again recalled the ill-fated battle at Pruth and the courage of his battle companion.[20] By that time Peter and Catherine had been together on many campaigns and had just returned from a long and dangerous military campaign to Persia, where Catherine had again displayed her calmness, perseverance, and good sense. She did not fare well on naval campaigns, apparently suffering from seasickness. So Peter often went to sea alone, but he sent notes regularly to his wife, who would be waiting for him on shore, in which he informed her of his endeavors and health, and thanked her for sweets, a bottle of good wine, or strawberries.

Upon their return from the Pruth campaign, in February 1712, the long-awaited event took place, the engagement and wedding of Peter and Catherine. It was unlike traditional royal weddings with pompous and long ceremonies; rather, it was the modest wedding of the rear admiral Peter Mikhailov—under this name Peter served in the Navy. Peter, as a respectful subordinate, invited his direct Naval chief, the Norwegian vice admiral Cornelius Cruys, to play the role of the proxy father, and other admirals and high-ranking officers were guests. Among the close circle of people invited to the wedding ceremony, which took place in the small chapel in Menshikov's palace, there were mostly sailors, shipbuilders, and their wives. Two winsome and graceful creatures, cognizant of their important role, made an appearance as bride's attendants, carrying Catherine's train. One was four and the other two years old; they were her daughters—Anna Petrovna and

Wedding of Peter and Catherine. From A. G. Brikner, *Istoriia Petra Velikogo* (History of Peter the Great) (St. Petersburg, 1882), p. 660.

Elizaveta Petrovna. After walking around the lectern, a rite performed in the Orthodox Church wedding ceremony, they would become the legitimate children of the spouses. "However, as the whole ceremony would have been too wearisome for the very young princesses, they appeared only briefly, and then were replaced by the tsar's two nieces," remarked with sincere disappointment Charles Whitworth, the English envoy.[21]

Many diplomats wrote of the extraordinary behavior of the Russian tsar, who showed his subjects, by personal example, how one should serve his country in battle, on the captain's bridge, or in the shipyard. All these graphic models of behavior were supposed to convince the lazy Russian noblemen that one must follow the tsar's example and gradually climb up the ladder. For Peter had started his service as a drummer boy, and by the end of his life he had attained the high rank of general-admiral. However, one must admit it was one thing to swing an ax in the shipyard or climb agilely on the ship's shrouds for pedagogical purposes, and another thing entirely to marry a former laundress and to acknowledge her children as heirs. For the wedding of Peter and Catherine was no farce; it was quite real. It was an incredible event in the history of the Russian dynasty. Peter violated all the conceivable and inconceivable mores and precepts of his regal ancestors.

The decisive act of violating accepted customs required a lack of inhibitions, internal freedom, and pluck. Thus, for the tsar-reformer who had been shaking the old foundations of life in Russia, it was a natural act. Also, such a mésalliance was impossible without deep and sincere feelings, that is, without love. Unlike the majority of his royal ancestors, contemporaries, and descendants, Peter was marrying for love, and he did not give a damn about anything else. An admiral's comparatively modest wedding suited him in every respect. He strove to separate his private life from the public life of the Russian tsar. According to his contemporaries, Peter used to tell his boyars that "the life of an English admiral is much more happy than the life of the Russian tsar."

That memorable February day in 1712 the tsar spent the way he had always dreamed. He was married in a cozy church in the presence of close friends, then hurried on ahead of everyone to his palace, where the wedding table was already laid; and assisted by his servants, he hung a six-candle chandelier made of ebony and ivory, which he had been turning on his lathe for many months. When all the guests were seated at the table he probably looked up and, as any skilled craftsman would have done in his place, proudly boasted more of his handiwork than of all the victories over his enemies, or his progress in legislative reforms, with his young wife in a beautiful dress smiling approvingly by his side.

"The occasion was splendid," commented Whitworth in his message describing the Russian admiral's wedding. "Fine wine from Hungary, and what was most pleasant is that no one was forced to drink to excess . . . The evening ended with dance and fireworks."[22] But the guests were unaware that the money spent on this celebration had not come from the counter-admiral's modest salary. An edict had been sent to every city with instructions to collect money for a wedding present for the tsar. And Russia has always been known as "a country of cities."

* * *

Thus, Cinderella became queen. No one had the right any longer to address her in any way other than "Your Royal Majesty," and all subjects, regardless of distinction, were considered her slaves and required to bow their heads in her presence.

Catherine was not a belle in the strict sense of the word, and this fact is confirmed by numerous portraits made by her contemporaries. She had neither the angelic beauty of her daughter Elizabeth, nor the refined elegance of Catherine II. Broad-shouldered and stout, her dark complexion gave a tinge of vulgarity to her appearance. The Markgravine Wilhelmina of Bayreuth looked at Catherine in vexed bewilderment when the latter visited Berlin in 1718: "The tsaritsa is a small, stumpy, very dark-complexioned, unimpressive and ungraceful woman. It's enough to look at her to see her humble origins. Her tasteless dress seems to have been bought at a junk dealer's: it is old-fashioned, covered with silver and dirt. A dozen orders are pinned on her and the same number of small icons and medallions with relics; all these jingle when she walks so that you have the impression that you are being approached by a pack mule."[23]

But we need not pay too much heed to the opinion of this catty woman: she was only ten years old when she saw the tsaritsa. Other contemporaries also left behind testimonies regarding Catherine. They remember her, splendidly dressed, dancing gracefully, easily, and merrily at balls; and one could not imagine a better pair than the tsar and Catherine.

Those who had seen Catherine were impressed by her endurance, patience, and strength. One eyewitness recalls a wedding party at which the Austrian envoy disgraced himself by losing to Catherine in a test of strength that involved lifting with one hand the wedding marshal's heavy baton. Another observer, Henning Friedrich von Bassewitz, after noting how naturally yesterday's laundress behaved amid St. Petersburg's high society, heard the tsar say that he himself was surprised by the ease with which Catherine was turning into a tsaritsa, meanwhile never forgetting her own origin. All these observations led Bassewitz to the conclusion that Catherine's success in life was due "not to her upbringing and education, but rather to her mental qualities. Having realized that the only thing she had to do was to carry out her important predestination, she rejected any other type of education except that based on her own experience and contemplation."[24]

Undoubtedly, Catherine possessed an inherently flexible mind and a sense of intuition which enabled her to act naturally, simply, and with dignity. For many years she enjoyed Peter's love. More that one hundred of their letters have survived. More than two hundred fifty years have passed, yet one cannot read them merely as historical documents: one still feels the intimate warmth and deep mutual love that united Peter and Catherine for two decades. Hints and jokes, often bordering on the obscene, touching concern for each other's health and safety, and most of all continuous melancholy and loneliness without the other close by, these are the universal themes about which lovers write all over the world. "I miss you so," "For God's sake, come soon; if, for some reason, it's impossible to be here soon, write, for I am sad not hearing your voice, and not seeing you," "I hear that you are lonely, and I feel lonesome, too." The tsar's letters are laced with such frank admissions of love. Catherine is just as lonely without Peter. "Whenever I go out," she writes about strolling in the Summer Gardens, "I regret that I do not have you by my side." He responds accordingly: "I believe you when you write that you feel lonely while walking alone in the Summer Gardens, though it's a beautiful garden, for I am feeling the same way. Just pray to God that this summer be the last one that we will be apart, and thereafter we will be together." And she picks up on this topic again in her letter: "Let us pray to God that He make it thus as you desire, that this summer be the last that we are apart."

Throughout all the ages this is what has been called love, and its traces have been preserved on faded and brittle paper. In 1717, while traveling in Brussels and wishing to make his wife a truly grand present, Peter decided to order some famous Brussels lace. He wrote to Catherine asking her to send him a pattern for the Brussels lace-makers. Catherine replied that she required nothing special, "only there should be two names worked into the lace, yours and mine, interwoven together."[25]

We cannot say that the tsaritsa Catherine led a serene life, and that the spouses, like two turtledoves, billed and cooed in love's blind raptures. This was not the case, for Peter was a man of difficult and even cruel character, and Catherine had to think constantly about how to maintain his affection. In keeping with the traditions of that time and his own temperament, the tsar never missed an opportunity for romance and, as before, he took mistresses with him wherever he traveled.

Catherine found the best possible solution for herself in this situation: she did not trouble her husband with useless jealousy and personally selected mistresses for him. On June 18, 1717, Peter writes to his wife from Spa, where he was taking mineral water treatments: "There is nothing to write to you about, only that we arrived here yesterday safely, and as doctors prohibit domestic fun [i.e., sex—E.A.] while drinking the water, I have sent my mistress back to you, for I would not have been able to resist the temptation if I had kept her here."[26] In her letter of July 3, Catherine answers that the reason for sending the mistress away was evidently not associated with the doctors' orders, but with the fact that the mistress had contracted an unpleasant disease "and I have no desire (and Heaven forbid!) to have this mistress's lover come home in the same condition as she."[27]

The existence of such an aspect in the spouses' relations tells us a lot about Catherine's character. Although she accepted and even encouraged Peter's marital freedom, yet it was as if she had drawn back the bed curtains of secrecy behind which her potential rival might gain power by using the tsar's weakness for women. Intimate liaisons often presuppose secrets of the heart. This was the last thing that Catherine wanted, and therefore she legalized the institution of mistresses in their married life.

But what worried Catherine more than mistresses was the future of her children. Years went by, some children died, new ones were born (Catherine gave birth to eleven children altogether), and as a mother she could not help thinking about their future. And their future was obscure, for Tsarevich Aleksei, Peter's and Dunia's son, had remained the official heir to the throne all these years. He was born in 1690 and at the age of eight was separated from his mother. This separation caused him great anguish; he even traveled to Suzdal' secretly to visit his mother. Peter did not love his oldest son, who was a stranger in the tsar's new family and lived all by himself, receiving no affection or attention. Nor did Catherine display any excess affection toward her stepson. Among the hundred or so letters exchanged by Peter and Catherine, the name of Aleksei is mentioned only two or three times, and there is not a single letter in which even so much as a greeting was conveyed to him. Peter's letters to Aleksei are cold, short, and impassive—lacking any words of approval, support, or affection. Whatever the tsarevich did was bound to result in his father's displeasure. Absorbed in the tumult of the wars, the fever of drunken pleasures, the long chain of urgent matters, Peter brushed the boy aside, entrusting him to the care of strange and petty people. As a result, ten years later, Peter had an enemy at his back, who accepted none of those things that his father was doing or striving for.

The tsarevich was not a limp and timorous hysteric as he is sometimes described. The son of his great father, he had inherited Peter's strong will and obstinacy, and he responded to the tsar with tacit disagreement and an impudence which he kept hidden behind a demonstrative obedience and formal respect. But they were enemies of the same stock. The ancient ghost of fate hovered over them. Like the heroes of Sophocles and Euripides, they could not live together on one earth. Yet the tsarevich believed in his lucky star, he felt absolutely certain: he was the sole legitimate heir, and the only thing he had to do was to clench his teeth and await the hour of his triumph.

In October 1715, the tragedy reached a climax. By that time, Aleksei, in keeping with Peter's will, had long been married to Charlotte Sophia, the princess of Wolfenbuttel, and on October 12 she gave birth to a son who was named after his grandfather Peter. Sixteen days later, Tsaritsa Catherine gave birth to a long-awaited boy who was also named Peter. He was a healthy and lively child. *Shishechka* (little pine cone), *Potroshonok* (particle of my blood)—these are the nicknames Peter and Catherine use in their letters when referring to their son. Just as a newly married couple admires their first son, so the not-so-very-young royal parents observed with pride the first steps of their son. "Could you, my master, stick up for me, for he quarrels a lot with me over you: he doesn't like to hear it when I tell him that papa has gone, but he is happy when I tell him that papa is here."[28]

The parents dreamed of their son's bright future. Having learned that Shishechka has cut his fourth tooth, Peter writes: "God grant that his others will cut through just as successfully, and God grant us the joy of seeing him a grown man in reward for all our previous sorrows over his dead brothers."[29] They vested all their dynastic hopes in Peter Petrovich. Catherine even called her son "the master of St. Petersburg," and she believed that she would have still more children. In the aforementioned letter of July 3, 1717, from Amsterdam, she added a joking postscript: "As to congratulations on the name-day of the Old Man and Shishechka [i.e., the name-day of the tsar and his son], I think that if that old man were here, then another 'little pine cone' would ripen for next year." It is clear from the letter that this particular name-day celebration does not include the third Peter, the tsar's grandson. The

Tsarevich Peter Petrovich, son of Peter the Great and Catherine. From A. G. Brikner, *Istoriia Petra Velikogo* (History of Peter the Great) (St. Petersburg, 1882), p. 363.

happy parents seem to have forgotten about Tsarevich Aleksei, the future master of Russia, and his little son, the same age as Shishechka, who were also living in St. Petersburg.

But actually Peter never forgot about them: it was not his style to leave problems unsolved, especially when it came to matters concerning the fate of Russia. And from the tsar's letters to Aleksei we can see that after the birth of Shishechka Peter's claims against his eldest son became more serious and accusations more grave. Peter demands the impossible from Aleksei: he wants him to "change his disposition," to become a reliable, eager helpmate in promoting the tsar's arduous cause. Otherwise, threatens the tsar, "I shall disinherit you; I will sever you like a limb infected with gangrene, and do not think that you are the only son I have and that I am writing this as a warning: I will really do it; I spared not nor do I now spare my own life for my native land and people, so why would I take pity on an indecent creature such as you?"[30]

This threat had revealed Peter's true and sinister intent of transferring the throne and his "St. Petersburg legacy" to Shishechka. But Aleksei was to be prevented from being his rival. Peter demanded that the tsarevich abdicate his right to the throne, and Aleksei obeyed the tsar. Then Peter demanded that his son join a monastery. And again Aleksei gave his consent. But the

Tsarevich Aleksei Petrovich, son of Peter the Great and
his first wife, Evdokia Lopukhina. From A. G. Brikner,
Istoriia Petra Velikogo (History of Peter the Great)
(St. Petersburg, 1882), p. 331.

tsar was still restless, he knew all too well that Russia was a country of traditions wherein the statement of abdication was merely a piece of paper, and,
unlike a grave, one can leave a monastery. So as long as Aleksei was alive he
was a danger to Peter's children by Catherine. Having left St. Petersburg for
Copenhagen on a military mission, the tsar quite unexpectedly summoned
Aleksei to join him there. As Aleksei feared Peter's fits of violent fury and a
possible attempt upon his life on the road (in his letter, the tsar demanded
that Aleksei specify in detail the places he would be passing through on the
way to Denmark and the dates of arrival at each), he fled to Austria.

A few months later, using false promises, the tsar lured Aleksei back to
Russia, where the torture chamber awaited him, with Peter personally pull-
ing out his son's nails. Then a trial took place in which the tsar's son received
the death penalty. One of the Guards officers who executed this verdict,

Aleksandr Rumiantsev, recalled that on the night of June 26, 1718, Peter had sent for them and, breaking into tears, gave the order to kill Aleksei secretly. According to Rumiantsev, when he entered the tsar's apartments he saw the following scene: Peter was seated and standing around him were Archbishop Feodosii, his personal confessor and the head of the Synod; Count Peter Tolstoi, the chief of the Secret Chancery (political police), which had made the case against Aleksei; Tolstoi's deputy, Major Andrei Ushakov; and Catherine.[31]

We do not know what she was thinking about or what she said in that awful hour that made Peter, like Ivan the Terrible, a slayer of his own flesh and blood. Of course, Catherine was there to ease the terrible lot of the tsar, who was about to sacrifice his own son on the altar of his Fatherland and free himself of an internal enemy. But we must keep in mind that at this late hour, not far from the room where the killers were meeting, Shishechka was sleeping soundly, and it was she, Catherine, the mother of "the master of St. Petersburg," who needed Aleksei's death. Besides, the tsaritsa was in the late stages of pregnancy, and the parents were probably thinking that in August of 1718 they would have one more son (but a girl was born that time, Natalia).

The murder was committed: the tsarevich was strangled in one of the casemates of the St. Petersburg citadel, the Peter and Paul Fortress. Peter and Catherine breathed a sigh of relief: the problem of succession had been resolved. Peter Petrovich was announced heir to the throne. The parents were moved as they watched him grow up: "Our dear Shishechka often speaks of his dear papa, and with the help of God, at this age, he is already enjoying perfecting his skills in play with toy soldiers and cannon fire,"[32] writes Catherine to her husband shortly after Aleksei's death. The soldiers and guns for now were made of wood, but the tsar was happy: the heir would grow up to be a soldier of Russia.

But Aleksei's death cries that night, as he struggled to break loose from his secret executioners (according to Rumiantsev, this was a horrible and revolting scene), turned into a curse which hung over Peter's home. In April 1719, the spouses were deeply shaken by a grave misfortune: their joy, their hope, dear Shishechka fell ill and died a few days later. He was not yet three and a half. This event rocked the very foundation of the family's future prosperity. Catherine's grief knew no bounds. When she herself died eight years later, Shishechka's toys were found among her things; there were no toys that had belonged to Natalia, who died later, or to any of the other children who had died in infancy; only those that had belonged to "the master of St. Petersburg." The items recorded in the Registrar's list are quite touching: "A golden cross, silver buckles, a whistle with bells, a glass fish, a jasper case of drawing instruments, a toy flint-lock rifle, a miniature sword (with a golden handle), a tortoise whip, a child's cane . . ." The inconsolable mother must have fondled again and again these priceless little objects.

An ominous event occurred during the funeral service in the Trinity Church in St. Petersburg on April 26, 1719. Stepan Lopukhin, a relative of the disgraced Tsaritsa Evdokia, said something to some bystanders and then laughed blasphemously. Later, witnesses testified to the Secret Chancery that Lopukhin had said the following: "The flame of his, Stepan's, candle has not gone out yet, there will be a future for him!"[33] Under torture, Lopukhin confessed that when he was talking about his burning candle he had meant the Grand Duke Peter Alekseevich. And that was the truth: although the light of life had died in the beloved Shishechka, this same light was thriving in the Grand Duke Peter, who was Shishechka's age. The orphaned grand duke (his mother, Charlotte Sophia, had died in 1715), deprived of anyone's love, was growing up; and this fact gave heart to those who were awaiting the tsar's death, that is, to the Lopukhins and other opponents of the reformer.

What consolation could Catherine find in this cruel turn of fate? She had two lovely daughters, Anna and Elizabeth, and a third, Natalia, was born in 1718. But still no son came. Actually, in 1723, Catherine did give birth to one last child—a son, Peter—but he died very shortly after birth. Catherine was approaching forty, the maximum age in those days for childbirth, so Peter had little hope of getting a male heir. But the tsar did not give up: he had no intention of transferring the throne to his grandson, the son of Aleksei, whom the tsar had cursed. On February 5, 1722, Peter issued the "Charter on the Succession to the Throne." The idea was clear to everyone: violating the tradition of transferring the throne from grandfather to father, son and grandson, the tsar had secured the right of appointing the successor from among *any* of his subjects. This was the boldest demonstration of absolute power yet. From that time on the tsar not only had full charge of Russia today, but assured himself a voice in ruling Russia tomorrow.

And on November 15, 1723, a manifesto announced Catherine's upcoming coronation. Peter had been proclaimed Emperor and Father of his Native Land earlier on November 22, 1721, in a celebration marking the end of the Great Northern War. (By the Nystad Peace Treaty, Sweden ceded to the Russians the Eastern Baltic countries, the region in which the cities of Riga, Revel [Tallinn], and Petersburg were located.)

At last on May 7, 1724, Catherine became empress. The event took place at the Assumption Cathedral in the Moscow Kremlin, in the presence of the highest-ranking government officials and a multitude of spectators. The cathedral, with its shiny gold domes and luxurious interior created by the fifteenth-century Italian architect Ridolfo Fioravanti, had long been the traditional site for coronation of the Russian tsars. Gold, velvet, gem-embossed armchairs, Persian carpets, a gold brocade rug leading from the tsar's place to the Holy Gates—all this Byzantine, Eastern splendor shone brightly and sparkled in the light of the hundreds of candles lit on that day, just as it had during the times of Ivan III or Ivan IV, known as the Terrible. Only never before had the cathedral seen such a variety of fancy European costumes, in which the men and women present were attired, and never before in Russia had the crown been bestowed on a woman of such common ancestry.

On this day even Peter himself, usually preferring to wear everyday clothing, stockings darned by his wife, and worn-out shoes, was dressed as finely as a French king—a sky-blue caftan embroidered with silver thread by Catherine and a hat with a white feather. Our heroine looked very beautiful. She was wearing a gold-trimmed purple dress brought from Paris, and diamonds sparkled in her tall hairdo. The bells of all Moscow cathedrals were pealing, salutes were firing, and army bands were playing as Catherine, surrounded by stately officers of household cavalry with golden eagles on their shoulders entered the cathedral, a sacred place for any Russian.

The ceremony was festive, long, and tiring. Peter and his attendants covered Catherine with an ermine-lined brocade mantle, which lay like a heavy weight across the strong shoulders of the emperor's comrade-in-arms. Then Catherine knelt and Peter placed the crown on her head, adorned with pearls, diamonds, and a huge ruby of marvelous beauty larger than a dove's egg. At that moment feelings of gratitude welled up in the heart of the Livland captive, and overcome, she began to cry and then tried to embrace the feet of her ruler, but he stepped away from her as this was not the time nor the place for such sentiments.

The celebration was followed by receptions, dinners, massive public feasting on roast beef, fireworks, and a salute. Watching the fireworks flashing against the blue May evening sky, many Muscovites must have thought the same as the Holstein courtier Bergholtz, who wrote in his diary: "One cannot help wondering at God's Providence whereby the empress has been elevated from the lowly position into which she was born and in which she lived to the pinnacle of human honors."[34]

Bergholtz, like most of the guests at the celebration, did not know of one important fact, namely, that on the eve of the coronation Peter destroyed the old will and testament and wrote a new one, in which he named Catherine his heir. This event was kept a dark secret and only the penetrating mind of the French envoy Campredon sensed the implications of the festive coronation not evident to the uninitiated. He alone understood the true meaning of what was happening under the vaulted ceiling of the cathedral: "Especially noteworthy is the fact that contrary to custom the ritual of anointing of the tsaritsa was also performed, which meant that she was acknowledged ruler and sovereign after the death of her spouse, the tsar."[35]

The decision to write the new will was the result of long contemplation on the part of the tsar, a whole chain of transformations that had taken place within him as well as in the world in which he lived. It is well known that Peter never intended Catherine to be either his successor or a politician. In all the tsar's many letters to his wife there is not a trace of his political matters ever being discussed by them. At no time had Catherine ever directed anything in Russia besides the royal kitchen. Even managing the populated land holdings to which she was entitled as tsaritsa was delegated to other people. Peter had his own plain and simple human reasons for this. He himself was obliged to live continually in the nervous, all-consuming world of politics, and had to consciously strive to separate his private life from his public affairs. In the evenings he would return to his small Dutch-style palace in the Summer Gardens, and awaiting him there was his thoughtful wife, surrounded by children and servants. Peter would have supper, meticulously checking a mark that he had made earlier to find out whether the impudent cooks had eaten too much from his favorite Limburger cheese. His wife would darn his underclothes, blazing firewood would crackle in the fireplace, the wind would howl outside the windows, the waves of the Neva would be lapping, and inside the small room all was warm and cozy. And suddenly this abrupt turnabout: he makes his humble affectionate housewife the heir to the imperial throne! Yes, it's understandable that his own cruel fate had compelled him to do so, but it was not just fate alone which guided his hand as he wrote the will.

"Katerinushka, my dearest friend, hello!" Dozens of Peter's letters to Catherine begin with these words. As the years pass these letters become warmer and more cordial. During the last five years of his life, Catherine's influence on Peter increasingly grew. She was able to give the tsar that which his entire external world, so complex and hostile, was unable to give. Peter, a severe and suspicious person, was transformed in the presence of Catherine and children. At balls guests would see how the tsar, excited by the last fast dance, would tenderly kiss his wife, a tireless and sensitive dancing partner. They also recalled startling scenes, when Catherine would drive a demon out of Peter. It is known that Peter suffered from bouts of deep depression, which could turn in a flash to fits of raving, all-destructive fury (one well-known story tells of how the tsar nearly killed a page with a naked dagger for having accidentally pulled the tsar's hair while removing his night cap one morning). These fits of rage were accompanied by muscle spasms in the face and convulsions of the arms and legs. Bassewitz recalls that upon first notice of the symptoms of a seizure (the tsar would begin to shake his head and make strange faces), those around would send for Catherine.

She would come immediately and even as she approached she would begin saying quiet and affectionate words to her husband; "the sound of her voice instantly calmed him, then she would seat him and hold his head gently stroking it and running her fingers through his hair. This had a magical effect on him and he would fall asleep in just a few minutes. In order not to disturb his rest she would hold his head on her breast and sit motionless for two or three hours. After this he would awake completely refreshed and in good spirits."[36]

Catherine knew to the last detail all of Peter's predilections, whims, and human weaknesses. She was sensitive, attentive, and knew how to please and oblige the tsar. Knowing how distraught Peter was over the extensive damage to the ship *Gangut,* she wrote to the tsar who had left on a campaign that the ship had arrived after successful repairs "to join its brother, *Lesnoy,* and they are now standing together in one place; I've seen them with my own eyes and they are truly a joy to behold!"[37] No, neither Dunia nor Anchen could ever have written so simply, sincerely, and with such sensitivity. But the former laundress knew what the dearest thing in the world was for the great skipper and shipbuilder of Russia, who referred to all the ships which he had launched as his "children." And Peter appreciated this very much. In a letter dated June 5, 1716, from the water resort Piermont he reports that he had received the bottle of wine sent from Catherine, "but I think that you have the gift of prophecy, insofar as you sent one bottle, for [the doctors] do not allow [me] to drink more than one glass a day."[38] Doubtless Catherine possessed, if not the gift of prophecy, the gift of knowing Peter.

In Catherine's letter of July 5, 1719, we see how cleverly the tsaritsa adapts to Peter's mode of thinking. In telling a mortal mishap that had taken place in the suburban palace-park of Peterhof she writes: "The Frenchman who was making new flower beds went walking, the poor fellow, at night across the canal and bumped into Ivashka Khmelnitskii [the Russian equivalent of the wine God Bacchus—E.A.], and he somehow pushed the Frenchman off the bridge and sent him to the next world to make flower beds."[39] Here Catherine even imitates Peter's characteristically black humor, his peculiar attitude toward people.

Now we can say with certainty that Catherine was not selfless in her love to Peter. In later years she skillfully took advantage of his weaknesses in achieving the goal, which was previously inconceivable for an ordinary Livland peasant. Purposefully and surely she nudged her husband into deciding to appoint her the heir to the throne for the sake of their daughters' futures. One must not forget that time introduced its own alterations into their plans. Peter's letters to Catherine are warm, but at the same time slightly sad notes can be heard in them, covered up at times by clumsy jokes, all focusing on one thing: Alas!, we're not an even match, you are young and beautiful and I am already old and sickly. What will become of us? Her half of the correspondence resembles a lover's game: Look, you're still strong, and therefore young, the future belongs to us! Having once received a package from his wife containing his badly needed spectacles, Peter reciprocates by sending her jewelry and these words: "Suitable presents for each of us: yours aids me in my old age, and mine adorns your youth."[40] In another letter, thirsting for a meeting and intimacy the tsar once again jokes: "Although I do want to see you, still I think that you want to see me more, for I know what it's like to be twenty-seven, and you do not know yet what it's like to be forty-two."[41]

Catherine takes heed of her husband's jokes, knowing what's behind them. We read in her letters quaint appeals to her "dearest friend and old-timer," and we see her ploy as she protests: "In vain you've started asserting that you're an old man!" She pretends to be jealous of the queen of Sweden, along whose shores Admiral Peter Mikhailov is sailing, or of Parisian coquettes, to which he answers in feigned offense: "I just received your letter filled with jokes. You write as if I were soon to find a lady here; however, this would be indecent at my age."[42]

This feigned game of playing the old man and young wife becomes a way of life by 1724: the fifteen-year difference in their ages that had been imperceptible earlier becomes more and more obvious and significant. Peter turns fifty in 1722 and begins to weaken. Long years of an irregular, wild, and unsettled life, perpetual moves, campaigns, battles, a continual emotional stress or "alteratsiia," as the tsar put it, all these had their destructive effects: Peter begins to age quickly. He is tormented by illnesses, especially by blockages of the urethral canal, either caused by adenoma of the prostate gland, a typical problem of old men, or the result of inadequately treated gonorrhea. He suffers severely and more and more often sets off to health resorts, where he diligently drinks mineral water, believing in its healing powers.

He had reached the sad threshold of old age, but, as we all know, the human soul is young, and the tsar's feelings toward Catherine not only do not wane, but flare up with a late burning passion. During the summer of 1718, the forty-six-year-old tsar, like an ardent young lover, writes Catherine in alarm: "This letter which I am writing to you is the fifth, and from you I've received only three, which cause me to worry about you—why have you not written? For God's sake, write more often!"[43] A cry of alarm can be heard in another letter: "It's been eight days already since I've received any letter from you, over which I'm deeply troubled."[44] And here's one of his last letters, dated June 26, 1724. Catherine was still in Moscow following her coronation, and Peter had already arrived in St. Petersburg. It was a warm summer, and the flower beds in the Summer Gardens were blooming, but the tsar felt restless in his paradise: "No sooner do I come into our rooms than I feel like running away—all's empty here without you."[45]

Such acute and desperate feelings always make a person vulnerable. Taking advantage of Peter's love, Catherine managed to convince the tsar on the eve of the coronation to destroy the version of his will written after the death of Shishechka, which named their eldest daughter Anna as heir, and replace her name with that of Catherine. At the same time the tsaritsa was pressing to give Anna away in marriage to one suitor close at hand, Charles Frederick, the Duke of Holstein-Gottorp, a small state in northern Germany, and nephew of the deceased Charles XII. Ironically, Anna had become Catherine's rival to the throne. Peter had contemplated the matter for some time, carefully weighing its implications. Such a marriage could have a serious effect on the entire political situation in the Baltic. He vacillates, saying

Tsarevna Anna Petrovna. From A. G. Brikner, *Istoriia Petra Velikogo* (History of Peter the Great) (St. Petersburg, 1882), p. 572.

neither yes nor no. But of one thing he is already certain, Catherine's name as the heir to the throne is entered in the will and she is officially crowned in Moscow. In the summer of 1724, Peter returned to St. Petersburg and impatiently awaited his wife's arrival, but she was in no hurry, she had gotten what she wanted!

And once again, just as in the classical drama, merciless fate destroys the hero's happiness: in the fall of 1724, Peter learns abruptly of his wife's betrayal, and of the name of the empress's lover. He is young and handsome and had been close to the tsar for many years. As fate would have it, in 1708 Peter included in his retinue the attractive youth Villim (William) Mons, Anchen's younger brother. We do not know the reasons for Peter's doing so, but I believe that he had not completely forgotten his first love; the tsar had to have near at hand a face that would remind him of Anchen's endearing traits. And, later, Anchen's sister, Modesta (married name Balk), entered the inner circle of Catherine herself. In 1716, Villim is named Catherine's gentleman of the bedchamber and, thanks to his charm and industriousness, launches a fast and successful career. He is appointed to manage the tsaritsa's estates and is promoted to court chamberlain. This young man, who in the words of the Danish envoy Hans Georg Westphalen "was among the most handsome and elegant people whom I have ever seen," became Catherine's lover.[46]

When in the fall of 1724 Peter was given a report on Mons's abuse of privileges and acceptance of bribes, he still had no idea of its wider ramifications. But papers confiscated at the arrest of the chamberlain opened his eyes. Among the vulgar verses and love letters from various ladies were dozens of humiliating letters from the emperor's closest associates: Menshikov, Iaguzhinskii, and Golovkin. Even the widowed empress Praskovia Fedorovna asked for help from Mons. They all called Mons "benefactor," "patron," "dear friend and brother," and gave him countless expensive gifts, money, valuables, and even villages! Only a fool could fail to see the secret of the chamberlain's great influence on the empress, the heiress to the Russian throne. The scales suddenly fell from Peter's eyes. Apparently everyone had known all along, had demeaned themselves behind his back before the favorite, and kept silent. This meant they were all awaiting the tsar's death!

On November 9 Mons was brought, under arrest, before his interrogator, who was Peter himself. He could not entrust this matter to anyone. As legend has it, Mons looked into Peter's eyes and fainted. This stately, good-looking man who had taken part in the Battle of Poltava, the tsar's adjutant general, was by no means a coward. He probably foresaw his death sentence in Peter's eyes. Frivolous and romantic, a tireless and skillful womanizer, he practiced his hand at poetry. In one of his poems we read a prophetic confession: "I know how I will die/I dared to love the one/Whom I should have only respected/I burn with passion for her."

Within a few days of the interrogation Mons was beheaded on Trinity Square after the trial's verdict condemned the former chamberlain for accepting bribes and other criminal abuses of power. Similar cases had usually taken months and years to resolve. Everyone knew the truth of the matter. Remembering the bloody ordeal involving Tsarevich Aleksei in 1718, which had swept into its orbit the lives of dozens of people, the capital froze with fear.

But Peter did not unleash terror. Only the unfaithful wife's closest associates were severely punished, those who delivered notes and stood guard over the lovers, namely: the lady-in-waiting Modesta Balk, the jester Ivan Balakirev, the page Solovov, and Mons's secretary Egor Stoletov. The executioner's ax passed close by Catherine's head, but did not harm her. Some contemporaries reported that Peter made scenes of jealous rage before Catherine, smashed Venetian mirrors. Others, on the contrary, who had seen the tsar during these terrible days at an anniversary party, described him as calm and in good spirits, at least on the outside. Often impetuous and impulsive, Peter was known to be able to assert his will and show self-restraint in moments of trial.

We will never know what the spouses were thinking when, returning from a visit through Trinity Square many days after Mons's death, they passed by the scaffold covered with Mons's blood beneath the blind gaze of his severed head on top of the pole.

It could not be said that Catherine fell into disgrace. As always she continued to make appearances with her husband at public events. But foreign diplomats noticed that the empress was not as cheerful as before. Like it or not the Mons incident compels us to reconsider Catherine's personality. The pellucid and simple image of the empress vanishes. Of course her affair with Mons could be regarded as a passing fancy, but why then did her young lover exercise such great influence at court? And where were Catherine's wisdom and knowledge of Peter? Surely such an affair could not help but have dramatic repercussions for the empress, heiress to the throne.

There is another possible explanation for Catherine's behavior. What if she had never been the blind admirer of her great benefactor-husband and had never really loved him? It just so happened that in her early youth she, a Livland captive, had been passed against her will from hand to hand and found herself in his embrace and in his household. Here, as in all previous places, she meekly surrendered to his will and began to live, readily performing all that was required of her. In time she grew close to the tsar, the source of her well-being, and eagerly took on the role of a kind, loving, and caring spouse, deriving pleasure from playing up to the whims of her master and ruler. But all the while, just as millions of subjects of the Russian autocrat, she remained his slave, whose lot it was to obey implicitly and unquestioningly. And God alone knows what is locked in the heart of a slave fluffing the pillows of the master's bed.

Mons, the object of Catherine's affections, the man for whose sake she underwent such risks, was an absolute nobody, an empty, conceited fop. She should have given some thought to her own security. Catherine knew Peter well and, on more than one occasion, had seen how he would sacrifice anyone's life for the welfare of Russia. Remember what Peter wrote to his son Aleksei! And during those November days this was exactly what was on the mind of the great emperor, the fate of the throne and of his reforms.

It is safe to assume that these were not happy thoughts. Betrayal had shadowed Peter throughout his life. He had been betrayed by exactly those people whom he trusted the most, whom he sincerely loved or respected: Anchen; the Polish king Augustus II, crowned "dearest brother," who in 1706, without Peter's knowledge, signed a secret pact with their common enemy, Charles XII; the hetman Ivan Stepanovich Mazepa, who in 1708 during the most critical hours of the Northern War, deserted to the Swedes; and Aleksandr Kikin, nicknamed "grandfather," who behind the tsar's back had become an accomplice of Tsarevich Aleksei. And, finally, Catherine, whom he had trusted more than anyone on earth, had also joined their ranks. All of his closest associates connived to keep quiet: Menshikov, Chancellor Golovkin, even General Prosecutor Iaguzhinskii, "the eye of the sovereign." They were also traitors. Each had been thinking of his own skin. And who would think of Russia? Campredon wrote back to France telling how suspicious the tsar had become. He "is extremely concerned that there are traitors in his household and among his servants. There is talk of complete disfavor with Menshikov and Major-General Mamonov, whom the tsar had trusted almost unconditionally. There is also talk of the tsar's secretary Makarov, and even the tsaritsa is afraid. Her relations with Mons were common knowledge, and although she tries hard to hide her grief, it is nevertheless evident on her face and in her manner of behavior. All of society tensely awaits what will become of her."[47]

The case of Catherine's betrayal was more serious than the others. And its essence lay not in a lack of matrimonial loyalty, although there can be no doubt that the "old man" was hard hit that his wife preferred a younger, more handsome man to him. The morals of those times allowed much freedom to both men and women of the noble classes. However, moral requisites became rigid when the matter concerned not a mere noblewoman, but the mother of potential heirs to the throne, the emperor's spouse. In this case his wife's unfaithfulness became a crime against the dynasty, the throne, the state. But there is no doubt that something else must have troubled Peter even more. In considering the future he probably felt his extreme isolation and the indifference of those around him to the work to which he had dedicated his life and which might turn to ashes. Who would rule the country after his death? Catherine or some opportunist whom a passing fancy allowed to jump into her bed? Was not that exactly how it had been with the tsar's half sister, the regent Sophia, vacillating between lovers Count Vasilii Golitsyn and Fedor Shaklovityi? But it is unlikely that Peter could imagine at that time what an endless obscene sequence of "night emperors" was begun with poor Villim Mons. Throughout history despotism and favoritism have always gone hand in hand.

Peter made up his mind to destroy the will benefiting Catherine, which had been signed on the eve of the celebration in the Assumption Cathedral. In the early morning of November 10, 1724, that is, on the day following Mons's interrogation, he sent Vice Chancellor Andrei Osterman to the Duke of Holstein, Charles Frederick. The young duke had come to Russia in the hope of securing Russia's aid against neighboring Denmark, which had at one time annexed part of Holstein's territory; he also sought the hand of one of the tsar's daughters. As we know, Peter vacillated for a long time, but suddenly the Mons affair had changed everything. Peter gave permission to issue a marriage contract, the signing of which took place on November 24. In it the tsar arranged for the lovely sixteen-year-old Anna to become Charles Frederick's bride. According to the marriage contract, the future spouses forfeited their and all their potential offspring's rights to the Russian throne. At the same time a secret agreement was signed, whereby Peter received the right to bring to Russia his would-be grandson born of the union between his daughter and the duke in order to make him the heir to the Russian throne.

This was the intent of Peter's new dynastic plan. In this marriage contract with the Holsteins he sought to solve a mind-boggling problem: how to avoid the accession of Grand Duke Peter Alekseevich (who would possibly avenge his father's death) and that of the fickle empress, and secure that of the son of the tsar's beloved daughter Anna. All that remained was to wait just a little bit longer. Obviously, the fifty-two-year-old tsar counted on living several more years and seeing his grandson. And this was within reason. Anna did in fact give birth to a son on February 10, 1728, calling him Charles-Peter Ulrich, who subsequently became the Russian emperor Peter III, husband of Catherine II. Peter had to wait only a little more than three years for this event, not a long period of time. But it was more time than he had: he was not destined to see his grandson—after the betrayal, death spoiled his game. On the night of January 28, 1725, he died in physical and mental agony, having resolved nothing.

* * *

Peter's death sent shock waves throughout St. Petersburg and Russia, which were also felt in other countries' capitals among the emperor's friends and enemies. With the tsar-reformer's death ended not only his thirty-five-year reign, but an entire epoch of Russian history, the time of reforms, sweeping changes in all spheres of Russian life. All were grief-stricken. Bergholtz wrote in his diary that even the Guards wept like children. "On that morning you scarcely met anyone who was not crying or whose eyes were not red and swollen from crying."[48] Soon the news of Peter's death reached Moscow and death knells summoned Muscovites to their parish churches. One contemporary recalls that when Catherine I's "Manifesto of Peter's Death" was read aloud, there was so much wailing and sobbing that it was some time before the words could be heard. This is no exaggeration—such are human beings, such is the mental and emotional state of a crowd at such a time. Just yesterday people gossiped spitefully of the tsar's indecent marriage to a Livland laundress, complained of his severe decrees, cursed his heavy taxation. And now the crowd, sincerely grieving, wept for its father, who had left his entire people orphaned.

Catherine ordered that every resident of St. Petersburg have the chance to pay last respects to the great ruler. Thus, forty days an endless stream of noblemen and serfs, workers, soldiers, beggars and merchants, ladies of fashion and market women filed through the mourning hall of the Winter Palace, where Peter's body was lying in state. There were so many hushed people passing through to kiss the tsar's calloused hand that the long black-cloth rug on the floor wore through and had to be replaced several times. People were awestruck by the mourning hall with its combination of luxury and great sorrow. The golden tapestries, sculptures, and gilt canopy, all that which had affirmed life and joy, was now covered with crepe and enveloped in sad semidarkness, the dim light of funeral candles. Upon approaching the coffin people saw their father transformed and unrecognizable. Earlier he had hurried along the city streets with his famous walking stick in hand, in a worn out camisole, wearing homemade shoes and twisted stockings. Now a tall man lay in a golden coffin dressed in a splendid costume of silver and lace. The luxury of the dress, of the coffin, of the entire hall reminded all that the man of simple and unpretentious tastes in everyday life was an emperor.

Catherine spent many long hours seated teary-eyed by the coffin. The whole of St. Petersburg witnessed her sorrow, and this was more than just a politically expedient public display of grief by an inconsolable widow: Catherine's suffering was real indeed. On March 4 yet another tragedy struck: her youngest daughter, Natalia, died of the measles. She was six years old. The tsarevna's tiny coffin was displayed not far from her father's.

The funeral took place on March 10, 1725. Cannon-fire signaled the beginning of the great emperor's final rounds through his capital. People flocked to Peter's Winter Palace on the Neva Embankment. On that day large snowflakes fell, turning at times to hail. It was cold, windy, and—as always in winter along the Neva—unpleasant. Trumpets and kettledrums announced the beginning of the funeral procession. The poignant sounds of the trum-

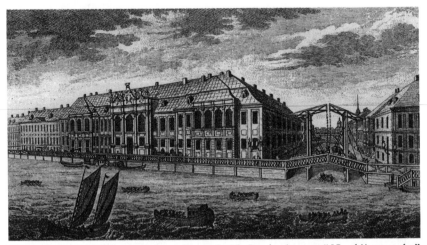

View of the Old Winter Palace. From I. N. Bozherianov, "*Nevskii prospekt.*" *Kul'turno-istoricheskii ocherk dvukhvekovoi zhizni Sankt-Peterburga* ("Nevskii Prospect." A Cultural and Historical Sketch of St. Petersburg at Two Hundred) (St. Petersburg, 1901–03), vol. 1, p. 64.

pets and drone of the large kettledrums combined with the rapid roll of regimental drums and the singing of dozens of choristers and priests, walking in snow-white mourning chasubles carrying gonfalons and icons. A funeral sleigh drawn slowly by eight horses arrayed in black trappings bore Peter's golden coffin. Priests carried the emperor's attributes of power: swords, scepter, an orb and crown.

Catherine walked first behind the coffin, surrounded by attendants who supported her at the elbows. Her face was covered by a black veil. She was followed by relatives, courtiers, generals, and servants. No one in the huge crowd lining the embankment and bridge across the Neva could help but be moved by this solemn and dismal rite—the mournful sounds of the funeral marches, the heavy beats of the kettledrums, the doleful singing of the church choirs, the flashing and clashing of weapons, and the sweet-smelling incense rising toward the sky. The incessant tolling of the death knell floated over the Neva and faded in the low-hanging clouds. All these noises were periodically muffled by the sound of cannon-fire. These rounds had an especially oppressive effect on those present. Throughout the entire hours-long ceremony shots were fired every minute from the bastions of the Peter and Paul Fortress. As Feofan Prokopovich wrote later, the blasts filled everyone "with a kind of wistful horror."

Torches lit the way as the coffin was carried into the wooden church which stood in the middle of the Peter and Paul Cathedral, which was still being built and where all Russian emperors of the eighteenth and nineteenth centuries would be buried. The bell tower of the cathedral with its tall spire and clock soared skyward, but the cathedral walls were no higher than the height of a grown man. This too was a symbol of Petrine Russia, "the incomplete shrine," as Menshikov called it later.

At Peter's graveside Feofan Prokopovich delivered a vivid, expressive eulogy, which later went down in all books on eloquence. The priest called on the Russian people to look back and appraise the greatness of the man whom Russia was about to lay to rest and to always remember that it was their duty to increase and reinforce the country's glory and wealth as Peter had done. "What he made of his Russia, thus it shall remain: he made it beloved for kind people, beloved it shall be; he made it frightening for enemies, frightening it shall be; he made it glorious throughout the world, then it shall never cease to be glorious. He left us in body, but his spirit remains." Addressing Catherine, who was standing by the coffin, Feofan exclaimed: "We see in you his helper throughout life . . . the whole world is witness that the female flesh has not hindered you in being like Peter."[49]

But Catherine was inconsolable. With great effort she was pulled from her husband's body and the coffin sealed and left under guard until the completion of the Peter and Paul Cathedral. It was not until the summer of 1733, following the dedication of the cathedral, that the coffin with Peter's remains was placed beneath the floor of the burial vault. At that time

Catherine's own coffin—she survived her husband by only two years—was placed next to his.

And as the funeral was ending and people were leaving the church, the terrible blast of the final salute from all guns at once rang out. Peter became a part of history. On the next day, things returned to normal.

* * *

After the funeral, spring came to St. Petersburg, its first spring without Peter. Travelers visiting the Russian capital for the first time in 1725 were struck by the purposeful energy, wide scope, and comprehensive planning with which Peter had built his city. It was still incomplete, but its future scale and beauty could already be felt. The broad and clean streets, rhythmic uniformity of the buildings and palaces, and the tall pointed spires of the churches were new and unusual for Russian cities. The city grew thanks to the will and love of one man, its founder, its gardener. And that spring, when the gardener returned no more to his young creation, it began an independent life of its own. More than twenty years had passed since its foundation, people had been born and grew up here as citizens of St. Petersburg. And no matter what happened to their city, it was and would remain forever their homeland, their childhood home, the dearest place to them on earth. This gave the city hope for a future even without Peter.

As empress, Catherine sought to demonstrate that her reign would be a humane one: many high officials who had fallen into disfavor and those imprisoned for crimes against the state were pardoned. All would remain as it had been during Peter's rule. And indeed life in St. Petersburg was measured and calm. Thousands of workers labored on its construction sites. Traditions and holidays instituted during Peter's reign continued to be observed. In the spring of 1725, a large new ship called the *Noli me tangere* was launched, the construction of which was begun by Peter. The launching of boats from the admiralty shipyard, located on the bank of the Neva in the center of the city, was a favorite event for Peter, a splendid shipwright. In the presence of his wife, the court, and diplomatic corps, he himself would usually direct the crucial and symbolic ceremony of launching a new ship. For Peter, politician, warrior, and engineer, launching a ship he had created was a test of his abilities, the accuracy of his calculations, and even more—a test of fate. Who knew whether all the calculations would prove correct, or whether he had made a mistake in devoting himself to such a complex and fine art as shipbuilding? But then, with a shake the ship, symbol of young Russia, would slide faster and faster from the building stocks into the water. The Neva would receive it into its lap. Yet another of the many sons of Master Shipwright Peter Mikhailov sails proudly, while its father, right again in his calculations, looks on in admiration.

That spring all was as it had been under Peter's rule. The empress observed the ceremony from a wooden barge anchored opposite the Admiralty;

CATHARINA IMPERATRIX
RUSSORUM

Catherine I. From I. N. Bozherianov, "*Nevskii prospekt.*" *Kul'turno-istoricheskii ocherk dvukhvekovoi zhizni Sankt-Peterburga* ("Nevskii Prospect." A Cultural and Historical Sketch of St. Petersburg at Two Hundred) (St. Petersburg, 1901–03), vol. 1, p. 41.

flags and pennants were waving, cannons blasted, and the ship entered its natural element. Catherine circled it twice, admiring its smooth contours and lines, raised the first glass for the fortune of her son, gave the sign to continue the feast, and returned home. Peter's celebrations on new ships, as a rule, turned into terrible days' long drinking-bouts from which the tsar reluctantly let his intoxicated and exhausted guests return home. Now that the main toastmaster was gone, the occasion passed quietly and ended early: by nine in the evening everyone had left for home. Apparently new times had begun after all.

"We desire that all that was begun through the emperor's efforts, with God's help, be completed"[50]—that was the empress's promise to her subjects in one of her first manifestos. And indeed at first glance that was the way it seemed. The short reign of Catherine I is famous in Russian history for the opening of the Academy of Sciences. Peter conceived this project, but did not live long enough to see it realized. An entire year was spent corresponding on the matter with specialists abroad. At that time Russia had no professional scientists. They all had to be invited from Germany, France, and other countries. One has to give credit to these people. They came on their own free will to Russia, infamous in Europe as a country of barbarians, savages, and religious schismatics. Leaving their illustrious positions in comfortable university towns in Europe, they were inspired by the wide horizons of serious work for the benefit of science and civilization in general. They believed Peter when he guaranteed them normal working conditions, high salaries, and the independence so necessary to a scientist, and without which he could never be successful. And the newly arrived scholars and scientists were not mistaken: Russia opened its doors and heart to them. For many it became a second homeland, where they won fame, honor, and respect. Their ashes remain in Russia to this day. These scientists are the glory of Russia. They, along with their Russian colleagues, elevated Russia into a country not alien to science and culture.

And it was under Catherine that the inauguration of the academy took place. The empress received the first academicians and benevolently listened to the speech of Professor Jacob Herman, delivered in Latin. He hailed the empress as one who would continue Peter's great educational endeavors. The Livland peasant girl sitting on the throne did not understand a word of Latin, but nodded her head in agreement, glancing occasionally at Aleksandr Menshikov, the field marshal and member of the British Royal Society, who was standing next to her and could not understand a single word, either. Everyone was quite pleased with what was happening, with themselves, and with each other.

From the earliest days of Catherine's reign, Menshikov became the most important man in government. The empress was not a statesman. She could only reign, but it was Menshikov who ruled. He had played a decisive role in Catherine's accession to the throne, and now he wanted his full due: power, honor, money, titles, and rank. Peter's death had freed Menshikov from the eternal fear of punishment for his numerous transgressions and graft. Now he was free! And instantly there emerged to the surface personality traits that he repressed during the life of the tsar and that the tsar was quick to punish: greed, boundless ambition, haughty confidence in his right to suppress other people.

Pavel Iaguzhinskii, the head of the highest state body, the senate, tried to oppose Menshikov. Impulsive and unrestrained, Iaguzhinskii was addicted to drink and took pleasure in publicly exposing the social shortcomings and

Pavel I. Iaguzhinskii. From A. V. Morozov, *Katalog moego sobraniia russkikh gravirovannykh i litografirovannykh portretov* (Catalogue of My Collection of Engraved and Lithographed Portraits), vol. 4 (Moscow, 1913), folio CDLXXVII.

the personal vices of those around him. Many documents that passed through his hands shed light on Menshikov's unseemly activities, and Iaguzhinskii was eager to expose him before the throne. The scandalous quarrels of these two principal officials could not but please the court cliques and grieve the tsaritsa, who rebuked them both by turns.

The head of the secret police, Peter Tolstoi, followed Iaguzhinskii and Menshikov's quarrels with keen attention. His aim was to convince the

Peter A. Tolstoi. From A. G. Brikner, *Istoriia Petra Velikogo* (History of Peter the Great) (St. Petersburg, 1882), p. 203.

empress to consult with him—an experienced and impartial politician. His detailed and cunning reports sometimes captivated the tsaritsa, sometimes put her to sleep. All other high officials remained in the background and relaxed with pleasure after decades of incessant work imposed on them by the tsar-reformer.

Moreover, several individuals of dubious intelligence within Catherine's circle began to think that now they did not have to stand upon ceremony with the empress herself, whose mild nature and lightheartedness was strikingly different from Peter's style of rule. A prominent religious figure, Archbishop Feodosii, turned out to be just such a fool. He once allowed himself to express in public his rather negative opinion of Catherine and certain practices taking place at her court. Such behavior on the part of the formerly obedient and obsequious church hierarch was regarded as mutiny. Just as swiftly as under Peter's rule an investigation took place and a trial was organized, which sentenced Feodosii to death. Catherine demonstrated her magnanimity: she commuted Feodosii's death sentence to confinement in a monastery prison.

This turned out to be more terrifying than execution on the scaffold. Feodosii was immured in an underground prison of a remote monastery located in the far north near Arkhangel'sk. He was given bread and water through a narrow window opening. Peter's former and very successful confessor survived only a few months in hunger and the filth of his own excrement, dying without confession in February 1726. This was just the way in which dozens of people had died who had disagreed with the official religion and who had been sent by Feodosii to similar prison cells when he was at the peak of power. The woman seated on the throne had shown everyone that in Russia autocratic power even in weak, female hands remained indisputable, and no one would be allowed to scorn it. This was the most striking feature of eighteenth-century Russia: a weak and incapable leader did not presuppose a weak regime, or a weak autocratic power structure.

The empress badly needed outside assistance in order to deal with affairs of state, something which she was unable to do on her own. Therefore, in February 1726, a new organ of power was formed, the Supreme Privy Council, which took on the entire burden of the routine functions of government. It comprised such prominent figures of the period as Aleksandr Menshikov, Gavriil Golovkin, Peter Tolstoi, Count Dmitrii Golitsyn, Andrei Osterman, Admiral-General Fedor Apraksin, and the empress's son-in-law Charles Frederick, the Duke of Holstein, who in May 1725 had married Tsarevna Anna.

The council was headed by the empress herself. The council's charter naively read that it had been formed "*by our side* for no other reason than that of relieving and helping with advice and impartial opinions on all state matters."[51] The empress could have found no better words for admitting her incapacity. After a few initial sessions, she stopped making appearances to listen to the ministers' boring discussions and only signed the decrees that they drew up.

But a minister's lot became more and more difficult: a position in the Supreme Privy Council looked like a sinecure only from a distance. Matters requiring responsible and serious consideration fell like an avalanche upon the councilors. When Peter was alive, he generated all ideas for reform and plans for their execution. As he was responsible for all government functions, he was the supreme guarantor for all that went on in the country.

Now Peter was dead. And the work of government that he left behind proved to be a heavy burden on the shoulders of his associates. One very important thing became clear after Peter's death: the country could not go on living any longer in keeping with his behests. Decades of war, numerous reforms, exorbitant taxes, and obligations had ruined the peasants and merchants. Hundreds of thousands of peasants had left their homes: some fled to the Don steppes in the south, others crossed the Polish border, and still others made their way to Siberia trying to escape the cruel tax-collector, thievish administrator, and merciless chastiser. Information reached the capital that there was a great increase of arrears in tax collections, that many villages were completely forsaken, and that many areas of the country were suffering from hunger. In short, knowing the real state of affairs in the country, the new rulers were compelled to change the former, Petrine, policies.

Catherine's government followed the principle: "*Petrus erat magnus monarcha, sed jam non est*"—"Peter was a great monarch, but he is already gone." He could not envisage all the consequences of his reforms, and he too could make mistakes. That is how Menshikov and his associates explained to themselves and to others their motives for discontinuing the Petrine reforms and projects. For many this was unconscionable: no sooner had the tsar closed his eyes than his successors began tearing down the idols they had worshipped for decades.

But cruel necessity compelled the Supreme Privy Council to take this action: expenses and taxes had to be reduced, many ambitious projects, which the impoverished country no longer had the resources to realize, had to be abandoned. Reducing the size of the army and the state bureaucracy and easing trade regulations were problems that came to the fore. Members of the Supreme Privy Council were kept busy carrying on continuous heated discussions and preparing decrees to be signed by the tsaritsa. The furious pace of transformation slowed abruptly, and the huge ship of the empire entered still waters.

Necessity and state expediency were not the only reasons that motivated the members of the Supreme Privy Council to retreat from Peter's reforms and suspend the realization of Peter's grandiose plans. They consciously based their policies on criticism of Peter's principles because to criticize one's predecessors is the easiest policy of all. The leaders of the post-Petrine government sought to earn political capital by pleasing those who had opposed the reforms all along. They thought not so much about their country as about themselves, their power, and their positions at the foot of the throne, occupied by Catherine.

Foreign diplomats who watched the changes at the Russian court with a vigilant eye agreed unanimously in their appraisal of Catherine: after Peter's death, she had become another person. Not a trace remained of the modest, thrifty keeper of Peter's house in the Summer Gardens. Catherine openly led a dissipated life that turned into one continuous holiday. Outdoor balls gave way to dances in palace halls; luxurious dinner parties followed lively picnics, and boat rides on the Neva River alternated with carriage rides around St. Petersburg.

Campredon noted in the spring of 1725 that mourning for the tsar was observed in form alone. Catherine often visited the Peter and Paul Cathedral, weeping beside her husband's coffin, but soon set out on yet another spree. "Those amusements constitute almost daily drinking-bouts which take place in the garden and continue the whole night through and well into the next day, and involve persons whose duties require them to always be present at court," wrote the French diplomat.[52]

The empress's tastes were not highly refined. The lessons of Peter's that she assimilated best were his rather vulgar forms of amusement. Peter had established a special club of drunkards, "The All-Joking, All-Drunken Synod of Fools and Jesters," whose rituals were founded on praise of Bacchus, God of wine, and his faithful priests, one of whom was the emperor himself. The frequent drinking-bouts of the Mock Synod knew no restraints. Catherine kept up this tradition. Princess Nastasia Golitsyna, an old confirmed drunkard and female jester, became the main "heroine" of Catherine's drinking parties at court. Her court register gives one account of when the empress, Menshikov, and other dignitaries were having dinner in the hall and drinking English beer "and Princess Golitsyna was offered a second cup into which Her Majesty had placed ten ten-ruble coins."[53] The reader may ask: What does that mean? There's only one answer—Golitsyna would get the gold coins only after emptying the entire contents of the huge cup. According to the entries in the register, the princess was a firm and steadfast contender in combat with Bacchus, although she lost at times as well: Bacchus proved to be stronger, and the princess would drop under the table to join the empress's other incautious guests who had collapsed there while others at the party roared with laughter.

Residents of St. Petersburg long remembered the "amusing" incident organized by Catherine on the night of April 1, 1726, when the order was given to sound an alarm throughout the city. Only when the frightened half-dressed people tumbled out into the dark streets did they learn that this was a way of celebrating April Fool's Day. We have no record of what they said about their sovereign after this incident, but it is not difficult to guess.

Most of her subjects knew nothing about these disgraceful drinking-bouts. On holidays, Catherine appeared before them in all her glory and beauty. "She wore a riding-habit of silver cloth, her skirt was trimmed with a gold Spanish lace, and a white plume fluttered on her hat,"[54] writes a French diplomat who had seen the empress at the celebration of Epiphany. Surrounded by her splendid retinue she was riding in a sumptuous golden carriage past crowds of onlookers. "Vivat!" cried the regiments formed up on the square; cannons fired; heads and banners bowed low to the ground. Power, glory, and the delight of her subjects—more than Cinderella could have dreamed of in her lowly Livland kitchen—were hers!

Yet sometimes, having had her fill of glory, the empress would descend to the palace kitchen and as in the aforementioned register "she did some cooking in the kitchen herself."[55] Peter was right when he repeated the saying: "Habit is second nature."

In early 1726, the sovereign's court began to buzz with gossip: an "invasion" of the empress's relatives from Livland had begun. The fact of their existence had been known for some time. As long ago as 1721, when Peter and Catherine were in Riga, Christina Skavronskaia, a peasant-serf, came to see them; embarrassing the courtiers and the guards with her villagelike appearance, she insisted that she was the tsaritsa's sister. And that was the case. Catherine talked with her, gave her some money, and sent her home. At that time Peter issued an order to seek out the rest of his wife's relatives, who had been scattered around the country by the war. They were all to be kept under watch and were not allowed to parade their kinship with the empress.

Although democratic in his manners, Peter knew measure, and those favors and gifts that he showered on Catherine he had no intention of extending to her barefooted family. Catherine's peasant relatives could damage the prestige of the dynasty, and cause people to cast aspersions on their children.

When Catherine came to power she did not think of her kinsfolk, but they reminded her of their existence themselves—probably deciding to act when the news of Catherine's succession reached them. Prince Repnin, the Governor of Riga, sent a message to St. Petersburg that a peasant Christina Skavronskaia had called on him with a complaint on the oppressions she had been subjected to by her landlord. Kristina also said that she was the empress's sister.

At first Catherine was obviously embarrassed. She gave an order to keep her sister and her family "in a modest place and to provide them with a sufficient amount of food and clothing";[56] then to take them away from their landlord on some pretext and "to appoint a confidential person to look after them who could keep them from idle talk" (that is, about our heroine's ragamuffin childhood).[57]

However, six months later, feelings of kinship prevailed and the Skavronskii family was brought to St. Petersburg—to the suburban palace in Tsarskoe Selo, to be exact, as far as possible from the curious eyes of ill-wishers. One can imagine what was going on in the Tsarskoe Selo palace! Catherine's relatives arrived in abundance. Apart from her eldest brother, Samuel, her second brother, Karl, came with his three sons and three daughters, also her sister Christina with husband and four children, and her sister Anna with husband and two daughters—so all in all about twenty hangers-on. It took the empress's village relatives, who had just come from their pitchforks and milk-pails, quite a while to learn to wash themselves clean, make curtsies, bow, and wear nobleman's clothes. Of course, there was no time to teach them Russian, and there was no need to do so—in early 1727, they were all granted the title of count; in addition to this, they received large estates and became very rich landowners. For some reason, however, no records have been found that testify to any particular closeness between the empress and her family.

A closeness, however, did arise between the empress and her smart handsome chamberlain Count Reingold Gustav Löwenwolde, who in some ways resembled the late Villim Mons. Times had changed and there was no reason to hide her affections; so Catherine kept the young lover by her side day and night. But at times he was also at a loss to cope with the feverish rhythm of life at court. The French diplomat Magnan reported that Menshikov and Bassewitz had visited the empress's fond friend, who "was tired of endless feasting." The poor count must have been suffering greatly, and the field marshal–general was good enough to sympathize with him.

Indeed, Menshikov, being an experienced courtier, was well aware that nothing good would come of the lifestyle which the empress was leading. There was firm evidence supporting this: at times the empress was said to be "in high spirits, eating and drinking as usual, and going to bed no earlier than four or five o'clock in the morning as she usually did,"[58] and at other times the feasts and drinking-bouts came to an abrupt halt, as Catherine could not get out of bed. She began to fall ill more and more frequently. No longer could she dance all night long—her legs became swollen and she suffered from asthma attacks. Frequent fits of fever prevented her from leaving home. Nevertheless, she would force herself to leave her bedroom, take a ride, dance, and drink, only to take to her bed again afterward. Sensing that the end was near, Catherine gave little heed to her life and health, and she set about squandering the little that remained.

In early 1727, Menshikov was thinking hard not so much about the Bacchante-empress's health as about his own future. What will happen to him if Grand Duke Peter ascends the throne after Catherine's death? It was he, Menshikov, who had blocked Peter's way to the throne in 1725. The Most Serene Prince realized that he did not necessarily have to struggle against fate: let Peter take his grandfather's throne, but something had to be done to ensure that he do so with Menshikov's assistance, Peter having been slated by that time to be his son-in-law and already engaged to one of his daughters.

Menshikov had two daughters, Aleksandra and Maria. Maria had been engaged to a Polish aristocrat, Peter Sapega, a delicate and comely man. The two became fond friends. But one day Empress Catherine noticed the handsome Sapega amid the crowd of courtiers and nodded to him favorably. That was enough for Menshikov to enter into negotiations with his old girlfriend: in return for freeing Sapega from his engagement obligation to Maria, Menshikov requested a suitable substitute for his daughter—namely, allowing her to become engaged to the twelve-year-old grand duke Peter. The well-informed Dutch envoy Hans Georg Westphalen referred to this particular "exchange" when he wrote: "The empress has literally snatched Sapega away from the princess and made him her favorite. This gave Menshikov the right to discuss with Catherine another suitable match for his daughter with the young tsarevich. The empress was obliged to Menshikov in many ways—an old friend of her heart. It was he who had introduced her, a simple servant girl, to Peter the Great, and later influenced the emperor's decision to recognize her as his spouse."[59] No, Martha could not refuse Aleksashka's request!

The veterans of the coup of January 28, 1725, did not like Menshikov's crafty plan. In seeking his daughter's marriage to Peter (whom he was simultaneously making the new heir to the throne), the Most Serene Prince was leaving to the mercies of fate those who had helped him to elevate Catherine to the throne in 1725. Peter Tolstoi was especially anxious. The chief of the Secret Chancery had many secret threads of power in his hands, and now one of these threads had been jerked and stretched—Tolstoi sensed danger: Grand Duke Peter's accession to the throne would mean the end for him, the inexorable executioner, and killer of Tsarevich Aleksei, the emperor-to-be's father.

Other dignitaries also worried about their future: General Ivan Buturlin, who had brought the guards to the Winter Palace on the night of Peter the Great's death; the chief of police, General Anton Devier; and others. They were aware that Menshikov was deserting to the enemy's camp, joining Grand Duke Peter's advocates, and in doing so betraying them.

Tolstoi and Catherine's daughters, Anna and Elizabeth, implored the empress not to listen to Menshikov and to write the will in favor of Elizabeth, but Catherine, enamored of Sapega, was adamant. And Menshikov himself was not sitting around doing nothing. He was taking action, decisive action. Once in a conversation with Campredon he had spoken candidly about Tolstoi: "Peter Andreevich Tolstoi is in all respects a very cunning person, in any case, in dealing with him it does not hurt to keep a good stone in one's pocket, in order to break his teeth in case he decides to bite."[60]

And the time had come for Menshikov to get out his stone: Tolstoi, Devier, Buturlin, and others discontent with his actions were arrested and accused of conspiracy against the empress. Desperation hurried Menshikov: The "conspirators" were interrogated on April 26, 1727, and as early as May 6 Menshikov had reported to Catherine about the successful uncovering of the plot. Conceding to his demands, she signed the order exiling Tolstoi and the others. This happened within just a few hours of Catherine's death. Menshikov celebrated his victory. But at that time, in May 1727, he did not know that it was a Pyrrhic victory, that a mere four months were to pass before the new emperor, Peter II, who had gained the throne thanks to Menshikov's efforts, would in turn send the former Serene Prince into exile. Tolstoi and Menshikov shared the same fate: they both died in 1729, Tolstoi immured in Solovetskii Monastery, located on the cold islands of the Northern White Sea, and Menshikov in the remote Siberian town of Berezovo.

"The empress has become so weak and changed so much, that it's almost impossible to recognize her," wrote the French diplomat Magnan in mid-April 1727.[61] Everyone was alarmed that she did not even appear in church on the first day of the Easter celebration, and there was no feasting on her birthday. It was unlike our Bacchante to miss any festive occasion. She was in a grave state. Menshikov did not leave the palace. He saw to it that the empress's will was prepared in time, according to which Menshikov's future son-in-law the Grand Duke Peter would become heir to the throne.

We do not know what ailed Catherine. Most likely it was consumption. Fits of a suffocating cough and total loss of strength alternated with sparks of feverish hectic activity and inexplicable cheerfulness. The forty-three-year-old woman, formerly of good health, did not believe the end was near. She was wearied of the fuss raised over her will, and she sent everyone to Menshikov, and signed all the papers that he gave her without so much as looking at them. In the spring not long before her death she made up her mind to take a drive along the sunlit streets of St. Petersburg, but soon turned back. She had not even the strength to ride in a carriage.

There is a vivid legend regarding Catherine's passing. Not long before her death she told of one of her dreams in which she was sitting at a table prepared for a feast surrounded by her retinue. Suddenly Peter's shadow appears and beckons his dearest friend after him. They fly away as if in a cloud. Catherine casts one last glance back and clearly sees her daughters encircled by a loud malevolent crowd. But it was too late for remedies. Faithful Menshikov was her last hope—he would not abandon them in time of need.

Catherine died at nine o'clock in the evening on May 6, 1727. The fairy tale of the Cinderella from Livland came to its sad end.

CHAPTER 2

The Poor Relative Who Became Empress

(Anna Ioannovna)

The night of January 18, 1730, was a sleepless one for many Muscovites. The Russian autocrat Peter II (Alekseevich) lay dying in the Lefortovo Palace, his imperial residence on the Iauza River. He had caught cold twelve days earlier, on January 6, while taking part in the Epiphany celebration on the frozen Moscow River. To complicate matters he came down with smallpox, a common disease in those days. At first the tsar became delirious, then his fever continued to rise, and by the night of January 18 he was in a grave state. The doctors, priests, and courtiers keeping constant watch at his bedside could do nothing to help their sovereign: Peter II died without regaining consciousness. According to contemporaries his last words were: "Harness the sledge, I want to drive to my sister's."[1] The tsar's sister, the Grand Duchess Natalia, had died in the autumn of 1728. The night of January 18 was a terrifying one for Russia. Not only had the tsar died, the autocrat, a fourteen-year-old boy who should have lived a long full life, but with him died the last direct descendant of the male line of the Romanov dynasty, which extended back to its founder and the first Romanov tsar Mikhail Fedorovich (1613–1645). Now Aleksei Mikhailovich's great grandson, Peter the Great's grandson, son of Tsarevich Aleksei, was dead. Everyone present that night in the Lefortovo Palace was thinking the same thing: "Who will inherit the throne?"

Many times in Russian history, after the death of a ruler who had left behind no direct heir, the horror of interregnum threatened the country. People remembered the terrible years of the Time of Troubles in the early seventeenth century when, following the passing of the childless Tsar Fedor Ivanovich and the mysterious death of the last of Ivan the Terrible's sons, Tsarevich Dmitrii, the country was beset by civil war, pillage, and ruin. In the words of one contemporary, the Russian people were locked in an "insane silence." It seemed to everyone then that the sky would collapse on the Russian land, ravaged by crime and sin, and Russia would cease to exist.

People remembered the events of the spring of 1682, when the childless tsar Fedor Alekseevich died. Then the strel'tsy, skillfully provoked and directed by Tsarevna Sophia, set about killing and robbing those siding with the family of the newly crowned tsar, ten-year-old Peter I. People also remembered what had happened in January 1725, when the death of Peter, who had left no will, had almost brought about an open confrontation between court factions. And now, five years later, it appeared that the specters of the Time of Troubles might once again rise from their graves. On that winter night, January 18, 1730, in the Lefortovo Palace in Moscow, the fate of Russia, a huge sleeping giant still unaware of what had come to pass, was being decided.

Peter II left neither heirs nor last will and testament. After rising to power in May 1727 thanks to Menshikov's efforts, he followed the advice of secret enemies of the Most Serene Prince and got rid of Menshikov as early as September of the same year, stripping him of ranks and exiling him to Siberia. Tall for his age and physically well-developed, young Peter had fairly early fallen into the bad company of that era's golden youth, befriending Count Ivan Dolgorukii, who was known as a profligate roisterer. After the court's move to Moscow in early 1728, Peter immersed himself fully in a world of diversions. Hunting became his passion. It is difficult to say what fate would have awaited Russia if Peter II had not died at the age of fourteen, but had lived to rule for a considerable time. Of course, personalities can change and character can develop, but still one cannot deny the impression that Peter II would have been for Russia what Louis XV had been as the king of France, a symbol of depravity and shamelessness.

But fate would have it otherwise, and therefore the people who were present in the palace on the night of January 18, 1730, were tormented by one question: Who would take power? Would it be the offspring of Peter the Great and Catherine I, their twenty-year-old daughter, Elizaveta Petrovna, or would it be their two-year-old grandson, Charles Peter Ulrich, the son of the already deceased Anna Petrovna and Charles Frederick, Duke of Holstein-Gottorp? Or maybe, as after the death of the last tsar of the ancient dynasty founded by Riurik, another dynasty would begin to rule in Russia.

The Dolgorukii princes were dreaming of just that. They were also of the Riurik lineage, belonging to a more distant branch, and they had almost always been shunted to the political sidelines. Only during the short reign of Peter II did they, thanks to Ivan Dolgorukii's status as favorite, assume leading roles in government and make gains in wealth, power, and high ranks.

Peter II. From the journal *Russkaia starina* (Russia of Old) (St. Petersburg, 1890), tip-in plate.

The favorite's father, Prince Aleksei Grigor'evich, was particularly successful. He courted the young tsar and eventually secured the ruler's betrothal to his daughter and Ivan's sister, the Princess Ekaterina Dolgorukaia. The festive engagement party had taken place on November 31, 1729. The wedding date was set for January 19, 1730. It seemed that the Dolgorukiis were on the brink of becoming related to the ruling dynasty, and out of any reach of their enemies and evil-wishers. How deep must have been their despair when they learned of their future bridegroom's fatal illness. They had to act quickly, do something.

Thus on January 18 Aleksei Dolgorukii's relatives held a secret meeting at his home. After some wrangling, a counterfeit will was written, which they had decided to read publicly as soon as Peter II had closed his eyes forever. According to this will, the tsar was supposed to have passed the throne to his future bride, Princess Ekaterina Alekseevna Dolgorukaia. Prince Ivan

Ivan A. Dolgorukii. From I. N. Bozherianov, "*Nevskii prospekt.*"
*Kul'turno-istoricheskii ocherk dvukhvekovoi zhizni Sankt-
Peterburga* ("Nevskii Prospect." A Cultural and Historical Sketch
of St. Petersburg at Two Hundred) (St. Petersburg, 1901–03),
vol. 1, p. 52.

Dolgorukii even signed one of the copies of the will on behalf of the tsar.
How did the Dolgorukiis dare to do such a thing? They were by no means
naive simpletons who did not understand that in creating this false document they were committing a serious national crime, for which exile to Siberia would have been a mild punishment. We do not know which motivated
them most, frivolity, arrogance, confidence that they could get away with
it, or desperation. But the opinion of contemporaries has been passed on to
us that the Dolgorukii clan had never been known for its intelligence, a
quality essential to successful politics.

Immediately following the death of Peter II, the Supreme Privy Council,
Russia's highest government body, convened in the Lefortovo Palace. In
addition to the four members of the Council—Chancellor Count Gavriil
Golovkin, Prince Dmitrii Golitsyn, and the Dolgorukii princes Aleksei and

Vasilii—two field marshals, Prince Mikhail Golitsyn and Prince Vasilii Vladimirovich Dolgorukii, and the governor of Siberia, Prince Mikhail Dolgorukii, were also invited. In total two represented the Golitsyn clan and four were from the Dolgorukii family. At the very beginning of the meeting Prince Aleksei Dolgorukii placed Peter II's "last will and testament" on the table. But the plan, which had appeared to the Dolgorukiis as being so brilliant and well-laid, fell immediately flat. Neither the Golitsyns nor even Field Marshal Dolgorukii, whose word as an old military leader carried great weight, supported the ruse. A scandal, however, was averted when the council's most authoritative and experienced member, Prince Dmitrii Mikhailovich Golitsyn, took the floor. For many years he had served Peter the Great. He was intelligent and educated. He condemned the excesses of Petrine reforms and was disturbed by the "humiliations" imposed upon the ancient noble families, which the great transformer of Russia had held in little regard. Dmitrii Golitsyn's speech was short and well thought out. Brushing aside the Dolgorukii's dynastic claims, he said that "we must choose from the illustrious Romanov family and no other. Insomuch as the male line of this dynasty has come to an end with Peter II, we have no other alternative than to consider the female line . . . and choose one of Tsar Ivan's daughters."

Ivan V, Peter the Great's older brother and co-ruler from 1682 to 1696, had sired three daughters: Catherine, the Duchess of Mecklenburg; Anna, the Duchess of Courland; and Tsarevna Praskovia. Golitsyn proposed making the middle sister, Anna, empress. All those present found this unexpected proposal satisfactory, including the slighted Dolgorukii family and other associates, whose main fear was that Peter the Great and Catherine I's children might rise to power. Therefore Prince Dmitrii's arguments in favor of this alternative seemed irrefutable. Anna was a widow, but still of an age to be married and bear heirs, and, most important, "she was born in our midst, from a Russian mother, and into a good old family [this was a slur on the Livland peasant-girl Catherine I—E.A.], we are aware of her kind heart and other splendid merits."[2]

The Supreme Privy Council members listened attentively to Prince Dmitrii: the candidacy of the widowed Duchess of Courland seemed ideal to them also because Anna had no influence whatsoever at court, no one feared her; on the contrary, they all counted on gaining great benefits for themselves from her rise to the throne. "Vivat, our empress Anna Ioannovna!" Field Marshal Dolgorukii was the first to exclaim, and the others joined him. The old military man probably reproached himself many times later for his impulsiveness and cursed his enthusiasm. In 1731, after being accused of insulting Her Majesty's honor, Anna stripped him of his rank and titles and imprisoned him for eight long years.

But Dmitrii Mikhailovich was not through giving his speech yet. Having waited for total silence to prevail, he went on to say something that caused all those present to open their mouths in awe and to fall into deep contemplation. And indeed there was something worth thinking about. Prince Golitsyn announced that it was time to "make our own lives easier, and provide ourselves more freedoms," by limiting the power of the new sovereign in favor of the Supreme Privy Council, of which all those present were members.[3] Prince Dmitrii Mikhailovich had long advocated the idea of restraining the power of the autocracy. He was well-read, liked to juxtapose and consider different ideas, and made friends with many scholars. He had seen a lot during his sixty-five years: he had been an ambassador to Istanbul, governor of Kiev, president of the Financial College, senator, and member of the Supreme Privy Council. He had been an eyewitness to the Petrine reforms, which had turned life in Russia upside-down. Prince Dmitrii saw the obvious advantages of the new state which Peter the Great had built. But as an aged noble grandee he was provoked by the scornful, disparaging attitude toward high-born nobles that Peter and his undistinguished cronies, such as Menshikov, Iaguzhinskii and their like, demonstrated. Many times in his life Prince Dmitrii had himself experienced humiliation and fear.

In 1723 proceedings were begun in the matter of breaches of conduct against Senator Peter Shafirov. Action was also brought against Golitsyn, who was relieved of his post and placed under house arrest. An interesting scene was recorded at this time in the diary of the Duke of Holstein Charles Frederick's *Kammer-junker* (gentleman of the bedchamber) Frederick William Bergholtz: when once his master entered Tsaritsa Catherine's chamber he saw that "at Her Majesty's feet lay the former chamber president and current senator Prince Golitsyn, who touched his head to the floor several times and most humbly thanked her for her intervention before the sovereign: In the matter of Shafirov, he, together with Prince Dolgorukii, had been sentenced to six months' arrest and had already spent several days in prison, but on that day, at the request of Her Majesty, he had been pardoned."[4] Of course the well-born, proud grandee could not forget such a humiliation.

And now, with the death of Peter II it had suddenly become possible to markedly change the situation in favor of the high-born nobility. Dmitrii Golitsyn's proposal of selecting a weak ruler for the throne, as precisely so Anna seemed to everyone, under the condition that the ruler's power be limited by the Privy Council, which consisted primarily of noble grandees, satisfied both the Golitsyns and the Dolgorukiis. Such a proposal even allowed them to forget the animosity and rivalry that had divided these two clans during Peter II's reign and earlier. The cautious Vasilii Lukich Dolgorukii did express some misgivings: "Although we may attain, we might not hold on to [power]!" "We'll hold on to it, all right,"[5] replied Prince Dmitrii confidently, and proposed reinforcing the limitations of autocratic power by special conditions, which the new sovereign would be required to sign before ascending the throne.

And then something unexpected happened: the Supreme Privy Council members summoned a secretary and began to dictate these conditions crowding around the table and interrupting one another. The poor official was overwhelmed by the feverish, flagrantly rapacious attitude of the power-hungry old men. He did not know which one he should listen to. Then they tore the draft out of his hands. And one after the other, the grandees themselves sat down and had a turn at writing. In less than an hour the conditions were ready. They prohibited the empress from initiating wars, imposing taxes, spending state funds, granting anyone villages or ranks, and commanding the army and Guards without the permission of the Supreme Privy Council. The document ended with the words: "Should I not fulfill any part of this promise, I shall be deprived of the Russian crown."[6] On the evening of January 19 Dmitrii Golitsyn's younger brother, Prince Mikhail Golitsyn, and Prince Vasilii Lukich Dolgorukii set out in haste for Courland to deliver the conditions to Anna Ioannovna.

* * *

On the evening of January 18, 1730, Anna Ioannovna, the thirty-seven-year-old Duchess of Courland, had gone to bed as usual. But upon wakening the next morning, she was already the empress of Russia, the ruler of one of the greatest powers in the world. Located in the territory of current-day Latvia, Mitau, the quiet snow-covered capital of the small duchy of Courland, was far removed from Moscow. It took a week for the delegation of the Supreme Privy Council to arrive in Mitau on the evening of January 25 in order to offer Anna the throne. She greeted the Moscow envoys immediately in the modest reception hall, where Prince Vasilii Dolgorukii informed the Duchess of Peter II's death and of her selection as empress—that is, of course, if she would agree to sign the conditions. Anna Ioannovna "deigned to mourn the passing of His Majesty," wrote Prince Vasilii in his dispatch to Moscow, "and then ordered the conditions to be read aloud to her, and, having heard them, deigned to sign them with her own hand thus: 'I pledge in accordance herewith to uphold everything without a single omission. Anna.'"[7]

Dolgorukii's letter reads routinely; it does not reflect the psychological aspects of what had happened. I do not believe that Prince Vasilii, an experienced diplomat and well acquainted with the duchess from previous meetings, was particularly worried. It was a fail-safe assignment. On behalf of the council, he dictated Anna the conditions: If you want to, sign the conditions and you will be empress; if you do not want to, keep living in Courland. You have two sisters; it is unlikely that they will decline the imperial crown!

We do not know what feelings Anna experienced at that time. But we do know that she had twenty-four hours in which to consider the matter. That which she had heard from Dolgorukii was not news to her. Despite the barriers set up around Moscow at the order of the Supreme Privy Council members, one courier managed to get through with a letter from Anna's long-time acquaintance, Count Karl Gustav Löwenwolde. It was he who had informed her of what had happened in Moscow. And then, as forever thereafter, having become the almighty sovereign, she never doubted her right to the throne: The daughter of a tsar, she was born in wedlock to a mother from an old family. In terms of purity of bloodline, Anna was indeed among the first. She was only expressing the facts of pedigree when she subsequently taunted Elizabeth so maliciously, the daughter of the Livland laundress Catherine I, and her numerous peasant relatives, members of the Skavronskii family.

Besides, Anna remembered well the prophecy of her mother's *iurodivyi* (God's fool) Timofei Arkhipych, which foretold that she, still a girl, was to have the crown and throne. Anna was superstitious, just like many of her contemporaries, and always heeded the mysterious and vague words of all kinds of God's fools and seers, believing that they really could see into the future. And events on the winding roads of history often unexpectedly confirmed the accuracy of such prophecies.

But still the main point was that Anna would have signed anything at all in order to finally get out of provincial Mitau, to cut short the long cheerless years of her wretched and uninteresting widowhood there; to enjoy, if not power, then at least honor, prosperity, and peace of mind. She longed to leave the Kremlin's Dormition Cathedral with the imperial crown on her head to the tolling of the bells, the thunder of a fireworks salute, and the enthusiastic cries of the crowd. Of course, she could not let this unexpected miraculous chance pass by. Anna designated January 29 as the date of departure, as it turned out, forever, from Mitau.

The royal train moved along the snow-covered roads eastward into the heart of Russia. Prince Vasilii, with the vigilance of Cerberus, did not leave the empress-to-be for a moment and even rode in the same sledge as she, fearing that she might hear something derogatory about the designs of the Supreme Privy Council members. Two weeks' traveling was time enough to enjoy the winter scenery, experience all the possible inconveniences of travel, and contemplate her fate thus far. And the time was ripe for doing so, as Anna found herself once again on the crossroads of life . . .

Up to now her life had been a failure. It had been warped by another's mighty will, subordinated to the interests of other people, passed in fear, humiliation, poverty, lacking warmth and family. Yet it had all begun so radiantly: On January 28, 1693, she was born in the Kremlin, the daughter of a tsar. The splendor of the Kremlin churches and palaces, which have survived to our times, help us to imagine what unearthly beauty surrounded the newborn tsarevna. The shining glimmer of gold and silver, the brilliant colors of the wall paintings, leather stamped with gold, oriental carpets, the ineffably beautiful combinations of yellow, light-blue, azure, and scarlet—

all this created the impression of a feast for the eyes, of a paradise. But there has long been no paradise on earth, we know, and life in Kremlin palaces and peasant huts conforms to the universal laws of love and hate, of hunger and satiation, of sickness and death.

It is unlikely that Anna remembered her father—Tsar Ivan V died when she was just three years old. Indications of degeneration were obvious in his entire appearance: feeble-minded, speaking with confused articulation, and sickly from birth, Ivan was ill fit to be tsar. But by will of his power-hungry elder sister Sophia, in 1682 he was made co-ruler along with his half brother Peter. Sophia always stood behind Ivan. It was she who had forced the eighteen-year-old tsar to marry in 1684. Sophia needed Ivan to produce an heir. This would allow her to extend her power as regent and remove Peter from the throne. A bride was chosen for Ivan, one who was healthy, as Russians say—all blood and milk, the twenty-year-old Russian beauty Praskovia (Parasha) Fedorovna from the noble Saltykov family.

Rumors circulated persistently that Tsar Ivan was even less suited to married life than to state rule, and that the real father of Anna and her sisters was a courtier named Vasilii Iushkov, to whom Tsaritsa Praskovia was indeed well-inclined, giving him expensive gifts, villages, jewels, and money beyond his rank. Who knows the real truth? The first five years of their marriage were infertile, and then Parasha began to bear children nearly every year: in 1689 Maria was born, in 1690 Feodosia, in 1691 Ekaterina, in 1693 Anna, and in 1694 Praskovia. Five daughters and not one son or heir!

Maria and Feodosia died in infancy; the rest of the girls survived. That only girls were born ceased to grieve Regent Sophia: in August of 1689 she had been removed from power by Peter and shut away in Novodevichii Monastery, near Moscow, under the name of Susanna. Her brother Ivan had been relegated to the backseat of political life. Rumors, which were investigated many years later during the reign of his daughter, Empress Anna, that someone had dumped firewood on Ivan while in the latrine, are very characteristic of his unenviable position. Ivan went to his grave quietly and almost without notice, not having reached his thirty-third birthday. The widowed tsaritsa together with her three daughters left the Kremlin for good and settled in the suburban palace of Anna's grandfather, Tsar Aleksei Mikhailovich—Izmailovo.

Anna's earliest and probably best childhood memories were those connected with the relatively serene years spent in Izmailovo not far from Moscow. In the late seventeenth century Izmailovo was a quiet green corner where time seemed to stand still. Having visited there, the Austrian diplomat Korb called it "a magic refuge." The wooden palace had a whimsical shape and stood on an island surrounded by a ring of ponds. All around it were flowerbeds with luxurious exotic flowers: lilies, roses, and tulips. And a short distance beyond the ponds, apple, cherry, and plum orchards bloomed as far as the eye could see along the Serebrovka River. There were green-houses in Izmailovo that produced mandarins, grapes, and even pineapples for the royal table.

The favorite parts of the estate were its menagerie and aviary with dozens of animals and birds. Shady groves, fragrant blackthorn bushes, and barberry bordered quaint pathways—in short, spaciousness, calm, and coolness. Surrounded by countless nannies and wet nurses the tsarevnas romped in the gardens and played on the swings. One can almost picture the three tsarevnas, clothed in bright dresses, slowly floating in a boat decorated with greens and colored cloth across the smooth surface of the ponds, throwing food to the fish that would swim up to them from the depths. The historian Mikhail Semevskii maintained that living in the Izmailovskii ponds were pike and sterlet that had gold rings in their gills put on during the reign of Ivan the Terrible, that is, 150 years earlier than the events described here, and that these fish were accustomed to swim out to be fed when a little silver bell was rung.

In bad weather the tsarevnas would sit in the attic rooms, embroider with silk and gold thread, and listen to tales and songs. The palace had its own orchestra, which Korb described: "the gentle melodies of the flute and horns combined with the quiet rustling of the wind which flowed slowly from tree-tops."[8] After she became empress, Anna remembered her years at Izmailovo. In honor of her childhood home she established the Izmailovskii Guards Regiment similar to the way in which Peter the Great had created the Preobrazhenskii and Semenovskii Guards Regiments, thus commemorating the name of those places dearest to him.

At an early age the tsarevnas were taught the alphabet according to Karion Istomin's *Alphabet with Moral Teachings in Verse*. They learned to write, copying short couplets from a copy book. It must be said that the tsar's daughters were poorly taught—all her life Empress Anna wrote unevenly and ungrammatically. Foreign teachers brought with them new ideas for educating the tsarevnas. Johann Christopher Dietrich (the brother of the future vice chancellor of Russia, Osterman) taught the girls German, and the French-man Ramburg instructed them in dance and the French language. But Anna never really learned the language of Voltaire and Molière. She was no better at dancing: clumsy with no talent for music, Anna could not execute dance formations, in contrast to her plump but well-coordinated and energetic older sister, Ekaterina.

When Peter the Great was in Moscow he visited Izmailovo. He got along well with his sister-in-law, Ivan V's wife, Praskovia. Although she was uneducated and not particularly intelligent, she had the good sense and the tact not to try to give him advice, not to become entangled with the tsar-reformer's enemies, and to submissively accept his incomprehensible (and often inconvenient) innovations in everyday life and leisure. And in his own way Peter was appreciative of this: after the exile of his wife Evdokia to a monastery, Tsaritsa Praskovia, his sister Natalia, and aunt Tatiana Mikhailovna remained his closest relatives. In 1708, by the tsar's decree, Praskovia and her daughters, like Peter's other relatives, moved to the tsar's "Paradise," St. Petersburg.

Having arrived from Moscow on a huge train of sledges, Tsaritsa Praskovia and her family settled in a house prepared for them in advance on the Petersburg side of the Neva River not far from the Peter and Paul Fortress. The house was built in the new Western style and therefore appeared to the natives of Izmailovo to be uncozy and inconvenient. This was an entirely different, unknown world vastly removed from their refuge at Izmailovo. But they had no choice. One does not go against the tsar's wishes, just as one does not admit to him that one is afraid of the water. Everyone remembered what Peter had said when he met his newly arrived relatives in Schlüsselburg: "I am accustoming my family to the water, so that in the future they will not fear the sea and so that they will grow to like the location of St. Petersburg, surrounded by water. Whoever wants to live with me shall be on the water often!"[9] If Tsaritsa Praskovia had to learn to sail on a yacht in her old age, she would do it! And no one had any doubts whatsoever, at least none that they voiced out loud.

For Praskovia's daughters childhood came to an end in misty, damp St. Petersburg, which had been founded only five years earlier. They entered their youth here and with it made their debut in society. Yesterday's Izmailovo recluses now took part in court celebrations, attended dances, sailed in sloops and yachts on the Neva, spent time with their royal uncle in Kronstadt. It was a new world for them to which they were entirely unaccustomed.

But Anna was not happy. Here in St. Petersburg her mother's hostility toward her began to manifest itself. For some reason her middle daughter was a constant source of annoyance for Tsaritsa Praskovia. Anna grew up to be a silent type, even morose, and not inclined to have heart-to-heart talks with her mother. It seems that the mere appearance of her awkward, unattractive daughter spoiled Praskovia's mood. Often animosity toward one child is a sure indication of excess love toward another. And such was the case with the tsaritsa: she dearly loved her oldest daughter, Ekaterina, whom she addressed in letters as "Katiushka-Dear." A lighthearted joker and chatterbox, Ekaterina was always by her mother's side.

In general the atmosphere in Praskovia's palace was heavily laden with courtiers' gossip and squabbles, which Praskovia herself took pleasure investigating. The tsaritsa's brother, Vasilii Saltykov, was particularly hard to get on with, and Anna feared his intrigues most of all.

"Truly my dear Sovereign, I tell you," wrote Anna to Tsaritsa Catherine I from Mitau, when she was already Duchess of Courland, "I can't bear the way they scold us! If I lived with my mother now, I think I would scarcely be alive from all their intrigues." Complaining about her life, the Duchess of Courland requests help from the tsaritsa, who is kindly disposed toward her, but at the same time cautions: "And I also ask you, my dear, that my mother know nothing of all this."[10] The reader who from a general course of Russian history knows the Empress Anna only as a sullen, capricious, and suspicious individual would do well to consider whether it was possible for her to become a woman of sincerity, warmth, and charm when she had spent her early life as an unloved child, a burden to her family from which her mother took the earliest possible opportunity to rid herself.

Had Anna been born not in the late but rather in the early seventeenth century, her life's course would have been known from the first to last hour: winters spent in the royal chambers, summers in a suburban palace; almost daily church visits, old age spent in a monastery, and final rest in the family burial vault in the Kremlin. At that time tsarevnas, the tsar's daughters and sisters, were not allowed to marry. The Russian Orthodox religion did not allow them to marry a foreigner and convert to another faith; and ancient custom forbade wedlock between a tsarevna and a Russian grandee because all subjects of the Russian tsar were considered his slaves *(kholopy)*. Grigorii Kotoshikhin wrote in his book about seventeenth-century Russia during the reign of Tsar Aleksei Mikhailovich: "Princes and noblemen are their [the tsarevnas'—E.A.] slaves. And it would be considered an eternal disgrace if a lady were to be given away in marriage to a slave."[11]

But beginning with Peter the Great, revolutionary changes came to pass in dynastic politics. Peter decided to form strong blood ties between the Romanovs and other foreign dynasties. In a meeting with the king of Prussia, Frederick I, in 1709, Peter agreed to the marriage of the king's nephew Frederick William, the Duke of Courland, to one of his own nieces. The tsar left the final choice of the bride up to the Tsaritsa Praskovia, and she, going against tradition, decided to marry off not her oldest, the beloved Katiusha, but her second daughter, Anna, instead. It seems that the future mother-in-law took a disliking to the bridegroom when he arrived in St. Petersburg in 1710: he was too young, thin and weak, and a heavy drinker. On top of that his duchy was a poor estate ruined by war. In short, he was an unenviable groom, so let Anna marry him!

No one asked how Anna felt toward the groom, which was not done back then: her royal uncle and mother had decided she would be married, that was that. "From Your Highness's kind letter . . ."—Anna, or rather the Embassy Chancery, replied to the duke's gallant correspondence—"I learned with particular pleasure of our present marriage by will of the Almighty and Their Royal Highnesses. Nothing could bring me greater pleasure than to hear your confession of love for me. For my part I assure Your Highness of precisely these same feelings . . ."[12] At the end of Anna's reign the Secret Chancery, an organ for political investigations, handled the case of one peasant woman who had been caught singing a song of the time of her youth about the bride of the Duke of Courland, who supposedly had asked her terrible sovereign:

Don't give me away, uncle dear,
To a foreign land, a non-Christian land;
A non-Christian land, a heathen land.
Give me away, O ruling Tsar,
To one of your Generals, Princes, or Boyars.

The peasant woman was whipped with a knout and sent home—a very mild punishment for those times. It is possible that the empress, who was invariably informed of all the cases handled by the Secret Chancery, took pity and softened the sentence of the incautious singer, whose song had reminded her of those long-gone years of youth and those feelings that filled her then . . .

The wedding was set for the fall of 1710. October 31 marked the beginning of the festive ceremony, the likes of which had never been seen before along the banks of the Neva. An entire squadron of barges and sloops floated down the river carrying the groom, the bride, and their numerous guests. They sailed from the Petrograd side to Menshikov's palace on Vasil'evskii Island, where the wedding ceremony and festivities took place. The tsar himself directed the whole affair, dressed in a fancy scarlet caftan (unusual attire for him) and adorned with a silver sword on a beautiful baldric. Music blasted, and soldiers and ships gave gun-salutes. Never before had our heroine, the "ugly duckling" of the Russian court, been the center of such grand attention. She was dressed in stunning royal splendor. Her pitch-black hair was set off by a diamond crown, and a white velvet robe and long white mantle, also of velvet and lined with ermine, flattered her tall and suddenly majestic figure. The young groom was clad in a white-and-gold caftan.

The guests ate, drank, danced, and smoked pipes until three o'clock in the morning. Every toast ended with a round of gunfire, and in keeping with Petrine custom, as the end of the celebration grew near, the firing of the guns came more and more frequently, so much so that the tipsy guests had a hard time holding their toasting cups. The night sky was lit up with fireworks that the tsar himself set off at risk to his own life. At last the tired newlyweds were led to their bedchamber.

The celebration continued the next day. With a dagger Peter cut a giant pie and out popped a female dwarf in fancy dress. A second one popped out of a second pastry shell and together they danced a minuet right on the table. This was by way of a prologue to the royal dwarf Ekim Volkov's grandiose wedding. More than seventy Lilliputians had been brought from all over the country especially for this mock wedding. I think that Anna, as all her guests, enjoyed both the wedding ceremony and the dwarfs' feast. The audience were all products of their times and laughed to their hearts' content at a variety of human misfortunes, seeing stunted growth as a *kunst* (curiosity), an amusing live caricature of a normal man. One eyewitness wrote: "It's hard to imagine the jumps, affectations and faces which were shown here! All the guests, and especially the tsar, were delighted and couldn't get their fill of the contortions and grimaces of seventy-two dwarfs and laughed until their sides ached. One had short legs and a large hump, a second had a huge belly, a third had legs which were crooked and turned outward like a dachshund, or a huge head, or a crooked mouth and long ears, or tiny eyes lost on a face layered with fat."[13] Anna's uncle's escapade had made such a memorable gift on the occasion of his niece's wedding that she copied it years later as empress when a similar mock wedding was staged in the famous Ice House, built on the Neva River in the winter of 1740.

We know nothing of how the seventeen-year-old newlyweds began married life together. Perhaps they had already become accustomed to one another and to their new status; perhaps they would have grown to love one another, if only . . .

Peter did not allow the newlyweds to idle in St. Petersburg. Two months after the wedding, on January 8, 1711, the ducal pair set off for their home in Mitau. But they got only as far as the first post relay station, Duderhof, for there, exhausted by the incessant Petersburg drinking-bouts, Frederick William died. The duke's body was taken to Mitau and placed in the family burial vault, and the unfortunate young duchess, who had been widowed two months after being married, returned in tears to her mother's palace, which, presumably, brought neither much pleasure.

True, Anna could give a sigh of relief now since she did not have to go to "a foreign heathen land." But her future looked gloomy. In Russia, the life of a childless widow was sad and degrading. If a new spouse was not found for her, she would have to join a monastery. However, Anna put her trust in her uncle—he would take care of her and come up with something. In the meantime she, her mother, and her sisters moved around, living in St. Petersburg, Moscow, and Izmailovo. And only a year and a half later Peter made the final decision regarding his niece's fate: he ordered her to go to live in Mitau. At first the tsar intended to send Anna's mother and two sisters, Ekaterina and Praskovia, along with her to Courland. But later he changed his mind, and in the summer of 1712, Anna once again set out for a foreign land—this time all alone.

It would be naive to think that the duchy became her own property, where she felt truly in charge. Courland was a state that bordered on Prussia, Poland, and Russia, and each of these powers dreamed of getting their hands on it. The tsar had done much to increase Russia's influence in the duchy, and Anna's marriage to Frederick William was but one step along the way. Peter would have occupied Courland long ago, but since he did not want to strain relations with Prussia and Poland, he acted circumspectly. The presence of his niece, the duke's widow, in Mitau satisfied the tsar because now he would always have grounds to come to her aid and thwart any encroachments upon the duchy.

The Russian resident Peter Mikhailovich Bestuzhev-Riumin went with Anna to Mitau. He became the true master of Courland and, by Peter's decree, could summon soldiers from Riga at any time, to protect the duchess's interests. The young widow's situation was utterly miserable. The self-willed Courland nobility met their new ruler without enthusiasm. Having arrived in Mitau, Anna was obliged to stay in an abandoned burgher house, as the ducal palace was not prepared for her arrival. Revenues from state lands were insignificant, barely enough to support the court. Collecting them was extremely difficult, as Courland had been completely ruined by the Northern War and had suffered greatly from repeated epidemics. For Anna this was a cold, harsh country. Living in Mitau she was uncomfortable and apprehensive, especially in the beginning.

Anna's life in Mitau could be described in three words: poverty, uncertainty, and dependence. Having dispatched his niece to Courland, the tsar neglected to provide her with money there. In the meantime, as a duchess she was obliged to maintain a court staff and spend money on apparel suitable for a ruler. Tsaritsa Praskovia, knowing all the details of her daughter's life in Mitau, wrote to the tsar's secretary, Aleksei Makarov, to find out how "she, the tsarevna, should conduct herself while in that duchy, should she go by the example of previous duchesses and maintain a court staff at home, or live more simply? What then should she live on if she should live well, and in keeping with ducal traditions, this is not stipulated."[14] Anna herself wrote to Tsaritsa Catherine: "You, my dear Sovereign, know that I have nothing other than the damask which you had ordered, and if the opportunity were to arise, I have neither suitable diamonds nor laces, neither linens nor a fine dress, and with the revenues from the villages I can hardly maintain my home and put food on the table during the course of the year."[15]

Every trip to St. Petersburg or Moscow became problematic. Each time she had to beg for horses and money to cover the travel expenses. Stingy Tsar Peter did not want to spoil his niece, so he would not give her any extra money. And he generally kept her within strict bounds. She could not spend a ruble without the knowledge of the tsar, his secretary, or Bestuzhev-Riumin. For example, among the documents of Peter's Chancery is an inventory of beverages available at the Duchess of Courland's court wherein the number of bottles and prices were shown. Nor was she at liberty to conduct the duchy's foreign affairs. Anna would forward any official letters received from abroad to St. Petersburg, where replies were made in her name. Before leaving for Moscow to take part in Catherine's coronation in the spring of 1724, she asked the tsaritsa to indicate the color of the dress she was to wear for the festive ceremony. And so it was, down to the most inconsequential matters.

Her life was a mixture of humiliating trivialities and large and small fears. Anna's greatest fear was her severe uncle, the tsar, who was quite strict with his niece; each time she came to Russia, he would relentlessly send her back to do her "state service" in Mitau. Anna's relations with her mother remained strained. Tsaritsa Praskovia was especially severe with her daughter during the last years of her life. Only in the autumn of 1723, shortly before her death, she wrote to Anna: "I heard from the Empress Catherine Alekseevna that you are greatly troubled wondering whether you live under my damnation; make no doubt of this now: for the sake of Her Majesty, my dear Sovereign daughter-in-law, I absolve you of all the sins you may have committed against me."[16] As we see, the tsaritsa absolves her unloved daughter's sins with great reluctance.

It was nettlesome for Anna to see her mother, so she tried to avoid visits. In 1720, she wrote to her patroness, Catherine I, that her mother "asks in great anger, why I do not seek permission to come to St. Petersburg or why I do not invite mother to come to see me."[17] And to save herself from suffering the indignities inflicted on her by her mother, Anna asks Catherine to play along with her in deceiving Praskovia: Anna would pretend to ask permission to come to St. Petersburg, and the tsaritsa would refuse to grant permission to leave Mitau.

Reading the nearly three hundred letters that Anna sent from Courland, it is clear that they are written by a poor widow, an impoverished relative, a totally vulnerable woman, taken advantage of, humiliated, and constantly forced to humble herself before the powerful. Servile letters to Uncle Peter and Aunt Catherine alternate with demeaning messages addressed to the new people of influence during the post-Petrine epoch, like Menshikov and Osterman. Anna never forgets to send congratulations on festive occasions to the family of the Serene Prince, to remind them of herself and of her sorrows.

Over the years Anna grew accustomed to Mitau and was even reluctant to leave: we have seen that she felt less at home in Russia. The uncertainty of her situation continued to worry her. More than once she asked the tsar and tsaritsa to find a suitable fiancé for her. "I ask you, my dear Sovereign, as if I were asking God himself, you, my dear aunt, show me your maternal kindness, ask our dear uncle to have mercy on me to finish settling the matter of my marriage, so that I shall not suffer more grief from family miscreants and settle quarrels with my mother."[18]

Anna wrote this letter to Catherine in 1719. Years had passed since Anna became a widow. It cannot be said that Peter did not consider a suitable match for his niece, but making a choice was no easy matter: Anna's husband would become Duke of Courland and could disturb the unstable equilibrium that had been established in the duchy and in the adjacent areas. It was for this reason that Anna could not marry Johann Adolf of Saxen-Weisenfall. In 1723, a marriage contract had finally been drawn up with a nephew of the king of Prussia; but later Peter withdrew his consent to this union, for he did not place much trust in the Prussian king, who dreamed of uniting Courland and Prussia. And once again the Duchess of Courland spent her days in waiting while the years slowly passed by.

In 1726, Anna was suddenly inspired with a gleam of hope: Count Maurice of Saxony, a handsome womanizer, born out of wedlock to Augustus II, the king of Poland, came to visit Mitau. Local noblemen found him suitable to occupy the Courland throne, which had been vacant for so many years, and they, despite warnings received from St. Petersburg, made Maurice Duke of Courland. And as to Anna, she liked his outward appearance very much indeed! The only thing that worried her was the prince's incessant philandering. Surprised to see so many beautiful women in this godforsaken corner of Europe, he tried not to miss a single opportunity. As is well known, Don Juans are the most sought-after grooms, and Anna immersed herself in sweet dreams.

Alas! She was in for a rude awakening: Anna's old patroness, Catherine, who by that time had become empress, issued an unrelenting verdict: "The choice of Maurice is at variance with the interests of Russia," for it would increase the influence of the king of Poland in the duchy.[19] Aleksandr Menshikov was hurriedly dispatched to Mitau. He himself had hopes of becoming Duke of Courland. Not knowing this, Anna nearly fell on her knees before the Most Serene Prince. Menshikov reported to the empress that from the first moment of their meeting, Anna "without wasting any words and with many tears" had asked his permission to marry Maurice.[20] But Menshikov was inexorable: the count was to leave Courland! Without permission, Anna hurried to St. Petersburg to beseech her aunt, the empress, to intervene on her behalf. But all her appeals were in vain. The empress refused her request.

Although Menshikov failed to be elected Duke of Courland—his methods being too crude and straightforward—with the help of Russian soldiers Maurice was successfully expelled from Courland. The frivolous count remained true to himself. The historian Peter Shchebal'skii wrote of Maurice: "War and love were his life's credo, but he never racked his brains over studying the former, and never found the latter to be a cause for suffering: he engaged easily in both."[21] On July 17, 1726, Maurice was informed that that night Russian soldiers would storm the house where he lived. And when the soldiers had penetrated into the garden near the house they saw a person wrapped up in a cloak descending from the window. They overtook him in the hope of capturing the impertinent count trying to escape from his enemies. How great was their surprise when they found out that it was not Maurice after all, but a girl who had climbed out of his window. As for Maurice, he and his people successfully repelled the attack.

Yet in 1727 he had no other choice but to secretly flee Courland, the place he had grown so fond of. He complained bitterly to a Spanish grandee he met when he had put a safe distance between himself and Courland that the Russians got his trunk full of love-letters and, most important, his "register of love affairs at the King's court, that is, his father's court." What grieved Maurice most was not so much the loss of the Courland throne as the inevitable scandal that would ensue the moment the Russians published that "terrible" document. But everything turned out all right in the end, his secrets remained intact, and subsequently Maurice of Saxony became a great French general, his name shining in the military annals of France. Unfortunately for Anna, Maurice's departure only added to her emotional suffering.

Maurice's "excursion" to Courland had sad consequences for Peter Bestuzhev-Riumin as well. An honorable dignitary, father of the outstanding future diplomats Mikhail and Aleksei Bestuzhev-Riumin, and an experienced courtier, he was not only the Russian resident in Courland and chief steward of the duchess's court, he was also her long-standing lover. Being nineteen years older than Anna, he seduced the young widow and made her his complete subordinate. This incidentally had become one of the reasons for the chronic conflict between Anna and her mother. In allowing her daughter to go to Mitau, Tsaritsa Praskovia expected to keep her under strict surveillance even at a distance. For this purpose she dispatched her relatives to Courland to play the infamous role of informers and spies at the duchess's court. But Bestuzhev-Riumin succeeded fairly well in driving Anna's mother's spies out of Mitau. On more than one occasion Praskovia Fedorovna requested Peter the Great "to replace the former court steward there (in Mitau), who is a most intolerable person." But Peter had his own opinion regarding Bestuzhev-Riumin—Peter knew him as an intelligent diplomat who gave Russia's interests higher priority than ordinary moral issues, which suited the sovereign just fine.

"It is impossible to justify Anna Ioannovna's lust for love," wrote the famous Russian upholder of morals at Catherine the Great's court, the historian Prince Mikhail Shcherbatov. "For it is a patent fact that Bestuzhev partook of her favors"—that is, was her lover.[22]

I have no desire to absolve Anna of the sin of lust, if that is the correct term for a love affair between an old widower and a widow. But let's be fair: our heroine had never been Messalina or Cleopatra. Anna Ioannovna was a simple, unpretentious, not especially bright, and unflirtatious woman. She lacked the ambition of Catherine the Great, and never laid claim to any honors for her beauty as did Elizaveta Petrovna.

She had dreamed all her life of the reliable protection and support she could receive from a man, the master of the house, the lord of her fate. Anna's letters to Peter the Great, to Catherine, to Peter II, as well as to dignitaries and relatives are full of requests for protection and "patronage," and with declarations of her readiness "to give herself to the will of a patron and protector." This is why she was so eager to get married. But as we have seen, life had always prevented her wishes from coming true. Gradually it was Bestuzhev-Riumin who became her protector, supporter, and master. Of course, this was not ideal, but it was better than having nothing at all. And

Anna lived life one day at a time, shutting her eyes to her favorite's trespasses, which were spoken about by all the people in Mitau. One anonymous informer put it quite bluntly when writing about the escapades of the old court steward: "He lures the ladies-in-waiting outside the court and makes children [with them]."

Menshikov put all the blame for his failed aspirations to become Duke of Courland on Bestuzhev-Riumin, who was eventually recalled from Mitau to St. Petersburg. And as we see from their correspondence after the resident's departure, Anna was overcome with despair, almost hysterical. From June to October 1727, she wrote twenty-six letters addressed to anyone she could possibly write to, including even his Most Serene Prince's sister-in-law, Varvara Arsen'eva, and daughter, Maria, Peter II's future fiancée. Anna implored them to return Bestuzhev-Riumin to Mitau, writing that without him the duchy's finances would fall entirely to pieces. But Menshikov, who had taken over the reins of power after Catherine I's death, ignored Anna's desperate pleas.

Then she began to bombard Vice Chancellor Osterman with letters, hoping that he would intervene on her behalf. In these letters to Osterman, a man of humble origin from Westphalia, the tsarevna, daughter of a Russian tsar, uses phrases that are more appropriate in a petition from a soldier's widow: "I humbly request of you, Your Excellency, to intervene for me, a poor woman, before His Serene Highness [Menshikov—E.A.] . . . Be merciful, Andrei Ivanovich, kindly heed the humble appeal of an orphan, give me cause for joy and save me from tears. Have mercy on me, as would God himself!" Despair and loneliness resound in the words: "Truly, I live in great sorrow, emptiness, and fear! Do not let me spend the rest of my life in tears! I have grown accustomed to him!"[23] She grieves for Bestuzhev-Riumin as if he had died. But this is not a special undying love for him in particular, as may appear at first glance. Anna simply could not bear the thought of returning to the loneliness and emptiness of her previous life.

In late 1727 and early 1728, significant changes took place in Anna's life. Her status as duchess remained the same as ever: helplessness, dependence, and uncertainty. Earlier she had sought the patronage of Menshikov, his wife, and his sister-in-law, but now, after the downfall of the Most Serene Prince in the autumn of 1727, Anna wrote her imploring letters to the Dolgorukii princes and to Tsarevna Natalia, Peter II's sister, informing them, as she had earlier in her previous entreaties, that "all my hopes rest on Your illustrious mercy."[24] She promises to send Peter II, a passionate hunter, a pack of hounds. Life went on as usual.

But changes did occur in her private life: she found a new favorite—Ernst Johann Biron. From this moment and till the end of her days she never parted with him. Bestuzhev-Riumin, who was allowed to return to Mitau following Menshikov's downfall, was inconsolable—his warm place by the duchess's side had been taken in the most insidious way. He wrote to his daughter: "My grief is unbearable, I can hardly live [when I think] that my dear friend has left me because of these evil people, while your friend [an ironical reference to Biron—E.A.] has gained even greater trust . . . Do you realize how I love this person [that is, Anna—E.A.]?"[25]

Bestuzhev-Riumin tore his hair in despair—he himself had nurtured this scoundrel, this rogue. "Neither a nobleman, nor a Courlander," Bestuzhev-Riumin wrote peevishly about Biron. "He came from Moscow without so much as a caftan on, and thanks to my effort he was admitted without rank to the Courland court, where year after year I, who was fond of him, fulfilled his requests, and promoted him in rank to make him what he is today. And now, in exchange for my being so kind to him, he so gravely offends me . . . and while I was away from [Courland] he came into the confidence of Anna."[26]

And although Biron was actually both a nobleman and a Courlander (in contradiction to the above assertion), many shadowy incidents sullied his past. It is a known fact that when he was studying at Königsberg University he was sent to jail for killing a soldier one night during a brawl between students and the guards. With great effort he managed to get out of prison, and around 1718, after an unsuccessful attempt to find work in Moscow, he joined Anna's court, where, in fact, thanks to Bestuzhev-Riumin's patronage, he gained a foothold within the duchess's inner circle. He worked diligently, doing all that the chief steward asked him to do. Without describing Biron's life in detail, suffice it to say that Bestuzhev-Riumin's rival (he was born in 1690, that is, he was three years Anna's senior) was a bright chap. He was quick to console the grieving and lonely widow, and Anna soon found herself under his sway. Knowing them both, Bestuzhev-Riumin felt insecure: "They might do me harm: though she may not want to, he would make her do it."[27]

These fears proved to be well founded. In August 1728, Anna sent her informant to Moscow with a request to ascertain "how it came about that Bestuzhev has robbed me of everything I had and put me in great debt."[28] Some questionable deals with the duchy's funds, sugar, wine, and raisin supplies came to light in which the former chief steward was involved. Of course, the stolen raisins were not the point; the point was his full and irrevocable retirement, for which the lucky man who took his place near the raisins and sugar began to take skillful action.

Biron was married to one of Anna's ladies-in-waiting, Benigna Gottlieb von Trotta Treiden, and they had three children: a daughter and two sons. According to some historical records, Anna Ioannovna was believed to be the mother of Biron's youngest son, Karl Ernst. Karl did enjoy unusual privileges at court during Anna's reign. At the age of four the boy became bombardier-captain of the Preobrazhenskii Regiment, at eight he became chamberlain, and at twelve the holder of the highest Russian orders, the Order of Saint Aleksandr Nevskii and the diamond-studded Order of Saint

Andrew the First-Called. But even more convincing than this was the fact that the empress and the child were inseparable. In setting out for Moscow at the invitation of the Supreme Privy Council members, she took a minimum of things with her and also Karl Ernst, who was only a year and a half old at the time. Why then would she have taken the boy with her? This was no excursion, but rather a long, difficult journey with unforseeable consequences. Probably this is precisely why she took him along with her. In 1740 the French envoy Marquis Chetardy reported that the young prince of Courland always sleeps in the tsaritsa's room. Other contemporaries knew of this as well. It is likely that the great influence which Biron exerted over Anna stemmed in part from the empress's having had a child by the favorite . . .

But just as she left that wintry road behind her, so Anna left her entire past life behind as the sledge on February 13, 1730, brought her to the village of Vsesviatskoe, on the outskirts of Moscow. Nearby were the noisy streets of a huge city—the heart of Russia, which awaited the arrival of its new sovereign.

* * *

And what had been happening in the capital while the new empress was making her way through the giant snowdrifts to Moscow? Events had been developing with unexpected rapidity and with great unpredictability. On the morning of the same day that the Supreme Privy Council delegation had set out for Mitau (January 19) with the conditions for Anna's becoming empress, the entire "state" had been invited to the Kremlin, including generals, high-ranking officials, the senate and synod, and all courtiers. The members of the Supreme Privy Council solemnly announced the Duchess of Courland's selection as heiress to the Russian throne. Awestruck by the importance of the moment, those present enthusiastically hailed the wise decision, pleased that the dynastic crisis had been resolved with such miraculous quickness and ease. There was a general sigh of relief for Russia—a new *Smutnoe vremia* (Time of Troubles) had been averted.

By evening, it had become known that the Supreme Privy Council members had failed to inform the public of one very important detail—the conditions. The contingent of noblemen was disturbed not so much by the actual writing of the conditions—the idea of reducing unbounded autocratic power was not new to anyone—but rather that the "limitation" of imperial power would have inevitably meant an increase in the power of two ancient noble and princely families—the Golitsyns and Dolgorukiis. At first in whispered private conversations, and then more and more boldly, other noblemen who had come to Moscow to attend Peter II's wedding and, as it turned out, were staying on to attend his funeral, began to express their dismay and discontent over the affair. The anonymous author of memoirs dating from the year 1730 expressed the opinion of many of his contemporaries about the intentions of the Supreme Privy Council members when he wrote bitterly that if they were thinking of society's best interests, why then did they so unscrupulously deceive everyone in hiding the conditions? "Are not we all," complained this nobleman, "loyal to and desiring of the best for our native land, or are they alone, the members of the Supreme Privy Council, wise and loyal? By their contempt for us, who in family honor and important service to the State are no less worthy of respect, they have disgraced us, or [do they] consider us fools and knaves?"[29]

Here one must elucidate the sensitive topic of the subordination of subjects to the ruling authority in Russia. How many times before in Russian history had it happened that those in power had deceived the people? Speaking in their subjects' name, Russian rulers impudently trampled on their subjects' rights and self-respect, treating them as fools, and thinking neither of the state, nor of their native land, but only of their own self-interests. And in 1730 no one had any doubts that the Supreme Privy Council's scheme was an attempt to establish an oligarchic order, to usurp power for its members, a clique of noble grandees from two prominent clans. The first actions of the Supreme Privy Council members corroborated these fears—they initiated two new members to the council, the two field marshals: Vasilii Dolgorukii and Mikhail Golitsyn.

Then something quite unanticipated happened: Moscow began to boil and churn; noblemen began to gather in circles and discuss what had happened. "Wherever one goes," wrote Feofan Prokopovich, "whichever meeting one drops into, you hear nothing but grievous reprimands of the schemes of those eight men [at that time the Supreme Privy Council had eight members—E.A.]; everyone reproved them cruelly, cursing their uncanny audacity, insatiable greed and lust for power."[30] Thus, an unexpected interlude of freedom came during those two weeks, while the Supreme Privy Council was waiting for the conditions signed by Anna to arrive from Mitau. Civic feelings welled up in hundreds of people. And on February 2, when the Supreme Privy Council again called the "state" to gather in the Kremlin and read aloud the conditions, pretending to be surprised as if they were seeing them for the first time, no one believed them.

Dmitrii Golitsyn's audacious plan to present the secretly prepared conditions to Anna as the opinion of the state, and then to the nobility as the empress's own initiative, fell apart. New people stood before the Supreme Privy Council. They, the Russian nobility, had long been preparing for this moment. The concepts of noble honor inculcated by the Petrine doctrine, of individual initiative, as opposed to the collective responsibility of the clan as it used to be in the old days, and an understanding of honest and dignified service to one's native land had not died out. On the contrary, they had taken deeper root. Society had become more open than before. Those who had traveled abroad had seen that there no one dared to lay a finger on or beat a nobleman without a court order, let alone execute him or confiscate his lands, as was common practice in Russia.

In addition, the death of Peter the Great dispelled the fear that had so constrained people. The Secret Chancery had virtually ceased to function, and the other political police organ, the Preobrazhenskii Department, had been liquidated in 1729. Russian society is known to react with great sensitivity to the slightest weakening of pressure from above, and to perceive any slight, almost imperceptible breath of freedom. And during these two weeks of secret discussions and arguments, important changes had taken place in peoples' minds. At the February 2 meeting with the Supreme Privy Council members, the nobility demanded that they be granted permission to present their own plans for the restructuring of the state, which differed from those offered by the council. Under extreme pressure, seeking to win time, the Supreme Privy Council members agreed to the noblemen's demands. The dam had burst. The most prominent aristocrats worked with a flourish in Kremlin halls and at home. Numerous circles of gentry met day and night all around Moscow, writing and rewriting various versions of plans for governmental reform. Leaders and experts on Western parliamentary practices appeared out of nowhere. For the first time political opponents engaged openly in polemic discussions without the fear of being informed on or sent to the torture chambers. In a very short time, more than ten plans for reform had been written and signed by no less than one thousand people.

The Danish ambassador to Russia, Hans Georg Westphalen, reported to Copenhagen that noblemen were meeting around the clock in the Kremlin and "so much had been said both good and bad for and against reform, and [they were] either criticizing or defending it with such bitterness, and that finally the commotion had reached such extreme proportions that there was danger of an insurrection."[31] An uprising did not take place; however, in all the noisy discussions, the Supreme Privy Council members heard not a single word of support for their intentions. To be sure, practically all of the nobles' plans for restructuring the country called for limiting the empress's power, but not as the Supreme Privy Council members wanted, whose intention was to concentrate all the power in their own hands. The gentry sought collectively to create a system of government that would protect the general nobility both from any excesses by the monarch as well as from the omnipotence of one or two aristocratic families. Never before had the Russian nobility so persistently demanded that its representatives partake in ruling the country.

But the Supreme Privy Council members wanted nothing to do with such planners. To share power with the entire body of the nobility and thus to actually serve the interests of their country—this was inconceivable to Prince Dmitrii and his cohorts. On February 13, having reached no agreement with the gentry, they learned of the sovereign empress Anna Ivanona's arrival in Vsesviatskoe.

Here in Vsesviatskoe, despite all Vasilii Lukich Dolgorukii's efforts to remain with Anna at all times, her isolation came to an end. Through her relatives, the Saltykovs, her sister the Duchess Ekaterina of Mecklenburg, Tsarevna Praskovia, as well as through other well-wishers, Anna began to find out about the true state of affairs in the capital. She understood two central facts: the Supreme Privy Council had deceived her in presenting the conditions to her as the decision of society in general; and there was no unity among those who wished to limit the empress's power.

This was largely the Supreme Privy Council members' own fault: they had allowed themselves to become entangled in fruitless arguments with the noblemen, and lost precious time before Anna Ioannovna's arrival. They had begun to lose their advantage. In addition, a split was imminent among the gentry. The deeper discussions probed, the more the success of the endeavor became doubtful. As had happened many times in Russian history, doubts arose as to whether it was even possible to accomplish anything rational in Russia using democratic methods. This mood was expressed most clearly by the governor of Kazan', Artemii Volynskii, the future Cabinet minister, in a private letter to a friend, in which he wrote that the noblemen's democracy was unlikely to benefit the country. In Volynskii's opinion, new democratic institutions would immediately become corrupted "because our people are so fawning and cowardly"; elections would merely be formal affairs, and the one "who receives the most votes in his favor will do whatever he pleases. They will elect and reward whomever they desire, and anybody weaker, no matter how deserving, will always be left out of the running."

In addition, Volynskii feared that freedoms of the noble class would have dire consequences for the fighting capacity of the army and of the country, for, in his opinion, without the threat of terror, no one would serve in the army in Russia, and "if one were to give total freedom to all noblemen, it's a fact that the people are in no way ambitious, but rather lazy and disinclined to work. For this reason if not compelled by some form of duress then, of course, there will be some who will sit at home and eat black bread rather than work to receive either honor or abundant food, but rather each preferring to lie around at home."[32]

There is much truth to Volynskii's arguments, but primarily they expressed the age-old conviction inherent in the Russian mentality that we Russians have not yet matured enough for a more judicial order, for democracy. And these doubts have always led to a nostalgia for a strict order, and a strong hand that would establish that order. The direct result was a reinforcement of the autocratic position, whose adherents began to press the reformers and advocates of limiting the empress's power. The slogan of a strong hand was quite popular among the Guards and army, who cherished order. At the same time a weakening of authority increased the Guards' praetorian mood and their confidence in their right to decide the fate of the country. A highly volatile situation had developed. All that

Artemii P. Volynskii. From I. N. Bozherianov, "*Nevskii prospekt.*" *Kul'turno-istoricheskii ocherk dvukhvekovoi zhizni Sankt-Peterburga* ("Nevskii Prospect." A Cultural and Historical Sketch of St. Petersburg at Two Hundred) (St. Petersburg, 1901–03), vol. 1, p. 64.

was lacking was a spark to make it all explode. And that is what happened on February 25, 1730, in the Kremlin.

On that day during the empress's first meeting with the "state," the gentry, led by Prince Aleksei Cherkasskii, submitted a petition, in which they complained of the Supreme Privy Council members' refusal to hear their proposals regarding governmental reforms. The petitioners asked the empress to intervene and allow discussion of the draft proposals. This escapade greatly displeased the members of the Supreme Privy Council and an argument ensued between them and the petitioners. Not expecting to be chosen the arbitrator in an argument over how to better limit her own power, Anna stood there in surprise. Suddenly her sister Ekaterina approached her with a feather pen and inkwell in hand: "Since they have come to you, empress, then you decide!"[33] Anna inscribed the traditional words "execute in accordance herewith" on the draft—in other words, she granted permission to begin offering and discussing opinions.

The gentry convened a meeting, and the empress invited the Supreme Privy Council members to dine with her. Prince Dmitrii Golitsyn and his associates were probably suffering from lack of appetite after seeing how they had begun to lose ground. Counter to their anticipation, Anna had refused to play their game and had begun one of her own. But they were as yet unaware of what awaited them next and that the moment had arrived when lady fortune would waver and begin to smile—not in their direction.

One contemporary, the Spanish ambassador de Liria, wrote in his report to Madrid about the events in the Kremlin: "Meanwhile large numbers of Guards officers and others present began a disturbance, crying that they did not want anyone prescribing laws to their Sovereign, who should be in every way as autocratic as her predecessors. The noise rose to such a level that the tsaritsa was compelled to threaten them, but they all fell at her feet and said: 'We are Your Majesty's loyal subjects, but we cannot bear this tyranny imposed on you. Give the order, Your Majesty, and we'll throw the tyrants' heads at your feet!' Then the tsaritsa ordered them to obey . . . Lieutenant-Colonel of the Guards Saltykov, who led them in proclaiming the tsaritsa the autocratic Sovereign. The noblemen who had been summoned did the same."[34]

Several significant points in de Liria's report require elaboration. In his version he describes what is virtually a palace coup. Just as in 1725 after the death of Peter the Great, in 1730 the Guards were once again deciding the fate of the throne. Indeed, more than the fate of the throne—the fate of Russia. There's no doubt that the Guards had been excited to patriotic fervor. Immediately upon her arrival in Russia, Anna began flirting with the Guards. When she was still in Vsesviatskoe, she gave a hearty welcome to the soldiers of the Preobrazhenskii Regiment, who knelt down before her, and she declared that she herself would be in command of them, in contradiction to the conditions which she had signed. She personally served wine to the cavalry guards as well, which signified the highest honor for the defenders of the throne. Semen Andreevich Saltykov, one of the tsaritsa's relatives, worked hard to create and maintain the right state of mind among the Guards' ranks.

When both high-ranking military commanders—the field marshals Golitsyn and Dolgorukii—heard the noise made by the Guards and rushed out from the dining hall following the empress, they realized that the Guards were in rebellion. They remained silent when Anna, despite the conditions, started giving orders to the Guards through Saltykov, whom she had placed in command. The two field marshals, fearless in battle, knew their Guards all too well and, therefore, did not dare raise any objections to the actions of the excited crowd of Russian janissaries: they, too, had only one life to live!

The noble schemers who were discussing their petition in the next room also listened attentively to the noise in the grand hall. They must have felt quite ill at ease. Numerous times in Russian history soldiers have cried out: "Enough! We're fed up with it! Away with your meetings, papers, voting! Away with all that! The Guards are tired!" And when the noblemen later entered the hall and approached the empress, they submitted to her not a plan for restructure of the state, but a petition begging "loyally and humbly to kindly reaffirm the autocracy in the form which had existed in the times of your glorious ancestors, and revoke the articles [that is, the conditions—E.A.] which were submitted to Your Imperial Majesty and had been signed by Your Majesty's hand." The lovers of liberty ended their petition with the words: "We, Your Majesty's obedient slaves, appeal to Your Majesty's inherent natural kindness that we shall not be despised and that we shall be able to live our lives in happiness and prosperity, in peace and in safety. We are Your Imperial Majesty's most humble slaves."[35] This was followed by signatures. And not a word about freedom, rights, and guarantees.

It is unfortunate that Artemii Volynskii was not present in the hall at that moment. He could have confirmed his assertion that the slave mentality had won out after all. The Guards' shouts and threats had done their job—what the noblemen had signed in the meeting hall was not a call for reforms, but a slavish appeal. With the jealous eyes of the Guards fixed on her, Anna listened to their capitulation, then ordered that the conditions be brought to her, and, according to the impassive entry in the official register of the Supreme Privy Council, "in plain view of everyone present took [the conditions] and tore [the sheet] in two."[36] The members of the Supreme Privy Council watched in silence: they had played their last hand and lost. It had taken only thirty-seven days for autocratic rule to be reestablished in Russia. . . .

One day while visiting the State Archives of Ancient Manuscripts I badgered the curator into showing me this sheet of yellow paper, torn in two from top to bottom, which was kept in a safe along with other rarities. It was hard to fathom it—before me lay a document which could have given rise to a new history for Russia, could have promoted the development of a state with a functioning legal system, and, perhaps, by this time Russia would have had an approximately 260-year-old tradition of parliamentary rule. Perhaps Russia would have become a different country and we, the Russians, would be different, had it not been for one group of peoples' blind lust for power, or for the discords and squabbles among other groups, the outright stupidity of others, the impudence of still others, and the cowardice of all.

On the first day of Anna's autocratic reign, Muscovites were struck by a mysterious natural phenomenon: the sky was lit up with scarlet northern lights of unusual brightness. "Fiery pillars emerged in the zenith forming a shining ball,"[37] read one newspaper report. Many considered it as a bad omen for the future reign.

* * *

Thus, to her own surprise, Anna Ioannovna became the empress of all the Russias. While supporters and opponents of restricting imperial power were engaged in their own power struggle, nobody gave much thought to the Duchess of Courland's personality. Neither faction was fighting for her; they fought rather for the triumph of their own political ideals, for their own precious principles of state rule. And when the fight was over and the autocracy had been restored, they all gazed at the throne with surprise, trying to discern just who it was that was going to rule and over whom they had fought so desperately?

Of course, those who used to visit the tsar's court had already met Anna and her sisters and had treated them without any particular respect. Princess Praskovia Iusupova told people who were close to her of how earlier, during Peter the Great's reign, Anna and her sisters were not referred to as tsarevnas; people called them disparagingly by their father's name, "Ioannovnas"—that is, Ivan's daughters. In his reports about the events of January and February 1730, de Liria, who had been closely connected with Peter II's court, at first confused the new empress with her sister Praskovia—

Anna Ioannovna Tears Up Concessions to Privy Council. From I. N. Bozherianov, "Nevskii prospekt." *Kul'turno-istoricheskii ocherk dvukhvekovoi zhizni Sankt-Peterburga* ("Nevskii Prospect." A Cultural and Historical Sketch of St. Petersburg at Two Hundred) (St. Petersburg, 1901–03), vol. 1, p. 57.

so insignificant was Anna's role at court. And now, to the court camarilla's surprise, "Ioannovna" had become not only empress but autocrat.

Not a single court flatterer, regardless of how servile and mendacious he was, could bring himself to call Anna a beauty. That would have been too much. In formal portraits, Anna is depicted as a somber corpulent woman in a lavish dress with a ribbon of the Imperial Order thrown over her shoulder. Locks of coarse jet-black hair fall on her short neck; her nose is long, and there's a malevolent look in her dark eyes . . . Oh, no! Not a beauty at all!

The emotional Countess Sheremeteva, who was then, in February 1730, engaged to the disgraced Prince Ivan Dolgorukii, was horrified when she saw the empress passing by her window: "Her whole appearance was awful and her face was repulsive; she was so big that she stood head and shoulders above any of the cavaliers who escorted her, and she was excessively fat." Count Ernst Münnich, son of the prominent field marshal, offered a more impartial view: "She had a grand and impressive figure. Her noble and majestic facial expression compensated for its lack of beauty. She had large penetrating brown eyes, a slightly long nose, nice lips, and good teeth. Her hair was dark, her complexion somewhat speckled, and her voice was strong and piercing. She had a strong build and could withstand many ordeals."[38] This can be confirmed, for we know of Anna's passion for shooting, and that not many women's shoulders could contend with the gun's strong recoil. But Anna went shooting every day for many years running.

Nastasia Shestakova, a simple noblewoman, and the somewhat timid guest of the tsaritsa, recollected: "The empress asked me to approach her to kiss her hand, and then in amusement she took me by the shoulders with such a firm grip, her fingers pressing my skin so tightly that it hurt." Indeed there was a touch of ruggedness in Anna. De Liria wrote that her "face is more like a man's than a woman's."[39] Other contemporaries also noted Anna's excessive stoutness, and lack of grace and charm. Of course, it would have been more pleasant to have an empress who was perfect in every way, one with a beautiful face, fine clothes, a sensitive soul, deep thoughts, a good ear for music, intelligence, and refined manners. But there was nothing to do about it: the empress proposed by the wily Prince Dmitrii Golitsyn was the one Russia was stuck with.

Once she was empress, Anna felt quite uncomfortable in Moscow. Obviously, she could not trust those who had brought her to the throne. And although the noble schemers had yielded under the Guards' pressure during that decisive moment in the palace, it took some time for them to calm down completely. They continued their attempts to establish a "general assembly for senior officials." Even though by the beginning of March 1730 it was clear that their cause was lost, still rumors and gossip about the possible repetition of the events of early 1730 did not subside and were a source of worry for the new empress. Seeking stable control at first, Anna could not deal immediately with her rivals for power from the Supreme Privy Council. In early March, she dissolved the council, but almost all of its members became members of the Senate and were decorated during Anna's coronation in the summer of 1730.

She could reveal her true intentions only in regard to the Dolgorukii princes. Formerly Emperor Peter II's favorite, Prince Ivan Dolgorukii, his wife, and father, Prince Aleksei, together with all their household, were exiled to the city of Berezov in Siberia, where the disgraced Menshikov had just died.

Nor could Anna fully rely on the Guards. Although it was the Guards who had made her autocrat, she could not trust this fickle and self-willed crowd of new strel'tsy. Quite accidentally Anna once overheard a conversation of the Guards returning from extinguishing a small fire in the palace. They regretted that in the ensuing fuss they "had not met up with the one whom they had it in for, otherwise they would have killed him."[40] They were referring to Biron, who had recently arrived from Courland. He had immediately taken the place closest to the throne, and the Guards did not like it. To magnify their displeasure, in August 1730, Anna hurriedly began to form a new Guards Regiment—the Izmailovskii Regiment. Commanding officers were mostly foreigners, with Karl Gustav Löwenwolde and Biron's brother Gustav at the head. As to soldiers, they were recruited not from the members of the Moscow gentry, as had been the case since the times of Peter the Great, but rather from the more minor and poorer nobles living on the southern borders of the country, these recruits being totally ignorant of the political games of the capital. Anna probably figured that she could rely on the loyalty of these people in crucial moments of her future reign.

Rumors that malcontents were going "to rectify the events of 1730" forced Anna to take unprecedented action in early 1731. All regiments, generals, and high-ranking officials were instructed to appear at the palace in the early morning. Anna addressed them with a speech in which she stated that "in order to prevent unrest such as that which took place after the death of her predecessor" Peter II, she intended to appoint her successor in advance, but since the latter had not been born as yet, the empress required that everybody swear an oath of allegiance to her choice as successor, whoever that might be.[41]

Anna sought to avert dynastic difficulties through her twelve-year-old niece Anna Leopol'dovna, the daughter of her elder sister, Ekaterina, and Charles Leopold, Duke of Mecklenburg. She brought her to court to live and intended to marry her suitably and then transfer the throne either to her or to her children. The Guards and dignitaries swore to the empress's strange whim without so much as a murmur.

Anna felt insecure despite this success. Moscow had turned out to be an unsafe place for her. A superstitious and mistrustful person, Anna was badly shaken when General Ivan Dmitriev-Mamonov, her younger sister Praskovia's morganatic husband, had suddenly died in her presence. And the empress felt especially queer when during a country drive she saw the carriage in front of hers suddenly disappear beneath the ground. Later an investigation revealed that it was a skillfully made trap.

The decision to move to St. Petersburg was made in late 1730. The architect Domenico Trezzini received a rush commission to make the imperial palaces ready to be occupied. On January 17, 1732, *Sankt-Peterburgskie Vedomosti* (St. Petersburg Gazette) triumphantly informed the world, "The day before yesterday in the evening Her Imperial Majesty deigned to have successfully arrived here from Moscow to the inexpressible joy of the local inhabitants." The empress was met by General Burkhard Christopher Münnich. The future field marshal, who remained from the first day of Anna's reign the principal chief in St. Petersburg, had faultlessly intuited the new trend from Moscow, and he immediately showed his loyalty to the new sovereign by arranging for the city, the army, and the navy to swear an oath of allegiance to her. Later he informed against Admiral Sievers, who had advised others not to be too hasty to swear allegiance to Anna, and who expressed his sympathies for Elizabeth, Peter the Great's daughter. This helped Münnich win Anna's favor, and she started to assign the faithful general other dirty work of a political nature.

So Münnich worked furiously preparing for Anna's arrival. Splendid triumphal arches had been constructed, the Winter Palace refurbished, the streets of St. Petersburg cleaned up. Unfortunately, it was wintertime and the empress could not view the ships. Anna's arrival was both a festive and a solemn occasion involving cheerful crowds, a salute given by the regiments lined up along the road, the roar of drums, and fireworks.

When Anna arrived in St. Petersburg, she went straight to St. Isaac's Church, where a celebratory service was held. Then the empress proceeded to her new home in the Winter Palace. The crown had returned to St. Petersburg after a four-year interval, when Peter II made Moscow capital of the country. Now, far from Moscow, Anna could breathe a sigh of relief. On the eve of the court's departure for St. Petersburg, the Saxonian envoy Lefort wrote that in leaving Moscow the empress wanted to "rid herself of many unpleasant people who will stay here [in Moscow—E.A.] or will be sent farther on into the interior of the country; she wants to have total freedom . . ."[42] "The one whom the [G]uards had it in for," namely, Biron, was also quite satisfied with the court's move.

Biron did not like "the barbarous capital" Moscow; moreover, he suffered unprecedented embarrassment in Moscow: an excellent horseman, he had been thrown by his horse to the ground right in front of the empress, courtiers, and many others. Disrupting the entire ceremony of the royal equipage, Anna jumped out of her carriage to help her poor, injured, but exceedingly dear chief chamberlain extract himself from the confounded Moscow mud.

The transfer to St. Petersburg was a strong move on the part of Anna's government. Foreign countries had interpreted the transfer of the capital to Moscow during Peter II's reign as a signal that Russia was deviating from Peter the Great's policies. Anna chose a new direction: her return to St. Petersburg was to symbolize the reestablishment of close relations with Europe. Many sensible politicians were aware of the importance of returning the seat of Russian government to the banks of the Neva. Anna heeded their advice. Her return to St. Petersburg symbolized the continuity of Peter the Great's political ideals and signified the reinforcement of both the empire and its new ruler.

And so Anna Ioannovna came to live in St. Petersburg. In 1732, the Secret Chancery investigated the case of Ivan Sedov, a soldier who had ventured to make insulting comments when his friend told a story of a remarkable scene he had witnessed near the palace: Her Majesty Anna was sitting by an open window when a man from the country wearing a torn hat happened to be passing by. Anna stopped him and scolded him for his unkempt appearance, and gave him two rubles so that he could buy a new hat. A praiseworthy act indeed. But this action is of note not because of its benevolence. In it the real nature of the empress is revealed: a bored estate mistress sitting by the window and watching the people pass by or enjoying a fight between a goat and a watchdog. Such an image could hardly be applied to someone like Catherine II. But as to Anna it is a perfect likeness. Indeed, she was a true mistress of an estate, though this estate was no longer a godforsaken village, but the huge expanse of Russia. A superstitious, petty, and capricious mistress, she stood by her Petersburg "window" and examined her vast yard with partiality and keen attention, duly punishing any servants and slaves responsible for any disorder she might happen to see. She even had her own foreman who was in charge of her largest "village"— Moscow. His name was Count Semen Andreevich Saltykov. The reader remembers that it was he whom Anna had appointed to command the Guards on the memorable day of February 25, 1730. Now he was in command of Moscow.

"Semen Andreevich! On receipt of this letter send someone to Khot'kov Monastery to take from there Iliushka, the foster-son of a legless Mother; provide him with a fur-coat and send him to us by post-chaise together with a soldier escort."[43] "Semen Andreevich! Go to Apraksin's and personally examine his storeroom; look for a portrait in which his father is depicted on horseback, and send it to us; he [Apraksin] is in Moscow, of course, and if he hides it [the portrait], they, the Apraksins, will be sorry."[44] Saltykov received such letters for ten years running.

On many occasions this respectable commander in chief of Moscow, the general in chief, count, and senator, had to climb into the dark storerooms of the empress's subjects, hitting his head on low beams looking for someone's "portrait" or "love-letters" buried among the cobwebs and rubbish. "Also find out," writes Anna to Saltykov, "whether Golitsyn's father [the courtier Golitsyn—E.A.] was really ill, as his son told us here, or whether he was in good health; if he was ill, then write what kind of illness he had and how long he had been ill."[45] Someone had informed the mistress of the count's feigned illness, and she ordered an investigation into this fact, and woe be to him who deceived her.

Letters addressed to the Moscow manager are full of phrases such as "I have heard," "We have heard," "It's been brought to my attention that," "People have said." Anna valued gossip above all else as an indispensable and universal source of information. When you read her letters, you get a funny impression that she knows everything, that her sharp eye and ear penetrate space and she knows, for example, that "in Vasilii Fedorovich Saltykov's village the peasants are singing a song which begins with the words: 'In our village of Polivantsovo there is a stupid boyar who filters beer through a sieve,'"[46] and that in a certain Moscow tavern "there is a cage with a talking starling," and that a certain Mister Kondratovich staggers about Moscow instead of going to work, and that, finally, in the village of Saltovka "there is a muzhik capable of quelling a fire."[47] And mistress Ioannovna gave strict orders: the muzhik, the starling, and words to the song should all be immediately dispatched to St. Petersburg, and Kondratovich sent to his place of work.

In order to do his mistress's bidding, Saltykov often acted in an underhanded way. This was Anna's favorite method of operation; she was, after all, the sole master of her subjects' lives and property. Incidentally Anna was not alone in using this method. Rummaging about subjects' dusty storerooms, secretly checking their purses, looking through keyholes, and opening others' letters had long been practiced by the Russian authorities. Anna saw herself as mistress of an estate inhabited by lazy and roguish servants; that was why she felt justified poking her "slightly oblong" nose into other peoples' business, her credo being: "The right is mine to decide who is to be pardoned and who is to be executed." And Anna was absolutely justified in this claim: That was exactly what the noblemen had asked for at the memorable meeting in the Kremlin in February 1730—to endow the tsaritsa with unlimited power. In their famous petition they asked the empress "to reaffirm the autocracy in the form which had existed in the times of your glorious ancestors."[48] And that is just what came to pass.

A portion of the correspondence between Anna and Saltykov can be characterized as the royal matchmaker's archive, a typical example from which would be: "Locate the whereabouts of the voevoda Kologrivov's wife, call her in and inform her that she is to give her daughter in marriage to Dmitrii Simonov because he is a kind man and we shall not deprive him of our favor."[49] The voevoda's wife was happy to hear these promises and claimed she "had no objections to giving her daughter away in marriage," but—to everyone's disappointment—the bride was not yet twelve years old. This means that the empress had been given the wrong information. The royal matchmaker experienced yet another failure in respect to the daughter of Prince Vasilii Gagarin. Anna interceded on behalf of her bedchamber gentleman Tatishchev and asked Saltykov to discuss with the prince himself all the necessary details concerning the marriage. Saltykov responded that Gagarin would have been happy to please the empress if only he had not been lying mute and motionless for the last three years.

But in other cases Anna's efforts were successful. And the reader should not think that the empress forced people to wed each time she planned a marriage! In Gagarin's case she wrote: "However, we are not forcing him, the prince, but it would please us if he acted by our will and without any compulsion."[50] And in fact, there was not a single case of refusal on the part of parents; on the contrary, all were happy to please the royal matchmaker.

Anna's efforts to see to the personal happiness of her subjects reveal the matchmaker's conceited vanity, the proud feeling of being "Mother of the Native Land," the mistress of a large estate who showers her subjects with good deeds, being confident that she knows better than they what is good for them. But that's not all. In 1733, Anna pleaded for two noble orphan girls, "one of which," she writes to Saltykov, "Matiushkin, has fallen in love with and asks my permission to marry her; but the girls are very poor, though they both are not bad-looking and are not stupid, I have seen them myself."[51]

The empress instructed Saltykov: "Call in his father and mother and ask them whether they want him to marry and whether they will allow him to take whichever of the two girls he likes most. And should they (the parents) become obstinate for the reason that the girl is poor and has no dowry then you give them this reply: Which of the wealthy would give their daughter in marriage to their son?"[52] Three months later Anna wrote with satisfaction to Saltykov informing him that Matiushkin's wedding had been a merry one and took place "in my home," that is, at the imperial palace. One sees nothing but benevolent feelings in this story. Perhaps in it there is an echo of this woman's own personal drama, whose life had been maimed by fate. Having become a widow at the age of seventeen, she strove vicariously to attain a happy and peaceful family life, but she did not in her own life put on a new wedding dress.

On the other hand, "the mistress Ioannovna" was excessively severe with her subjects when it came to any kind of sexual liberties, unsanctioned love affairs. On May 17, 1731, the following appeared in *Sankt-Peterburgskie Vedomosti*, the only newspaper published during that time: "The other day one officer of the household cavalry fell in love with a Russian girl and decided to abduct [her]." Then the story described how the girl had been abducted from under her thoughtful grandmother's very nose and a secret marriage ceremony held in church. "Meanwhile news of this had reached the court [One can imagine Anna's reaction.—E.A.] and a man was sent immediately to the newlyweds' house to catch them in the act. The man sent to the newlywed couple [I think it was the Chief of the Secret Chancery Andrei Ushakov himself.—E.A.] arrived at their home just in the nick of time when the bridegroom was undressing, and the bride was already in bed." All those involved in this affair were immediately arrested and the article concluded with the words: "Now everyone is eager to find out how this amusing love affair is going to end." There is no doubt that the empress herself, as the unwavering upholder of national morals, personally conducted the operation for extracting the newlyweds from their nuptial bed. It was within her power to nullify any church marriage, for since the time of Peter the Great the emperor or the empress was the head of the Russian Orthodox Church.

It would be a mistake to think that Anna had nothing else to do but to investigate her subjects' personal lives. She had other riveting tasks. For instance, the matter of jesters called for her constant concern. She was especially strict and captious in this matter—after all, the jester became almost an adopted member of the large court family. When the empress was considering Nikita Volkonskii as a jester she ordered Saltykov to provide her with complete information about his habits: the way he lived; whether he kept his rooms clean; whether he ate cabbage-stumps; whether he spent too much time lying on the stove; how many shirts he had and how many days he wore one shirt before changing it. Anna was a mistrustful and fastidious woman and her concerns were quite understandable: she was taking a stranger into her house and she did not want him to be untidy or unclean, to spread bad odors in the palace quarters, to breathe too heavily, to snore, or to champ. After careful consideration the empress selected a troupe of six professional fools, which did not include numerous voluntary jesters. Among the jesters were two foreigners: Jan d'Acosta and Pietro Mira, nicknamed Pedrillo; and four Russians: Ivan Balakirev, Princes Nikita Volkonskii and Mikhail Golitsyn, and Count Aleksei Apraksin. They were all outstanding fools of rare talent and despite later searches no better fools could be found in all Russia.

Of course, jesters were kept chiefly for laughs and amusement. Let us leave to fiction the image of a fool sitting at the foot of the throne and exposing social vices. In real life everything was simpler and more prosaic. The jester's craft provided a source of constant entertainment, an unrehearsed comedy played close at hand, and salvation from boredom during long winter evenings and opulent dinners.

This spectacle was often quite obscene and a modern viewer would not like it much. The historian Ivan Zabelin described jesters' pranks as the special "elemental force of laughter" wherein "the nastiest cynicism was not only appropriate and in order, but even merited universal approval."[53] The jester lived outside of the prevailing system of ethical standards, which were often hypocritical. By exposing his body and soul, the jester provided a release for the physic energy repressed by strict principles and social morals. "This was precisely the reason for keeping a fool in the house in order to personify the

The Jester Jan d'Acosta. From I. N. Bozherianov, "*Nevskii prospekt.*" *Kul'turno-istoricheskii ocherk dvukhvekovoi zhizni Sankt-Peterburga* ("Nevskii Prospect." A Cultural and Historical Sketch of St. Petersburg at Two Hundred) (St. Petersburg, 1901–03), vol. 1, p. 68.

foolish, or essentially, the free impulses of life."[54] Buffoonery with all its obscenity, free of any taboo, was, probably, very important and necessary for Anna: it helped relieve the strain this woman must have experienced on the subconscious level. A bigot, upholder of social morals, strict judge of others' faults, she had no qualms about her own unsanctioned liaison with Biron, who was already married. And this bond was censured by custom, by faith, by law, and by the people. Anna knew all about this from the reports of the Secret Chancery, which she read regularly.

The fool was a conspicuous member of the large court family. Jesters and their rulers often became close friends during the years they spent under one roof. The jesters' own life stories amused the tsaritsa and court and would be savored for months and even years. For instance, Ivan Balakirev's acute family problems were especially funny and evoked much laughter from everyone who became involved in solving them: the empress, various dignitaries, and even the Synod. Sometimes reports of the jester's struggle with his father-in-law, who did not want to pay his son-in-law the agreed dowry, were discussed; and at one point the Most Holy Synod considered seriously the problem of Balakirev's "returning to his former married life" with a wife who was not accommodating in bed. Suddenly a new problem arose: the jester had lost half of his horse at cards, and a lottery was held among the nobility in order to save the tsaritsa's favorite's mare.

Golitsyn-Kvasnik was also very popular at court. He was as talented as Balakirev, and having become a jester under rather dramatic circumstances, he wore the jester's cap with due honors. After having seen him in his first performance, Anna wrote to Saltykov that the Prince "is the best one here and has outdone all of the other fools."[55] One should not think that Russian princes and counts felt humiliated or oppressed when they became jesters. They looked upon this service as a type of duty to their sovereign, to their master, a service not just anybody could perform: in Russia it was easier for a fool to become a general than for an intelligent man to become a jester. When Anna decided to appoint Prince Volkonskii (who had become famous for his foolish tricks) a court fool, she wrote to Saltykov: "And tell him that he is ordered to be jester [at court] as a sign of favor, not anger."[56] And so they all lived together—the tsaritsa and her fools.

One favorite winter pastime in St. Petersburg was the construction of towns and fortresses made of ice out on the frozen surface of the Neva River. But in February 1740 numerous workers came to the Neva to build something out of the ordinary. The curious townspeople watched as day by day a fairy-tale-like ice palace began to take shape. A grandiose wedding was planned at court to top all previous escapades in this genre, such as the marriage of the jester Pedrillo to a goat, which he, to Anna's delight, took to bed with him. This time the jester Prince Mikhail Golitsyn and a young Kalmyk woman, Avdotia Buzheninova, were the nuptial pair. Prince Golitsyn had been appointed jester as punishment for his marrying a Catholic woman during his stay in Italy. His wife, who was brought to Russia and abandoned by all to her fate, eventually died in that foreign land, but Golitsyn became a prominent jester. Now Anna, the all-Russia matchmaker, had decided to arrange his family life for him in a most unusual way.

A decree went out ordering that a man and woman be brought to St. Petersburg dressed in their native costumes representing each national minority group, that is, all of the tsaritsa's "non-Russian" subjects, in order to take part in the wedding festivities. The tsaritsa found the idea of these people trailing in a procession through the streets of St. Petersburg very amusing.

The ice palace was intended for the newlyweds. It blended in with the culture of that time when "curiosities," tricks, and optical illusions were in vogue, and spectators appeared to see real objects when in fact they were only plaster casts, models, or wax figures. In this case everything was made of ice. The palace was surrounded with bushes and trees made of ice and painted green, on the branches of which sat different-colored ice birds. A life-size ice elephant stood in front of the palace; a man blew through the upraised trunk as if it were a trumpet. During the day a fountain of water sprayed from the trunk, which was replaced at night by a fountain of flaming oil.

But most impressive of all was the way the palace was built and decorated. The windows, walls, doors, and furniture of the luxurious rooms were made of ice skillfully painted to look natural, even to the point where playing cards seemed to be lying on the table. The bedroom for the new couple was an exact replica of the real royal bedchamber: with an ice bed and canopy, ice sheets, pillows, and an ice blanket. When the wedding ceremony was complete, the new couple was delivered in a cage, and solemnly put down to bed here. The court poet Vasilii Trediakovskii dedicated verses to this wedding march of many nationalities.

The newlyweds, who were frozen through to their bones, were released only toward morning, when Anna Ioannovna and her retinue questioned Golitsyn about the delights of his first wedding night, to the great amusement of those at court.

Jesters made up only a small part of the court community and its staff. There were also many other people at court, who, to a stranger, might be taken for a collection of freaks, residents of a large almshouse, or specimens from a wax museum: such seemed the invalids, cripples, dwarfs, giants, and repulsive old women at Anna's court. Yet there was some order and sense in all this. One should keep in mind the epoch in which Anna lived and the strange twist of fate she had encountered on her life's path. Originally a seventeenth-century Moscow tsarevna, she unexpectedly became the Duchess of Courland one day, retained this title for twenty years, and then awoke one morning as the empress of Russia. These three periods left their mark on her psyche, tastes, and habits. Anna lived at the crossroads of two epochs, and the mixture of styles and a peculiar sort of eclecticism were characteristic of that time.

Undoubtedly, Anna felt a deep attachment to the past, to the seventeenth century, when she was born. When she became tsaritsa, she not only fondly recalled the heavenly place of her childhood, Izmailovo, but even reconstructed the old tsaritsa's room, where hangers-on at court would group around the Russian tsaritsa during her leisure time. Of course, one cannot turn back time, and Anna had no intention of bringing back the old system of ranks at court. The *rynda* (tsars' bodyguards), *stol'nik*, and other close attendants had long since been replaced by gentlemen of the bedchamber, chamber menservants, and chamberlains. No, what was more important for the empress was the spirit of "the tsaritsa's room." And it was not an interest in historical documents, but rather nostalgia that prompted her many requests that Saltykov search for and send her some old portrait of her mother Praskovia or of her father tsar Ivan, old books with illustrations, and various other things from her previous life in the Kremlin or in Izmailovo.

But as we all know, people remain the most important element in any endeavor. The tsaritsa's letters to Saltykov reveal her attempts to gather together her late mother's aged court attendants and servants. Once they had been so numerous that they filled the entire Izmailovo palace, making the fastidious Tsar Peter's flesh creep. And now soldiers began to deliver old women and widows, storytellers and bedtime heel-scratchers, to the empress's court in St. Petersburg. Anna's inner circle now featured such characters as "the Legless Mother," "Tall Dar'ia," "Grandma Ekaterina," and "Noblegirl." Anna instructs Saltykov in her letter to "Find a girl in Pereslavl" who resembles Tatiana Novokreshchenova (who, we think, will die soon) to become her replacement; she may be a poor noble girl or a city girl. You know our tastes: we like girls around forty years old who are talkative like Novokreshchenova, or like Princess Nastasia and Anisia Meshcherskaia."[57]

Jesters and ugly dwarfs of both sexes, God's fools (those "touched" by divine grace or just plain retarded), the deformed, the crippled, the dumb, and the legless—all these made up the company in the empress's room. This contingent also included "Arab women," "foreign female orphans," "Kalmyk women," "German women," and other foreign women representing various races. In 1734 Anna instructed General Levashov, commander in chief of the Russian forces on the Caucasus, to send two girls to St. Petersburg, either Persian or Georgian, "only that they be white and clean, good-looking and clever." During Anna's reign the old concept of "going to the top" was revived, which had seemed to have been lost forever in the European city of St. Petersburg, as it is situated on flat terrain.[58] In previous centuries this expression used to mean visiting the Kremlin Palace, where on the "top" of the Kremlin Hill the tsars lived. There was neither Kremlin palace nor Kremlin hill in St. Petersburg, but the term "top" came into use again. There the empress lived among gossip and quarrels, spending long evenings at storytelling with numerous servants and hangers-on. This corresponded to the old traditions of life in Moscow, and it was the world which Anna Ioannovna cherished.

Old customs reappeared at court as if of their own accord, though without displacing new ones. On the contrary, they combined fancifully with customs that had come to Russia from the West. The years Anna had lived with Biron in Courland were not spent in vain—she was not indifferent to such European pastimes as theater, ballet, and opera. Itinerant Italian theater troupes doing commedia dell'arte were especially popular at court. Their humorous mimicry of real life, noisy fights, punches and cuffs, and the simple subjects of their plays closely resembled the tricks and acts of Russian jesters and *skomorokhi*. The interludes' main characters, Harlequin, Pierrot, and Esmeralda, always seemed to be in conflict with one another. With great pleasure Anna—a rather unsophisticated viewer—watched plays whose names speak for themselves: "The lovers who oppose one another, with Harlequin, as the insincere Pasha," "Esmeralda [who has become] filled with hatred," "Climbing over the fence," "Amusement on the water and in the field," "Harlequin changing clothes," and other such popular pieces of the open-air theater.

Music historians have noted that Anna's reign marked a turning point in Russia's musical culture. Theater and concert music came to Russia during her reign mostly by way of itinerant Italian troupes and took its place alongside martial music, ceremonial music, and the mandatory dances of the Petrine soirées. Italian-born Francesco Araia became the first court composer. A large court choir was formed which consisted almost entirely of Ukrainian boys notable for their rare musical talent and beautiful voices. In 1737 a French-born choreographer, Jean Baptiste Landez, founded the St. Petersburg Classical Dance and Ballet School, which remains world famous to this day. Music set the mood at ceremonial court dinners, and had a positive effect on appetites as well. Thus, in 1735 at the dinner given in honor of bearers of the Aleksandr Nevskii Order, Anna dined with them at one table, while "accomplished Italian musicians and [female] vocalists gave a music concert, which immensely pleased Her Imperial Majesty."

Her Majesty also enjoyed listening to and watching operas, which, although staged rather rarely in St. Petersburg, still evidently brightened up life at court and in the capital. A huge theater with one thousand seats was built especially for staging operas, which all were welcome to attend, except those who were drunk or unkempt. The residents of St. Petersburg, unaccustomed to such shows, were enchanted by the grandiose stage sets, music, singing, recitation, ballet pieces, and also by the well-coordinated work of theatrical devices and mechanisms, hidden from the spectators' view, which could raise the main characters up to the canvas clouds or make the walls of the theater and spectators' hearts quake with the thunder of "hell's chasm" or the brightness of "Jupiter's lightning bolts." As Jacob von Stählin, a music expert and a prominent art connoisseur explained in a newspaper article— "action performed in song" was, as a rule, timed to coincide with specific events: the empress's birthday, the anniversary of her accession to the throne, her coronation, and so on.

Thus, the opera *The Pretending Ninus, or Semiramis Recognized* was staged in 1737 in celebration of the Tsaritsa's forty-fourth birthday. The stage decorations and costumes were lavish, and the Italian music was beautiful. Although this opera's plot has not survived, there is no doubt that it was full of lofty feelings, and its sentimental scenes brought tears to the spectators' eyes. In the end Good triumphed over Evil, and Love overcame Hatred. According to *Sankt-Peterburgskie Vedomosti,* spectators enjoyed all of this as much as the empress.

In recalling life in St. Petersburg in the 1730s one writer's memoirs read: "Her Majesty, being unable, on account of bad weather, to take delight in shooting as was her custom almost every day during the summer period which she spent in Peterhof, visited the theater regularly with all her court whenever they were staging an opera, comedy, or interlude."[59]

Indeed, hunting—or to be more precise, shooting—was Anna's true passion. A rather unusual sport for any other Moscow tsarevna, it came quite naturally to the somewhat masculine and rough empress. Anna not only took part in chasing the wild beasts, nor was her role limited to unleashing the dogs. She herself fired a gun and did it splendidly. Rarely a day passed in the park of the suburban palace at Peterhof without shooting. If the weather was bad the tsaritsa would shoot at targets placed for her in the park or in the riding arena. But most of all the tsaritsa enjoyed shooting at live targets, and did it regularly. Various kinds of wild game were brought from all over the country and kept in special enclosures and aviaries near Peterhof. This enabled the empress to shoot at will while strolling in the park at the wild beasts, which were there in plenty.

On her hunts during the summer of 1739 she personally shot nine deer, sixteen wild goats, four wild boars, one wolf, three hundred seventy-four hares, and six hundred eight ducks! In addition, among our Diana's one thousand twenty-four trophies there were sixteen large inedible seagulls. One can imagine how it must have been: the tsaritsa did not lose her ardor even inside the palace, but would grab one of the loaded guns that were kept along the walls between the windows, and shoot out of the window at passing seagulls, crows, or jackdaws. Wherever she went, the empress always took her carbine with her.

During Anna's reign barbarous hunts from *jagdwagens* (hunting-wagons) were in fashion; these were special carriages placed in the middle of a glade to which beaters pursued beasts from the entire surrounding forest. During the final stage of the methodical and uninterrupted chase, which might continue for weeks and cover an immense forest area, the animals would be driven into a canvas shute which led them straight to the *jagdwagen,* where the hunters, sitting in safety, picked off at point-blank range deer, wolves, and bears chased out of their dens as well as other big and small denizens of the forest.

Thanks to the tsaritsa's fondness for shooting, this sport became quite fashionable in society. The fawning nobility schooled their young daughters by having them shoot at doves, and when the empress questioned one Muscovite lady who was a guest at court, "Do the ladies in Moscow shoot?" the latter replied reassuringly, "yes they do, Your Majesty, indeed they do!" What else could one expect? If Her Majesty were to take to bathing in a hole cut in an iced-over stream, then all the young and not-so-young countesses and princesses would be obliged to climb into the ice-cold water only to please the crowned naiad.

Of course, Anna's passion for hunting and shooting tells us a lot about her. Such bloodthirsty deeds required that Diana of Peterhof possess a firm hand, a sharp eye, physical strength, presence of mind, and an appetite for risk. Probably a combination of Amazonian traits correlated well with the empress's psyche, which was free of intellectual quests and introspection.

However, in order not to mislead the reader and cause him or her to draw doubtful conclusions, it must be noted that no matter how great was Anna's passion for hunting, it was still overshadowed by yet another passion, her main one, the object of which was a man, namely, Biron.

"Never in the world, I think, was there a more harmonious couple than the empress and the duke, who, in sorrow and joy, displayed complete mutual understanding!" wrote Ernst Münnich in his memoirs. "Neither one of them could ever completely conceal their feelings. If the duke came frowning, the empress immediately took on a worried air. If he was gay, the monarch's face showed obvious pleasure. If someone failed to please the duke, then that someone would immediately detect a marked change in the eyes of the monarch and in the way she received him. All favors were to be sought from the duke, and only after his approval would the empress make her decision."[60]

From the moment Biron arrived in Moscow in mid-March 1730 he and Anna never parted, not for a single day, until the empress's death in October 1740. Moreover, they were always seen holding hands, which made them the object of social ridicule, and this accordingly became the subject of an investigation by the Secret Chancery. Biron's influence on the tsaritsa was profound. Its roots lay not so much in the favorite's personal qualities (although he was a handsome, imposing, and undoubtedly a strong-willed and clever man) as in the emotional makeup of Anna Ioannovna, who gladly became the subordinate of her lord and master. They were so close that they even fell ill at the same time or, to be more exact, Biron probably passed his illnesses on to the empress.

The English resident Claudius Rondeau, reporting to London that Anna was "not so well," added, "a few days ago they let her blood as well as that of her favorite, Count Biron. [He received the title of Duke in 1737.—E.A.] While the count was ill Her Majesty took her meals in his room."[61] At times she received visitors there or refused to receive anybody due to Biron's indisposition. Field Marshal Münnich wrote that "the sovereign held no table whatsoever, but she had her dinner and supper with Biron's family, and even in her favorite's apartments."[62]

As I have already mentioned, Biron was married to Anna's lady-in-waiting. They had three children: Peter, Hedviga Elizabeth, and Karl Ernst. The children were absolutely uninhibited at court, playing excessive pranks and taunting the courtiers. The empress was kindly disposed toward the young Birons. They were showered with awards and ranks as if from the horn-of-plenty. I have already suggested that it is possible that Karl Ernst was Anna's son. But she loved her favorite's other children as well.

One gets an impression that Anna and the Birons made up a single family unit. Together they attended festivals, visited theaters and concerts, rode sleighs along Nevskii Prospekt, and played cards in the evenings. This triangle might have surprised contemporary observers, but history has known many similar combinations wherein each is aware of the situation and each has his or her own role, own niche, and a common fate to share.

Biron once complained to his close friends that he was obliged to spend days at a time with the empress, while pressing state affairs demanded his attention. But this statement was made either in a moment of weakness or out of slyness. Keeping in mind the sad fate of his predecessor Bestuzhev-Riumin, Biron did not leave Anna unattended for even a single day. If he had to leave, his wife or one of his informers would stay with the tsaritsa. This is what he wrote to his friend Count Herman Keiserling, the Russian ambassador to Poland: "It is of the utmost necessity to use caution in asking great favors of great persons so as not to cause ill-fated changes."[63] And Biron observed this rule during the entire life with Anna. As she lay dying she gave her lover the most valuable thing she had—her power; and she is not to blame that he was unable to hold on to this invaluable gift.

Anna's rise to power opened vast horizons for Biron. As early as June 1730 she petitioned the Austrian emperor to obtain the title of Count of the Holy Roman Empire of the German nation for her favorite; later Biron received the highest Russian Order, that of St. Andrew the First-Called, and became chief gentleman-in-waiting. Amendments were made to the Table of Ranks, which regulated the official promotion of military personnel, functionaries, and courtiers, so that the newly fledged chief gentleman-in-waiting "skipped" from the fourth class directly to the second class.

But Biron's secret dream was to become Duke of Courland, to occupy the throne in Mitau, which still remained vacant. This was no easy task. The Prussians and Poles held Courland under close scrutiny. Besides, the Courland nobility would not hear of passing the throne to a relatively lowborn member of the nobility such as Biron. The detailed correspondence between the favorite and Keiserling has survived to our days. Biron tried everything he could to lull the vigilance of his potential rivals, figures sent to Courland by the Prussian and Polish kings. He wrote to Keiserling: "They try to find out whether I am pursuing any special aim in Courland. Your Honor knows how little interest I have had in it before, and I have even less as regards the future, for I am quite satisfied with my position, but if God should see fit to provide us [Courlandians] with a duke, then it should make no difference to me who it might be, if only the country could be happy with him." And further: "My only incessant desire is to forget all the world and spend the short time remaining of my life in peace . . . I am no longer one who seeks to gain glory for his labors."[64] But of course glory and power were exactly what he was after.

When the crucial moment arrived in the spring of 1737 Biron was ready for it. Quite to the surprise of political plotters, Biron, who had pretended to be indifferent and relaxed, began to act decisively and boldly. He set into motion the powerful machine of the Russian Empire: diplomatic pressure was applied, and the Russian army entered Courland. The Courland nobility convened the Seim, which was reliably "protected" by the Russian dragoons. The Seim delegates were warned that while each was free to vote for or against Biron, those who did not support his candidacy could pack their things for Siberia. The decision was unanimous in favor of Biron, whose dream had come true. Feeling like a gambler who had just won the last, decisive hand, he wrote to Keiserling about the thwarted Prussian king: "[Now] his fox won't grab at my goose."[65]

Biron had no intention of moving to Courland. His place was near Anna. Mitau was prepared as a potential base should retreat be necessary. In order to make it more comfortable, Biron sent to Courland the brilliant architect Francesco Bartolomeo Rastrelli, who had been working in St. Petersburg. He was allowed to work without any budget constraints, and the Russian treasury opened wide to cover expenditures for erecting palaces in Mitau and Ruhental. Within a few short years ornate palaces had sprung up in rather poor Courland. True, they had to wait long enough for their master to come home, for Biron did not leave the empress's side even for a minute, and later, after her death, he was sent as a state criminal in the opposite direction . . . Only in 1763, after his release from exile in Iaroslavl' did he, a man past seventy, celebrate his house-warming in Mitau.

The reader has a right to ask: What kind of a statesman was Empress Anna Ioannovna after all? The answer is quite simple: None whatsoever! An absolute nonentity! One did not need much political acumen to append instructions on a diffuse report or mark a petition "Be it so enacted," "Give it to him," "Approved." Anna repeatedly demonstrated her unwillingness to attend to political affairs, especially on the days when she was relaxing. And she relaxed almost continuously. The empress often reprimanded her ministers for forcing her to make decisions, especially when it came to so-called minor matters. Thus, in 1735 Anna notified members of the Council of Ministers that "We are not to be disturbed with minor matters."[66]

It cannot be said that the empress totally turned her back on state affairs. But she preferred listening to reports to working on the papers herself. Andrei Osterman and Artemii Volynskii were the two ministers who submitted reports most often. And it was only after consultations with Biron that Anna made her decision. A short resolution or an approving nod was enough to set into motion the enormous machinery of state. And even that was sometimes difficult for Anna. After one visit to the palace, an annoyed Artemii Volynskii told his friends: "Our sovereign is a fool, you cannot get a decision from her on any matter!"[67]

Persistent petitioners and plaintiffs were a particular headache to the sovereign. After years of persecution and torment in various chanceries and offices they came to St. Petersburg as a last resort, where they would wait patiently for the tsaritsa near her palace and fall at her feet with a cry of despair holding out a tear-stained complaint about some injustice. There were bold spirits who contrived to face the rain of the tsaritsa's bullets at Peterhof or catch Her Majesty while she was having a stroll in the Summer Gardens in order to submit their petitions to her. But only a very few were successful, as almost all of the plaintiffs were caught by the guard. In 1736 the Secret Chancery investigated a case against one informer whose howls and appearance had frightened the empress nearly to death when he tumbled out of the shrubs in the Summer Gardens. The poor fellow was sent to jail. Another case is known when a woman petitioner seized the opportunity to hand the tsaritsa her petition complaining on the delay in payment of her husband's salary. Anna reprimanded the woman severely: "Do you know that it is forbidden to address me with complaints?"[68] Then she ordered that the poor noblewoman be taken to the square and whipped. This was meant to be a lesson to others, of course.

In 1738 Anna decided to finish with the problem of complaints once and for all. She ordered that the Senate should collect all complaints and "after giving them due consideration, make a decision, in accordance with the appropriate decrees, such that poor people's cases be examined justly and without procrastination and that in the future Her Imperial Majesty be not disturbed with petitions containing this type of complaints."[69] A very wise solution: in one fell swoop to establish order, justice, and most important— peace! I believe that Anna made this decision on her own.

Among materials dating back to the eighteenth century I have often seen special imperial decrees "in anger." And they all refer to the time of Anna's reign. "Landlady Ioannovna" was firmly convinced of the effectiveness of shouting and loud cursings-out. "You invite that priest," wrote Anna in one of her letters to Saltykov, "and shout at him a little . . ."[70] Iakov Shakhovskoi, procurator-general of the Senate, recalls how ominous the Petersburg police chief Vasilii Saltykov had looked when he had come to deliver "an angry decree." He summoned the officials and "told us in a loud and menacing voice [a necessary touch when reading a decree 'with anger'!—E.A.] that Her Imperial Majesty had been informed that we are not attending well to our duties and therefore had instructed him to express her monarchic anger and to warn us that we shall not escape punishment."[71] Anna presumed that the officials, frightened by her loud threats, would immediately stop stealing, idling, and impudently cheating petitioners.

In the summer of 1738, Artemii Volynskii notified the Cabinet that Anna, "before leaving St. Petersburg for Peterhof, issued an oral imperial edict wherein she announced that she was going to Peterhof for her own amusement and a rest; therefore, Her Imperial Majesty is not to be bothered by reports about state affairs and the Cabinet is to consider by itself all matters which arise."[72] And only matters "of the utmost importance" could be brought to the empress's attention in Peterhof. Like all Russian autocrats, Anna never defined the range of her duties. Otherwise, the principle of autocracy as unlimited power would have been violated. Neither did she specify which matters were to be considered "of the utmost importance" and which less important. The ministers' level of skill was determined by their ability to correctly prioritize all matters by their degree of importance.

The Cabinet was established in 1731 for "the execution of all state affairs." The necessity for such a body had become evident immediately after Anna Ioannovna's rise to power and the dissolution of the Supreme Privy Council. As early as February 1730 Vasilii Tatishchev, nobleman, designer of new social structures, and historian, wrote in a draft: "Regarding Her Majesty, the Empress. Although we are confident of her wisdom, high morals, and ability to rule justly, however, she is still a female and thus ill-adapted [to carry out] so great a number of duties . . ." Thus, "it is necessary to establish a new entity to help Her Majesty."[73] And this "new entity" became the Cabinet, which was established in 1731. Highly trusted dignitaries were appointed members of the new body, among them Chancellor Gavriil Golovkin, Vice Chancellor Andrei Osterman, and Cabinet ministers Aleksei Cherkasskii, Pavel Iaguzhinskii, and Artemii Volynskii, who joined the Cabinet later.

This new body was endowed with great power: A minister's signature had the same authority as that of the empress, although Anna alone had the right to decide which matters she would attend to herself and which things she would charge to her ministers. The Cabinet dealt with a vast amount of work that Anna was not only unable but also unwilling to attend to. It was a functioning body of state administration. Cabinet members had been selected carefully enough: timorous Golovkin (who died in 1734) and Cherkasskii were not very perspicacious but they followed through on all matters assigned to them. Count Osterman was the driving force of the institution—the major burden of work fell on him. Biron did not trust Osterman, the latter being two-faced; but valuing the vice chancellor's serious work habits, Biron was forced to put up with him.

To counterbalance Osterman, the favorite named Peter the Great's former procurator-general Iaguzhinskii to the Cabinet, a blunt and straightforward person. He was replaced at this post after his death in 1736 by Artemii Volynskii, a clever and ambitious dignitary who was just as hot-tempered and blunt as Iaguzhinskii had been. Biron hoped that Volynskii would provide a check on Osterman's power and would duly inform him regarding all of his activities. Biron himself was not a member of this organ, his only official position being that of chief chamberlain. However, not a single important decision was made in the Cabinet without his knowledge and approval. While reporting to Anna in her apartments the ministers correctly assumed that they were being listened to not only by the yarning empress but also by the favorite, who was sitting behind the screen.

He had the last word in all matters. He appointed the ministers and other officials. On April 5, 1736, he worriedly wrote to Keiserling: "Iaguzhinskii will probably die tonight and we should try to find a substitute for him in the Cabinet . . ."[74] Officials waited hours to be received by Biron. He could get anything moving. For no one dared to contradict him. But, of course, to be successful one had to "oil the wheels." No, the chief chamberlain never took any bribes. And why should he, the empress's servant, stoop to such a thing? Benevolent people simply gave him nice presents like a thoroughbred horse for his stable or a bunch of sable furs or jewelry for his wife. That was all.

If we were to imagine for a minute a group portrait with the empress, it would have to look somewhat like this. Several persons looking severe and intent would be depicted against a background of heavy crimson velvet. In the middle, seated on a gilded armchair, is the stout uncomely woman we already know, wearing a small crown in her thick black hair and with a blue ribbon flung over her right shoulder. Biron is standing on Anna's right, holding her hand. He is a tall, handsome man with a puffy fretful face. He is dressed in his usual clothes: a bright, light-colored caftan with diamond buttons, with the long curls of his magnificent white wig thrown behind his back.

Three other men are depicted in our imaginary portrait. One of these is a tall, courageous, and elegant man. He is standing with one hand on his hip, in the other he is casually holding a marshal's baton. This is Field Marshal Burkhard Christopher Münnich. In early 1730 he was staying in St. Petersburg, which had been abandoned by the court, and was thinking of how to get the best price for his sword, or, more precisely, his compass. An excellent engineer and fortification specialist who had served in four different armies before coming to Russia, he was about to set out on a voyage as a mercenary in search of fortune and high rank when suddenly Anna came to power, and she was looking for people like him—those who were not connected with boyar circles, who were neither Privy Council members nor noble schemers, but simply faithful servitors. And so he threw himself into Anna's service with great zeal, paying little heed to moral problems.

Münnich made a pleasant impression on imperceptive people; he could be both charming and endearing. His tall, lean figure was elegant and attractive. However, those who knew anything at all about people could see that Münnich was insincere and deceitful. Excessive ambition and self-admiration were the distinguishing features which stood out in the field

Burkhard Christopher Münnich. From I. N.
Bozherianov, "*Nevskii prospekt.*" *Kul'turno-istoricheskii*
ocherk dvukhvekovoi zhizni Sankt-Peterburga ("Nevskii
Prospect." A Cultural and Historical Sketch of St.
Petersburg at Two Hundred) (St. Petersburg, 1901–
03), vol. 1, p. 75.

marshal's character. He imagined himself to be a great general and in the
name of this fantasy he vainly forfeited the lives of many soldiers during the
Russo-Turkish war of 1735–1739. In his memoirs he admits "modestly" that
his glory knew no boundaries and that the Russian people called him the
"eagle with the all-seeing eye" and the "pillar of the Russian Empire." From
the files of the Secret Chancery, however, it is known that his soldiers called
him a butcher.

He was indeed a good-for-nothing general. Ill-considered strategic plans,
poor logistical thinking, routine tactics, all of which resulted in unjustified
loss of human life—that is what can be said about the military talents of
Münnich, who himself narrowly escaped by some strange hoax of fate or
stroke of luck.

Münnich did have a rare talent for making enemies. He was a classic troublemaker: wherever he appeared he brought quarrels and discord with him. When addressing others (especially with his subordinates), he chose his words in such a way that they were ready to eat him together with his jackboots. At first he would charm a person, getting on his good side, then suddenly change his tone and begin insulting and humiliating him, and the latter would never forgive such abuse. In 1736 Anna was very anxious about the state of the army, which was on march at the time. The source of her worry was not their defeats on the battlefields. More terrible than the Turks was the fighting going on in Münnich's headquarters; rumor had it that the generals were engaged in a conspiracy against their commander in chief. It was with great effort that a potentially explosive situation in the Russian forces general headquarters was kept under control.

But Münnich remained safe in his position despite these scandals. He could always smooth things over back in the capital, and the empress shut her eyes to all of his faults. Anna knew very well that as long as she had Münnich, the army would be hers. In her letters to the field marshal she even addressed him as "Our dear and trustworthy [one]." And these words were indeed accurate: he would do anything for the sake of the monarch's favor and a successful career. Münnich wrote numerous denunciations and acted as interrogator in political investigations. Cynical and unscrupulous, he organized the murder of the Swedish diplomatic courier Malcolm Sinclair outside Russia following Anna's secret order, and committed numerous other crimes in order to please his ruler and to receive various medals and honors.

Biron saw through Münnich's ambitious aspirations early on and tried to prevent him from winning the empress's confidence. Being a civilian with no military ties, the favorite was afraid that he might lose out in Anna's eyes to this knight in shining armor—we all know that women in past centuries found military men most attractive. Münnich's efforts to become a member of the Cabinet were repeatedly thwarted by Biron. Having confronted Münnich's excessive ambitions and pretensions time and again, Biron did his best to direct the field marshal's enormous energies toward reaping military laurels in the place where they grew, that is, primarily in the south, far removed from St. Petersburg. Münnich was first dispatched to the Russo-Polish front from 1733 to 1735, and then fought almost continuously against the Turks on the southern frontier. And it was not until 1740 that he was able to finally trade in the rugged steppes for the smooth parquet floors of the palace, at which time he did skillfully trip up his old benefactor after all, arresting Biron, the ruler of Russia, on the night of November 9, 1740. But that part of the story will come later.

Yet another main character is depicted in the picture. Hardly able to withstand exposure to bright light, he seems to be just about to dash behind the crimson curtain—so strong is his desire to avoid the public eyes. His clothes are untidy and unattractive, but his eyes show a piercing intelligence. This is Vice Chancellor Andrei Ivanovich Osterman—another key figure during Anna's reign. A modest man from Westphalia who started his service as a translator during Peter the Great's reign, he gradually grew to become an extremely influential figure of the Russian political elite.

He was notable for his incredible efficiency, and according to contemporaries, he worked all the time: day and night, weekdays and holidays, something that any self-respecting minister could not permit himself to do. His vast administrative experience helped him to navigate in both domestic and foreign policy. He was particularly strong in diplomacy. He conducted Russian foreign policy for at least fifteen years, and the results of his efforts were not bad at all for the empire. But Andrei Ivanovich lived in isolation. His associates found it very unpleasant to work with him. His secretiveness and hypocrisy were the talk of the town, and his pretenses the object of many jokes. As a rule, he would malinger at the most critical and delicate moments of his career. Suddenly he would start to develop gout in his feet, or severe pains in his hands, or some other disease that was difficult to treat, from which he would remain safely bedridden for a long time, it being virtually impossible to get him to attend to his duties. In his letter to Keiserling in April 1734 Biron wrote sarcastically: "Osterman has been bedridden since February 18 and has shaved only once during all that time [Osterman did not live up to the standards of cleanliness even for his own nonhygienic times.—E.A.]; he complains of earaches [thus being unable to hear questions put to him—E.A.], and his face and head are bound up with bandages. As soon as this condition gets better he has another attack of gout, and thus, accordingly, he has not left the house. The nature of his illness may be: first, an unwillingness to give an unfavorable answer to Prussia . . . , and second, the war against the Turks is not going as desired."[75]

And here is what the English envoy Finch wrote about Osterman: "While I was talking the Count appeared to become gravely sick, he felt nauseous. This was one of the tricks he played whenever difficulties arose during a conversation and he did not want to give an answer on them. Those who know him allow him to continue with this wretched game, which frequently goes to extremes, while they keep on talking; seeing that the speaker will not be persuaded to leave, the count instantly recovers as though nothing were the matter."[76] Osterman did, in fact, know when to stop pretending: his keen sense as a seasoned courtier always prompted him to appear, albeit at times moaning and groaning, at the palace.

Anna respected Andrei Ivanovich for his reliability, erudition, and meticulousness. When it was necessary to get advice on foreign policy, one could not do without Osterman. It just took patience to coax from him the best solution to a problem, disregarding all of his numerous stipulations, digressions, and vague allusions. Osterman suited Anna as a person who was fully dependent on her favors. He was a foreigner, and owing to his personal disposition and post he did not mix with the Russian nobility despite the fact that his wife came from the old Streshnev family. And this only intensified his focus on the country's most powerful people. Menshikov was his first patron, one whom he betrayed when Peter II and the Dolgorukiis came to power. Later, during Anna's reign, at first he allied himself with Münnich, and then had to curry favor with Biron for quite some time before eventually becoming his indispensable assistant and consultant.

And, finally, we come to the last person pictured in our imaginary group portrait. He is standing behind Anna's armchair, and it appears as if they had just been hurriedly discussing some matter but were cut off the moment the grandees arrived to take their places. They did have a common secret: Anna needed this general who faded into the background whenever Münnich, Osterman, or Biron was present; she needed him just as she needed Andrei Ivanovich Osterman. Incidentally, this man's name was also Andrei Ivanovich—but his last name was Ushakov. It is no exaggeration to say that as the chief of the Secret Chancery, General and Count Ushakov held his hand on the country's pulse. Thanks to Ushakov, all cases of any importance were brought to the empress's attention. Of course, she did not read the voluminous notes taken during interrogations. Short extracts were prepared for her, which Ushakov brought to the empress, providing detailed oral reports on each, after which he waited humbly to hear her instructions or final verdict.

Ushakov was an experienced man, and like all people in his profession, an inconspicuous one. He had begun as a special messenger of the Guards Regiment during Peter the Great's reign, then got training under Peter Tolstoi while assisting him in investigating Tsarevich Aleksei and working on other delicate assignments in the Secret Chancery. Perhaps, the reader remembers him standing near the weeping emperor on the night of June 26, 1718, when Peter ordered the officers to execute his son. In 1727, the winds of fortune shifted and Ushakov was arrested in the Tolstoi-Devier case (the so-called plot against Menshikov) and exiled, but by the end of Peter II's reign, he had resurfaced. It is well known that this kind of person never disappears completely and can reappear and become useful to any regime. During Anna's reign he reached the peak of his career, becoming chief of the political police.

A loyal servant, cold-blooded and able to obey orders unquestioningly, he saw the world in one very narrow focus. The case of Baroness Solov'eva is a well-known example. While dining in Ushakov's home she berated her son-in-law and between courses mentioned that he had written a letter that offended the honor of Her Imperial Majesty. Ushakov's guest was arrested the very next day and all letters found in her home and that of her son-in-law, a high state official, were confiscated.

Count Ushakov quickly understood Anna's tastes and interests and soon learned how to satisfy them. This was not at all difficult to do. On the one hand, the empress had a strong dislike for her political opponents or for those whom she considered such, and persecuted them without mercy, while on the other hand, she loved prying into her subjects' private lives, especially if they represented high society. In Baroness Solov'eva's case, for example, Ushakov submitted excerpts from her son-in-law's letters for review "at the top" which had nothing to do with any political crimes; however, they were full of complaints about the frivolous behavior of the baroness's daughter, descriptions of quarrels and squabbles in the family, and so on. The empress was keenly interested in all this.

Andrei Ushakov's department was a frightening place. The Secret Chancery's papers are stained with the sweat and blood of those who died in its torture chambers. During this time the system of "word and deed" prevailed: informers were arrested together with those on whom they publicly informed. And the mechanism of political investigation was set into motion to accomplish its unhurried and terrible work. Few escaped torture and trial by ordeal before being set free. Not only those who had been suspected of committing a crime were tortured; but the informers were, too, if the suspects endured the torture and made no confession. Nevertheless, people hurried to inform on one another, for their fear was greater of being named noninformers (hence, accomplices) and in this capacity being taken to the Secret Chancery.

Reading investigative reports from those times is both disturbing and oppressive: fear of the rack and red-hot pincers loosened anyone's tongue, and under torture people lost all honor, conscience, and humanity. Anna was not repelled by the exposure of human inadequacies and vices; she found it fascinating to learn the whole truth, including all the nasty and disgraceful secrets about her subjects. Andrei Ushakov always remained close to the empress. He had impressed her with his steadiness and loyalty, and as often happens, a specific relationship had developed between the head of the government and the chief of political investigations. It was a relationship of accomplices, a partnership, for only these two persons knew so many secrets, saw so much dirt.

It should be noted that those cases which Anna received from the Secret Chancery convinced the empress that the Russian people in no way deified her; on the contrary, they held a most unfavorable opinion of her personally and also of her reign. One idea stands out in dozens of cases investigated by the Secret Chancery: With a woman in power, Russia will soon perish. "A woman cannot rule the country, because she was born a woman." And many other versions of the same: "A woman is long of hair but short on intellect." Many people were detained for discussing "the problem of carnal intimacy" between the empress and Biron. And woe to the many people who were taken to the Secret Chancery for a crime so petty as proposing a silly toast at a festive table: "Long live Our Imperial Majesty, even if she is a woman!" Anna reacted calmly to such criticism—she knew her own worth, yet she mercilessly ordered that all those who were caught talking such nonsense have their tongues cut out, for she was convinced that morals could be corrected through terror.

The time of Anna's reign has been represented by some historians as a period of boundless German predominance in Russia: even in our imaginary group portrait, three out of the four highest-ranking statesmen are of German descent. Indeed there were many Germans in high government positions during Anna's reign, but almost all of them had lived in Russia a long time and begun their careers during Peter the Great's reign. Russia had opened its doors wide for foreigners. Having earned enough money, some returned home to their own countries, others stayed in Russia and put down roots. Among these were not only the scholars of the Academy of Sciences, who were mentioned earlier, but also numerous military leaders, engineers, artists, actors, and doctors. Many of those people were talented; some were even geniuses. Among the foreigners who settled for good in Russia were the Italian architects Domenico Trezzini, Rastrelli senior and Rastrelli junior, the German mathematician Leonhard Euler, the French astronomer Joseph Nicolas Delisle, and the Danish navigator Vitus Bering, to name only a few who lived during Anna's reign, and not those who became famous at other times in Russian history.

Many officials, politicians, and courtiers also came from abroad. Almost all of them, with the exception of Biron, had settled in Russia long before 1730: Osterman and Münnich had occupied key government posts in the empire for many years. It should also be taken into account that having been confronted early in her reign with an attempt to limit her power Anna realized that she had to include in her team only reliable people—those on whom she could depend. This is the natural desire of any ruler. Therefore, relying on foreigners who had weak contacts with "boyars" and noblemen was also a natural thing to do.

In speaking about the "German domination" of Russia during Anna's reign these historians forget that together with the Germans there were a great many Russians in the upper echelons of government, such as Iaguzhinskii, Feofan Prokopovich, Volynskii, Ushakov, and Cherkasskii. No special "German party" existed at Anna's court. The Germans had never been united. Biron from Courland, Münnich from Oldenburg, Osterman from Westphalia, and the Löwenwolde brothers from Livland were all ready to cut each other's throats in the struggle for privileges, salaries, and power. "The tangle of friends" at the foot of any throne has no nationality. This is how the Spanish envoy de Liria characterized Count Karl Gustav Löwenwolde, one of the key figures in the beginning of Anna's reign: "He barred no means and stopped at nothing in pursuit of personal gain, even at the sacrifice of his best friend and benefactor: personal welfare was his life's goal. Deceitful and dishonest, excessively ambitious and vain, he had no faith, and it is unlikely that he believed in God."[77] These same words could apply to many of those who crowded around the throne, be they of Russian or other origin.

Many facts testify to the absence of any extraneous, foreign influence on the policies of Anna's government. Thus, Russia's foreign policy during Anna's reign did not undergo significant changes as compared with that of Peter the Great's time, and in no way was it a deviation from his imperial principles. On the contrary, one can clearly see the further evolution of these principles. In 1726, thanks to Osterman's efforts, Russia signed an alliance with Austria. The Petersburg-Vienna axis enhanced the stability of Russian foreign policy: this alliance was based on long-term interests in the war against Turkey in the south as well as common interests in Poland and Germany. This was the primary direction laid out for Russia's foreign policy, to which it adhered throughout the entire eighteenth century. The 1730s, that is, the epoch of Anna's reign, was no exception.

It was in the 1730s that a serious step was taken toward the future partition of Poland. On February 1, 1733, the king of Poland, Augustus II, died at the age of sixty-four. A "kingless" period beset Poland, a period of desperate power struggles. This fight was regulated by the well-coordinated actions of Russia and Austria. The allies had nurtured the noble democracy in Rzeczpospolita (after 1569 the Commonwealth of Poland and Lithuania) in order to prevent Polish royalty from regaining power and, by extension, the idea of statehood from gaining strength. The situation was complicated by the fact that the ex-king Stanislas I Leczczynski, who had been banished from Poland by Peter the Great, became engaged in the struggle for the throne. Having enlisted the support of his son-in-law, the French king Louis XV, he moved back to Poland. Russia's reaction was resolute and uncompromising: "Following from our firm [policy of] goodwill toward Rzeczpospolita and our intention to maintain peace therein as well as taking into account our own natural great interests, we will never allow that [Stanislas be elected king]." After the Russian government's resolution, the Russian army was immediately dispatched to the Polish border.[78] On July 31, the Russian forces invaded Poland from two different directions; and the Austrians followed suit in August. The allies could not prevent the election of Stanislas at the meeting of the entire *szlachta* (the Polish gentry), but almost immediately the reelected king had to flee to Gdansk, for the Russian forces commanded by the General Peter Lacy had already reached Warsaw. The free city granted asylum to Stanislas, hoping for the timely arrival of a French squadron with infantry forces. This reckoning proved to be incorrect: the advantage of the Russian and Austrian forces was overwhelming. The siege of Gdansk began and Lacy was replaced by Münnich. In May 1734, the French troops landed but almost immediately were crushed by the Russian forces, after which the French fleet left the Baltic for good.

In late June, Gdansk surrendered, but Leszczynski had already escaped abroad disguised in peasant's clothes. By that time civil war was raging in Poland. Russia's adherents, encouraged by money, had hurriedly elected the son of the late king Augustus II to occupy the Polish throne. The new king, Augustus III, supported by the Russian corps, commenced battle against Stanislas's advocates. The enemies ransacked and burned whole cities and villages, killing and robbing their inhabitants. By the autumn of 1734, Augustus III, with the support of the Russian army, mounted the Polish throne. It became clear then that the fate of Polish statehood depended little on the Poles themselves. During this war, which came to be called the war "for Polish heritage," Russia and Austria had taken a decisive step toward the future partition of that heritage, which belonged entirely to the Poles.

The successful end of the Russo-Polish war of 1733–1734 resulted in one more increment in the extension of the Russian Empire. Poland, Courland's suzerain, was greatly weakened by the war, and Biron, ignoring the grumbling of a discontented Prussia, was able neatly to lay his hands on Courland's crown. From that moment on, Courland ceased to be considered a disputed territory. It became clear to all: Courland's masters reside in St. Petersburg. And when in 1762 Catherine II came to power, she returned the ducal crown to Biron. His loyalty to Russia was beyond question: Courland had become Russia's!

In the autumn of 1735, Russia, quite unexpectedly, recommenced the war against Turkey. This was Russia's second war against Turkey during the eighteenth century, the first one being the previously mentioned Pruth campaign of 1711. And during roughly two centuries of confrontation, from 1676 to 1878, the Turks and the Russians shed each other's blood in eleven wars which lasted a total of thirty years. It was a struggle for supremacy over the Black Sea, the Balkan lands, and the Caucasus, as well as for dominion of one faith over another. For the Turks it was a fight against "infidels" for the expansion of Islam; for the Russians it was a fight against Mohammedans, in order to drive them out of Constantinople, which by that time had been the Turkish capital Istanbul for over a dozen generations of Turks.

According to a plan designed by Münnich, the commander in chief of the Russian army, the war was to last four years and to be crowned with the triumphant march of the Russian forces into Constantinople and the restoration of the cross on the St. Sophia Cathedral, the profaned sanctuary of the Orthodox faith. As it turned out many times in later years, these plans proved unrealistic, though the beginning of the war was successful enough. In the spring of 1736, the strong Azov Fortress at the mouth of the Don River surrendered; and in May, Turkey's vassal, the Crimean khanate, followed suit. The Russian forces passed through Perekop and invaded the Crimean peninsula.

This was the beginning of the next act in the drama of Russo-Crimean relations. It was preceded by periodic raids of cruel Tatar hordes across Russia's southern borders, as well as by periods of relatively peaceful coexistence. But never had these relations become friendly. Russia viewed Crimea as a "robbers' nest," and now Münnich had received the order to destroy it totally. Russian forces pushed deep into the Crimea, meeting no resistance, the Tatars retreated into the mountains, the Crimean auls (villages) and cities were ravaged, and the marvelous Palace of the Khan in the capital of the Crimean khanate, Bakhchisarai, was plundered and set ablaze. But soon massive outbreaks of dysentery among the soldiers, heat exhaustion, and malnutrition caused the Russian army to call a hasty retreat from the Crimea, leaving a long trail of dead Russian soldiers behind them.

Later, in the course of the war, the Russians invaded the Crimea two more times, destroying everything they failed to destroy during the first invasion. In the course of military operations in the northern Black Sea littoral and Moldavia, the Russians maintained an advantage over the Turks. In 1737, the Russians captured the Ochakov Fortress, which was the Turks' primary defensive site in the area, and in 1739, the Turks were defeated near Stavuchany and yielded the Khotin and Jassy Fortresses in Moldavia.

Yet the war did not go the way Münnich had planned it. The Russians had suffered heavy losses—no less than one hundred thousand men, the majority of the victims dying not from the Turks' bullets or the Tatars' arrows, but from disease and the effects of the unusually hot climate. The strategy of military operations was poorly thought out, and soldiers were ill-equipped and could not count on new supplies. Münnich could not adapt the army to functions under the special southern warfare conditions; he was not sparing with the lives of his soldiers, who, following the field marshal's order, moved over the steppe grouped in a square formation, many collapsing in a dead faint from the heat, fatigue, and hunger.

But the gravest of Münnich's shortcomings was his absolute inability to make use of the results achieved in victories. All the fortresses taken (except Azov) were eventually abandoned, and each new campaign was commenced from the deep home rear rather than from the newly gained front. No coordinated military operations were conducted with the Austrian forces that had entered the war.

Russia's diplomatic policy was equally unsuccessful. At the peace congress held in 1738 in the small Ukrainian town of Nemirov, Russia's territorial claims submitted to Turkey were excessive and were not supported by the appropriate military victories, which led to the total breakdown of negotiations. The Belgrade Peace Treaty of 1739, signed by French diplomats on behalf of Russia, was not a victorious one. Russia received only Azov, some territories in the Ukraine, and a hope for future success in a new war for the Black Sea coastline, as southern advances in imperial policy had become the most promising for Russia at that time.

Now let's consider the internal affairs of the country, which were unbearably boring for the empress. The principles of internal policy were formulated under the strong influence of the events that took place in early 1730, or to be more precise, under the influence of the nobility movement. Of course, the tsaritsa could not agree to a political compromise with the nobility and share her power with them; yet she did not dare to neglect their numerous claims against autocratic rule. And this is what determined the direction of internal policy in Russia during the 1730s. It was at this time that Russian nobility began receiving indulgences of which they would never have dreamed during Peter the Great's reign (although according to those who claim that Anna's was merely a regime of German favorites, the nobility was supposed to have been languishing under the yoke of foreign exploiters).

To start with, in 1732 Münnich, a German, initiated a proposal for making the salary of Russian military officers equal to that of foreign officers, for until then the Russians were paid half as much as the foreigners occupying the same posts. In 1736, a decree was issued that, according to the historian Sergei Solov'ev, "marked an epoch in the history of Russian nobility."[79] By that decree the burdensome conditions imposed on the nobles during the reign of Peter the Great, which committed them to lifelong service, were abolished. Now a nobleman could idle away his time at home until the age of twenty-five instead of joining the army at the age of fourteen or fifteen, as required during Peter's reign. The new law limited the duration of military service for a nobleman to twenty-five years; moreover, a nobleman was entitled to leave one of his sons at home "to run the household."

This was a real revolution in the military obligations of a Russian nobleman. He could enter the military school established by Münnich in 1731 and graduate from it as an officer, escaping the long and painful suffering of common soldiers in the army. Still more favorable for members of noble society were other decrees issued in 1730 and 1731. These abolished Peter the Great's decree on primogeniture, by which the right of inheritance of property went to the eldest son only, obliging younger sons to earn their living serving the state. Now, under Biron, this Petrine law, which had been so onerous for the nobility, was abolished. Important restrictions of land and property were lifted. These decrees extended the rights of the nobility almost to the extent reached by the famous 1762 Charter of Freedom to the Russian Nobility.

During the years of Anna and Biron's power, the economic situation in Russia was stable; it even improved, and any assertion that the national economy suffered is untenable. Thus, in 1720 there were smelted 10,000 tons of cast iron in Russia (17,000 in England), and in 1740 as much as 25,000 tons were smelted (compared to no more than 17,300 tons in England). Between 1729 and 1740 iron smelting in the Ural Mountains increased from 253 to 416 thousand poods (1 pood = 16.38 kg). During

Anna's reign, iron exports grew more than fivefold, and the export of wheat at the end of her reign was twenty-two times greater than it had been at the beginning of her reign. The volume of trade conducted through the port of St. Petersburg and other ports rose sharply.[80]

In 1739, the Berg Regulation was adopted, a new mine-industrial legislative act worked out by the Saxonian specialist Schemberg. This law stimulated new industrial ventures, and mass privatization of the state industries began, following the strategy that Peter the Great had adopted toward the end of his reign. On the whole, Peter's economic policy, based primarily on the use of serf labor, continued to develop during Anna's reign, reinforcing both the autocratic regime and the entire structure of social relations.

The 1730s brought a new lease on life for St. Petersburg, which was again declared the official capital and from that time on began to flourish. Construction was given just as much attention during Anna's reign as it was under Peter the Great. The city became for Anna what it was for other Romanovs—the imperial residence and the showcase of the empire. They spared neither money nor labor in making it beautiful.

Not all has survived of Empress Anna's St. Petersburg. Her Summer and Winter Palaces have long since been demolished, and one can no longer ascend the white-stone staircase leading to the Throne Room of the Winter Palace, in which the ceiling was painted by the French artist Louis Caravaque, beautiful cut-glass chandeliers sparkled, and blue tile stoves warmed the room. Seated there on the throne, Anna received ambassadors and held formal receptions and celebrations. The so-called Spyglass Palace, built in 1731 on a small island at the mouth of the Neva River, has vanished as if it had dissolved in the water. From that palace one could watch through a telescope the ships bound for St. Petersburg. It looked like a fairy-tale castle rising up out of the deep waters. At dusk its plate-glass windows seemed ablaze with the fiery tones of the marine sunset.

However, other parts of Anna's St. Petersburg have survived to our days. In the summer of 1733, the Sts. Peter and Paul Cathedral was consecrated, and in a vault under its floor the great founder of the city was finally laid to his eternal rest. The Twelve Colleges designed by Domenico Trezzini and the first Russian museum, the Kunstkammer (Chamber of Curios), opened. Ivan Korobov completed construction of the new Admiralty, whose golden spire was crowned with a ship, which has become the symbol of St. Petersburg.

In 1736 and 1737, two great fires destroyed the central part of the city near the Admiralty. A special team headed by Eropkin, a talented pupil of the Italian architect Chipriani, developed a new project for reconstruction of that part of the capital. It was Eropkin who devised the three-ray layout of the main part of the city, that is, three long streets—Nevskii Prospekt, Voznesenskii Prospekt, and Gorokhovaia Street—radiating from one center, the Admiralty; these three rays going in three different directions intercon-

Spyglass Palace, 1731. From I. N. Bozherianov, "*Nevskii prospekt.*" *Kul'turno-istoricheskii ocherk dvukhvekovoi zhizni Sankt-Peterburga* ("Nevskii Prospect." A Cultural and Historical Sketch of St. Petersburg at Two Hundred) (St. Petersburg, 1901–03), vol. 1, p. 23.

nected with squares and streets, so that even today while you move along streets that intersect them, for example, Sadovaia Street, you will be able to see the Admiralty's golden spire three times, shining brightly in the blue sky over the Neva River. Regular and skillfully planned streets and embankments gave the city its characteristically austere and well-proportioned appearance. Foreigners arriving from the Baltic Sea could view a magnificent panorama of St. Petersburg.

The tsaritsa could often be seen out on the streets of the city, especially in winter. Anna was particularly fond of sleigh rides along Nevskii Prospekt, the capital's main thoroughfare; a light frost and a speedy ride were good for the health and the appetite. In summer, the city stood empty and deserted as the court would move to the suburban palace of Peterhof situated on the Gulf of Finland. At the same time, life on the Neva picked up: hundreds of ships and boats sailed down the river bringing innumerable goods; Russia's rich natural resources came by river to the capital from Lake Ladoga; foreign ships sailed up the Neva from the west to moor in St. Petersburg's trading port.

Not far from Nevskii Prospekt, the area on the river between the split of Vasil'evskii Island, the Sts. Peter and Paul Fortress, and the Winter Palace formed a vast natural aquatic square, which in winter became the site for public prayers near an ice hole on the day of the Epiphany, and also a parade ground and a spacious setting for fireworks, festivals, and public merrymaking. In summer, this aquatic square was dotted with bright flags, sails, and the colors of variegated ships and boats. State-sanctioned and Russian Orthodox holidays had always been celebrated in a special way in the capital, and the sky over the city, which was often naturally aglow with the luster of northern lights, exploded with marvelous flashing fireworks. From her high balcony a tall, stout woman dressed in a splendidly regal fur coat approvingly looked out on the public merriment which would envelope the entire city below and the fiery magnificence of the sky above. Her life was tied forever to this city, to these shores . . .

The city took great pride in its Academy of Sciences. Although Anna herself had little use for science and could have got on well enough without any academy whatsoever, still it had been brought to Russia by Peter the Great and did enhance the empress's prestige. Ultimately, Anna became convinced that scientists could be useful; for instance, they could regulate the sawmill in the shipyards; they could locate ores; they could create festive fireworks; and they could draw the first map of Russia. And what wonderful things one can see through a telescope! For example, the rings of Saturn or spots on the moon.

The empress enjoyed visiting the Kunstkammer, where she could examine the specimens brought from Siberia by the Messerschmidt expedition, touch mysterious fossils, or sit on a bench inside the gigantic rotating Gottorp globe admiring the celestial map of the universe all around her. Filled with disgust and curiosity, Anna would look at the human body parts and em-

Kunstkammer (cross section), 1734. From *Russkaia arkhitektura pervoi poloviny XVIII veka* (Russian Architecture of the First Half of the 18th Century) (Moscow, 1954), p. 147.

bryos preserved in alcohol, which made up the famous Ruysch collection. The empress felt uneasy each time she passed the wax figure of Peter the Great, which the architect Carlo Bartolomeo Rastrelli had made immediately after Peter's death using the exact measurements taken from the body of the deceased tsar. And now this doll, dressed in Peter's original clothing, with real hair, and with a wax mask for a face, instilled fear and anxiety in the tsaritsa, for her uncle the emperor had never showered Anna with kindness.

For Anna, as for many of her contemporaries, science was valued primarily for its secondary purpose, namely, that of providing entertainment. Although the empress looked through the telescope and sat inside the huge Gottorp globe, it is most unlikely that she was an advocate of Copernicus's heliocentric concept of the universe. Let science remain science and let the rings around Saturn be, but in the case of the witch Agatha Dmitrieva, the empress signed a special decree establishing a committee to ascertain whether or not the witch could really transform herself, as she claimed, into a goat or a dog. During Anna's reign it was common practice to burn people at the stake who were suspected of witchcraft or who had adopted the Jewish or Islamic faiths. Thus, one of the last remaining Muscovite tsarevnas continued practices rooted in the Russian Middle Ages . . .

The empress also loved literature in her own way. Evidently she needed something more than just the fairy tales and epic poems narrated and sung to her during the long evenings by storytellers especially invited for that purpose to the palace. And so she brought the poet Vasilii Trediakovskii to court and listened to his translations of classical works. He was the first Russian to graduate from the University of Sorbonne, and later he often recalled with some sadness "the dear shores of the Seine." Being a well-educated man of great intellect, he wrote poems, translated contemporary Western authors and ancient poets, and was known as Russia's first theorist on prosody. But his knowledge and talent were not appreciated at Anna's court, as no one could understand them. Trediakovskii was valued merely as a versifier who could write an inscription on a triumphal arch, or an ode or a hymn on the occasion of an official holiday. He also wrote indecent verses when commissioned by the tsaritsa. "I had the privilege of reading verses for tsaritsa, sitting by the fireplace," wrote the poet later. "Upon finishing the reading I was favored with a most gracious slap in the face rendered by her own hand."[81]

Anna's epoch was cruel and unjust to Trediakovskii, one of the first Russian poets of the imperial period. He did not fit in well in its stuffy atmosphere; his talent was not appreciated by a society that took pleasure in jesters' dirty jokes and Esmeralda's slapstick comedies. Weak and defenseless, he could not fight for a more deserving place in life. He became a peevish failure, a whiner, berated by critics, laughed at by the public, and despised by courtiers and servants. But despite the universal mockery and humiliations at court, and fear of the Secret Chancery, Trediakovskii remained true to his

Vasilii K. Trediakovskii. From I. N. Bozherianov, "Nevskii prospekt." *Kul'turno-istoricheskii ocherk dvukhvekovoi zhizni Sankt-Peterburga* ("Nevskii Prospect." A Cultural and Historical Sketch of St. Petersburg at Two Hundred) (St. Petersburg, 1901–03), vol. 1, p. 64.

industrious muse. Nevertheless, nothing could protect him from the contumely and scorn of those who honed their skills through study of his imperfect verses. Before long new, more talented poets, such as Aleksandr Sumarokov and Mikhail Lomonosov, took over Trediakovskii's place as the foremost Russian poet.

* * *

The empress's interest in the arts and sciences, however, was lukewarm compared with her interest in the reports made by the Chief of the Secret Chancery, Ushakov. In the late 1730s she would even interrupt her hunts to listen to them. The time had come for rancorous Anna to get even with her main enemies, namely, the Supreme Privy Council members who had offended her in 1730. The first blow was dealt to Prince Dmitrii Golitsyn, who had then headed the Supreme Privy Council. Although he was old and sick, in 1736 he was brought to trial and sentenced to death. The merciful empress softened his sentence to life imprisonment, which he was to serve out in the Schlüsselburg Fortress located on a lonely island near the headwaters of the Neva River, right at the spot where the river flows out of Lake Ladoga. Golitsyn lasted only till the next spring, dying on April 14, 1737.

Next in line for retribution came Anna's other offenders—the Dolgorukii princes. As already mentioned, the Dolgorukiis, Peter II's favorite, Ivan Dolgorukii, and his father, Prince Aleksei, together with two children, were exiled to a village in Penza province far from Moscow. On the way to their destination a Guards officer caught up with the Dolgorukiis and, following the empress's personal instructions, stripped them of all their orders, decorations, and jewelry. The exiles had scarcely settled in the village when new troubles arose. This is how Princess Natalia Borisovna, Ivan's wife, described what happened: "I looked out of the window and saw the dust rising over the road; it could be seen from afar that a large group of people was approaching and moving at great speed."[82] A detachment of soldiers had arrived to arrest the Dolgorukiis and take them farther away, to Siberia, in accordance with Anna's new decree . . .

Here we must digress to say a few words about Princess Natalia Borisovna, who was a woman of sterling character. In the autumn of 1729, shortly before Peter II's death, Ivan Dolgorukii announced his desire to marry her, a fifteen-year-old countess, daughter of the late field marshal Boris Sheremetev. Ivan had earned a bad reputation as a decadent, drunk, and philanderer. But this did not daunt the young countess. She immediately fell head-over-heels in love with Prince Ivan, an agile, handsome nobleman and a major of the Preobrazhenskii Regiment. She was charmed and captivated by his sweet talk and without hesitation gave her consent to become his wife. The official ceremony of betrothal took place in the Sheremetev's palace on Christmas Eve of 1729 and was attended by the tsar, his court, and numerous relatives. Natasha dreamed blissfully of the rosy future that lay ahead. The wedding date was set for some time in January 1730 and was approaching fast. But on January 19 misfortune dealt them a staggering blow—Peter II died. Prince Ivan instantly lost all favor at court. He and his father moved to their country estate Gorenki, where he remained waiting for his fate to be decided.

It was clear to many, including the bride's relatives, that Prince Ivan was in for hard times. And they all advised Natasha to dissolve the betrothal and return the engagement ring to the fallen bridegroom. But quite unexpectedly that delicate girl, in age still a child, rejected their advice. Many years later in her memoirs Natalia appealed to her readers: "Put yourself in my place: was it a consolation to me, and would my conscience remain clear (to live with the thought) that I was happily willing to marry him when he was great, and when misfortune struck I rejected him! I could not follow such dishonest advice and decided in this way: once I had given my heart to one [man] then I would live and die with him, and no other man could hope to capture my love . . . In all mishaps I was my husband's comrade. And now I shall tell the real truth: having gone through all these troubles I have never regretted the fact that I married him . . ."[83]

Let's ask ourselves: What was on this girl's mind when she resolved to take such a step—to follow her bridegroom without looking back into exile, and perhaps even to her death? But is there really any need to guess? Of course, love is the answer, that deep, selfless feeling that makes a human being courageous, kind, and ready for self-sacrifice for the happiness of another. But this is not the only reason that Natalia came to Gorenki and later followed her husband to Siberia, where they spent many years in exile. Compassionate women have often graced the course of Russian history. Love guides them not only in the form of a fond attachment or carnal passion, but also in the form of empathy, and the need and obligation for self-sacrifice in order to help a loved one. I think that seventeenth- and eighteenth-century Irish, English, and French women must have felt the same when, following their husbands and bridegrooms, they climbed the shaky gangplanks boarding frail ships that were to take them across the vast ocean to the unknown shores of America in order to begin to weave their nests in the virgin forests amid unfriendly native tribes.

But we should keep in mind that most of these immigrants moved to the West of their own free will; they were free people and went there in the hope of making a better life for themselves. It is quite another matter when your loved one has been condemned to penal servitude and is conveyed, in shackles, along Vladimirka—the main road leading from Moscow to Siberia. For many centuries, crowds of women have been seen shuffling along behind guarded groups of male exiles—their husbands, sons, bridegrooms, and brothers—until they reached the next stop, where they could feed the sufferers, give them drink, dress their wounds, and lend a few words of encouragement. The reason for such behavior on the part of hundreds of thousands, even millions, of women, common and noble, young and old, lay in the traditions of Russian life: it was customary. One must not forget that in Russia in those days a woman who was left without a husband lost all status in society, and life became very difficult for her. But more than anything else Russian women were governed by the indisputable sacred Orthodox laws, which required self-sacrifice in the name of God, for the sake of goodness. To sacrifice oneself for the sake of a loved one, to suffer with him was a joy, for it was the path to the soul's salvation. And everything else was trivial. In climbing the gangway to board the ship that was to take the exiles in the direction of Siberia, a priceless pearl necklace of Natalia's fell into the water.

"I was not even sorry. I could not be bothered by it when life itself had already been lost," wrote Princess Dolgorukaia.[84]

She spent seven difficult years in the small Siberian town of Berezov, cut off from the world by endless snows in the winter and impenetrable marshes in the summer. During this time Natalia's father-in-law, Prince Aleksei Dolgorukii, died. In 1738 a local official, Tishin, sent a letter to St. Petersburg denouncing Ivan Dolgorukii; he wrote of his reprehensible conversations, all-too-free mannerisms, and friendship with local inhabitants. This was sufficient for Anna to order that Ivan and his brothers and uncles be moved to Schlüsselburg. Here under torture Ivan told of the forging of Peter II's will and other events which took place in 1730. If it were not for Ivan's faltering testimony from the rack, the Dolgorukii affair would not have had such a bloody outcome. On November 8, 1739, Ivan, his uncles Sergei and Ivan, as well as Vasilii Lukich Dolgorukii were executed in Novgorod after being tried and sentenced. All remaining male relatives were exiled to the Pacific, and the women sent to Siberian monasteries.

Several months later, Princess Natalia was horrified to learn of her husband's death. And when she was allowed to leave Berezov together with her two children, the eight-year-old Mikhail and one-and-a-half-year-old Dmitrii, she found no help from friends in her native city of Moscow, no sympathy from relatives, who sought to avoid disgraced Prince Ivan's wife. With great difficulty she raised her elder son, Mikhail, and in 1758 she entered a monastery near Kiev. There she lived as the nun Nektaria together with her younger son Dmitrii, who was mentally disturbed and who died in 1769 in the arms of his selfless and infinitely kind mother. Nektaria's own sorrowful life ended just three years after her son's death.

No less dramatic was the fate of yet another person entangled in the Dolgorukii affair, Peter II's unfortunate fiancée, Catherine Dolgorukaia, who was exiled together with her relatives to Berezov. In December 1740 Archimandrite Lavrentii of the Alekseevskii Monastery in Tomsk received an order to force "maid Catherine," who was sent there under guard and whose identity was known to no one, to take a nun's vows. He was to keep her in the neighboring convent under heavy guard, and not to allow her any contact with the outside world. This "maid Catherine" was twenty-eight-year-old Princess Dolgorukaia.

She had spent the previous ten years in Berezov, where she had made life miserable for her family. Unhappy with fate, she unleashed her temper on close relatives, particularly on her father, who initiated the marriage to Peter II. One has to admit that the accusations she made against her father were justified. For the sake of the Dolgorukii clan's political ambitions, he disregarded the close relationship which had sprung up between the eighteen-year-old Catherine and Count Mellesino, the nephew of the Austrian ambassador. Once he even rudely drove the enamored young man out of the house, destroying thereby an advantageous and mutually acceptable ready-made marriage arrangement in order to make his daughter (in de Liria's words) into a "coquettish siren for trapping Peter II."[85]

One can appreciate Catherine Dolgorukaia's horror when she arrived in that same cursed Berezov, where not so very long before, in late 1729, Peter II's previous fiancée, Maria Menshikova, had died on her eighteenth birthday, having been brought there along with her once prominent father. Long years passed in wretched exile, and Catherine was in despair. Unlike Princess Natalia Dolgorukaia, she did not have a love, a family, or children to bring her comfort in exile. She was horrified to discover that a local drunkard sought to win her favor, a simple clerk by the name of Tishin. After she refused this suitor, and her brother Ivan gave a good thrashing to the impudent plebeian, Tishin took vengeance in his own way on all the Dolgorukii family—writing a letter denouncing them all. This denunciation was the starting point of the entire Dolgorukii affair of 1738–1739.

And thus Catherine ended up in Tomsk, where she was forced to take the veil and although she had blasphemously refused to answer the priest's questions of whether she had freely decided to forsake the world and devote herself to God, an answer was not requisite, and the sacred ceremony which for another might have been full of divine meaning was played out quickly and formally. Soldiers stood next to the girl ready to apply force if necessary to dissuade her from resisting. Then they dressed the weeping girl in a black robe and gave her a rosary and led her to a low cottage in which stood a small table and bench in place of a bed. The young nun was kept under continual surveillance by one of the other nuns. A legend has survived of Catherine's proud, unapproachable behavior in the monastery and of an unsuccessful attempt on the part of the monastery authorities to remove the engagement ring which had at one time been given by the Russian emperor to his fiancée. During the long years of exile in Berezov, the ring had grown into the finger and could only be removed by chopping it off, finger and all, something that the authorities stopped short of doing.

In late 1741 Catherine was released from the monastery. She took off the nun's robe and returned to St. Petersburg. There Elizabeth Petrovna was already in power, and she graciously met yesterday's prisoner and even helped her to marry a rich and influential man, Count Bruce. But a long and happy life did not follow. Soon after the wedding Catherine died. Legend has it that, anticipating the end, the countess collected all her strength and began cutting and throwing all of her expensive toiletries into the fireplace—so that no one else would come by them.

But let us return to Anna's reign. The execution of the Dolgorukiis made a profound impression on Russian society. It was clear that the bloody reprisal inflicted on one of Russia's most distinguished families was not called for by any real dangers which threatened the empress from remote Siberia, but rather by her rancorous thirst to avenge all the humiliation which she, the widowed Duchess of Courland, would have had to endure at the hands of the Dolgorukiis and their allies.

Vindictiveness and suspiciousness were characteristic traits of the empress's personality and had made themselves manifest long before the bloody Dolgorukii affair. As early as 1730 she had exiled the young and beautiful Praskovia Iusupova to Tikhvinskii Monastery (without making her a nun), after accusing her of reprehensible chatter. And even behind the high monastery walls the empress did not relax her vigilant watch over the impudent sharp-tongued princess. Someone informed on her and the Secret Chancery launched an investigation, which entailed an interrogation of the princess's servants and Praskovia herself. The case had sad implications for the beauty—she was sentenced to beating with a knout and was forced to take the veil right in the Secret Chancery and then sent to a distant monastery in Tobol'sk.

It was spring of the year 1735. The willful cruelty with which the princess had been treated—spoiled as she admittedly was and accustomed to the comforts of a prosperous life—was intended to humiliate and trample her human dignity. She repeatedly asked to be given roasted chicken on the road to Tobol'sk, but her guard refused the girl even when, according to his report, she said: "I will not eat, but at least [let me] look at the chicken and I will be satisfied."[86] At the monastery, in reply to Prokla's (that became Princess Iusupova's name as a nun) discontent and tantrums, it was ordered that she be placed in leg-irons and thrashed with a whip and that it be announced "that if she does not stop, she will be even more cruelly punished."[87] We know nothing more of her later life. It is most likely that she did not withstand the severe conditions in prison and soon died there.

Anna, of course, was behind all these cruelties, apparently taking pleasure in the suffering of others. She was like a cruel landlady who, having given the necessary instructions regarding kitchen and home, goes out to the stables, where in her presence a young servant girl who has committed some minor trespass is being mercilessly flogged. Anna was this same kind of landlady, only her estate was larger and the servant girls of more distinguished families.

Talk of the Dolgorukiis' execution had barely died down when another political affair, this time in St. Petersburg itself, deeply distressed Anna's subjects. It began in the winter of 1740 when, on the eve of the famous House of Ice Festival, a most unpleasant incident took place, one that had serious repercussions for one of its participants.

Anna's Cabinet minister Artemii Volynskii cruelly beat the poet Trediakovskii, who had come to Biron with complaints about Volynskii's arbitrariness. This was the straw that broke the empress's favorite's patience. Biron had already noticed that Volynskii, who owed his career to him, had long since ceased to be a loyal and grateful servant, and had distanced himself more and more from his patron. Proud and ambitious people like

Volynskii soon take for granted those who have helped them climb the career ladder. Having become a member of the Cabinet in 1738, thanks to Biron's efforts, Volynskii was dissatisfied with his dependence on the favorite, who had helped Volynskii with the very design of having his own reliable man in the government.

An enterprising and experienced administrator, Volynskii had begun his government service at the age of fourteen as a soldier in the Guards during Peter the Great's reign. He advanced quickly and soon became one of Anna's main counselors. This displeased Vice Chancellor Osterman, who held the Cabinet in check. Volynskii and Osterman quarreled on a regular basis, and sly Osterman awaited his chance to trip up his young, hot-blooded colleague. And that chance presented itself following the incident with Trediakovskii. Biron was furious, and Osterman managed to direct all of the favorite's rage on Volynskii.

The investigation, which was headed by obedient Ushakov, delved into the details not of Trediakovskii's treatment, but rather of the parties that took place at the home of the widowed Volynskii. These were attended by the Cabinet minister's old friends, many of whom were high officials, such as the senator Platon Musin-Pushkin, the counsel Andrei Khrushchov, the seaman Fedor Soimonov, and the architect Peter Eropkin. As often happens within a circle of friends, they discussed current political events, and Volynskii began to read them excerpts from his draft document "On the Correction of Affairs of State," which included proposals and recommendations for improving the administrative system, economics, and politics. It was precisely this draft that became the primary evidence against Volynskii when he was accused of antigovernmental activities.

Anna valued her intelligent counselor and was unwilling to turn him over to the Secret Chancery, but Biron was unrelenting and insisted that the tsaritsa remove the obstinate minister. Anna reluctantly agreed to the demands of her beloved chamberlain, and later, by force of habit and owing to her characteristic curiosity regarding political cases, she herself became involved in the investigation, read Volynskii and his friends' interrogations, and even gave orders to the inspectors and wrote questions for Volynskii.

Beginning on May 7, 1740, Volynskii and his acquaintances were tortured. Under torture Volynskii was forced to confess that he had devised a conspiracy to take the Russian throne. At first Artemii Volynskii begged to be pardoned, wept, and threw himself at the feet of his interrogators. But later, faced with imminent death, he changed drastically, taking the entire blame on himself with courage and dignity, not implicating anyone else. On June 20 Volynskii was sentenced to be impaled, and his six acquaintances to quartering, breaking on the wheel, and other cruel forms of execution.

Who passed this verdict? Neither Biron nor Osterman—they only secretly led the investigation. Volynskii was sentenced by noble Russian grandees—

Empress Anna Ioannovna. From I. N. Bozherianov, "*Nevskii prospekt.*" *Kul'turno-istoricheskii ocherk dvukhvekovoi zhizni Sankt-Peterburga* ("Nevskii Prospect." A Cultural and Historical Sketch of St. Petersburg at Two Hundred) (St. Petersburg, 1901–03), vol. 1, p. 56.

Field Marshal Ivan Trubetskoi, Chancellor Aleksei Cherkasskii, senators, generals, almost all of them acquaintances and guests of the hospitable Volynskii. They probably patted Volynskii's twelve-year-old daughter on the head whenever they came to his house to visit. And on June 20, 1740, they sent the innocent girl into exile and forced her to take the veil in a remote monastery in Siberia. Fear motivated them, while feelings of patriotism, friendship, or any other human emotion remained silent. It was well known that one of the judges in the Volynskii affair (who earlier together with Volynskii passed judgment on Dmitrii Golitsyn), the chief of police and

Empress Anna's own relative, Count Vasilii Saltykov, had signed an earlier verdict sentencing Golitsyn's son Aleksei to exile together with his wife to the remote and deadly location of Kizlar. And the wife of the exiled man was the Saltykovs' only daughter, Agrafena Vasil'evna! And so be it! He remained silent, bore it well and probably thought, like all the other judges: "Lord, let this cup pass me by!"

Anna, as before in similar cases, displayed her mercy: Volynskii had his tongue cut out and then was beheaded on the market square. Peter Eropkin and Andrei Khrushchov were also beheaded. The rest were beaten with a knout and sentenced to hard labor. Anna was in Peterhof enjoying hunting on execution day. Volynskii and his friends were of no concern to her. She carried on as usual, hunting, strolling, being entertained by jesters and actors, and cooks prepared abundant, rich dishes which were not the healthiest for the forty-seven-year-old stout woman.

She had tired of many of life's previous attachments, except her passion for Biron. In order to spend more time with him, a fanatical horseman who spent many hours each day in the ménage, she began to learn to ride horseback, since her chief chamberlain had wonderful stables.

On August 12, 1740, an important, long-awaited event took place: Anna Leopol'dovna, Empress Anna's niece, wife of Prince Anton Ulrich, gave birth to a son. He was named Ivan. Everyone was convinced that he would be heir to the throne but assumed that he would have to wait a long time for that moment. Anna's health was excellent, and as the Prussian envoy Axel Mardefeld wrote not long before the onset of her grave illness: "Everyone cherishes the hope that she will reach advanced old age." But he was the very one to announce on October 5 that Anna was beset by an illness, throwing up blood, and that "her health had gotten worse and worse."

Anna was known to have suffered from kidney stones. It is possible that in the fall of 1740 her condition had become acute after she began to spend much time on horseback. Perhaps this had caused the kidney stones to change position (an autopsy revealed that they resembled a branching coral), and the kidneys began to die. Suffering from agonizing pain, Anna became bedridden and, as Mardefeld describes it, hysterical. Maybe her fear was connected with a strange event which occurred in the palace one night not long before Anna's death.

The Guards officer who was on watch at night in the palace noticed a strange figure in white in the darkness of the Throne Room who closely resembled the empress. It wandered around the room and did not respond to words addressed to it. This seemed odd to the vigilant watchman, as he knew that the empress had gone to bed. He woke Biron, who confirmed Anna's having retired. The figure remained despite the ensuing uproar. Finally, Anna was awakened, and went to look at her twin. "That is my death," said the empress and retired to her room.[88]

And indeed, death soon came for her. She died on October 17, 1740, having lived for forty-seven years and reigned for ten. But even at her last moments she did not take her eyes off Biron, who stood weeping at her feet, and—as the English envoy Edward Finch recorded—"Her Majesty, looking up, said to him: *Nie bois!*—the ordinary expression of this country, and the import of it is: 'Never fear.'"[89]

CHAPTER 3

The Secret Prisoner and Her Children

(Anna Leopol'dovna)

This story begins long before Anna Leopol'dovna was born in 1718, and of course that much earlier than her son Ivan Antonovich's birth in August 1740. We must immerse ourselves in the military and political events which were shaking Europe during 1700–1721, the years of the Northern War.

In 1711–1712, Peter the Great's Russian army, in alliance with the Saxons and Danes, had entered the Duchy of Mecklenburg-Schwerin in Northern Germany. Thus, the Northern War, which Russia, Saxonia, Poland, and Denmark had begun against Sweden in the regions near Riga and Narva, had reached the borders of Germany. The allies' aim was the Swedish crown's possessions in German Pomerania. By 1716, only the town of Wismar located on the Mecklenburg shore of the Baltic remained in Swedish hands. The allied forces laid siege to Wismar, and a Russian corps commanded by General Anikita Repnin was dispatched to assist them.

By that time Tsar Peter and Charles Leopold, Duke of Mecklenburg, had established rather friendly relations. Having ascended the throne in 1713, the duke considered friendship with the great tsar, the victor of Poltava, advantageous. First, Peter had promised his aid in returning to Mecklenburg the town of Wismar; second, the presence of Russian forces in the duke's domain suited Charles Leopold just fine, for his relations with the local nobility were strained, and he was hoping that with the help of the Russian club he would be able to subdue the noble-born freethinkers who were discontent with his tyrannical ways.

Peter also pursued his own interests in Mecklenburg. The tsar did not intend a quick and easy departure from Northern Germany, to which he had taken a great liking. From this important strategic zone Russia could pose a threat not only to Sweden but to Denmark as well, which had levied imposts on all Russian trading vessels passing the straits of Oresund on their way from the Baltic Sea to the North Sea.

On January 22, 1716, the Russo-Mecklenburg marriage alliance was signed in St. Petersburg, which marked the beginning of the story of Anna Leopol'dovna. According to this treaty Charles Leopold was to marry Peter the Great's niece Ekaterina Ioannovna, and Peter would provide security to the duke and to his heirs against all internal disruptions by sending to Mecklenburg several regiments from Russia that would be placed at Charles Leopold's own disposal in order "to protect the duke from all unjust complaints of the hostile Mecklenburg nobility and to coerce them into obedience."[1] In addition, Peter promised with the end of the war to turn over the port of Wismar to his future in-law. Since matters needed to be settled quickly, it was decided that the wedding would be performed without delay in Gdansk, where Peter was headed on business right after Easter in 1716.

Peter the Great had truly reformed Russia. Everything he had laid hands on in the land of his forefathers had immediately changed its appearance or substance. He ended Russia's ideological, religious, political, and economic isolation, and nudged her out of the "window" that he had cut into the West. One of his many innovations that shocked Russian contemporaries was the contracting of foreign marriages. The first such undertaking was selecting a bride for his own good-for-nothing son, Tsarevich Aleksei. She was Princess Charlotte of Wolfenbuttel and came from an old German ducal family. Moreover, she was a sister of the Austrian empress, Elizabeth, Charles VI's wife. The wedding took place in Torgau in 1711. A little earlier, in 1710, as we know, Tsarevna Anna Ioannovna, Peter's niece and the future Russian empress, married Frederick William, an offspring of Courland's famous family of Ketler dukes. Peter also tried to arrange a marriage between Louis XV of France and his daughter Elizabeth. He married his elder daughter Anna in 1725 to Charles Frederick, the Duke of Holstein-Gottorp.

Petrine "matrimonial expansion" was a policy aimed at the distant future. The tsar was well aware that political alliances were temporary and short-lived, while blood relationships might be far more reliable and long-lasting. And to jump ahead a bit, we can say that Peter's successors followed his policy—so much so, in fact, that the last Russian emperor, Nicholas II, had a very insignificant percentage of the Romanov family blood running through his veins, the major portion of it being inherited from other European dynasties. Incidentally, this was what had led to Nicholas II's family tragedy: Tsarevich Aleksei's affliction with hemophilia.

Charles Leopold's (the Duke of Mecklenburg's) marriage to Tsarevna Ekaterina Ioannovna was just another instance of this dynastic policy. According to an entry in the *Zhurnal, ili podennaia zapiska Petra Velikogo,* Peter the Great's official diary, "On the morning of the 8th [of April 1717], while in Gdansk the Sovereign presented the Duke of Mecklenburg with the Order of Saint Andrew, thereby confirming the marriage contract, and at four in the afternoon the marriage ceremony of Her Majesty Tsarevna Ekaterina Ioannovna and His Highness Duke of Mecklenburg was happily performed in the presence of the Sovereign and the tsaritsa (Catherine I), His Majesty the King of Poland (Augustus II), generals and ministers from Russia, Poland, and Saxony, as well as other distinguished persons; and in the evening there was a fireworks display,"[2] which Peter, himself an expert in and great lover of these amusements, personally set ablaze on the market square of Gdansk.

In the eighteenth century, women often got married at the age of fourteen or fifteen, so Ekaterina Ioannovna, the young wife of the Duke of Mecklenburg, was not all that young a bride: she was born on October 29, 1692, and when she married Charles Leopold she was twenty-four years old.

She led a happy life up to her marriage. She came from the family of Peter the Great's elder brother, Tsar Ivan V and Tsaritsa Praskovia. After her father's death in 1696, four-year-old Catherine together with her mother and two young sisters—three-year-old Anna (the future empress) and two-year-old Praskovia—moved to Izmailovo, an estate located near Moscow.

Here, in the peace and quiet of a comfortable wooden palace, surrounded by gardens and fields, Catherine spent her childhood. At the age of fifteen she left the comfort of Izmailovo and together with other relatives of the tsar-reformer moved to St. Petersburg, which had already become by that time the unofficial capital of Russia. Here, of course, she found herself in a strange and totally new environment. But unlike her sisters and many other Muscovites who, living on the unfriendly marshy shores of the Neva River, missed the more cozy atmosphere of dear old Moscow, Catherine quickly adapted to the way of life in the windy young city. This was largely because of her extremely cheerful personality and also because she, like other young ladies of the Russian capital, was thrilled with the freedoms provided by a European-style social order with its holiday parties and balls and emphasis on fashions.

Indeed, one gets the impression that Russian women of the seventeenth century were not too suppressed by Domostroi and seemed to have just been waiting for the Petrine reforms to take place in order to make a break for freedom. This movement was so powerful that the authors of *Iunosti chestnoe zertsalo* (A Mirror of Honor for Youth)—a code of conduct for young people—which appeared in 1717, had to warn young girls that in spite of the new opportunities offered by life in high society, they should observe modesty and chastity, not allowing themselves to run in the living rooms, nor to sit on young men's laps, nor to drink to the state of drunkenness, nor to jump on tables and benches, and finally not to let men squeeze them "as a slut" in every corner.

Catherine especially enjoyed Peter's soirées, where she danced with her partners until she dropped. She was a short, red-cheeked, and excessively plump but lively and energetic woman. When she danced she rolled around like a dough-ball, and her laughter and chatter were heard all the evening long. And Catherine's ardent character didn't seem to change with the years: "*. . . die Herzogin eine überaus lustige Dame ist, und alles wegspricht, was ihr in den Mund kommt*" ("The duchess is a very cheerful woman, and she always says whatever crosses her mind"), wrote Bergholtz, Duke Charles Frederick's chamberlain.[3] The Spanish diplomat de Liria echoed Bergholtz's words: "The Duchess of Mecklenburg is a woman of unusually lively character. She has little modesty, she never troubles herself over anything, and blurts out everything that comes to mind. She is excessively stout and loves men."[4]

Catherine was the complete opposite of her tall and sullen sister Anna, and was adored by the tsaritsa Praskovia Fedorovna, who, as we have seen, disliked her second daughter. Even though, according to tradition, the oldest daughter should have been married first, the tsaritsa married Anna off to the Duke of Courland, in order to keep her favorite eldest daughter at home longer. Leaving St. Petersburg in late January for Gdansk to negotiate with Charles Leopold, Peter took his niece with him, and Catherine went bravely along to meet her fate.

The thirty-eight-year-old bridegroom had actually been expecting a different bride—the younger "Ioannovna"—widowed Anna, the Duchess of Courland. But Peter had his own plan in mind, and vexed, he even threatened to dispatch the Duke of Mecklenburg's envoy to Siberia for his insistence on the duke's demand. Hence, the diplomats were forced to accept Catherine's candidacy and give up designs on the Duchess of Courland.

The bride herself did not dare to disagree with her stern uncle. Before the wedding Peter gave his niece a short brief almost in the form of a military order, instructing her on how she was to live abroad: "Keep our faith and laws without fail until the end. Don't forget your people, hold them in love and respect above all others. Love your husband, respect him as the head of the household and show your obedience to him in everything, except in the above mentioned. Peter."[5]

Of course, this was not a marriage of love, for Charles Leopold aroused this kind feeling neither in his subjects, nor in his first wife, Sophia Hedviga, whom he had not managed to divorce prior to marrying Catherine, so Peter had not only to hurry him on this account, but even to pay money to cover the fee for his divorce. According to contemporaries, Charles Leopold was a rude, uncouth, despotic, and erratic man and a terrible miser who never paid his debts. The duke's subjects were the unhappiest people in all Germany—he tormented them without reason, inflicting cruel punishment on those who complained about his dictatorial ways. Charles Leopold's attitude toward his young wife was cold, aloof, and at times even insulting. Only the presence of Peter, who accompanied the newlyweds to Rostok, the capital of Mecklenburg, compelled the duke to be more polite with Catherine.

However, as soon as the tsar had left Mecklenburg, the duke could no longer conceal his antipathy toward Catherine, and her life became extremely difficult. This is evident from Praskovia Fedorovna's letters written to Tsar Peter and Tsaritsa Catherine. If in her first letters she thanked the tsar "for the special favor granted to Katiushka," her subsequent letters were full of complaints and entreaties. In her letter to the tsaritsa she writes: "Be so kind,

Praskovia Fedorovna. From the journal *Russkaia starina* (Russia of Old) (St. Petersburg, 1882), tip-in plate.

[our] Sovereign, as to request of his Royal Majesty, on my daughter Katiushka's behalf, that he relieve her of her sorrows. She sent me an oral message that she is not happy with her life."[6] Apparently, the ever-cheerful Catherine had to bear hard times in her husband's home, for her mother's letters implored her: "Do not kill yourself with grief, and [likewise] don't destroy your soul."[7]

The duchess was in a complex predicament. Charles Leopold believed he had been deceived—he did not attain the promised town of Wismar, and the allies prevented the Russian army from advancing to that point, which became the cause of international friction. An even bigger scandal arose after Peter arrived in Mecklenburg and unceremoniously arrested the ringleaders of the local nobility, who had revolted against his niece's husband. This and the Russian army's presence in Mecklenburg annoyed many German rulers and especially its nearest neighbor, the elector of Hanover, who was at that time also the king of Great Britain. In addition, Mecklenburg was an integral part of the Holy Roman Empire, and the Mecklenburg nobility, as well as that of its alarmed neighbors, began to complain of the duke's behavior to their common supreme suzerain—the kaiser, that is, the Austrian emperor of Germany. Seeing how many serious problems had been caused by his attempt to intervene in Mecklenburg affairs, Peter decided to retreat, and essentially abandoned the duke to his fate. In any case, he decided to postpone aid to Charles Leopold until the end of the Northern War.

After signing the Nystad Peace Treaty in 1721 the tsar, not known himself for soft-talk, wrote to Catherine: "And from this day we can freely help you in your affairs, if your spouse would only act more mildly."[8] In another letter the tsar advised that the duke "not do what he wants, but rather act in accordance with circumstances."[9] But Charles Leopold was not capable of compromise and continued his destructive struggle against his own nobility and the entire German world.

From Catherine's correspondence it is clear that she had been raised in the tradition of a wife's unquestioning submission to her husband. And in the beginning she did not seek to run away from Mecklenburg, perhaps being even more afraid of disobeying her terrible uncle the tsar. At the order of her despotic husband she even wrote Peter a letter in his defense: "In this I ask Your Majesty not to discontinue your favors to my spouse, as my spouse has heard that Your Majesty is angry with him, and hearing this has left him in great sadness."[10] She asked Peter not to forget her husband's interests as well in the course of his great political game on the Baltic.

The Duchess of Mecklenburg's abject lack of rights can be seen in everything: in her unenviable position as the wife of a person who would have been more at home in the Middle Ages than in the enlightened eighteenth century; in the scornful treatment she received from the nobility living in German provinces who called the Moscow tsarevna "*Die wilde Herzogin*" ("the wild duchess"); in Peter's peremptory and imperious letters to her; and finally, in her own servile letters to St. Petersburg. On July 28, 1718, she wrote to Empress Catherine: "By God's grace I've become pregnant, and am already at the halfway point, but during the earlier half, I didn't dare to write Your Majesty, for I was not sure of it."[11] On December 7 of the same year she gave birth in Rostok to Princess Elizabeth Katerine Christine, who after conversion into the Orthodox faith in Russia would be called Anna Leopol'dovna, by which name we know her in Russian history.

The baby girl was sickly and weak, but was loved dearly by her distant grandmother, Tsaritsa Praskovia, who showed incessant concern over her granddaughter's health, education, and pastimes. When Anna turned three, Praskovia began to write letters addressed directly to her granddaughter. They still preserve the human warmth and tenderness that often arise in relationships between the very old and the very young: "Write in your own hand to me about your health and about your father and mother, and kiss your father and mother for me—father on the right eye, and mother on the left. I am sending you gifts, my dear: a warm caftan to keep you warm when you come to visit me. Comfort your father and mother, my dear, so that they will not become engrossed in their sorrows, and invite them to be my guests, and come with them yourself, and I believe that I will see you because you are constantly on my mind. My old eyes can hardly see anymore, but your old grandmother wants to see you, my little granddaughter."[12]

The ducal pair's visit to Russia becomes a central theme in the old tsaritsa's letters to Peter and Catherine. Praskovia passionately wants to lure her daughter and granddaughter to St. Petersburg to stay since Charles Leopold's affairs were going from bad to worse: the united forces of the German states had driven him out of the duchy and Charles Leopold and his wife left no stone unturned in an effort to make peace with the emperor in Vienna. It was difficult to help him. Peter wrote in annoyance to his niece in the spring of 1721: "My sincere sympathy, but I don't know how to help. For if your husband had heeded my advice, none of this would have happened, and now he has gone to such extremes that nothing can be done."

By 1722 Tsaritsa Praskovia's letters voice desperation. Feeling her own approaching death, she asks, begs, even demands that her daughter and granddaughter be with her whatever the cost. "My dear granddaughter! I wish you all the best with all my heart, and want so very much to see you, my little one, and to be your friend: An old one and a young one can live very well together. Invite your father and mother to come visit me, kiss them for me, and make sure they bring you, for I have to speak with you about some private matters."[13] The tsaritsa threatened Catherine with her parental curse if she did not come to her sick mother. She also wrote to Peter asking him to help her good-for-nothing son-in-law, as well as returning dear Catherine to her.

In the summer of 1722 the old tsaritsa finally got what she wanted; Peter summoned the Mecklenburg ducal pair to Riga. The emperor wrote that if Charles Leopold could not come, then the duchess should come alone "since our sister-in-law and your mother is sick and wishes to see you."[14]

As we know, the will of the sovereign was law, so having left her spouse to fight with his own vassals, Catherine and her daughter traveled to Izmailovo, where Tsaritsa Praskovia impatiently awaited them, sending couriers to meet them en route with such messages as: "How soon will you arrive? Send news of where you are now. I am so sick just waiting for you!"[15] And when Charles Frederick, the Duke of Holstein, visited Izmailovo on October 14, 1722, he saw there a happy Tsaritsa Praskovia sitting in a wheelchair: "*Bei sich auf dem Stuhl hatte sie der Herzogin von Mecklenburg kleine Tochter auf dem Schoße sitzen, welche ein gar munteres kind, und ungefähr vier Jahre alt war.*" ("She held the Duchess of Mecklenburg's small daughter on her knees, a very cheerful child about four years old.")[16] Indeed, Catherine and her daughter Anna had arrived in Izmailovo in August of that year. Once again Catherine found herself among relatives and servants in the familiar old home of her grandfather. And just as during the tsarevna's childhood, she heard Izmailovo's orchard, heavy with autumn fruits, rustling beyond the palace windows.

Looking at dear Catherine, neither her mother nor the courtiers could refrain from smiling—none of life's problems, sorrows, or illnesses had daunted her undying optimism, or changed the cheerful character of everyone's favorite. She was the same as always—carefree and gay. Almost immediately upon her arrival she indulged in dancing and merrymaking, doing it to the point of exhaustion. In October of 1722 Catherine put on a performance for her guests. She selected actors from among her ladies-in-waiting and servants, commissioned court tailors to sew the costumes, borrowed wigs from the Duke of Holstein, and enthusiastically directed the performance, which, as Bergholtz wrote, was made up of nothing but trifles. It is noteworthy that during the frequent closing of the curtains, when the auditorium, full of invited foreigners, plunged into total darkness, somebody stole Bergholtz's expensive snuffbox. Other guests from Holstein also had their pockets lightened as well.

The girl-princess felt herself in a Russian seventeenth-century environment, though it had gradually begun to lose its distinctive features under the impact of eighteenth-century culture. On October 26, 1722, Bergholtz made an entry in his diary describing his visit to the Mecklenburg duchess in Izmailovo. Catherine led the visitors from Holstein into her bedroom, where the floor was covered with red canvas and the beds of the mother and daughter stood next to one another. The guests were shocked by the presence of one "half-blind, dirty mandora-player, reeking of garlic and sweat," who sang the duchess her favorite songs, which, as Bergholtz understood, were not entirely decent. "*Allein ich wurde noch bestürzter, als ich ein altes, blindes, schmutziges, hessliches [?] und närisches Mensch im Zimmer bei ihnen barsuß [?] herumspazieren sahe, welches fast nur im Hemd war, und die Erlaubniß hatte . . . die Prinzeßin dieses Mensch öfters vor sich tanzen liesst, und das man demselben nur ein Wort sagen dürste, so höbe sie ihre paar alte stinkende Lumpen von vorne und hinten in die Höhe, und zeigte alles was sie hätte. Ich konnte mich also nicht darein finden, das die Herzogin, welche so lange in Deutschland gewesen ist, und daselbst ihrem Stande gemäß gelebet hat, hier ein solches Weibstücke um sich leiden kann."* ("But I was even more surprised when I saw that they had some kind of old, blind, dirty, wretched and stupid woman who wandered barefoot from room to room in nothing more than a shirt. The princess often made this hag dance for her, and it sufficed to say one word and she would immediately lift her stinking old rags in front and back and show all that she had underneath. I could not at all imagine how the duchess, who had been so long in Germany and had lived there in keeping with her title, could bear this hag being near her here.")[17]

Oh, naive and slow-witted gentleman of the bedchamber! Ekaterina Ioannovna grew up in her mother's room and the mores and manners of those who traditionally surrounded the Russian tsaritsa—the jesters, fools, and squalid cripples—had not disappeared at Izmailovo Palace, which preserved the old way of life, despite the winds of Peter's reforms. The girl-princess found herself in the very same environment in which her mother and grandmother had lived.

We know very little about the years which Catherine spent with her daughter after her return from Mecklenburg to Russia and before Anna Ioannovna's accession in 1730. We cannot say anything definite about the little girl's personality but believe that she was a normal child. In 1722 Bergholtz wrote that once when taking leave of Tsaritsa Praskovia, he was lucky enough to see the little naked legs and knees of the princess, who, "dressed in a short evening housecoat, was playing and rolling about with another little girl on a mattress which had been laid on the floor" in her grandmother's bedroom.[18] The young beauty apparently liked the handsome gentleman of the bedchamber very much. On December 9, 1722, Bergholtz wrote in his diary that the Duchess of Mecklenburg sent to him one of her courtiers who *"bat mich auf heute Nachmittag nach Ismailof hinaus, um mit der kleinen Prinzeßin zu tanzen, welche sehr nach mir verlange, und mit keinem andern tanzen wolle"* ("asked that I come to Izmailovo after dinner to dance with the little princess, as she keeps asking about me and does not want to dance with anyone else").[19]

We know that the princess and her mother moved from Izmailovo to St. Petersburg, where Tsaritsa Praskovia died on October 13, 1723. The tsaritsa's funeral took place two weeks later and was as solemn and tiresome as that of any ruler, complete with a canopy of violet velvet adorned with an embroidered double-headed eagle, an exquisite royal crown, a yellow state banner with crepe, the sad toll of the bells, Guards, the emperor and his family, and all the Petersburg nobility in mourning. Finally, the signal was given and the tall black chariot drawn by six horses covered with black cloths moved slowly down the street that would later be called Nevskii Prospekt. Accompanied by her mother and her aunt Praskovia, five-year-old Anna went the entire way to the Church of the Annunciation in the Aleksandr Nevskii Monastery to bid farewell to Tsaritsa Praskovia. Although she rode in a carriage, it was damp, dirty, slippery, and cold—what else could one expect from fall in St. Petersburg?

The affairs of the Mecklenburg family got no better after the death of Tsaritsa Praskovia. Word came that Catherine's husband Charles Leopold did not intend to change his suicidal policies, and the German emperor had threatened to transfer the rule of the duchy to his brother Christian Ludwig. And Catherine was distressed that Charles Leopold had refused to come to St. Petersburg, to Peter, who could help the "Wild Duke." All of the duchess's pleas were in vain. Finally, after a long struggle, Charles Leopold, who had not changed, was relieved of the throne in 1736, arrested, and died in November of 1747 in the dungeon of the ducal palace. He never saw his wife and daughter again after their departure for Russia.

However, Catherine's sorrows were not deep or long lasting—her optimism and levity invariably triumphed over any sad thoughts, and she enjoyed herself and grew even more stout. As Bergholtz wrote, once the duchess complained to him that the emperor, seeing her stoutness, advised her to eat and sleep less, and she was hurt by such inhumane advice. But, Bergholtz noted, "the duchess soon gave up fasting and vigilance which she could not have long endured just the same."[20]

Anna was always with her mother, who lived in obscurity after Catherine I ascended the throne in 1725 and under Peter II, Russian emperor from 1727 to 1730. The "Ioannovnas" were of no interest to anyone at that time.

As a matter of fact, the names of our heroines would have been lost in time just like the cozy palace at Izmailovo if a miracle had not occurred in January 1730: Peter II died and the widowed Duchess of Courland, Anna Ioannovna, Catherine Ioannovna's sister and the aunt of the eleven-year-old princess of Mecklenburg, was invited to take the throne of the Russian Empire.

In no time Anna Ioannovna became a full-fledged autocrat, having rid herself of the restrictions imposed on her by the members of the Supreme Privy Council, who had invited her, on certain conditions, to ascend the throne of her ancestors. The question of succession inevitably arose. Anna had no children, at least no children born in wedlock, and her death might open the way for either Tsarevna Elizabeth Petrovna, or "the little devil"— that's what the court called the tsarevna's nephew, the two-year-old Karl Peter Ulrich, prince of Holstein and son of Peter the Great's older daughter, Anna Petrovna, who had died in 1728. Under no circumstances could Anna Ioannovna let that happen. The empress, who had long nurtured a liaison with her favorite Biron, did not want to marry. When in 1730 a prospective husband suddenly turned up, the Infante Emmanuel, brother of the king of Portugal, he was made a laughing stock, presented with a sable coat, and hurriedly sent home. No one in Russia could even imagine the autocratic empress with a husband. "Who then," they all thought, "would rule us?"

In 1731 a rather complicated solution to the problem of succession was devised by the cunning vice chancellor Andrei Osterman and Karl Gustav Löwenwolde. Anna accepted it, but insisted that her subjects swear allegiance to the empress's personal choice as heir. Her subjects obeyed, but wondered: Who would be the successor to the throne after all? It soon became clear—and that is why Osterman's and Löwenwolde's plan was so cunning—that the throne would belong to the child of the empress's niece, the princess of Mecklenburg, and her as yet unknown spouse. The empress immediately dispatched Löwenwolde to Germany under orders to find a suitable bridegroom for the young princess of Mecklenburg. Meanwhile, miraculous changes began to take place in the princess's life.

The girl was taken from her mother and sent to live with her aunt Anna Ioannovna at court, where she was granted a suitable allowance and a retinue of court servants. But most important, a crash course in the Orthodox faith ensued, for now her name had come to be involved in a political game on a grand scale. The learned monk Feofan Prokopovich took charge of the girl's education. Having been christened Elizabeth Katerine Christine in Mecklenburg, she was converted to the Orthodox faith in 1733 and received the name Anna. To outside observers it appeared as if the empress had adopted her niece and had even given her her own name. But this was not the case. It is most likely that Anna Ioannovna became Anna Leopol'dovna's godmother. Her own mother, Catherine, attended her daughter's christening ceremony on May 12, 1733, and died only one month later. Throughout her married life she had suffered from serious feminine disorders and had developed dropsy. Death came when she was only forty years old. The Duchess of Mecklenburg was buried at the Aleksandr Nevskii Monastery next to the grave of her mother, Tsaritsa Praskovia.

Still, she lived long enough to have a good look at the bridegroom whom Löwenwolde had found for Anna in Germany. It was Anton Ulrich, prince of Brunswick-Bevern-Luneburg, the nineteen-year-old nephew of the Austrian empress Elizabeth, wife of Charles VI. He arrived on February 5, 1733, just in time to celebrate the name day of the empress and, accordingly, of his bride. He joined them to watch a magnificent spectacle: the ice field in front of the Winter Palace was decked out as a garden illuminated by thousands of green and blue artificial lights, and in the middle of it stood a large "flower-bed" in the form of a crown with the empress's monogram made up of red lamps. The Peter and Paul Fortress and the building of the Academy of Sciences were also sparkling with illuminations. There was a total of one hundred fifty thousand lamps and lanterns burning that evening; the prince could see for himself that he was visiting the capital of a powerful empire . . .

Princess Anna did not impress people favorably. As Lady Rondeau, the wife of the English resident, wrote in 1735: ". . . she is neither handsome nor genteel, and her mind has not yet displayed very shining qualities. She is very grave, seldom speaks, and never laughs; which to me is very unnatural in one so young, and, I think, her gravity rather proceeds from stupidity than judgment."[21]

Ernst Münnich, Anna Leopol'dovna's future head chamberlain, had a different opinion of her. He wrote that people considered her cold and arrogant, allegedly despising everyone around. In actual fact, however, she was tender and compassionate, generous and forgiving, and her coldness was a form of defense against "the unctuous manners" so habitual at her aunt's court. In any case, a certain aloofness, sullenness, and unfriendliness on the part of the princess was evident to everyone. Many years later, the French

Anna Leopol'dovna. From A. G. Brikner, *Istoriia Ekateriny Vtoroi* (History of Catherine II) (St. Petersburg, 1885), p. 199.

envoy Jacques-Joachim de la Chetardy recounted that when she was a child the duchess had to use all her motherly authority to make her daughter show up in high society. Incidentally, one must not lay full blame for Anna Leopol'dovna's lack of social appeal on her personality alone. Also significant were the circumstances in which she lived, especially after 1733.

Anna's bridegroom had arrived and been a disappointment to everyone, including his fiancée, her mother, the empress, and the court. The slim, fair-haired, effeminate son of Duke Ferdinand Albrecht felt uncomfortable before the hard, unfriendly gaze of the elite of Anna's court. As Biron wrote in his memoirs, "Prince Anton had the misfortune of failing to please the empress, who did not like Löwenwolde's choice. Yet the blunder had been made, and it was impossible to correct it without bringing grief to herself and to others."[22] The empress told the Austrian ambassador, who was the official matchmaker, neither yes nor no, but she allowed the prince to stay on in Russia so that he could get accustomed to the new country while waiting for the princess to come of marrying age. He was granted the rank of lieutenant-colonel in the Cuirassier Regiment and a corresponding allowance.

The prince tried repeatedly to become friends with his future spouse, but to no avail as she indifferently refused his advances. As Biron wrote later: "His zeal was rewarded with such coldness that for many years to come he could flatter himself neither with the hope of love, nor with the possibility of marriage."[23] In the summer of 1735 a scandal arose that partly explained Anna's marked indifference toward Anton Ulrich.

Anna, a sixteen-year-old girl at that time, was suspected of having intimate relations with a certain ladies' man, the handsome Count Maurice Karl Lynar, the Polish-Saxonian ambassador to St. Petersburg, and Mrs. Adercass, the princess's governess, was named an accomplice in organizing their secret meetings. In late June of the same year she was put with great haste on a ship and deported; later on, at the Russian government's request, Augustus II recalled Count Lynar from Russia. As the English resident Claudius Rondeau wrote, the reason for this scandal was very simple: the princess was young, and the count handsome. Punishment was also imposed on the gentleman of the princess's bedchamber, Ivan Brylkin, who was exiled to Kazan'. Nothing else can be said about this incident. We only know that Anna's coming to power in 1740 immediately brought Lynar back to the St. Petersburg court, where he soon felt quite at home, attended meetings, received the highest decoration in Russia—the Order of St. Andrew, a diamond sword, and other rewards. This fact speaks for itself, as does the fact that the former gentleman of the bedchamber, Brylkin, earlier completely unknown to anyone, was appointed Chief Procurator of the Senate. Finally, we know that, after the scandal, Empress Anna Ioannovna established a very strict and vigilant watch over her niece. There was now no possible way for unauthorized persons to penetrate her quarters.

Isolation from all possible contacts with people her own age, her girl-friends, high society, and even the court, which she visited only for official ceremonies, lasted five years and could not help but leave its mark on Anna Leopol'dovna's mind and morals. Naturally, not a very lively and sociable person, Anna now became even more reserved and inclined to seclusion and doubts. According to Münnich, she grew very fond of reading books, which in those days was considered a most unusual pastime and one that could bring young girls to no good. She got up late, dressed slovenly, fixed her hair carelessly, and displayed reluctance and fear when stepping out onto the shining parquet floor of palace halls. Even in the days of her reign Anna could hardly endure the company of more than four people, even if they were all well known to her, and nobody dared to speak of noisy, merry festivals and masquerades in her presence.

Princess Anna's isolation came to an end only in July 1739. On that day, the Austrian ambassador Marquis Antony de Botta, speaking on behalf of Prince Anton Ulrich and his aunt, the Empress of Austria, asked Empress Anna for Princess Anna's hand in marriage and finally received her consent.

Empress Anna had no choice. At first, the empress did not want to think about any heir at all—she had become empress at age thirty-seven after so many years of humiliation, poverty, and expectation, and it seemed to her that her own life had just begun. Moreover, the empress did not at all like either her niece or her niece's future husband; therefore, she kept putting off making a decision in this banal matter of marriage.

It so happened that Princess Anna's future was of more concern to the empress's favorite, Biron, than to anyone else. Seeing Anna's demonstrative contempt for her bridegroom, in 1738 the duke had launched a *ballon d'essai*: through one of the court ladies who acted as a mediator, he tried to find out whether the princess would agree to marry his eldest son, Peter Biron. To be sure, he had enlisted the empress's support for the idea in advance, and the fact that Peter was six years younger than Anna did not bother Biron in the least, for if his plan had succeeded, the Birons would have become related to the ruling dynasty and outdone such cunning manipulators of earlier times as Menshikov and the Dolgorukiis.

But Anna Leopol'dovna had long since developed an aristocratic frame of mind. She rejected Biron's pretentious idea by saying that she was more inclined to marry Anton Ulrich, a prince descending from an old family. Incidentally, the prince, her bridegroom, had matured somewhat by that time; he had fought as a volunteer in the Russo-Turkish War, had earned the rank of general and been decorated with the Order of Andrew for bravery at the Battle of Ochakov.

The empress personally urged the future bride and bridegroom to expedite their wedding. According to Biron, she once told him: "Nobody wants to consider that I have a princess on my hands who has to be given away in marriage. Time is passing, she is in her prime. It's true, neither I nor the princess like the prince; but ladies of our status do not always marry out of love."[24] There was another, still more important point. According to Claudius Rondeau, "The Russian ministers think it is high time to marry that princess, who begins to grow fat, which may prevent her having children in case she remains long unmarried."[25]

Having evaluated all these circumstances, the empress had decided that there was no need to delay the betrothal any longer. On July 1, 1739, the young couple exchanged rings. Anton Ulrich entered the hall where the ceremony was taking place, clad in a white gold-trimmed satin suit; his long blond hair had been curled and covered his shoulders. A strange thought occurred to Lady Rondeau, who was standing next to her husband at the ceremony, one that she shared with her girlfriend living in England. "I could not help thinking he looked like a victim,"[26] she wrote. It is amazing how this seemingly casual phrase would turn into a prophecy. For Anton Ulrich indeed fell victim to the dynastic interests of the Russian court.

Anton Ulrich. From A. G. Brikner, *Istoriia Ekateriny Vtoroi* (History of Catherine II) (St. Petersburg, 1885), p. 197.

But at that moment it was the bride-to-be who considered herself the victim. She gave her consent to marry the prince and "on this . . . clasped her hands round her aunt's neck and burst into tears. Her Majesty stood some time with a grave composure, but at length melted into tears also. Thus they continued some minutes, till at last the ambassador [Botta—E.A.] took hold of the empress, and the great marshal [Löwenwolde] of the princess."[27] When the ring-exchanging ceremony was over, Tsarevna Elizabeth Petrovna was the first to congratulate the bride-to-be. Tears flowed in plenty again. It looked more like a funeral than a betrothal.

The wedding took place two days later. The splendid procession set out for the Church of the Nativity on Nevskii Prospekt. The empress and the bride, the latter clad in silvery dress, traveled in a luxurious carriage sitting opposite each other. Then came a gala dinner followed by a ball. In the end, they dressed the bride in a satin nightgown; Duke Biron led the prince into the room, clad in a dressing gown, and the doors of the nuptial suite were closed on the newlyweds.

The wedding celebration continued at court for the whole week and included dinners and suppers, a masquerade with the newlyweds dressed in orange dominos, an opera at the theater, a fireworks display, and an illumination in the Summer Gardens. Lady Rondeau, who was among the guests, later wrote to her girlfriend that "Everybody was dressed to their own fancy, some very pretty, and some very rich ones. And thus ended this grand wedding, from which I am not yet rested, and what is worse, all this rout has been made to tie two people together, who, I believe, heartily hate one another; at least, I think, she showed it throughout all this week's feasting in a shocking public manner, and continues to treat him with the utmost contempt when out of the empress's sight."[28] It was also said that on their wedding night the young wife had run away from her husband into the Summer Gardens. Nevertheless, thirteen months later this unfortunate marriage bore fruit: on August 18, 1740, Anna Leopol'dovna gave birth to a boy, who was named Ivan in honor of his great-grandfather.

The English envoy Edward Finch noted that the artillery was firing in honor of Princess Anna having borne a prince, that he had to put on new clothes, and to go to make his compliments at court.[29]

The birth of a son to the young couple made Empress Anna very happy. The risky dynastic gamble conceived as far back as 1731 had been crowned with success. As if by special order a boy had been born, and he was healthy and strong! The peace of the dynasty had been assured, and Anna, having become the baby's godmother, began to take meticulous care of him. To begin with, she took Ivan away from his parents and lodged him in rooms next to her own. Nobody took any interest in Anna Leopol'dovna and Anton Ulrich any longer—they had done what they had to do. However, Empress Anna did not have long to nurse her grandnephew or to devote herself to his upbringing: on October 5, 1740, while she was having her dinner, she experienced a painful seizure caused by a disease, which would result in her death in two weeks' time.

On the very first day of the empress's illness, Biron called a meeting of high-ranking dignitaries. Münnich writes that the favorite sobbed not only over his own future (of which he had cause to be sincerely concerned) but also over Russia's future, which appeared to be in danger because Ivan Antonovich was still so young and Anna Leopol'dovna was so weak-willed. He finished his speech saying that the administration of state should be entrusted to an experienced person who "has enough strength of spirit to keep the unruly disobedient people quiet and restrained."[30] The dignitaries, or "zealous patriots," as Biron called them later, declared enthusiastically that they saw no person capable of assuming the role of ruler other than Biron himself. At first he tried to decline. But Aleksei Bestuzhev-Riumin, who had, by Biron's will, taken the post in the Cabinet of Ministers previously held by Artemii Volynskii, resorted to a perverted form of toadying: in a strident tone he reprimanded Biron for his ingratitude to Russia, the country that had brought him glory and prosperity, and that he was about to abandon at such a desperate hour. Ashamed, Biron gave his consent to become regent, but only on the condition that this decision be endorsed by all the higher ranks of the empire. On the next day a joint petition requesting the appointment of Biron as regent was ready, and Field Marshal Münnich was the first to solicit the empress on Biron's behalf.

Quite unexpectedly, however, Biron encountered resistance from Anna herself. She did not seem to be willing to pass away as yet or sign any will. A superstitious woman, she was afraid that once she had signed a will she would die shortly thereafter. Anna Leopol'dovna also displayed unexpected firmness by telling Biron that she would not ask the empress to write a will, for she had no doubt that her aunt would secure Ivan Antonovich's and his family's future without any special fuss. In the end, the situation had taken an unfavorable turn for Biron. If the empress died without signing the version of the will that he wanted, then the regency for the heir to the throne, Ivan, would most likely go to his parents, not to Biron.

Kneeling before the empress, Biron entreated her to sign the will, or, as Münnich noted maliciously, "the duke found himself compelled to finagle on his own behalf."[31] And he had to do it quickly, at all costs, for Anna's life was waning even as he spoke. Biron remained by Anna's bedside until she signed a decree declaring Ivan heir to the throne and appointing Biron regent to the young emperor, Ivan VI, until the latter reached the age of seventeen. The duke could wipe the sweat from his brow—his scheme had succeeded, but not for long.

How many times in the course of history has it happened that a person who had reached the peak of power suddenly, as a result of one false move or someone's slight nudge, plunged headlong into the state of political nonentity. That was exactly what happened in 1727 to the Russian political Goliath, Menshikov, who had overcome all barriers on his way to the top. And now Biron's turn had come: one cannot hide from one's fate! Who could have known that the regency that Biron had planned for years would last three weeks?

In the beginning everything appeared to be going well. Worries about some unrest among the Guards during the swearing-in ceremony turned out to have been false alarms: "All this has been transacted with more tranquillity than a regiment of guards would have passed in Hyde-park"[32] (from Finch's report). Biron could rely on his people everywhere: Münnich in the army; Bestuzhev-Riumin and Prince Cherkasskii in government; and Ushakov in the political police. Numerous spies and volunteer informers served the regent. When they informed Biron that Anton Ulrich, the emperor's father, had censured the regent and was plotting a conspiracy, Biron acted quickly and decisively. All those suspected of being connected with the emperor's father were arrested, and then Anton Ulrich underwent a humiliating interrogation in the presence of high officials and Biron himself, who treated the confused prince unceremoniously. After this ordeal he was removed from all governmental posts and placed under house arrest. This was to demonstrate to everyone what awaited the average conspirator if the future tsar's own father received such severe treatment. We also know that Biron threatened Anna Leopol'dovna that if her spouse continued this behavior he (Biron) would exile the entire Brunswick family to Germany.

In a word, the regent was active, and he got his way. He often met with his close associates and discussed business. At their meeting on November 8, the regent was slightly absent-minded and at the end of the discussion suddenly asked Münnich: "Tell me, Field Marshal, in the course of your military ventures, did you ever have cause to accomplish something significant during the night?" According to his adjutant Christoph Herman Manstein, Münnich answered that he could not recall, but "the rule which he went by was to take advantage of all circumstances, especially when they seemed favorable."[33]

I believe that Münnich lied as usual when he retold this story to his adjutant after the coup. More than likely he froze in his tracks out of fear and mumbled something incomprehensible. Unknowingly Biron had hit the bull's-eye: that very night Münnich was planning "a military venture" to overthrow his patron. Perhaps Biron suspected something was up. Later he said that he had never trusted Münnich and considered him an ambitious and desperate man.

Münnich had formed his plan to remove Biron much earlier. The main reason for his discontent was the regent's stinginess in rewarding the field marshal with decorations and rank. Münnich got on well with Anna Leopol'dovna. Not well versed in the game of intrigue, she complained of Biron's rudeness and oppressive behavior, which the field marshal took full advantage of. Conflict was inevitable. As Finch wrote, Biron understood that Princess Anna would never forgive the favorite for preventing her from ascending the throne and usurping the regency himself to the prejudice of her interests. This is why Anna and Münnich so quickly formed an alliance.

Encouraged by Anna Leopol'dovna on the night of November 8, Münnich and his adjutant Manstein together with eighty soldiers set out for the Summer Palace, the residence of the regent. As they approached the palace, Münnich ordered Manstein to arrest Biron. Manstein entered the palace without resistance, passed by the saluting guards and bowing servants, then calmly and confidently he walked through rooms and suites on the pretext that he was carrying an urgent message for the regent from the emperor. But suddenly he broke into a cold sweat and his heart filled with terror as it became apparent that he was unfamiliar with the floor plan and had lost his way in the maze of rooms. To ask one of the servants where the duke was sleeping might have seemed too strange and risky. Manstein later described the situation in his memoirs, where he referred to himself in the third person: "After having crossed the apartments, he found himself all of a sudden in a great embarrassment: he did not know the duke's bedchamber, and neither did he want to ask the servants who were awake in the antechambers, so as not to raise the alarm.

"After a moment's reflection he resolved to push forward, in the hope of finally finding what he was looking for. After having passed through two more rooms, he found himself in front of a locked door: luckily, it was made up of two panels, and the servants had neglected to close the bolts on the top and bottom, as a result of which he did not have any great trouble in forcing it open. There he found a large bed where the duke and duchess were sleeping so deeply that the noise he had made in forcing the door had not awakened them.

"Manstein, having approached the bed, opened the curtains and asked to speak to the regent; then both of them awoke with a jump and began to yell with all of their strength, doubting that he had come there to bring them good news. Manstein, finding himself on the side where the duchess was sleeping, saw the regent throw himself to the ground, apparently with the intention of hiding under the bed; to stop him he immediately went around the bed and threw himself on the regent; and held him tightly in his arms until the guards arrived. The duke, having finally gotten up, wanted to rid himself of the soldier's hands, and threw out punches to the right and left. The soldiers in their turn gave him great blows with the butts of their rifles, threw him to the ground, put a handkerchief in his mouth, tied his hands with an officer's scarf and carried him completely naked before the Corps de Garde, where, having covered him with a soldier's coat, they put him in the carriage of the field marshal, who awaited him there."[34]

The noise, shouting, and turmoil of this classic palace coup scene awakened the entire court, and only the deceased empress showed no sign of interest in what was happening as she lay quietly in her coffin in the palace's state hall as Biron was carried out past her bellowing and kicking. She could do nothing more to help her beloved chief chamberlain. Her funeral took place on December 23, 1740.

Here is how Manstein concludes his story: "While the soldiers had taken the duke, the duchess had left the palace in her nightgown and run after her husband through the streets, where a soldier took her by the arm and dragged her to Manstein, whom he asked what he was to do with her. He ordered him to take her back to the palace, but the soldier, not wanting to take the trouble, threw her into the snow and left."[35]

The next morning a manifesto was read on behalf of the three-month-old emperor, listing all the crimes of the regent who had been so coarse with Ivan VI's parents. Now it was Biron's turn to be the guest of General Fedor Ushakov, the head of the all-powerful political police. In the spring of 1741 the sentence was pronounced: Biron and his family were to be exiled for life to the town of Pelym in Siberia. Münnich himself made plans for the house in which his vanquished enemy's family would live, and he dispatched a special officer to oversee the construction.

Immediately following Biron's overthrow, the Guards were summoned to the Winter Palace, where they pledged an oath of allegiance to the "Sovereign Ruler of All Russia, Grand Duchess Anna." This title equaled Anna Leopol'dovna's power to that of the emperor. Field Marshal Münnich stood next to the ruler. His hour of triumph had come along with an opportunity to realize all of his great plans. "M. le Marechal de Munich," wrote Manstein, "had only arrested the Duke of Courlande in order to raise himself to fortune's summit on the ruins of the Birons . . . he wanted to seize all of the authority and give to the grand duchess only the title of regent; he imagined that no one would dare undertake anything against him. He was mistaken."[36]

Yes, Münnich was mistaken. A quiet, absent-minded woman—Regent Anna Leopol'dovna—was to throw him, the Russian Mars, vanquisher of terrible Biron, from the peak of the political Olympus. And it happened in this way. Münnich had figured on being named generalissimo for the "feat" carried out by his adjutant on the early morning hours of November 9, 1740, but he figured wrong. The highest military title was awarded to the tsar's father, Anton Ulrich. As there cannot be two generalissimos in one army, Münnich was terribly offended by the "greedy" spouses. In addition, having named Münnich first minister, Anna Leopol'dovna left him virtually without a job to do, as she had appointed Osterman to manage foreign policy and Mikhail Golovkin to take charge of domestic affairs.

The field marshal could bear this only until the spring of 1741. In early March he submitted a resignation request—a device to which he, who considered himself irreplaceable, had resorted often enough in the past. After slight hesitation, the ruler, to Münnich's surprise and dismay, signed the decree on the resignation of the field marshal, who had after all requested it himself, citing as the reasons his age and his "illness." Münnich had made a gross error in his calculations, assuming that by threatening to resign he would receive all that he desired. Anna informed the field marshal of her decision. "This news was, at first, a lightning bolt for him . . . but he was thanked [for having served well—Trans.] at the very time that he had imagined better establishing his power."[37] Here we see the well-known principle at work: "The Moor has done his duty, let him go," or another Latin version of the same: *Proditionem amo, proditorem odi* (I love treason—the traitor I hate).

Münnich was provided with a pension and guard at his house, which the retired statesman, still full of strength and plans, obviously mistakenly regarded as a guard of honor. At least so he wrote in his memoirs, even though we know that Münnich had been placed under house arrest.

It would be wrong to exaggerate Anna Leopol'dovna's independence in this whole affair. Her weak feminine hand was being guided by Vice Chancellor Andrei Osterman, who finally felt that his hour had come. He was accustomed to acting behind the scenes, insidiously exposing others to dangers while himself always remaining in the shadows safe and unharmed. And now for the first time, he found himself in the limelight of the political stage, becoming Anna's chief adviser. Accordingly, after Elizabeth's coup on November 25, 1741, Osterman was the first of Anna's government to be exiled to Siberia. Münnich soon followed him. He set out for Pelym as his place of exile, to take over the house which he had built for Biron. Münnich and Biron met in Kazan'. The former regent was being moved from Pelym to Yaroslavl' to continue his exile. This meeting on the road was unpleasant for both men, although, probably, it was less unpleasant for Biron than for Münnich.

Once she had declared herself "Grand Duchess and Ruler of Russia," and essentially become an autocratic empress, Anna Leopol'dovna continued to live just as she had earlier. As ever she despised her husband and often would not allow her unlucky spouse into her apartments. It is difficult to understand why their relationship was that way, why Anton was so unsympathetic to her. Of course, the prince was quiet, timid, and unobtrusive. He lacked Count Lynar's elegance, spirit, and masculinity. Münnich said that he had conducted two campaigns with the prince, but still did not know whether he was fish or fowl. When Artemii Volynskii once asked Anna Leopol'dovna what it was about the prince that she did not like, she answered: "He is too quiet and hesitant in action."

Indeed, the story of Biron's brief regency had shown that at critical moments, which required him to defend his own and his family's honor, the prince had demonstrated no backbone and not without reason did a laughing Biron tell the Saxonian diplomat Petzold that Anton Ulrich had plotted a conspiracy and enlisted the court jester, and later in answer to the regent's threatening questions he had responded naively that he "had wanted to rebel a little."[38] Even earlier Biron had told Petzold with more than a little cynicism that Anton Ulrich was "mainly ordained to produce children in Russia, but he did not have enough intelligence even for this," and one can only hope that the children he sired would take after their mother and not their father.[39] In short, it was unlikely that poor Anton Ulrich could count on the passionate love of his young wife.

On the other hand, the drama of Anna's situation was that she was in no way cut out for the job of king—that is, ruling a kingdom. She had not been groomed for this post, and nothing but fate and chance had led her to it. She lacked many qualities that might have allowed her, if not to actually rule the country, at least to nurture the illusion that she was ruling and doing so for the common good. Anna lacked a love for work, ambition, energy, willpower, and the ability to either please her subjects with a smile or, on the contrary, to set them trembling with her stern glance, as her aunt Anna Ioannovna had done so well. Field Marshal Münnich wrote: "She was naturally lazy and never appeared in the Cabinet; and when I presented myself to her in the morning with something that had been sent by the Cabinet or something that demanded some resolution, she felt her inadequacy and often said to me: 'I wish that my son was already of an age to rule by himself.'"[40]

Further, Münnich writes something that is confirmed by other sources, such as letters, memoirs, and even portraits: "She was naturally sloppy, wore a white handkerchief over her hair, went thusly to mass and without a whalebone skirt, and appeared in the same way in public and at her table and in the afternoons to play cards with a chosen party, made up of the prince her husband, Count Lynar, minister of the king of Poland and a favorite of the grand duchess; Marquis de Botta, minister from the Court of Vienna, her confidante . . . Mr. Finch, minister of England, and my brother [Baron Ch. B. Münnich]."[41] Only in this environment did she feel free and happy in society, adds the field marshal's son Ernst.

These card parties took place behind closed doors in the apartments of the ruler's closest friend, her lady-in-waiting, Julia Mengden. Anna and Julia were so close that Anna could not live without this olive-skinned beauty for even a day. Their relationship was unusual and arrested the attention of many. Finch, who knew all the company of card players well, wrote that Anna loved Julia as passionately as only a man could love a woman, and noted that they often slept together. Anna gave Julia priceless gifts, including a fully furnished home.

Many observers reported that besides Julia, Anna also fell under the influence of Count Lynar, who appeared on the political scene immediately after her coming to power. There was talk of Lynar's pending marriage to Julia: it was aimed at covering up the ruler's liaisons with one of the two. In any case the French envoy Chetardy saw a note from Lynar to Anna

Leopol'dovna that had been intercepted by Elizabeth Petrovna's people. Its tone and context left no doubt as to the real reasons behind his influence. In the fall of 1741 Lynar went to Dresden to resign from his post in order to become Anna Leopol'dovna's chief chamberlain. Biron had played this key role in governing Russia during Anna Ioannovna's reign. Now Lynar was preparing to do the same. Poor Russia! But Lynar was too late. On his return journey to St. Petersburg he heard of Anna Leopol'dovna's overthrow and turned back. And he did the right thing, for otherwise his trip would surely have been lengthened as far as Siberia.

While they waited for Lynar, Anna and Julia spent long evenings doing needlework by the fire: they removed the gold braids from Biron's numerous camisoles before sending them to be melted down. At the same time Julia gave her dear friend advice on how to rule Russia.

Anna Leopol'dovna was a kind and inoffensive creature. To be sure, as Manstein put it, "*aimant à faire du bien, il ne lui manquoit que de savoir le faire à propos*" ("loved to be good, but failed to do it at the right time").[42] Naive people, like Anna, simpleminded and trustful, could not hold their ground in the political wolf pack. Sooner or later these accidental people perish. And that is precisely what happened to Anna Leopol'dovna. In late October and early November of 1741, after receiving reliable news of a conspiracy inspired by Elizabeth Petrovna, Anna acted naively and stupidly. But that will be discussed in the next chapter. Now we shall say only that at this time Ivan VI had been emperor of Russia for almost a year.

Let's approach the infant emperor's cradle. What can be said of a boy who had become autocrat at the age of two months and five days and was overthrown when he was one year, three months, and thirteen days old? No wordy decrees were signed by him, no military victories won by his army. There's simply not much which can be said about an infant who is just an infant lying in his cradle, sleeping or crying, drinking milk and dirtying diapers. An engraving has survived depicting a cradle surrounded by the allegorical figures of Justice, Prosperity, and Science. Covered by a luxurious blanket, a round-cheeked infant looks sternly at the viewers. Around his tiny neck hangs the heavy chain of the Order of St. Andrew the First-Called. Almost at birth the heir to the throne had become the bearer of this highest order. That was Ivan Antonovich's fate: his entire life, from the first breath to his last, he spent in chains.

Perhaps the only existing document that provides an idea of little tsar Ivan's life is the systematic inventory of the imperial living quarters. Passing through numerous rooms and halls, we enter Ivan's bedchamber. The tsar's senior nurse, Anna Iushkova, was in command here, never leaving the infant's side; she slept in an adjoining room. The tsar's wet nurse, Ekaterina Ioannovna, carefully chosen from among numerous candidates, lived next door together with her son, Ivan's foster brother.

The tsar had two oak cradles covered with brocade on the outside and lined with green taffeta. The cradles were specially made by the Admiralty's best craftsman. Soft pillows covered with scarlet broadcloth lay on small benches. Miniature armchairs upholstered with raspberry-colored velvet and gold braid were just as beautiful. The tsar's first throne was an armchair with a high back and, as suited his age, it had wheels. Both the furniture and interior decor were the work of artists and craftsmen. The wallpaper embroidered with silver and gold threads was especially splendid. The curtains of the windows and doors matched the tone of the wallpaper combining all the colors of the rainbow: green, yellow, red-violet, and blue. The floor was covered with red or green broadcloth, in order to absorb extraneous noise. Only noises as subtle as the chiming of the clock or the rustling of the skirts of the maids and ladies-in-waiting could be heard in this room, where they whisked away every dust speck from the infant sovereign.

A description of the emperor's first "journey" from the Summer to the Winter Palace, which took place on Saturday, October 21, 1740, was recorded by Finch, and has survived to our day: "In my way I met the young monarch, who was removing from the Summer to the Winter Palace. His Majesty was escorted by a detachment of the guards, proceeded by the grand-marshal, the other great officer of the court, and chamberlains on foot; he himself was in a chair lying on his nurse's lap and followed by his mother, the princess Anne, who was in the first coach; there were several more in the train. I immediately stopped mine and got out to make His Majesty and Her Highness my bows."[43]

It's possible that the emperor was also taken to behold the strange and wonderful gifts—enormous elephants and camels—that had arrived from Persia. On October 10, 1740, St. Petersburg residents turned out in droves to stare at an amazing spectacle—the entry into the capital of the embassy of the Persian Shah Nadir, who by that time had reached the peak of his power, having conquered India, the empire of the Great Mogul. He left after pillaging Delhi laden with fantastically rich trophies, and decided to share part of them with his great northern neighbor, Russia, which, like Nadir, had fought against the Turks.

The long multicolored caravan stretched out along Nevskii Prospekt. The ambassador, dressed in gold-embroidered clothes, pranced ahead on a splendid steed, and fourteen elephants followed majestically behind, live gifts to Tsar Ivan. An unending procession of mules and camels carried the presents and supplies of the embassy. But this was not the entire embassy. When the Persian caravan had entered Astrakhan, a panic had ensued in the capital. The sixteen thousand–man embassy more resembled an army merely using the olive-branch as a cover. After great effort the Persians were persuaded to send only one-fourth of their contingent on to St. Petersburg, but even at that it remained enormous.

But even more improbable were the Persian shah's fantastic gifts: priceless oriental fabrics, exquisitely shaped vessels, gem-studded weapons and horse harnesses, sapphires, diamonds, and rubies of rare beauty. Anna and her maid, Mengden, probably abandoned Biron's meager camisoles and began sorting gems from Nadir. If his presents were so lavish, how much amazing wealth there must be in his capital, Meshed.

Nadir's embassy reached Russia's capital after Biron's overthrow, although they probably had set out when he was still in power. Curiously, a year prior to the events described here, when the French ambassador Chetardy learned of Biron's appointment as regent, he wondered at the similar fates of these two men who were almost the same age. To a certain degree their life paths coincided surprisingly. Nadir in Persia, like Biron in Russia, was a foreigner, a Turk from the tribe of Afshar, a runaway slave from Khwarazm. Yet he managed to gain total control over Tahmasp II of the Safawid dynasty. Then through slyness, force, and perfidy he managed to depose his master and proclaim eight-month-old Abbas III, Tahmasp's son, shah, for whom he became regent. After four years of regency Nadir decided to take over the throne as well. Grand elections were arranged, wherein Nadir's paradoxical public declinations of the throne alternated with secret intrigues and the murder of those who took his refusals seriously. Finally, after much pleading, Nadir agreed, of course reluctantly and only for the sake of the country's interests and prosperity, to ascend the throne. Soon Abbas III and his father Tahmasp were murdered. The Safawid dynasty ceased to exist, and a few years later the assassin's knife also found Nadir's chest.

Curiously enough, in dispatching his envoys to St. Petersburg Nadir hoped that the Russians would give their consent to his marriage to Elizabeth. Word of the beauteous blue-eyed tsarevna, the daughter of Peter the Great, had spread as far as Meshed and Delhi. It was she whom he had intended to dazzle with the glitter of gold and the radiance of diamonds and sapphires. However, the shah's ambassador did not have the chance to see Elizabeth's beautiful eyes, as Osterman refused him access to the tsarevna. This so enraged Elizabeth Petrovna that she sent a message to Osterman in which she accused him of forgetting who she was and who he was—a former scribe who had become minister thanks to her father, Peter the Great, and assured him that she would never forgive him any of this. And, indeed, Elizabeth did not forgive Osterman for this offense.

Of course, Elizabeth felt no eagerness to join Nadir's harem. Rather, she was eager to gain power. Her time was approaching, she sensed an increase in her political strength, and this was clearly reflected in her rage.

The summer of 1741, the first summer of Anna Leopol'dovna's regency, ended in fireworks and fanfare. In July, she had given birth to her second child—Princess Catherine, and on the 23rd of August the Russian forces under Field Marshal Peter Lacy's command had dealt a crushing blow to the

Swedish army near the Vilmanstrand Fortress in Finland. In July 1741, Sweden had declared war on Russia. The death of Anna Ioannovna, the toppling of Biron, and later the removal of Münnich had served as signal for the Swedes, who dreamed of regaining the eastern Baltic lands, which they had lost in the Northern War. Sweden had given three reasons for the declaration of war: first, the assassination of the Swedish diplomatic courier Baron Malcolm Sinclair by Russian officers in Poland; second, refusal of the Russian government to provide Sweden with grain; and, finally, the liberation of Russia from foreign oppressors. This is exactly what was stated in the Swedish manifesto referring to the German favorites at the Russian court. This historically unprecedented reason for starting a war concealed a much more prosaic attempt to aid Tsarevna Elizabeth Petrovna's "patriotic" conspiracy, which was nearly ready to be hatched in St. Petersburg.

Incidentally, neither the Russian soldiers nor their predominantly foreign commanders—German, Scottish, and English generals—were aware of the Swedish army's lofty aims. Under Lacy's leadership they had accomplished their task quickly and professionally: a swift march from Vyborg, an attack on rugged terrain that forced the Swedes to abandon their positions, and hot on their heels the Russians penetrated the Vilmanstrand Fortress. Most of the Swedes were killed; the rest were taken prisoner, along with their commander. According to foreign observers, the Russians had reaffirmed their reputation as excellent fighters. The Saxonian envoy Suhm wrote: "I believe that in a defensive war this country is invincible. A Russian becomes a soldier as soon as he is armed. He can be led with certainty into any venture, for his obedience is blind and beyond any comparison. He is satisfied with poor and meager rations. He seems to have been born especially for great military undertakings."[44]

The stunning and unexpected victory over the Swedish lion beneath three crowns (the emblem of the Kingdom of Sweden) was festively celebrated in St. Petersburg. The young Russian poet Mikhail Lomonosov wrote an ode to Russia's victory, containing the following words:

> As Russian army's fame is spread
> Impertinent hearts all quake with dread
> The young eagle's already tormenting the lion!

"The young eagle" remained lying in his crib and those who ruled the country did it very poorly. They failed to make use of the victory in Finland to strengthen the regime and thereby sealed their doom. Osterman held the reins of government at that time. He tried to prevail over Anna and prevent her from listening to anyone else's advice. But she suspected her prime minister's true intentions and considered the opinions of others as well, like Minister Mikhail Golovkin and Chief Procurator of the Senate Ivan Brylkin, who urged her to immediately take the title of empress and with it assume absolute power. The necessary documents were already in preparation, and on December 7, 1741, on her twenty-third birthday, the regent of Russia, Anna, was to become the empress of Russia, Anna II. One last step remained to achieve this goal, but it was never taken . . .

We cannot say now what kind of empress Anna Leopol'dovna would have been. Her inertness, reserve, lack of character and preparation would have made her chances for a successful reign over a country such as Russia doubtful. However, anything is possible; power and a crown on a person's head may transform him or her beyond recognition: action, ambition, and intelligence can suddenly appear. Suffice it to recall Austrian archduchess Maria Theresa when she became the empress of Austria. She was almost the same age as Anna Leopol'dovna when in 1740 she inherited the throne of her deceased father, Charles VI, and was compelled to immediately start fighting with Austria's old enemies, who dreamed of tearing the empire to pieces. Frederick II, the ingenious king of Prussia, had become Maria Theresa's most formidable and implacable enemy. Nevertheless, young and inexperienced Maria Theresa proved to be worthy of her destiny; she not only managed to preserve the empire but also to strengthen its position in the world. She invited talented ministers to work for her, effected important reforms, and when the time came for her to transfer power over the flourishing country to her son Joseph II, who was born almost at the same time as Ivan Antonovich, Maria Theresa did so. However, let's stop fantasizing—Russia is nothing like Austria, and nothing like any other country, for that matter.

By November 1741 plans for a coup d'état were being actively worked out by those surrounding Tsarevna Elizabeth. Information about the conspirators and their foreign patrons reached Anna's government via different channels. However, nobody at court seemed to attach much importance to this alarming news; Anna and her ministers remained unconcerned and shortsighted in their actions. No one could imagine that Elizabeth, a delicate, capricious beauty and woman of pleasure, was capable of such a masculine and dangerous enterprise as a Münnich-style coup d'état.

While Anna and her ministers thought one thing, events took a very different turn. On the night of November 25, 1741, Anna Leopol'dovna was awakened by noise and the thunder of soldiers boots, as they came for her and her small son. Two versions exist of the Brunswick family's arrest. According to the first, Elizabeth entered the regent's bedchamber together with soldiers and announced loudly: "It's time to get up, sister!"[45] Mengden was also in Anna's bed. According to another version, which sounds more plausible, the Tsesarevna, assured that the palace was completely surrounded by soldiers loyal to her, sent a detachment of grenadiers to arrest the regent. When Anna saw the soldiers, she cried out: "Oh, we're finished!"[46]

But one thing is confirmed by all sources, namely, that she offered no resistance; she dressed without a murmur, got into the waiting sleigh, and allowed herself to be driven away from the Winter Palace.

As is known, the ancients had always paid heed to omens and signs, those hardly noticeable symbols of fate that sometimes could tell a person some-thing about his or her future. Later the ages of rationalism, pragmatism, atheism, and the mind-boggling strides of technology have made a laugh-ing stock of such practices. We continue to live in this state of ignorance, only occasionally wondering at the insights of old men and the secret voice of our own premonitions. Anna Leopol'dovna received a sign of her fate when, on the eve of the coup, she made an embarrassing gaffe. Approach-ing the Tsarevna Elizabeth, she tripped on a fold in the carpet and suddenly fell at Elizabeth's feet in full view of the entire court. One eyewitness affirmed that this was a bad omen.

Prince Anton Ulrich was not allowed to dress and was taken to the sleigh half-naked and wrapped in a blanket. This was done intentionally: that is how Biron was arrested, as well as his brother, a general, and many other high-ranking victims of other coups. The reason was simple enough: without a uniform and trousers one is most unlikely to start giving commands, regard-less of rank.

Things did not go as smoothly during the "arrest" of the one-year-old emperor. Soldiers were instructed not to make noise and to take the child only after he had awakened. So they spent about an hour at the side of the cradle before the boy opened his eyes and screamed in fear at the sight of the fierce faces of grenadiers. In the ensuing turmoil in the bedroom they dropped the emperor's four-month-old sister, Princess Catherine, on the floor, which resulted, as it turned out later, in her loss of hearing. But no-body paid it any mind—she was the only victim of Elizabeth's bloodless revo-lution.

They brought Emperor Ivan to Elizabeth, who took him in her arms and allegedly said: "You are not guilty of anything, little one!" Elizabeth, who had become empress in the course of a few short hours, pressed the child tightly to her breast, for this was her prize, her enemy, her destiny. Nobody knew for sure what to do with the infant and his family. All were aware that Elizabeth was a usurper who had dethroned the legitimate ruler of the Rus-sian Empire, the latter being a blood relative to many foreign sovereigns, including Frederick II and the Danish king Christian VI. It did not take the new empress long to decide. With the joy of a quick and easy victory still fresh in her mind, she decided simply to deport the entire Brunswick family once and for all. A manifesto was issued on November 28 and that same night a string of *kibitki* (covered wagons) hurriedly left St. Petersburg and moved along the road leading to Revel and Riga, heading toward the eastern bor-der of Russia. Traveling in the wagons were the emperor and all his rela-tives and retinue. They were accompanied by a large convoy of soldiers under the command of the chief of police Vasilii Saltykov.

Before departure Saltykov received special orders authorizing him to ur-gently take the ex-emperor Ivan first to Riga, then to Mitau, and from Mitau

Ioann Antonovich (Ivan VI Antonovich). From A. G. Brikner,
Istoriia Ekateriny Vtoroi (History of Catherine II) (St. Petersburg, 1885), p. 188.

to Germany. But the convoy had scarcely left the outskirts of St. Petersburg
when a special courier caught up with the travelers and handed new orders
over to Saltykov, which obligated him to do just the opposite of what had
been stated in the first instruction: "Owing to certain circumstances, the
previous order [that is, a fast trip to Mitau—E.A.] is hereby canceled and
now you are obliged to move as slowly as possible, and take a two-day rest
at each station."

The "certain circumstances" lay in Elizabeth's second thoughts on her
generous act and fear that once the Brunswick family joined its powerful
relatives abroad, it would present a grave threat to her. The prisoners' train
moved more slowly with each passing day, while orders delivered from St.
Petersburg became more and more strict, and the conditions under which
the prisoners were held became more and more severe as compared with the

first days of the trip. Finally, after spending a year on this strange journey, the unfortunate family was incarcerated at Dünamünde, a fortress near Riga. It was clear that these unhappy people were to be trapped forever. They spent over a year in the Dünamünde Fortress. There, in 1743 Anna gave birth to her third child—Elizabeth—and in January 1744, Saltykov received an order to urgently dispatch his prisoners far away from the border to the town of Ranenburg in Voronezh province in central Russia. The empress further required that Saltykov inform her whether Anna Leopol'dovna and her husband were "dissatisfied or satisfied" to be moving to a new place of residence. In his reply Saltykov wrote that when the family members were offered seats in different wagons they had wept "for about a quarter of an hour" and probably thought that they were going to be separated. The fear of separation was now hanging over them. They lived with the expectation that things would get worse.

By mistake the new chief of the convoy, Captain Maksim Vyndomskii, set off not to Ranenburg in Voronezh Province, but to Orenburg—a town located a thousand miles farther east, almost in Siberia. Only on the way was the mistake discovered and the route adjusted. The Brunswick family lived in Ranenburg until late August 1744, when Elizabeth's own personal envoy, Guards Major Nikolai Korff, arrived unexpectedly with secret instructions from the empress.

These instructions were cruel and inhumane, obliging Korff under the cover of night to take the ex-emperor from his parents and give him to Captain Miller, who was under orders to remove the four-year-old boy in a closed coach to the north; under no circumstances was he to show the boy to anyone nor to even let him out of the coach. Also noteworthy is the fact that from this moment on Miller was to call Ivan by a new name—Grigorii. Perhaps this choice of names was coincidental, perhaps not. In Russian dynastic history the name Grigorii has definite negative overtones, as it was the true name of the pretender Otrepev, who seized power as False Dmitrii I in 1605, and whose shady ventures cost the Russia grave suffering and ruin. It was as if Elizabeth were equating the former emperor with this dangerous pretender.

Judging by his letters, Korff did not blindly follow orders. He had a kind heart and understood that he was being used to do something wicked. Therefore, he wrote to Petersburg for instructions on how to act if the boy is distressed due to the separation from his parents and asks the guard about his mother or father.[47] Petersburg replied that Korff was to act on his orders: to call the boy Grigorii and, refusing to answer any questions, take him to the place of destination. And that place was a terrible one. It was called Solovki.

In the historical memory of the Russian people there are many geographical places that evoke a wide spectrum of emotion. This is a phenomenon familiar to every nation. One can come across people who remain unmoved at the mention of place-names that mean so much to Americans and that have become imprinted in the developing historical memory of the nation, such as Concord, Massachusetts; Fredericksburg, Virginia; Monticello and Mt. Vernon, Virginia; Ford's Theater, Washington, D.C.; Pearl Harbor, Saigon, Alcatraz, and Sing-Sing.

There are place-names that mean as much to the Russian consciousness, like Borodino, the site of the battle against Napoleon in 1812; Stalingrad, the site of the battle against the Germans in 1942; Mikhailovskoe and Iasnaya Poliana, where the Russian geniuses Aleksandr Pushkin and Leo Tolstoi lived; the Catherine Canal Embankment, where tsar-reformer Aleksandr II was assassinated in 1881; Straits of Tsushima in the Sea of Japan, near which the Russian navy was destroyed in 1905; the Salang Pass in Afghanistan, a place synonymous with death for Soviet soldiers; Butyrki, Lefortovo, and Schlüsselburg, infamous for their criminal and political prisons. And Solovki could be added to the latter, the place where the Ranenburg prisoners were to go.

The huge monastery, built in the early fifteenth century by ascetic monks on a rocky island in the middle of the White Sea, remains to this day severe and impregnable. Almost throughout its history it served as a prison for ordinary prisoners and famous ones alike, who, upon learning that they were being dispatched to Solovki, confessed and took communion as if prior to death, for life in the cold, dark silence of the underground prison did not last long, and could not really be considered life, anyway. The Solovetskii prison camp, opened in 1920, marked the beginning of the vast Gulag system in the Soviet Union, which devoured the lives of millions of people.

But let us return to Ranenburg. Korff thought not only of the fate of the child. He also asked the empress what should be done with Julia Mengden, as she was not on the list of future prisoners at Solovki, and "if the princess were to be separated from her lady-in-waiting, she will fall into utter despair."[48] But Petersburg remained deaf to Korff's concerns: Anna was to be taken to Solovki and Mengden was to be left in Ranenburg. It's difficult to imagine what Anna must have experienced saying good-bye forever to her bosom friend and soul-mate. When she left St. Petersburg, Anna had made but one request of the empress: "Do not separate me from Julia!" At that time Elizabeth reluctantly had agreed, but now she took her promise back. Korff wrote that the news of the separation of the two girlfriends and the upcoming journey to an unknown destination was for the prisoners a bolt from the blue: "This news brought them extreme grief, which burst out in tears and cries. But despite this and the princess's ill condition [she was pregnant—E.A.], they answered that they were ready to comply with the Sovereign's will."[49] The prisoners were taken slowly northward along muddy roads, facing bad weather, cold, and snow.

This princess's stunning humility deserves special mention, just as the empress's taunting vengeful cruelty, which was determined neither by state

necessity nor by the potential danger that could be caused by these harmless women, a child, or a generalissimo who had not won a single battle. This
story clearly reveals Elizabeth's own passions. In March 1745, when Anna
and Julia were separated by hundreds of miles, Elizabeth wrote to Korff: "Ask
Anna to whom she gave her diamond things, many of which were not found.
And if she, Anna, starts to say that she did not give anyone any diamonds,
then tell her that I will be forced to torture Jul'ka, and if she pities her, then
she should not expose her to such sufferings."[50]

This was not the first letter of this kind to be received from Elizabeth.
As early as October 1742 she wrote to Saltykov in Dünamünde, entreating
him to explain how and why Anna complains about him. A rumor to this
effect had reached Elizabeth. Saltykov answered that this was slander: "I go
to see the princess each morning and except for her courtesy, neither myself nor any of the officers have ever heard any unpleasant words, and when
she needs something, she requests it with respect."[51] Saltykov was telling the
truth—this type of behavior would have been typical of Anna. She was a
gentle and harmless woman, a strange, quiet guest in this country and on
this earth. But Saltykov's answer obviously displeased the empress: her jealousy toward this woman seemed to know no bounds. Much will be said in
the next chapter about Elizabeth's personality, but now we will just note that
taking into account the empress's character and habits, her attitude toward
Anna is understandable.

Elizabeth could not stand to know or to hear that somewhere there was
a woman who was surrounded, unlike she herself, the empress, by children
and family, and who had friends from whom parting would grieve her,
yesterday's regent of the Russian Empire, more than the loss of power, and
that she does not need power at all, but needs only the person dear to her
heart. Deprived, as it seemed, of everything—freedom, normal living conditions, her son, and her close girlfriend—this woman did not, contrary to
Elizabeth's expectations, writhe in hysterics, throwing herself at the guards,
did not write the empress letters with humiliating requests, but simply, humbly accepted all that the new day offered her, even if it was more sad than
the previous day.

For over two months Korff tried to deliver the Brunswick family to the
White Sea. But owing to impassable roads, he failed to do it and entreated
St. Petersburg to allow them at least temporarily to stop this journey, which
was exhausting for everyone—the prisoners, the guard, and Korff himself—
and to settle in Kholmogory, a small town on the Northern Dvina upriver
from Arkhangel'sk. In the spring of 1746 it was decided in Petersburg to
extend the prisoners' stay here for some time. But no one could have expected that the empty house belonging to the Kholmogory bishop would
become their prison for thirty-four long years.

Anna Leopol'dovna's life there was not destined to last more than two
years. On February 27, 1746, she gave birth to a son, Prince Aleksei, her

fifth and last child (the fourth, a son who was named Peter, had been born earlier in Kholmogory in March 1745). The births of all these children gave Elizabeth yet another reason to hate Anna. All of them were princes and princesses, who, in accordance with Empress Anna Leopol'dovna's will, had a greater birthright to the throne than did Elizabeth. And although the right of Peter's daughter was in force, word of the birth of yet another potential rival so annoyed the empress that upon receiving news of Prince Aleksei's birth from Kholmogory, Elizabeth, according to the courier, "having read it, tore up the report."[52] News of the births of Anna Leopol'dovna's and Anton Ulrich's children was carefully withheld from the public, and the prison commandant was categorically forbidden to mention the children in any correspondence. After Anna's death the empress demanded that Anton Ulrich himself write a detailed account of his wife's death, while never mentioning that she had given birth to a son. However, as is often the case in Russia, to find out all about princes and princesses one had only to go to the Kholmogory market, a fact corroborated by numerous documents from the Secret Chancery.

The full report on twenty-eight-year-old Anna's death came shortly after the news of Prince Aleksei's birth. The former Russian regent died as a result of childbirth, from a so-called postbirth fever. In official documents the cause of Anna's death was identified as "fever," or general infection. Commandant Ivan Gur'ev of the Kholmogory prison acted on orders which he had received long before Anna's death: "If, by God's will, death comes to one of the persons concerned, especially Anna or Prince Ivan, then perform an autopsy of the dead body, put it in alcohol, and send it immediately to us via courier officer."[53]

That is exactly what Second Lieutenant Lev Pisarev did, delivering Anna's body to St. Petersburg, or more exactly, to the Aleksandr Nevskii Monastery. In the official notice of Anna's death she was called "Princess Anna of Brunswick-Luneburg." Neither the title Regent of Russia nor even grand duchess was granted her, just as the title of emperor was not granted to her son. In routine documents they were most often referred to using the neutral "persons concerned." And now after death Anna became again, as in her youth, simply a princess.

She was buried as a secondary member of the Romanov family. The funeral service and burial took place on the morning of March 21, 1746. All high-ranking government officials and their wives came to the monastery. Everyone wanted to have a last glimpse at the woman whose dramatic fate gave rise to many rumors and legends. Elizabeth stood by Anna's coffin. She cried, perhaps even sincerely. She was envious and petty, but never known as a villain who would take pleasure in another's death.

Anna Leopol'dovna was buried in the Annunciation Church. Two other women lay there in eternal rest as well—Tsaritsa Praskovia Fedorovna and Catherine, Duchess of Mecklenburg. Thus, on March 21, 1746, three women bound by blood and love—grandmother, mother, and granddaughter—were united for eternity in one grave.

* * *

Our story is not finished yet, for Anna's children and husband were still left to suffer on earth. As she lay dying in the bishop's house, Anna had not the slightest suspicion that her firstborn, Ivan, had been living right next to her for more than a year, behind a thick wall that divided the house into two parts. But it may well be that we are mistaken, for a mother's heart can divine her child over a distance of thousands of miles. We do not know how Captain Miller brought the boy here and what he had answered to the endless and worried questions of a child who had been taken from his parents and whom everyone had now begun to call Grigorii, or what kind of a relationship had developed between the two during the long weeks of riding in a small coach without windows. We only know that the young prisoner and his guard arrived at Kholmogory before the rest of the members of the Brunswick family, and Ivan was placed in an isolated part of the bishop's house. The ex-emperor's chamber-cell was situated so that no one except Miller and his servants had access to it. Ivan was treated with strictness in prison. When Miller asked Petersburg whether his wife, who was due to arrive soon, could see the boy, the answer that followed was—No! Thus, for the remainder of his entire life, Ivan saw only two women: two empresses—Elizabeth and then Catherine the Great.

Many facts tell us that Ivan was a normal, agile boy at the time he was separated from his parents at the age of four. There is no doubt that he knew who he was and who his parents were. This can be verified by the official correspondence from the time he was in Dünamünde. Colonel Chertov, who had been dispatched to Solovki to prepare a cell for Ivan, received instructions that the room should have no windows, to prevent the "agile boy from jumping out the window."[54] Later, in 1759, one of the guards reported that the secret prisoner called himself emperor. An eyewitness to Emperor Peter III's conversation with Ivan in 1762 in Schlüsselburg recalled that Ivan answered that his parents and soldiers had called him emperor. He also remembered a kind officer by the name of Korff who took care of him and even went on walks with him.

All this testifies that the boy was not an idiot who was physically and mentally handicapped, as he is sometimes portrayed. From this the terrible conclusion can be drawn that his childhood and youth, those magic moments of spring in a person's life, were spent in an empty room with a bed, table, and chair, and the expressionless face of Miller's servant, who treated the boy rudely and roughly. He probably heard muffled sounds through his cell walls, waited impatiently for the day or, more exactly, night, when he would be led out blindfolded into the courtyard of the house, and quickly taken to the bathhouse. The fresh air of the garden, the rustling of unseen trees, and the call of a night bird might have evoked associations with another world—one of freedom, which he was never to explore.

Of course, Elizabeth would have breathed a sigh of relief if she were to have received a report from the commandant telling of the death of the ex-emperor. Elizabeth's personal doctor, Lestocq, asserted authoritatively in 1742 that Ivan was small for his age and would inevitably die at the onset of his first illness. A time did come when in 1748 the then eight-year-old boy contracted two diseases that were terrifying for both children and adults. He fell ill with small-pox and the measles at the same time. Upon seeing the boy's grave state the commandant asked the empress for permission to allow a doctor, and if death was imminent, then also a priest, to see the boy. The answer was unequivocal. A monk could be allowed in, but only at the boy's last hour. In other words, don't treat the illness, let the boy die! But nature turned out to be more humane than the tsaritsa, giving Ivan a chance to live.

One eyewitness who saw Ivan as an adult wrote that he was blond, even with tints of red in his hair, average height, "with a very white face, an aquiline nose, he had large eyes and stuttered. His mind had been damaged. He aroused compassion, and was poorly dressed."[55] The subject of his "damaged mind" will be taken up later, but for now we note that in early 1756 Ivan's life underwent drastic changes. Unexpectedly in the dead of one January night the fifteen-year-old youth was secretly taken from Kholmogory and transferred to Schlüsselburg. The guards of the house in Kholmogory were strictly instructed to intensify their watch over Anton Ulrich and his children, "in order to prevent escape."

The circumstances surrounding the secret prisoner's hasty move from Kholmogory to one of the most gloomy prisons in the Russian Empire remain shrouded in mystery. A half year prior to these events an incident had occurred on the Russian-Polish border, which had some mysterious connection to Ivan, Elizabeth, and Frederick II, and many other people involved in this story. Russian border guards arrested a certain merchant from Tobol'sk named Ivan Zubarev while he was crossing the border. They knew that he was a fugitive criminal who had escaped to Poland. Soon Zubarev was giving such interesting testimony that his case came to be handled by the most powerful people in the Russian Empire.

Zubarev told of how he had found himself in the city of Königsberg in Prussia after having escaped from guards on the border. Here an attempt was made to recruit him into the Prussian army, and then he fell into the hands of that same Manstein who had dragged Biron out from under the bed and who by that time had become a general-adjutant to King Frederick II. Manstein took Zubarev to Berlin, and then to Potsdam. On the way he met Prince Ferdinand of Brunswick, Anton Ulrich's brother and a leading general in the Prussian army. The prince supposedly convinced Zubarev to return to Russia, make his way to Kholmogory, and inform his brother that in the spring of 1756 Prussian naval vessels will enter Arkhangel'sk disguised as merchant ships and try to free Anton Ulrich from imprisonment.

After some time the Siberian merchant was received in the palace at Sanssouci by Frederick II himself, who rewarded him with money and the rank of colonel. After this Manstein gave Zubarev gold and special medallions, which Anton Ulrich might recognize, and the newly recruited agent was sent back to Russia. Upon crossing the Polish-Russian border Zubarev was detained by Russian guards.

The story told by Zubarev to the investigators of the Secret Chancery is puzzling. No doubt Zubarev was a reckless adventurer and rogue, who had a ready tongue and could invent anything at all. But along with the completely fantastic details of his stay in Prussia, he cites absolutely accurate information, which suggests that Zubarev may indeed have been at Frederick's palace in Sanssouci. Also somewhat suspicious is the fact that Manstein plays the main role in his stories, and is organizer of the entire adventure. This is extremely important. As soon as Elizabeth ascended the throne Manstein left supposedly for a vacation in Prussia, but immediately engaged in Prussian service. This was not out of the ordinary for those times. But Elizabeth's reaction to this was unusual: she demanded Manstein's return to Russia, and when it became clear that he would not be returning, a military tribunal gave Manstein the death sentence for desertion. Meanwhile, Manstein became the king's best expert on Russian affairs, and possibly was in charge of the activities of Prussian spies in Russia.

It cannot be ruled out that Manstein, Prince Ferdinand, and Frederick II had intended to free Anton Ulrich and his family from prison, which would have answered Prussia's political purpose in destabilizing the situation in Russia. The entire plan may have been proposed to the Prussians by the foolhardy Zubarev. One witness who saw Zubarev in Königsberg testified that in parting with him and other Russians Zubarev had said: "Farewell, brothers. I'm going to ask to be taken to the Prussian King himself; I have a deal for him, the King."[56] That deal, no doubt, was what brought the Siberian merchant to Sanssouci. To be sure, Manstein and Frederick were risking nothing if Zubarev tried to contact Anton Ulrich. Taking the present facts one step further, we can infer that Zubarev was carrying out an assignment of the Russian government, which was disturbed by rumors circulating among the people of the unhappy emperor in prison and of his inevitable liberation, and which sought to provoke both the Prussian and the opposition forces in Russia to act in order to nip the conspiracy in the bud. A reckless adventurer like Zubarev would have been the perfect man for this job.

As it happened, war broke out between Russia and Prussia in 1756, no ships from Prussia came to Kholmogory, and the guards' worries were all for nothing. But the secret prisoner was nevertheless transferred to a new island prison.

* * *

In Schlüsselburg Ivan Antonovich lived eight years in a special barracks under the watch of a special team of guards. Without doubt his existence created headaches for three consecutive rulers of Russia: Elizabeth, Peter III, and Catherine the Great. After dethroning the toddler in 1741, Elizabeth, as she was dying in 1761, passed on this dynastic sin to her nephew Peter III, and from him Catherine "inherited" the sin in 1762. No one knew what to do with this young man.

Meanwhile rumors of Ivan Antonovich's life in prison continued to circulate among the people. To a great degree the authorities themselves facilitated this. After ascending the throne Elizabeth resorted to a surprisingly ineffective means of quelling the memory of her predecessor. The empress issued decrees requiring that all documents be removed from records depositories, wherein the Emperor Ivan VI and the Regent Anna Leopol'dovna were mentioned, and that all laws that were passed during the period of Anna's regency be declared null and void. All depictions of the emperor and regent were to be destroyed, as well as all coins, medals, and title pages of books with an address to the young emperor. Books from abroad that referred "to the former reign of the persons concerned" were burned.

Naturally, the effect of such measures was the exact opposite of that which was desired. (One might recall here the play by twentieth-century Russian playwright Grigorii Gorin. Its main character, the ruler of the ancient Greek city of Ephesus, demanded that his subjects forget forever the name of the worthless Herostratos, who had set fire to the splendid Temple to Artemis in Ephesus, one of the wonders of the world, and for this purpose had ordered that a grant obelisk be erected in the main square with the short inscription: "Everyone forget Herostratos!") Once forbidden, the name of the infant Ivan gained incredible popularity among the people.

Ivan was remembered: people told one another of his innocent suffering and asserted that one day his time would come and with it a time of justice and kindness. It's widely known that to become a celebrity in Russia one must suffer. To become the victim of a historically hated authority, which was cruel and alien to average persons, meant to gain the popularity and even the love of the people. The popular imagination created an image of Ivan, wherein he was suffering on behalf of the people, for the "true" faith, which stood in vivid opposition to the official, and therefore dead, "untrue" faith of the church.

Rumors about Ivan disturbed the authorities, despite the fact that "gabbers" who were caught had their tongues cut out and were sent into exile in Siberia. At the same time the boy himself aroused the interest of Russia's rulers. They wanted to see him. That is why Ivan was brought to St. Petersburg in 1756, into the home of Elizabeth's favorite, Ivan Shuvalov, where the empress saw Ivan for the first time in fifteen years. In March 1762 the new emperor, Peter III, rode to Schlüsselburg and conversed with the prisoner. In August of 1762 Catherine the Great went to visit Ivan.

There is no doubt that Ivan made a disturbing impression on his high-ranking visitors. As his guards Captain Stepan Vlas'ev and Lieutenant Luka Chekin wrote, "his articulation was confused to such a degree that even those who constantly saw and heard him could understand him with difficulty. In order to pronounce at least partially intelligible words he had to hold his chin with his hand and raise it upwards."[57] And the prison guards write further: "His mental abilities were disrupted, he had not the slightest memory, no ideas of any kind, neither of joy nor of sorrow, and no special inclinations."[58]

It's important to note that this evidence of Ivan's insanity comes from officers of the guards, people entirely incompetent in psychiatry. It was in the authorities' interest to present Ivan as a madman. On the one hand, it justified the severity of keeping the prisoner, as during those times the mentally ill were kept like animals, in chains in tiny closets without care and human compassion. On the other hand, Ivan's alleged insanity could provide justification for killing the unfortunate fellow, who, being mentally ill, was not responsible for himself and therefore could easily become a puppet in the hands of adventurers.

Of course, twenty years of imprisonment could not have had a beneficial effect on the development of the boy's personality. A young human is not like a kitten, which even in total isolation will grow into a cat. Isolation and what doctors call "pedagogical neglect" turned out to be deadly for Ivan. More likely than not he was neither an idiot nor a madman. Isolated and deceived, his life experience was deformed and defective.

As proof of his madness, the prison guards write of his abnormal, in their opinion, reaction to their behavior: "In June [1759] his fits became more violent: the patient shouted at the guards, quarreled with them, attempted to fight, twisted his mouth, and threatened to hit the officers."[59] From other sources we know that the officers of the guard treated him rudely, punished him, deprived him of tea, warm clothes, possibly beat him for his obstinacy, and quite probably teased him like a dog on a chain. Captain Oftsyn wrote in April 1760 that "the prisoner is healthy and agitated from time to time, to which state he is driven by the officers [Vlas'ev and Chekin—E.A.] who are always teasing him."[60] Of course, Ivan hated his tormentors and scolded them, and this was only the natural reaction of a psychologically normal person to inhumane treatment.

In general, the prisoner's situation was deplorable. He was held in a small narrow room with tiny windows, which were always closed. For many years he lived by candlelight and, as he did not have a watch or a clock, he could not tell the daytime from the night. One eyewitness wrote: "He did not know how to read or write, solitude had made him pensive, and his thoughts were not always in order."[61] To this one can add an excerpt from the instructions given to the commandant in 1756 by the head of the Secret Chancery, Count Aleksandr Shuvalov: "Do not allow the prisoner to leave the barracks; when someone will be let in to clean up all manner of dirt, the prisoner is to remain behind a screen so that he cannot be seen." In 1757 clarification followed: Do not allow anyone to enter the fortress without an order from the Secret Chancery, including generals and even field marshals.[62]

It is unknown how long this most unhappy of unhappy lives would have dragged on if it were not for a tragedy that occurred in 1764. On the night of July 4 nearby residents suddenly heard shots being fired irregularly within the fortress. A totally unexpected attempt to liberate the secret prisoner Grigorii, the former emperor Ivan Antonovich, had taken place.

The endeavor was led by Lieutenant Vasilii Mirovich of the Smolensk Infantry Regiment. Lack of success in life, poverty, and envy tormented this twenty-three-year-old officer, and he had decided in this way to remedy his affairs. He found out about Ivan when in the course of his service he had been obliged to keep the outer watch at the Schlüsselburg fortress. He planned to free Ivan, then to take him to St. Petersburg and raise the guards and artillerymen to rebel against Catherine II. During his regular watch Mirovich called the soldiers to arms, arrested the commandant and positioned his soldiers to storm the barracks where the secret prisoner was being held. Mirovich's daring scheme nearly succeeded: when the barracks guards saw the cannon brought by Mirovich's people, they laid down their guns. And then, as the prison officers Vlas'ev and Chekin wrote in their report: "Seeing the superior force of the enemy, we killed the prisoner."

The jailers, frightened by the assault, came running into Ivan's room, who had already been awakened by the shots, and started stabbing him with their swords. They felt nervous and were in a hurry; the prisoner fought back desperately but soon collapsed to the floor under the murderers' blows. That is how Mirovich found him when he burst into the room a minute later. He commanded that the dead body be put onto the bed and taken out into the fortress courtyard; after that he surrendered to the commandant. He had gambled and lost. The stakes had been high, he would pay with his life. A month and a half later, Mirovich was publicly executed in St. Petersburg; the scaffold with his body was burned and the ashes thrown to the winds.

Ivan Antonovich's murder raises an age-old problem of the balance between morals and politics. When Vlas'ev and Chekin were murdering Ivan, they were acting on orders they had received on such a possible turn of events: performing their duty they committed a crime. But is the matter that simple? Two contradictory truths, God's law and the law of the state, clashed in irreconcilable conflict. It appears that the mortal sin of murder can be a justifiable action if it is anticipated in written instructions, if the oath of allegiance obliges one to do so, or if the sin is committed for the welfare of the state or for the sake of society's greater majority. This contradiction seems to be insoluble. We cannot automatically reject the assertions put forth in

Catherine II's manifesto regarding these events, which claims that Vlas'ev and Chekin were not guilty, because these officers merely fulfilled the conditions of the oath they had sworn and managed to stop "by sacrificing the life of one man, who was unfortunately born," the inevitable bloodshed that would have ensued if Mirovich's harebrained plan had succeeded.[63] The facts indicate that the political situation in the capital at that time, when Catherine was out of the city, was unstable. In any large Russian city a number of people can be found who are willing to support any insurrection, for the sake of material gain, from a desire to act outside the law, and out of pure irresponsibility. No doubt the rebellion organized by Mirovich would have been crushed, but how much blood would have been shed, how many lives lost? How difficult a problem to weigh!

Ivan's dead body was kept in the fortress for several days, and then, at the special order of Catherine II, it was secretly buried somewhere in the courtyard. Today, more than two hundred years later, we approach Schlüsselburg Fortress's only gate aboard a small ship. Ancient and mighty, the fortress walls run along the entire perimeter of the tiny island, located in the middle of a dark fast current of cold water rushing from Lake Ladoga into the Neva and beyond into the Baltic Sea. It is warm and quiet in the fortress courtyard. Groups of tourists crowd around a guide, people walk among the ruins well overgrown with grass. They laugh, sun themselves, buy ice cream for children unaware that somewhere here, right under their feet, lie the remains of a most unhappy person, a martyr who lived and died never knowing for what purpose God gave him so wretched a life and so terrible a death at the age of twenty-three.

At the time that Ivan died, Anna Leopol'dovna's husband, Anton Ulrich, had been in prison for twenty-two years. His two daughters and two sons lived with him in the bishop's house, which stood on the bank of the Northern Dvina. The river was somewhat visible from one window of the house, which was surrounded by a high wall enclosing a large courtyard with a pond, vegetable garden, bathhouse, and carriage shed. The women lived in one room, the men in another. The rooms were small with low ceilings. Other premises were occupied by soldiers of the guard and the prisoners' servants.

Living as they did for years or even decades together under one roof (the last guard was not changed for twelve years), these people quarreled, reconciled, fell in love, and reported on one another. Scandal followed scandal: a soldier would be caught stealing, or officers carousing with maids. As always Prince Anton Ulrich was quiet and timid. He grew fat and flabby with age. After Anna's death he found comfort in the embrace of his daughters' servants. He had illegitimate children in Kholmogory, who grew up and became servants to the Brunswick family. On rare occasions the prince would write letters to the Empress Elizabeth, and later to Catherine II, thanking them for a bottle of wine or other items which had been sent out of charity. He especially suffered if coffee ran out.

It has been reported that in 1766 Catherine II sent General Bibikov to Kholmogory to offer Anton Ulrich on the empress's behalf the opportunity to leave Russia. But he refused. A Danish diplomat wrote that the prince, "accustomed to his confinement, sick and low in spirits, had declined the freedom which was offered him."[64] This is inaccurate. The prince did not want freedom for himself alone: he wanted to leave Russia together with his children. But Catherine would not agree to his conditions. She was afraid to free Anna Leopol'dovna's children, who, according to Empress Anna's will, could assert a claim to the Russian throne. The promise was simply made to the prince to free them all together as soon as circumstances permitted.

But Anton Ulrich did not live to see the fulfillment of Catherine's promise. By the age of sixty he had grown blind and decrepit. After thirty-four years of confinement he died on May 4, 1776, surviving his wife by more than twenty years. The coffin with his body was taken out into the courtyard at night and he was buried there without a funeral service, like a suicide tramp or drowned man. We are not sure whether his children were allowed to say farewell to him at his graveside.

They lived for another four years in Kholmogory. By 1780 they had all long since grown up. Catherine Antonovna was the oldest, deaf, and almost thirty-nine years old; Elizabeth was thirty-seven; Peter was thirty-five; and the youngest, Aleksei, was thirty-four. They were all sickly, weak, and with obvious physical handicaps. An officer of the guard wrote of Anna Leopol'dovna's elder son, Peter, that "he has a sickly and consumptive constitution; he is a little lopsided and bow-legged. The youngest son, Aleksei, is sturdily built, but suffers from seizures." The elder daughter, Catherine, "has a sickly and nearly consumptive appearance, besides being somewhat deaf; her speech is low-pitched and indistinct; she suffers from various attacks of painful seizures; and she has a very mild temperament."[65]

Although they lived in isolation and lacked any schooling (in 1750 Empress Elizabeth's decree arrived in Kholmogory forbidding that Anna's children be taught how to read and write), they all grew up to be clever, kind, and likable persons; writing and reading they mastered on their own.

After visiting the children, Governor Aleksei Melgunov wrote a message to Empress Catherine II about Catherine Antonovna wherein he stated that in spite of her being deaf "her manners show that she is timid, shy, and polite; she is quiet and cheerful, with a bashful disposition. Seeing others laughing during a conversation she joins in the laughter, although she actually does not understand its cause. The brothers and sisters alike are friends with one another, all of them being good-natured and humane. In summer, they work in the garden, looking after hens and ducks, and feeding them, while in winter they race with one another on the lake, ride horses, read psalm books and play chess and cards. In addition, the girls sometimes keep busy embroidering."[66]

Their lifestyle was humble and unassuming, as were their requests. Elizabeth was the head of the family. She was a plump and energetic girl, reliable and talkative. She told Melgunov that "father and we, when we were still very young, used to ask for freedom; but when father went blind and we grew older, we requested permission to go sledding in the street, but we received absolutely no reply."[67] She also spoke about her unrealized dream "of living in high society," and of learning good social graces. "However, in the current situation in which we live," Elizabeth Antonovna went on, "we may wish for nothing more than to continue living here in seclusion. We are completely content, we were born here, have become accustomed to this place and have grown old here."[68]

Elizabeth Antonovna made but three requests, which must have shaken Melgunov, a sensitive, humane, and warmhearted person: "We ask you to seek Her Majesty's favor so that we would be allowed to leave the house and take walks in the meadow; we have heard that flowers grow there that do not grow in our garden."[69] They also wished that officers' wives be allowed to visit them—life was so boring without society. And their final request: "We receive corsets, caps, and toques from St. Petersburg, but we do not use them, as neither we nor our servants know how to put them on or how to wear them. Please do us a favor, send someone to us who could help us learn to dress properly."[70]

In concluding her conversation with Melgunov, Elizabeth said that if these requests were honored, they would be satisfied with everything and would not ask for any more favors, "we do not wish anything else, and we will be happy to remain in this situation forever."[71] Reading Melgunov's report, Catherine was moved. She had probably only seen Anna Leopol'dovna one time—in her coffin in 1746. Now she gave orders for her children to prepare to leave their prison home.

Catherine II began correspondence with the Danish queen Julia Margaret, Anton Ulrich's sister, and the aunt of the Kholmogory captives, and she asked her to allow them to live in Norway, which was a province of the Kingdom of Denmark at that time. The queen gave her consent for them to settle in Denmark proper. Preparations for the journey began. All at once the glitter of gold, silver, and the sparkle of diamonds started to appear in the modest rooms of the Bishop of Kholmogory. These were gifts from the empress which kept arriving one after the other: a gigantic silver service, diamond finger-rings for the men and earrings for the women, marvelous unknown powders, lipsticks, shoes, and clothing. Seven German tailors and fifty in Iaroslavl' hurriedly sewed clothing for the four prisoners. Relatives in Denmark must know Empress Catherine's generosity and benevolence.

On June 26, 1780, Melgunov told the Brunswick family that they were being sent to their aunt's in Denmark. They thanked Melgunov for their freedom, but requested that they be settled in a small out-of-the-way spot in Denmark, where there were fewer people. On the night of June 27, for the first time in their lives, they were led out of the prison. They boarded a yacht and floated down the wide and beautiful Northern Dvina, a tiny gray patch of which they had seen all their lives from their window. When in the twilight of the northern night they saw the gloomy fortifications of Novodvinskaia Fortress near Arkhangel'sk, the brothers and sisters began to cry and bid farewell to one another, thinking that they had been deceived and that they were actually going to be separated and confined to the solitary cells in the wide openings of the fortress casemates. But they soon calmed down, being shown the frigate *Poliarnaia Zvezda* (Polar Star), which stood by preparing to sail.

On the night of July 1 Captain Arsen'ev gave the order to set sail. Anna Leopol'dovna's children left their cruel homeland for good. They cried as they kissed Melgunov's hand in farewell. He had come to see them off on the journey, which turned out to be especially difficult in rough weather. Nine long weeks of incessant storms, fog, and head winds prevented the *Polar Star* from reaching the shore of Denmark. We do not know what the frigate's passengers were thinking or what they said. But probably in calm weather they looked at the ocean and watched the free sea birds flying over the ship; and in bad weather they sat huddled close together praying in Russian to a Russian God desiring only that they all die together.

But fate was kind to them. On August 30, 1780, the Cape of Bergen came into sight. Here a Danish vessel was waiting for Anna's children, aboard which they became free. But here too they faced an ordeal, for stupid and cold-blooded bureaucratic laws forced them to leave their servants, their stepbrothers and stepsisters, on Russian territory—that is, on the deck of the *Polar Star.*

Freedom came a whole lifetime too late for the princes and princesses. Torn from their accustomed environment, surrounded by strangers speaking a foreign language, they were unhappy, and clung even more tightly together. Their aunt the queen settled them in the small town of Horsens in Jutland, but did not bother to visit her nieces and nephews even once. And they, like old birds set free to live in the wild, were ill-adapted and began to die one after the other. The first to go, in October 1782, was their leader, Princess Elizabeth. Five years later Prince Aleksei died, and in 1798 he was followed by Prince Peter. The oldest sibling, Catherine, outlived all the rest, reaching the age of sixty-six. She was the one who had been born in freedom, and who had been accidentally dropped in the confusion of the coup on the night of November 25, 1741.

In August 1803 the young Russian emperor Aleksandr I received a letter that came as if from the past. Princess Catherine Antonovna of Brunswick had sent him a letter, which she had written herself in poor Russian, begging him to bring her home to Russia. She complained of her Danish servants, who, taking advantage of her illness and ignorance, were stealing from her. "Every day I cry," Catherine concludes her letter, "and I do not know why God has sent me here and why I live so long on Earth. Everyday I remember Kholmogory, because for me that was paradise, and this is hell."[72]

But the Russian emperor did not respond. And on April 9, 1807, the last daughter of the unfortunate Brunswick family died still waiting for an answer.

CHAPTER 4

The Russian Aphrodite
(Elizabeth)

In the dead of night on November 25, 1741, Iakov Shakhovskoi, the senate procurator-general, was awakened by a loud knock at the door. "You can imagine, my benevolent reader, what a confused state I was in!" wrote Shakhovskoi in his memoirs. "Having no information about such undertakings, nor even expecting them to ever take place, my first thought was that the official must have gone mad to disturb me so and then to leave abruptly; but soon I saw many people, crowded in unusual bunches, running past my windows and heading in the direction of the palace, and I made immediately for that place myself . . . I did not have to think long about which palace to go to."[1] Everybody was hurrying in the direction of the Tsaritsyn Lug—the Field of Mars, where the palace of Tsarevna Elizabeth Petrovna was located. On that dark and frosty night the palace shone with lights. The merry shouts of the Guards, grouped around bonfires made right in the street, and a huge crowd of idlers who had blocked all approaches to the residence of Peter the Great's daughter—all this gave testimony that while the procurator-general had been asleep a coup d'état had taken place in the capital, and power had passed into Elizabeth's hands. That is how the glorious era of Empress Elizabeth began . . .

I believe that the experienced courtier Shakhovskoi was being somewhat disingenuous when he spoke of the confusion that had overwhelmed him that night: like many others, he had probably known well in advance about the impending coup. It had long been an open secret. Grand Duchess Anna Leopol'dovna, regent of the infant-emperor Ivan Antonovich, and her

Summer Palace of Elizabeth Petrovna. From I. N. Bozherianov, "*Nevskii prospekt.*" *Kul'turno-istoricheskii ocherk dvukhvekovoi zhizni Sankt-Peterburga* ("Nevskii Prospect." A Cultural and Historical Sketch of St. Petersburg at Two Hundred) (St. Petersburg, 1901–03), vol. 1, p. 118.

ministers had been warned several times about their aunt Elizabeth's ambitious intentions. This information had been procured by Anna Leopol'dovna's spies, and foreign diplomats had also written as much. But a certain letter from Breslau in Silesia had worried the prime minister Andrei Ivanovich Osterman most of all. A well-informed agent had reported that Elizabeth's conspiracy had definitely taken shape and was very close to realization; the letter called for the immediate arrest of the tsarevna's personal doctor, Johann Herman Lestocq, who held all the threads of the conspiracy.

Anna Leopol'dovna did not listen to those who advised her to detain Lestocq. She acted in her own way: naively and stupidly. At the nearest Courtag, or reception day at court, which took place on November 23, 1741, the regent interrupted the ongoing card game, left the table, and asked her aunt to proceed with her into the neighboring room. Holding the letter from Breslau in her hands, she confronted Elizabeth, attempting to deal with the matter of conspiracy on a family basis. When the two women rejoined the guests, both appeared flurried, which was immediately noted by the foreign diplomats present at the Courtag. Shortly thereafter, Elizabeth went home. As General Christoph Herman Manstein wrote in his notes: "Princess Elizabeth was not at all disconcerted. She protested to the grand duchess that she had never had the thought of undertaking the least thing either against her or against her son; that she was too religious to break the oath that she had sworn; that all of these reports came only from her enemies, who wanted to make her unhappy; that . . ."[2] In a word, tears began to flow, and all suspicions were drowned in their streams, for even the simpleminded investigator Anna Leopol'dovna joined Elizabeth in her weeping, and actually was made to believe, to her misfortune, in the tsarevna's innocence.

When Elizabeth returned to her apartments she was horror-stricken. She knew all too well that if Lestocq were arrested the plot would be foiled—the talkative and weak-willed French surgeon would have told everything he knew in the Secret Chancery at the very first sight of the rack. And then prison or a remote monastery, taking the veil, and farewell forever to the sweet life! No, Elizabeth could not bear the thought of all that! Having set out on the road of falsehood and sedition, she decided to see it through to the end. Approximately twenty-four hours later, in the dark early morning hours of November 25, 1741, after the tsarevna fervently and tearily prayed to God, she put on a cavalry cuirass, climbed into a sleigh, and rode hurriedly through the dark and blizzard-swept streets of the capital to the barracks of the Preobrazhenskii Regiment.

The Preobrazhenskii Regiment was waiting for Elizabeth. Her face flushed from the frost and anxiety, she was beautiful as Venus, but laconic as Julius Caesar, when she addressed the grenadiers: "My friends! Just as you served my father faithfully, in the present situation likewise show your loyalty to me!" The grenadiers answered in chorus: "We will be glad to die for your majesty and for our motherland!"[3] And they rushed behind their charming leader toward the Winter Palace.

It goes without saying that the grenadiers were not raised from their beds as suddenly as Procurator-General Iakov Shakhovskoi. They had been prepared for Elizabeth's coup long in advance. Tentative talks, hints dropped by trusted proxies, and finally money and promises had done their work. But all the same, so successful a beginning could be explained primarily by a political state of affairs that worked largely to Elizabeth's advantage. Troubled times had ensued following Anna Ioannovna's death in the autumn of 1740. Standing at the head of state (or more exactly, lying in a cradle) was the two-month-old emperor Ivan Antonovich, son of the regent Anna Leopol'dovna and Anton Ulrich, prince of Brunswick. A desperate struggle immediately broke out around the tiny emperor's throne. At first Empress Anna Ioannovna's former favorite, Ernst Johan Biron, took power into his hands; three weeks later he was overthrown by Burkhard Münnich, who was then replaced by Andrei Osterman.

Many Russians, and primarily the Guards, were indignant at this reshuffling around the throne, often led by foreigners in Russian service. They were disgusted with Anna Leopol'dovna's and the whole Brunswick family's lack of authority. Tsarevna Elizabeth Petrovna was able to take advantage of this discontent. She was especially popular among the Guards of lower ranks—simple soldiers: of 308 rank-and-file men who set out with Elizabeth to the Winter Palace there were only 54 noblemen, less than twenty percent. The remainder were the descendants of peasants, clergy, small landholders, and even *kholopy* (slaves). And although they had already broken their previous class ties and acquired a typically praetorian mentality of dull-witted solidarity, unceremonious disdain toward high officials, and overweening pride in their own role in the fate of the throne and country, their sympathies were on the side of the daughter of the great tsar Peter I and the Livland laundress.

The nobility, and especially its highborn members, now as earlier scorned Elizabeth, whose lowly and illegitimate origin (Elizabeth was born before Peter and Catherine were married) and commoner's behavior jarred upon them.

But the soldiers of the guards liked this good-looking young woman. She consorted with them easily, as her great father had done. Moreover, Elizabeth had even become related to many of the grenadiers, willingly responding to their invitations to be godmother of their children. And the relationship of godparents, according to Russian Orthodox tradition, entitled one to use the familiar form of address, and was considered very close because it came from God. And so we can read in the reports of the French envoy Chetardy how Münnich came to deliver his New Year's greetings to the tsarevna in 1741 and was dumbfounded by the spectacle he witnessed: "The vestibule, stairway, and lobby were packed full of Guards unceremoniously calling the princess their godmother. For over a quarter of an hour he was unable to come to his senses in Princess Elizabeth's presence, neither hearing nor seeing anything."[4]

The strength of the Guards' godmother, Elizabeth, lay in the fact that she was Peter the Great's daughter, who, in the guards' opinion, had been unjustly deprived of the throne after Peter II's death. And having seen the crowds of Guards in Elizabeth's palace, the old field marshal Münnich rightly appraised the situation.

The Guards' dissatisfaction with the regent's weak regime combined with their idealization of Peter as a severe but just ruler, who took care of his subjects, in contrast to the nonentities who flocked around the throne of Ivan Antonovich. This idealization spread in full measure to his daughter, in whom the Guards saw the heir of Peter's great but interrupted policies. Almost a third of the Guards who helped Elizabeth seize the throne had begun their service under Peter, according to an extant list of participants in the coup. By 1741 they were gray-haired veterans around fifty years old, who told stories of the glorious summers spent side-by-side with the great tsar, and of the blond girl who was his favorite daughter and had grown up before their eyes. The younger soldiers (120 of them in number, more than a third of the regiment) greedily drank in these stories. They had been inducted into the Guards toward the end of Anna Ioannovna's reign. Biron had been the initiator of this. Fearing noble freethinkers in Guards' uniforms, the favorite began renewing the Guards with recruits from the peasantry and other nonnoble strata. It was this very combination of daring veterans and raw naive youths who hung on every word of the veterans that would propel the coup. Elizabeth ignited the fuel herself by coming to lead them personally.

There is one page in the history of the coup of November 25, 1741, that Elizabeth would have preferred to forget, one that told of the active participation of foreign powers in the conspiracy in the figures of the French envoy to Russia, J.-J. Marquis de la Chetardy, and the Swedish envoy, Eric Mathias Nolcken.

Chetardy arrived in Russia in 1739 with the specific task of breaking the Russo-Austrian alliance of 1726, which had reinforced the position of Louis XV's enemy. Achieving this goal entailed undermining Anna Leopol'dovna's government.

Nolcken had the same aim. There were strong sentiments in Stockholm to revise the Nystad Peace Treaty of 1721 and thereby regain the Eastern Baltic territories. Nolcken and Chetardy searched for and supported those forces that were capable of overthrowing Anna Leopol'dovna's government. In the autumn of 1740, Nolcken was the first to make contact with Elizabeth, who entered into negotiations, or more precisely into political bargaining, with him, an endeavor not befitting Peter the Great's daughter.

Nolcken offered her a clear and simple plan: the tsarevna was to sign a document to the king of Sweden requesting his help in ascending the throne; in response the king would declare war on Russia, and his forces would attack St. Petersburg, thereby facilitating a coup in favor of Elizabeth. Elizabeth would be given one hundred thousand écus to execute the plan, in exchange for the promise that if it succeeded she would honor all of Sweden's territorial claims.

The tsarevna had agreed to all of the conditions, but she had asked for the money in advance, being, as usual, in dire need of funds. Nolcken insisted on doing the opposite: first, a written commitment, then the money. Elizabeth did not object; she was ready to sign the required document on the spot, but said that the money should come first. Chetardy, who had found out about the tsarevna's ambitious intentions from Nolcken, came on the scene just as the conspirators had reached an impasse, and he immediately went into action.

Let's make a short digression. Of course, what Nolcken and Chetardy were doing was a crime, but foreign diplomats' involvement in intrigues at their appointed courts was not an unusual practice at that time. A whole saga can be written about how Russian envoys paved the road with gold before Russia's political henchmen in Poland, Sweden, and other countries. In general, it was a rare occasion when an international treaty contained no secret articles on interference by the chief contracting parties into the internal affairs of other countries. Nolcken and Chetardy were no exceptions to these dirty rules. Unlike the cautious Nolcken, Chetardy spared no money for the tsarevna. He became deeply involved in the conspiracy, considering himself its prime mover or, to use a more modern phrase, its chief coordinator. An ardent and romantic man by nature, Chetardy was also frivolous and foolish. He employed signals, passwords, notes passed while dancing the minuet or cotillion, cloaks, and other disguises, the darkness of night, and all other manner of the conspirator's conventional attributes. As Catherine the Great's mother, Princess Johanna Elizabeth, wrote, the conspirators "met on dark nights, during thunderstorms, heavy downpours, and snowstorms in places people used for dumping garbage."[5] Spies regularly informed their superiors of the French envoy's secret nightly escapades, when he would steal through kitchen gardens to Elizabeth's palace, but obviously "not for Cupid's games."

Chetardy and Nolcken sent wordy reports to their ministers assuring that negotiations with the tsarevna were on the verge of a successful conclusion. But alas! for some unknown reason, Elizabeth began to buy time; she hesitated, having second thoughts, delaying, and most important, she refused to sign any papers. Finally, Nolcken and Chetardy concluded that Elizabeth shrunk from signing any commitments concerning future concessions of formerly Swedish territories conquered by her father because, according to Chetardy, she would run the risk of "becoming odious to the people if it turned out that she had called on the Swedes" to help her ascend the throne.[6]

It soon became clear, however, that it was impossible to stop this machine once it had been set into motion: the diplomats' triumphant reports of successful negotiations with Elizabeth played their fatal role—the Swedish government decided to take action without waiting for the documents signed by the tsarevna, which Nolcken failed to provide. In the summer of 1741, Sweden declared war against Russia over Finland and immediately suffered a crushing defeat near Vilmanstrand on August, 23, 1741. Any hopes Elizabeth had for Swedish assistance evaporated. Hotheaded Chetardy was of no help, either. Elizabeth could rely on no one but herself. After the Courtag on November 23, 1741, she decided to take action independently.

However, Marquis de Chetardy continued to believe until the very end that it was he who was heading the conspiracy in Elizabeth's favor, so one can imagine his horror when on the night of November 25 soldiers tried to force their way into his house, which was located on Admiralty Square, almost opposite the emperor's residence. He thought that he had been exposed and that Siberian exile awaited him. In actual fact, the soldiers had made a mistake—part of the Guards who were accompanying Elizabeth were given orders to arrest Osterman, Mikhail Golovkin, and other officials of Anna Leopol'dovna's government. But in the dark the soldiers arrived at the wrong building and in so doing frightened the entire French mission and its head, Chetardy.

We can assume that, standing by the window in his nightcap and gown, the marquis had himself seen the "storm of the Winter Palace," for which he had so vigorously been preparing at balls and secret meetings near garbage dumps. Elizabeth got out of the sleigh on Admiralty Square. Then, accompanied by 300 Guards, she proceeded to the Winter Palace on foot in order to make as little noise as possible. The soldiers were nervous and in a hurry. The tsarevna got tangled up in her skirts, and bogged down in the snow, and on top of that she felt awkward in her heavy cuirass. In short, she was delaying the whole company. And it was precisely then that an episode took place unprecedented in the history of all revolutions and coups: without a moment's thought the grenadiers picked up the beautiful Venus, like a lovely feather, and she rode into the Winter Palace upon the broad shoulders of her soldiers.

In his sermon on the day of Elizabeth's coronation, the archbishop Arsentii, amazed at what the empress had done on that memorable night of storming the Winter Palace, mentioned her courage when circumstances had forced this girl "to forget the delicacy of her sex and in the company of a small group of people run the obvious risk of her own life, ready to shed her own blood for the integrity of our faith and motherland, to act as a leader and a cavalier of fighting men, to gather together faithful soldiers, to form ranks, and take on the enemy headlong."[7]

On the night described by the eloquent pastor, Elizabeth's enemy was sleeping blissfully in his crib, having had his fill of milk at the breast of his wet-nurse Katerina Ioannovna, and he had not the slightest notion that someone had begun "to form ranks" to fight against him. Likewise, the emperor's parents, entire retinue, and servants were all sleeping. After Elizabeth had forced her way into the palace she wasted no time: all the entrances and exits were cut off. The watch immediately turned and joined the mutineers, and then the soldiers rushed into the imperial apartments on the second floor, where they awoke and arrested the regent Anna Leopol'dovna and her husband, Prince Anton Ulrich. Neither the prince nor his spouse offered any resistance, as mentioned already. They surrendered to their bitter fate without so much as a murmur and allowed themselves to be driven to Elizabeth's palace, where they arrived not long before its mistress. It was time for her, the lucky one, to receive congratulations—couriers woke up their chiefs, who hastily dressed and hurried like Shakhovskoi to make their bows.

To conclude the description of "the storming of the Winter Palace" we should note that although the coup came off on the whole as an easy and bloodless event, there were certain crucial moments when Elizabeth had to display will and character. It was not easy for one who had grown accustomed to a gay and carefree life to resolve to undertake a coup d'état.

At that moment, when she got into a sleigh to go to the Preobrazhenskii Regiment barracks, accompanied by only three persons—Lestocq, Mikhail Vorontsov, and the music teacher Schwartz—there was no one who could guarantee that the conspirators' plan would succeed, that they would meet with no resistance, and that Elizabeth would not ultimately come to trial for high treason. The night of any coup is always dark and frightening as a yawning chasm, into which one must step without hesitation. And to overcome this fear, even the strongest of men must possess courage. The tsarevna, a tender woman, proved to possess such courage and demonstrated it twice. First, she instigated the rebellion among the soldiers and, second, she led the storm of the palace herself. She had no other alternative since there were no officers among the mutineers to give orders to the soldiers. Therefore, Elizabeth did forget "the delicacy of her sex" and for the first and last time in her life she took on the role of a military leader.

Later in the brightly illuminated palace there was champagne, and crowds of silver-tongued courtiers fell at her feet. By morning a manifesto declaring her accession to the throne and an oath were ready. The army and citizens swore their allegiance, and the new empress entered the Winter Palace to a cannon salute and shouts of "Vivat!" Out of the window of her new residence Elizabeth could see the Peter and Paul Fortress, and the spire of its cathedral, under the floor of which her parents lay in eternal slumber.

Medal depicting Elizabeth's coup. From I. N. Bozherianov, *"Nevskii prospekt."* *Kul'turno-istoricheskii ocherk dvukhvekovoi zhizni Sankt-Peterburga* ("Nevskii Prospect." A Cultural and Historical Sketch of St. Petersburg at Two Hundred) (St. Petersburg, 1901–03), vol. 1, p. 101.

Perhaps amid the hustle and bustle of the housewarming events Elizabeth found a moment's repose by the window to remember them. The ice floes of the Neva River flowed by her new palace, separating it from the city's nucleus, where the fortress and cathedral stood; so too had thirty years of the tsarevna's life passed by, and now she had become empress.

* * *

Elizabeth was undoubtedly born under a lucky star. Her birthday fell on December 18, 1709, when the Russian army was triumphantly entering Moscow after the victorious campaign of 1709. Engravings show the beauty and grandeur of the event, in which Russian soldiers carried captured banners and some of the personal belongings of King Charles XII, who had fled the battlefield. The Russian army led their highborn captives into St. Petersburg. Among them were numerous generals, the king's retinue, and thousands of officers and soldiers. Peter the Great, who was in charge of the entire ceremony, had received news of Catherine's successful delivery of a daughter just before the spectacle began. He gave the order to postpone the entry of the victorious army into the old capital for three days and called for a feast to honor his daughter's birth. She was called Elizabeth, a name quite uncommon in Russia in those days.

Elizabeth's childhood and youth were spent in Moscow and St. Petersburg. She was brought up together with her older sister Anna, born in 1708. Their father was away on campaigns most of the time, and their mother often accompanied him. Peter's younger sister, the tsarevna Natalia, or the Menshikov family looked after the tsar's daughters. Today, walking through the neat and cozy suites and halls of the Menshikov Palace Museum, one involuntarily thinks about Elizabeth's childhood. It could not have been quiet and orderly here in those days with the commotion of the tsar's daughters and Menshikov's children, Masha and Aleksandr. And then the solicitous hunchbacked Varvara Arsen'eva, Dar'ia Menshikova's sister and the mistress of the house, would have to give the children their dinner or put them to bed. In his letters to Peter and Catherine, Menshikov would write: "Thank God, Your precious children are healthy."

One of the first references to Elizabeth is found in her father's letter of May 1, 1710, in which he sends his regards to his five-month-old daughter. In his letters addressed to his daughters, as well as in those in which he wrote about them, severe Peter, who was preoccupied with hundreds of important matters, appears in a new light—tender, cheerful, and sensitive: Annushka and Lizan'ka, playing and turning somersaults, had penetrated his iron heart. He regularly sent his regards to his children, especially to the little one, and gave them presents as well.

Elizabeth's first official appearance took place on January 9, 1712. This day was crucial to the fate of the future empress. Both Elizabeth and her sister were bastards until January 9, 1712, when Peter legalized his relations with Catherine by marrying her in church; the two girls followed their parents in a walk around the lectern and became the legitimate children of the royal pair. After the marriage ceremony, Anna and Elizabeth sat for a while at the feast table in the palace as the "bride's maids" before they grew tired and sleepy and were taken off to bed.

On June 11, 1717, Catherine informed her husband that Elizabeth had come down with smallpox, but it turned out to be only a light case of it, and soon the girl had "recovered from the disease without harm to her face."[8] It can be said with certainty that if Elizabeth's face had been left pocked from the disease, the story of her life and probably the whole history of Russia as well would have turned out differently. Indeed, the beauty of the tsarevna,

ELISABETA   PRIMA ,
Imperatrix et   *Autocratrix*
Omnium   *Rossiarum*

Empress Elizabeth. From I. N. Bozherianov, "*Nevskii prospekt.*" *Kul'turno-istoricheskii ocherk dvukhvekovoi zhizni Sankt-Peterburga* ("Nevskii Prospect." A Cultural and Historical Sketch of St. Petersburg at Two Hundred) (St. Petersburg, 1901–03), vol. 1, n.p.

and later of the empress, had a great influence on her character, habits, actions, and even her politics.

The tsar's daughters were taught how to write and read rather early. As far back as 1712 Peter had begun writing notes to Elizabeth and Anna without any particular hope, however, of receiving a response. But by 1717 they corresponded with their parents quite actively. Catherine, who was accompanying Peter on his journey, wrote to Anna asking her "for God's sake to try to write well so we can praise you and send presents as a reward for your diligence, and see to it that your younger sister also tries to merit presents."[9] And soon the younger daughter did indeed earn a present. In early 1718 Elizabeth received a letter from her father: "Lizetka, my dear friend, hello! Thank you for your letters. God willing, I wish you joy. Kiss the big man, your brother, for me."[10] The tsarevich, Peter Petrovich, was a little more than two years old at that time.

Elizabeth was officially declared to have attained her majority in a ceremony that took place on September 9, 1721, when she was not yet twelve. According to tradition Peter cut off small white wings (symbol of angelic innocence) from his daughter's dress and she entered a new stage in her life—she was now a marriageable bride. Many years had been spent preparing the tsarevnas for this occasion.

In 1716–1717, in addition to the customary army of nurses, a Frenchman entered the tsarevnas' circle who was to instruct them in dance, and the countess Maria Magnani and the tutor Glück taught the girls Italian, German, and French, the last of which the grown-up Elizabeth spoke perfectly. Besides reading, writing, and speaking several languages, Anna and Elizabeth could discern good music and dance gracefully; they dressed with taste and were familiar with the rules of etiquette. What more did one need, given such dazzling beauty, to become the queen of France?

For that was precisely what Peter had planned for his middle daughter (by that time another daughter, Natalia, had been born). In 1721 he wrote to the Russian envoy to France, Vasilii Dolgorukii, that when he had been in Paris in 1719 he had spoken with the mother of the future king Louis XV "about arranging a match between the king and one of our daughters, especially the middle one, for she is his age [Louis was born in 1710—E.A.], but we did not discuss it at length as I had to leave soon, and now I am entrusting you to make as much progress as possible in this matter."[11]

The tsar's special task proved to be a difficult one for Dolgorukii and, practically speaking, impossible—Versailles was not at all eager to accept an offer of marriage to a laundress's daughter who, moreover, had been born before the tsar's marriage. The French pleaded the king's tender youth, and after Peter's death in 1725, the wishes of his successor, Catherine I, were disregarded. King Louis XV was wedded to Maria, the daughter of the ex-king of Poland Stanislas Leszczynski, and Russo-French marriage negotiations came to an abrupt end. So Elizabeth was not destined to become lewd

Louis XV's wife and Marie Antoinette's mother-in-law. Her fate was to remain uncertain for a very long time.

When Elizabeth's mother, Empress Catherine I, was dying in May 1727, she willed her daughter to marry Charles Augustus, the younger brother of the Duke of Holstein, Anna Petrovna's husband. By that time Charles Augustus, a handsome and affable young man, had come to Russia and been engaged to Elizabeth. But unfortunately he fell ill and died in the summer of 1727. Much later, in 1744, Empress Elizabeth broke into tears at the sight of Johanna Elizabeth, the mother of the future Catherine II, so striking was the resemblance between her bridegroom, Charles Augustus, and this, his younger sister.

However, at that time the tsarevna's grief did not endure; she became the cynosure of the young emperor Peter II's court. Peter II had in the autumn of 1727 threw off Menshikov's importunate tutelage and was enjoying the taste of absolute power. But the young emperor, the son of Tsarevich Aleksei, who had been killed in the Peter and Paul Fortress, was still a boy and could not rule the country on his own. He was strongly influenced by his favorite, the nineteen-year-old prince Ivan Dolgorukii, and consequently by the entire family of Dolgorukii princes, who strove to reinforce their power at court. With this as their aim, they indulged the emperor's every fancy, constantly gratifying and entertaining him. Hunting became Peter II's main occupation. After the court had moved to Moscow, Peter and Ivan Dolgorukii spent weeks at a time hunting in the game-filled forests around Moscow. Prince Ivan, a man of deplorable morals and a lady-killer, had introduced Peter to his amusements. The emperor did not resist and began himself to show unpleasant traits presaging the rule of an arrogant, callous, and indolent man lacking schooling and self-discipline. As Lady Rondeau wrote: "He is very tall, and large-made for his age . . . he is fair, but much tanned with hunting, has good features, but a down look and though he is young and handsome, has nothing attractive nor agreeable."[12] Many other foreigners wrote about Peter's hard-heartedness, mediocrity, and obstinacy as well as of his inclination to idleness and weakness for entertainment, and unwillingness to study.

In late 1727, rumors began to circulate regarding a love affair between the emperor and his beautiful aunt. And indeed where there is smoke, there is fire. The eighteen-year-old Elizabeth was no Puritan, and the twelve-year-old emperor was unusually mature and strong for his age, and in the company of Ivan Dolgorukii he had learned quite a lot about sin. For a time, Peter and Elizabeth were inseparable. They had much in common: they both liked to live at a furious pace and were absorbed in holidays, trips, dances, and hunting. The Spanish envoy Duc de Liria wrote to Madrid: "The Russians fear the great authority Princess Elizabeth has over the tsar: Her intellect, beauty, and ambition frighten everyone . . ."[13] We have no desire to ferret out the full extent of the friendship between Aunt Elizabeth and her nephew. Let Peter and Elizabeth remain in our memory as the Russian art-ist Valentin Serov depicted them in his painting: two exquisite riders astride magnificent horses galloping through the autumn fields, with the young emperor trying to catch up to the alluringly smiling belle.

This friendship did not last, however, and before long others were seen accompanying Elizabeth on her rides in the fields near Moscow. At that time Elizabeth was especially lighthearted and gay. As typical for youth, life seemed to consist of an endless line of years which lay before her. She realized early enough all the advantages of her divine beauty and its bewitching effect on men. She was a real and devoted disciple of her hedonistic age, indulging in all forms of delight and pleasure, becoming utterly absorbed in the volup-tuousness of merrymaking and idleness. The level of interests of the tsarevna and her retinue can be inferred from a letter that Mavra Shepeleva, the tsarevna's closest girlfriend, sent from Kiel, where she had gone together with Anna Petrovna: "Mother-Tsarevna, How handsome Prince Or'dov is! It's true, I had never thought he would be as handsome as he is now: he is as tall as Buturlin, and just as slim, his eyes are the same color as yours and just as large, his eyelashes are black; his eyebrows are dark brown . . . ; his cheeks are always a ruddy scarlet, his teeth are good and white, his lips are nice and always scarlet, and he speaks and laughs the way the late Bishov did, his car-riage resembles that of the sovereign [i.e., of Peter II—E.A.], his legs are slim, for he is still young, only nineteen years old; he wears his own hair, which is so long that it reaches his waist . . . I can also inform you of the following: I have bought a snuff-box and the person [depicted] thereon re-sembles Your Highness when you are naked."[14]

Aleksandr Borisovich Buturlin is mentioned in this letter. A handsome man of gigantic height, he was chamberlain at Elizabeth's court and her lover. The Supreme Privy Council members, who ruled the country for the boy-emperor, observed Elizabeth's behavior closely, and frightened by the ru-mors of drinking-bouts of the tsarevna and her chamberlain in Elizabeth's estate near Moscow, Aleksandrova Sloboda, they found a pretext for induct-ing Buturlin into the army and dispatching him far away from Moscow, to the Ukraine. But this did not disturb the tsarevna too much. Distracted by her own fast life, she took the separation from Buturlin quite easily—he was quickly replaced by another.

In the spring of 1728, Elizabeth lost the person closest to her. She re-ceived a message from Kiel that her sister Anna had died. The life of Peter the Great's eldest daughter was a tragic one. In 1725, according to the late father's will, she had been given in marriage to Charles Frederick, the Duke of Holstein. It had taken Peter some time to decide which of the two daugh-ters he was to part with. Thus, Anna's fate might well have been Elizabeth's, and vice versa. Anna languished in the capital of Holstein, where she and her husband had lived since the summer of 1727. Peter's daughter felt lonely among the people of this foreign land; in the unanimous opinion of her contemporaries her husband proved unworthy of a treasure such as Anna. The duke was a drunkard, a profligate, and an idler. Anna's letters to her sister and Peter II are full of melancholy, tears, and complaints. But nothing could be changed. In the autumn of 1727 Anna became pregnant. Mavra Shepeleva wrote to Elizabeth that the Court at Kiel was busy sewing baby's clothing, and that Anna had "something moving in her belly."

In February 1728 Anna gave birth to a boy who was named Charles Peter Ulrich. Shortly thereafter Anna came down with galloping consumption and died, having left a will in which she requested burial in St. Petersburg next to her parents' grave. Anna must have wanted her younger sister, whom she loved tenderly, to attend her funeral, as during the whole period of their childhood and youth they had been inseparable. However, her body reached St. Petersburg only in autumn, and autumn being the hunting season, Elizabeth could not sacrifice even a couple of days to come to the capital to attend her sister's burial. We know for sure that she was healthy and not ill at that time.

Elizabeth was also in the country when Peter II fell ill and died in early 1730. The French diplomat Magnan wrote to Paris that Princess Elizabeth did not show up in Moscow during talks regarding a successor to the throne. She remained in the country despite the requests of friends who were ready to support her and came to the city only when Anna Ioannovna had already been elected.

Some observers saw this as the deliberate tactics of Peter's ambitious daughter, who was waiting for her hour to come; others hissed that right at that particular moment she was pregnant. The answer would appear to be a simple one: ambition had not as yet awakened in the tsarevna; she was not interested in power yet. There was just young blood pulsing in her veins. At that moment she had in fact only the remotest chance of taking the throne, and there was no time for deliberation, as right after Peter's death, the Supreme Privy Council members had announced that Anna Ioannovna, the Duchess of Courland, was to ascend the throne. It is noteworthy that while discussing the succession, the head of the Supreme Privy Council, Prince Dmitrii Golitsyn, the old aristocrat who had proposed the candidacy of Anna Ioannovna, this "purely Russian" daughter of Tsar Ivan V and Tsaritsa Praskovia Fedorovna, had merely made snide reference to the offspring of the Livland laundress, and that sufficed to prevent the tsarevna's name from being mentioned again.

The reign of Anna Ioannovna, who was Elizabeth's cousin, proved to be for the tsarevna a long, uneasy, and unpleasant one. According to court protocol, Elizabeth was the third-ranking person in the country after the tsaritsa and her niece Princess Anna Leopol'dovna, a very lofty position indeed. She had a palace of her own, a retinue and servants, estates, and an allowance. But she no longer enjoyed the privileges of the beauteous and spoiled daughter of the reigning tsar, as she had from her birth to 1727. She was no longer a pet, adored by all, whose fancies were the law: the new empress did not favor her cousin. Many things contributed to Anna Ioannovna's hostility toward Elizabeth. Elizabeth's "poor bloodline," fear of her future intentions, and most important, Anna Ioannovna's envy of the happy fate and carefree joviality of the young girl who had experienced neither the poverty nor the humiliation she herself had had to bear.

In fact, Elizabeth didn't have to do anything to arouse the tsaritsa's hatred: it was enough for her to appear in the dance hall dressed in a new gown, smiling, diamonds in her exquisite coiffure. The resulting wave of admiration that her presence sent rippling through the crowd of guests and courtiers was reward enough for Elizabeth. But sitting high on her throne, the empress's heavy gaze followed Elizabeth, the star of the ball. The tsaritsa, pockmarked, and overly stout, felt herself an old woman (Elizabeth was seventeen years younger) who could not compete with the tsarevna in the dance hall. Lady Rondeau describes the visit of one Chinese ambassador to a court ball. He and his interpreter were led into the hall just as the ball began. Anna asked one of them which of the ladies present in the hall he considered the prettiest. He said: "It would be difficult in a starlit night to say which star was the brightest," but observing that she expected him to say which he thought, he bowed to the princess Elizabeth: among such a number of fine women he thought her the handsomest.[15] It is not difficult to conceive how Empress Anna must have felt in moments like that.

Anna found ways to vent her spleen: she oppressed Elizabeth economically and morally. She granted the coquette an allowance of thirty thousand rubles a year and never gave a kopeck more. This was a shock for Elizabeth, who had never had to count money before. The tsarevna was very uncomfortable at Anna's court, feeling unwanted in the royal family. Her relations with Anna are revealed by the petition that the tsarevna submitted to the empress in 1736. Elizabeth had placed her estate manager under arrest on suspicion of theft. But he was unexpectedly released on Anna's order. This had frightened the tsarevna so much that she decided to forestall the manager's possible denunciation. The petition is written in the traditionally self-deprecating manner of eighteenth-century correspondance and ends with the signature: "Your Imperial Majesty's *obedient slave Elizabeth*." That's the way things were in reality: just like any other subject Elizabeth was at the total mercy of the autocrat, and Anna could treat her cousin as she liked.

Anna Ioannovna was determined to keep power out of the hands of Catherine I's descendants. Although Elizabeth had publicly pledged to obey all of the empress's decisions regarding succession to the throne, Anna and her entourage always worried about the threat to their power represented by Peter the Great's daughter. The calculating Vice Chancellor Andrei Ivanovich Osterman wrote that "there cannot be any doubt that they [i.e., Elizabeth and her nephew Charles Peter Ulrich—E.A.], while perhaps lacking the right and strength, will always have the desire" to ascend the throne.[16]

The easiest way to solve "the problem of Elizabeth" was to marry her off to a foreign prince. And a long line of bridegrooms courted the tsarevna one after another: Karl of Brandenburg-Bayreuth; Prince George of England; Infante Manuel of Portugal; Count Maurice of Saxony; Infante Don Carlos of Spain; Duke Ernst Ludwig of Brunswick. The Persian shah Nadir had also sent his matchmakers. Perhaps the fastidious tsarevna might even have found some of the bridegrooms to her liking. However, none of them satisfied the empress, who, together with Osterman, wanted to marry Elizabeth "to a prince . . . who would never present any danger to them."[17] The thought of a grandson of Peter the Great growing up somewhere in Madrid or London with designs on the Russian throne was too much for Anna to endure. Therefore, she put off continually the matter of Elizabeth's marriage.

During the entire period of Anna's reign, Elizabeth was under constant surveillance. When in 1731 the tsarevna began to live permanently in St. Petersburg, Münnich received a secret order from the empress, instructing him to watch Elizabeth day and night and keep a record of the places she went and of the people who came to visit her. Aware of the surveillance, Elizabeth sought to keep her distance from politics; yet her name is mentioned in almost every political trial during Anna's reign. The cases of the Dolgorukiis and Artemii Volynskii show that neither Anna Ioannovna nor Biron took the tsarevna seriously as a political figure; nevertheless, they continued to treat her suspiciously. For this reason, many courtiers avoided meeting and talking with Peter the Great's daughter, as they feared arousing the mistrustful empress's suspicion. Life at Anna Ioannovna's court was radiant with luxury, but the lively and fun-loving Elizabeth found it boring there. Dances and masquerades were held only rarely since the empress and her courtiers preferred to spend their time playing cards and amusing themselves with jesters' antics. No wonder Elizabeth sought shelter in her palace near Tsaritsyn Lug (later *Marsovo pole*, Field of Mars) or in her country house, among those she held dear and far away from the empress's hostile gaze.

The tsarevna's court was not a large one: about a hundred persons including servants. Three gentlemen of the bedchamber—the Shuvalov brothers, Peter and Aleksandr, and Mikhail Vorontsov—stood out among the other courtiers. Elizabeth's close relatives, the countesses Skavronskaia and Gendrikova, served as ladies-in-waiting at the court. They were the daughters of those same Livland serfs—Catherine I's brothers and sisters—who, having left behind their pitchforks and milk-pails, were brought to St. Petersburg in 1726 and made landowners and counts. After Catherine I's death in 1727, they were all shunted to the sidelines and away from the throne occupied by Anna Ioannovna, a real tsar's daughter, who disdained yesterday's barefooted counts and countesses. Elizabeth had become the only source of support for Catherine I's kin. The tsarevna had to think continually about their welfare and upbringing, help them advance in their careers, settle their arguments, lend them money—in short, carry the burden of a high-ranking relative, whose power and influence always seemed boundless to provincial kinsfolk.

Life at Elizabeth's court differed markedly from that at the empress's. The tsarevna's courtiers were not given titles and orders or burdened with state duties. And more important, they were all young. In 1730 when Elizabeth turned twenty-one, the Shuvalov brothers were about twenty, the future chancellor of Russia, Mikhail Vorontsov, was sixteen, and the tsarevna's closest friend, Mavra Shepeleva, was twenty-two. They were all the children of the Petrine epoch; life in the European-style city of St. Petersburg seemed to them both natural and comfortable. Like Elizabeth they enjoyed merry-making, dances, and strolls. Elizabeth herself initiated all festivities, journeys, and entertainments. She was the best rider, dancer, singer, and even excelled all others in writing verses and songs. Her creative talent was awakened quite early, and one of her works, with imperfect but sincere verses, is a lament for a lost lover written in the early 1730s and has survived until our days.

The verses reflected a tragic love story that Elizabeth experienced early in Anna Ioannovna's reign. At that time the tsarevna fell in love with her chamber-page, Aleksandr Shubin. Their whirlwind romance was rudely interrupted by the empress, who, in January 1732, gave orders to Münnich to arrest Shubin and exile him to Siberia. Shubin's exile was to break off all connections between Peter's daughter and the Guards, who, according to an informant, had demonstrated their "devotion" to Elizabeth on more than one occasion. And though no documents had been found compromising Shubin, Anna remained inexorable. It is possible that in addition to political motives, Anna's actions were a result of the malicious envy which she felt toward her beautiful cousin.

Poor Shubin spent ten years in Siberia. In early 1742, immediately following the manifesto announcing her ascension to the throne, Empress Elizabeth Petrovna liberated her former beloved. However, the officer who was sent to Siberia on this special mission had a hard time locating Shubin in Siberian prisons, for Shubin's name was not mentioned on any list of prisoners. Having learned that he was being sought, Shubin was afraid to identify himself. He did not know that Elizabeth had become empress and feared that a more severe punishment from Anna Ioannovna was in store for him. Not so long before this Empress Anna had summoned the Dolgorukii princes from Siberia only to execute them. It was by sheer chance that Shubin was finally found. He returned to St. Petersburg and was received cordially by the court as well as by the empress herself. But the heart of his beloved then belonged to another man.

After she had exiled Shubin to Siberia, Anna Ioannovna did not relax her vigilance. She was eager to know what the tsarevna was doing, what her thoughts were, and what she spoke of with her intimate friends behind the closed doors of her small palace. The cheerful daughter of Peter the Great, known for her joie-de-vivre, was often quite sad. In one of Elizabeth's own songs, she appeals to the fast-running water in a stream, beseeching it to wash away the heaviness from her heart.

There seemed to have been no reason for such a young beauty to be melancholy and depressed. She might go and stay at the country residence in Tsarskoe Selo, or ride in the fields, or hunt with her hounds, or plan a sea cruise or a masquerade ball. Youth can find many sources of joy when there's time and imagination. Elizabeth could also have taken up housekeeping. It is evident from her letters that although she spent large sums of money, she was a zealous and even stingy mistress of the house. "Stepan Petrovich," she writes to a city manager, "please make an announcement regarding the sale of apples in Tsarskoe Selo and Pulkovo for those who may wish to buy; one merchant has already come to us and offered fifty rubles for the two gardens, but we refused him because he did not pay well; therefore, give instructions to sell the apples right now, while we are here, for they are already falling to the ground."[18]

But despite all these diversions, Elizabeth felt sad. According to a record found in the Secret Chancery archives, one day a guardsman named Pospelov, who stood watch at the tsarevna's palace, heard the mistress come out onto the porch steps and sing a song: "Oh my life, my poor life!" Back at the barracks, Pospelov told this story to his fellow soldier Ershov, who, without giving a second thought to what he had heard, blurted out: "She's a woman . . . And sings women's songs!"[19]

It was bluntly said, but it was the absolute truth. The well-being of an unmarried girl in the society of those days was unstable, and Elizabeth was no exception. The empress had only to say one word and you were off to a remote German province to become the wife of a German landowner or a duke and spend the rest of your life watching how your husband pinches pennies on candles or—just the opposite—how he squanders your fortune entertaining his mistresses. Just one word from the sovereign and you will find yourself a nun in some remote monastery, and the fate of the obstinate Princess Iusupova, who rotted in a dark, cold cell in the 1730s might well become your own. The most effective distraction from all these dangers for Elizabeth was the theater, the seventh wonder of the world.

In 1735, the precentor of the tsarevna's court choir, Ivan Petrov, was unexpectedly arrested by the Secret Chancery, and all of his papers were seized. Count Ushakov, chief of the Secret Chancery, interrogated Petrov, and then released him with a warning that he was not to tell anyone about his arrest, including Elizabeth.

Petrov's unpleasant ordeal stemmed from his participation in the theatrical performances staged at Elizabeth's court theater, and the papers confiscated by the Secret Chancery were the scripts of the roles he played. Anna sent these texts to Archbishop Feofan Prokopovich, a great theater connoisseur and an amateur political investigator, to see if there was anything in the comedy that might insult the honor of Her Imperial Majesty. This form of political accusation was quite common in those days. Only after cautious consideration did Feofan state that he saw no criminal implications in the papers, and Petrov was released.

It was obvious that the empress's interest in performances at the tsarevna's palace was of a nontheatrical nature. She knew that the performances were given behind closed doors, and according to Petrov's testimony, "no outsiders were admitted to those performances except for courtiers."[20] It was true, Elizabeth had formed a tight company, a sort of "closed world," into which no stool pigeons or spies from "the grand court" could penetrate. Only intimate and reliable people gathered around the tsarevna, those who shared partial disgrace with her and who knew for sure that they would never be able to make a career for themselves at Anna's court.

Now a small group of spectators—only friendly and reliable people—gathered in the tiny hall, with their eyes fixed on the stage, where before them in the faint candlelight the drama of Diana, "the splendid tsaritsa of the Palestinian countries" was played out. Diana, Tsar Geograph's wife, was a beautiful, kind, and merciful woman—just like the tsarevna. She is mercilessly tormented and oppressed by her vicious, stout, and freckled mother-in-law. And the spectators do not even have to exchange glances—it is obvious whom the homebred playwright Mavra Shepeleva has depicted on the stage. The audience weeps, for they cannot help Diana, who is slandered by her mother-in-law, disgraced, and banished to the desert. And to add insult to injury, a lioness makes away with her infant son.

But still there is a God in heaven and truth on earth! Travelers find the unfortunate woman and her child, and bring them to Geograph, who had been deceived by his mother. Everything is cleared up, the lies and schemes of the pernicious mother-in-law are exposed, and Diana triumphantly takes her place on the throne by her husband's side. Other performances staged in this theater, which later became known as "the opposition theater" in the tsarevna's court, took on the same allegorical form.

Theater has indeed both magic and force. The miracle of the victory of good over evil, beauty over wretchedness, and truth over injustice that theater makes possible took place before our heroine and her young friends time after time, and very likely they all believed that just such a miracle was about to happen to them.

And it did on November 25, 1741: Empress Elizabeth Petrovna stood before the window of her Imperial Winter Palace looking out at the city and the country of which she had become the sole sovereign. It was the first day of her twenty-year reign. And the first day had brought with it problems and cares the tsarevna had not imagined during Anna's reign. She had to decide immediately what to do with the detained Brunswick family. She had to forestall any unrest in the army, and secure her recognition in Moscow, Russia's old capital. A manifesto had to be issued announcing the accession of Peter's daughter to the throne, which, in fact, was no simple matter. It would be necessary to explain to the people of Russia and the world just how it came about that Elizabeth now occupied the throne. The whole world knew that Ivan Antonovich had ascended the throne in 1740 in accordance with the late empress's will, and all Russians, including Elizabeth, had sworn allegiance to him. Consequently, Ivan's power was legitimate and Elizabeth's had yet to be established. Among the royal families of Europe, usurpers, of course, had never been regarded with favor.

The first manifesto signed by the empress, on November 25, 1741, was ingenuous; it lacked the experienced hand of Andrei Osterman, who had been indispensable in such situations. But his time had passed, and he pined in the dungeon of Peter and Paul Fortress, from where he would be sent into eternal exile in Siberia. According to the manifesto, what had led Elizabeth to enter the Winter Palace riding on the Guards' shoulders were, first, the persistent requests from all "loyal subjects both ecclesiastic and secular," and the Guards in particular; and, second, "blood kinship" to Peter the Great and Empress Catherine I. Three days later another manifesto was issued that specified that Elizabeth had taken the throne in accordance with the last will and testament of Catherine I. However, this justification was imaginary: according to Catherine I's testament, preference was actually given not to Elizabeth, but to Elizabeth's nephew Charles Peter Ulrich, the thirteen-year-old Duke of Holstein.

Reference to the humble requests of loyal subjects disappeared from official documents just as quickly—the Guards' godmother did not want to be reminded of those who helped her ascend the throne. Elizabeth now strove to convince society that she had owed the throne to God's will and her own successful efforts. In the spring of 1742, the Triumphal Gates in Moscow were decorated with an allegorical depiction of the sun in a crown with the inscription: *Semet coronat* (self-coronation). The following commentary was provided in a pamphlet with engraved views of the Triumphal Gates: "This sunny event originates from the sun itself, just as Her Imperial Majesty, having an absolute right [to mount the throne] has performed the act of self-coronation."

It is clear that the picture for the Triumphal Gates had been prepared well in advance, as had been Elizabeth's demonstrative gesture made during the coronation ceremony which emphasized her absolute independence. *Sankt-Peterburgskie Vedomosti* reported on the festive ceremony, which had taken place in the Dormition Cathedral of the Moscow Kremlin: "Her Imperial Majesty placed the Imperial crown on her head with her own hand: *Semet coronat!*"

The coronation ceremony took place in the Moscow Kremlin according to the tradition that now added Peter the Great's daughter to the long line of Russian rulers. The Kremlin is a special place not only in Moscow but in the whole of Russia. It is not just a group of national monuments, magnificent ancient cathedrals and palaces, with Ivan (III) the Great's imposing bell-tower hovering over them. It is not just a high hill on which the foundation of Moscow's first wooden fortress was laid. The Kremlin represents a most important page in the history of Russia. The ground on which the Kremlin stands and the land around it are saturated with the blood of those who assaulted and defended its ancient walls and of those who were executed on its scaffolds and torn to pieces by raving mobs. The Kremlin has seen popular uprisings, fires and epidemics, the tartar khans and Napoleon. Within its walls people wove plots and committed murders; the Kremlin has witnessed the treachery of some and the courage of others. But primarily the Kremlin has always been the citadel of *power*. Power, its alluring and repulsive force, has always imparted a magic to this hill, and when a Russian steps onto Kremlin territory, he experiences incomprehensible agitation and fear. The apple orchard in full blossom on the slope of the hill and the swallows' cries above it in the sky seem odd and out of place here where the stately bell-tower of Ivan the Great is shining with gold.

Elizabeth was crowned in the Kremlin, in order to ensure her recognition by the Russian people. In the spring of 1742 she stood on the same spot in the Dormition Cathedral where her mother, Catherine I, had stood eighteen years earlier, in the spring of 1724. At that time Peter the Great had placed the crown on the head of his spouse, and now Elizabeth Petrovna placed the imperial crown on her own head herself, the very same crown with which Anna Ioannovna had ascended the throne in 1730. Elizabeth Petrovna's coronation ceremony was a festive, beautiful, and magnificent sight in accord with tradition that went back centuries. The ringing of countless bells, the glitter of gold church vessels, the song of the choir glorifying the empress, the heavy royal mantle lined with white ermine, the touch of the cold droplets of myrrh, with which the archbishop anointed Elizabeth's face—all this was to signify that God and, accordingly, the people recognized their new earthly ruler. Feasts and balls and the enthusiastic shouts of the Muscovites followed the coronation. The people of Moscow remembered how the young tsarevna, gay and slender, had pranced through the streets of the old capital mounted on a white steed on her way to hunts in the fields near Moscow.

In the very first days and weeks of Elizabeth's reign something arose that was unusual for the eighteenth century, a surprising combination of ideas, dogmas, and clichés that could be called only one thing: ideology. Of course, the empress alone could never have hit on this fine mix of ideas—she had advisers among the learned people, bishops, and faithful disciples of the late archbishop Feofan Prokopovich; then writers, playwrights, actors, and other credulous people developed and spread it.

Elizabeth's ideological platform was a very simple one: seeing the unbearable suffering of the Russian people under the rule of odious foreign favorites, those who spoiled Russia's welfare, she, Peter the Great's daughter, rose up against them and happiness would dawn once more. Yesterday's gloom and today's light, former ruin and current prosperity—this antithesis was proclaimed repeatedly throughout Elizabeth's reign. Never before had patriotic motifs been so fruitfully used to the advantage of the ruling regime as it strove to establish the legality of the power which it had usurped. "Indeed, old man, if Elizabeth the Great had not arisen, we Russians would have remained in pitch darkness and would never have lived to see the light," stated sincerely one of the characters in a propaganda play titled *Conversations of Two Russian Soldiers* (1743).

In his sermon published and circulated widely in 1742 Archbishop Dmitrii Sechenov stigmatized those whom he had until recently so faithfully served: "They had taken over our entire Fatherland; what spiteful poison they had spewed upon the faithful children of Russia; what persecution they had started of the church of Christ and the pious faith; theirs was a dark time and regime." Patriots probably got goose pimples as they read the above. But as if by magic "the purple-clad maiden" began to rule and everything took its normal course:

> O mother of your people!
> Nature created you
> To finish what Peter had begun.[21]

Thus proclaimed the Russian poet Aleksandr Sumarokov. And in another work, the prologue to the opera *Titus' Charity* titled "Following Sorrow Russia Rejoices Again," the goddess Astrea descends from the clouds to the unfortunate Rutenia (Russia), who is sitting among the ruins in the dark. Astrea "reassures Rutenia that the time of Peter the Great will be restored and complete prosperity will be returned to her children, and she persuades Rutenia to praise and glorify the supreme name of Her Imperial Majesty and to erect monuments in her honor."

It would be a mistake to assume that Elizabeth spent a lot of time thinking about the ideological aspects of her rein. Like Anna Ioannovna, she in no way aspired to be a philosopher queen. She had other things to worry about: what dress should she wear at the ball and did she really have a blemish on her cheek?

The empress was hopelessly in love with herself. Narcissus gazing at his reflection in a brook seems modest compared with Elizabeth, who spent her entire life among an ocean of mirrors in her palaces. But it is impossible for a male author to judge—was there no woman in the whole world more beautiful than Elizabeth? That is what her contemporaries thought regardless of their political views and temperaments.

In 1728, for example, the Spanish envoy Duc de Liria wrote to Madrid regarding nineteen-year-old Elizabeth: "I have seldom met a woman as beautiful as Princess Elizabeth. She has a marvelous complexion, beautiful eyes, excellent neck, and an incomparable figure. She is tall and very lively; she is a good dancer and rides a horse without any fear. She is quite intelligent, graceful, and extremely coquettish."[22]

Princess Sophia Augusta Fredericka of Anhalt-Zerbst (the future Catherine the Great) first saw Empress Elizabeth when the latter was thirty-four: "It is true that then one could not see her for the first time without being struck by her beauty and majestic bearing. She was a large woman, who, even though she was very stout, was not at all disfigured by it, nor did she experience any embarrassment from it in any of her gestures; her head was very beautiful as well . . .

"She danced with perfection and had a particular grace in all that she did, whether dressed as a man or a woman. One would have liked to be always looking at her, and only regretfully turned the gaze away, because no object could be found to replace her."[23] This account is of particular value. In her youth, Catherine II suffered from Empress Elizabeth so much that she could not help feeling angry with her in the years to come.

At this point, readers might like to leaf through illustrations and confirm these assertions. Alas! Almost all of the portraits of Elizabeth were painted when she was about fifty, and they all were made in the prevalent style of those days, heavy, motionless, and formal. Russia had no Velázquez or Rembrandt at that time to capture for us the lively charm of her beauty, the deep-blue color of her large eyes, or the elegance of her movements and poses.

Hard work on the part of tailors, jewelers, hairdressers, and the tsaritsa herself, who was the most strict judge of her appearance, added to Elizabeth's natural beauty. She had exquisite taste; her sense of proportion and harmony was superb, and she was meticulous concerning both her apparel and jewelry. Every public appearance was for her a major event for which she prepared herself as a general prepares himself for a battle.

Jean Favier, who had seen Elizabeth during the last years of her life, wrote that "she appears in public dressed invariably in court attire made of a rare and expensive fabric of the most delicate color, sometimes silver on white. Her head is always 'laden' with diamonds, and her hair is usually combed back where it is pulled up and tied with a long pink ribbon the ends of which dangle freely. She probably attaches to this hairdo the significance of a diadem for she alone appropriates the right to wear her hair thus. No other woman in the empire is allowed to wear her hair the way she does."[24]

Elizabeth's beauty faded with the years. Eighteenth-century women knew nothing about diet or physical exercise. Favier saw the empress when she was turning fifty and wrote that Elizabeth "is still fond of wearing fancy clothes, and with each passing day she becomes even more particular and fastidious in this respect. No woman has had a more difficult time reconciling herself to the loss of youth and beauty. It often happens that, having spent a good deal of time at the dressing-table, she becomes angry with the mirror, and gives orders to remove the headpiece and other articles of clothing which she had put on, cancels the theatrical performance or dinner she had planned on attending, and locks herself in her room refusing to see anyone whoever it might be."[25]

Elizabeth could not accept the fact that her time had passed, and new beautiful women were on the horizon who could compete with her. Of course she resisted succumbing as long as she could. In her memoirs, Catherine the Great wrote that the empress did not like to see elaborately dressed ladies at the balls. At one ball, Catherine recalls, Elizabeth called Naryshkina to come up to her and in front of everyone in the hall cut off the ribbon decoration that suited the hairdo of the young woman. Another time she herself cut off half of the hair curled up on the forehead of two ladies-in-waiting on the pretext that she did not like that style of hairdo. Later the two girls complained that while cutting off their hair the empress had scratched their skin as well.

Finally, in 1748 an edict signed by the empress was issued expressly forbidding the style of the hairdo worn by her majesty. The empress did not restrict herself to regulation of hairdos. One day, as Catherine the Great recalled, the outrageous idea occurred to Elizabeth to have the court ladies shave their heads. Weeping, the women obeyed the order; Elizabeth sent them black, poorly combed wigs, which they were forced to wear until their own hair had grown back. The fact is that in pursuit of beauty the tsaritsa had ruined her own hair while dyeing it, and as a result had to cut it all off. She wanted the other women to bravely share with her in this unfortunate mishap, which resulted in the issuance of a decree unprecedented in the history of world legislation. Until the end of her days Elizabeth Petrovna wanted everyone to play the role of the Chinese ambassador admiring her beauty as ardently as ever.

Masquerades, usually evening affairs, were a very special part of court entertainment and the highlight of Elizabeth's life: she simply could not do without them. They were a complicated form of amusement. Costumes, masks, dances, and music were only part of the affair. Guests would arrive wearing costumes and masks in accordance with the invitation cards that had been sent to them in advance. People without masks were also admitted but they could only occupy boxes along the side and observe people moving on the dance floor and on the stage. The guests in masks were treated to drinks and snacks in separate rooms, where they also played cards and participated in lotteries. The famous adventurer Casanova, who had attended a court ball in St. Petersburg, though already in 1765 during Catherine the Great's reign, wrote that tables were groaning with food, and the whole scene was a spectacle of "fanciful splendor" in terms of the decoration of the rooms as well as the guests' costumes.

Masquerade Ball. From I. N. Bozherianov, "*Nevskii prospekt.*" *Kul'turno-istoricheskii ocherk dvukhvekovoi zhizni Sankt-Peterburga* ("Nevskii Prospect." A Cultural and Historical Sketch of St. Petersburg at Two Hundred) (St. Petersburg, 1901–03), vol. 1, p. 144.

At masquerades, as at other festivities and holidays, court orchestras and singers with widely ranging repertoires could be heard. Music, mostly Italian, which prevailed in Europe in those days, was played constantly throughout the palace balls and feasts.

On rare occasions Elizabeth gave masquerades at which men dressed as women and women disguised themselves as men. According to Catherine the Great, everyone looked terrible, awkward, and ridiculous, except for the empress: men's clothing suited her perfectly, and such masquerades were intended to make her stand out.

"Ladies [are to] wear white caftans made of taffeta; cuffs, edgings and skirts are to be green, and lapels trimmed with a fine braid; [they are to] have on their heads a papillon-like embellishment with green ribbons; hair drawn up smoothly. Gentlemen [are to] wear white caftans, camisoles with small, slit cuffs; green collars, with buttonholes trimmed with braid, and these buttonholes decorated with small silver tassels."[26] These are not a designer's recommendations from a fashion journal for 1752, but rather an imperial edict that was to be strictly observed by all those who would show themselves at court.

Knowing her subjects' careless and lazy nature, Elizabeth saw to it that those participating in court masquerades demonstrated initiative and ingenuity in preparing their costumes, but only within the limits set forth in the regulations. In November 1750 an imperial decree was issued strictly requiring every member of noble families, "except minors," to attend public masquerades. Moreover, "no pilgrim or harlequin costumes . . . [these costumes were inexpensive and could be easily made—E.A.] and no one dare, under fear of penalty, to put on indecent dress of any kind."[27] The Guards at the entrance to the palace checked everyone's costumes, and there were as many as fifteen hundred guests.

The empress kept abreast of fashions. According to contemporaries, Elizabeth never put on one dress twice and, moreover, she changed her dresses several times a day. This may be so, as suggested by the account of a fire in her palace in Moscow in 1753 in which four thousand of the empress's dresses are said to have been destroyed.

Jacob Stählin, teacher of the heir to the throne, recalled that when Elizabeth died the new emperor found over fifteen thousand dresses in her wardrobe, "some of which had been worn but once while others never worn at all, two chests filled with silk stockings, several thousand pairs of footwear, and more than one hundred untouched lengths of splendid French fabric."[28]

In addition to performing their assigned duties, Russian diplomats accredited at courts in European countries were also busy purchasing fashionable novelties for the empress. Diplomats stationed in Paris, the capital of European fashion, found themselves in an especially difficult situation. In November 1759 Chancellor Mikhail Vorontsov wrote to his subordinates that the empress had learned about "a special shop" in Paris known as the "Au très gallant" where "the best articles for every season" were sold. The chancellor ordered that "a reliable person" be engaged who would buy the most fashionable items available there and send them without delay to St. Petersburg. Twelve thousand rubles were allocated to cover these expenses, an insignificant amount, considering the empress's appetite for splendor. The widow of Fedor Bekhteev, the Russian envoy to France, wrote to Elizabeth that her husband remained a debtor in Paris, for he had impoverished himself buying silk stockings for her majesty.

All ladies in high society were to follow the example set by Elizabeth. Every time they attended a court festivity they had to wear a new dress. As rumor had it, in order to prevent them from any deceptions, the Guards would mark their dresses with indelible ink or even the state seal when they left the palace so they could not wear a dress a second time!

But in spite of the displeasure this caused their husbands, the ladies did not cry over the spoiled dresses—the empress's example was so bewitching that everyone had become engrossed in problems of attire, and luxury had reached the point where apparel was changed twice a day. And although the ladies understood that they were supposed to dress modestly, enabling the empress to be the most dazzling of all, still in this atmosphere of "contrived coquetry," as Catherine the Great wrote, it was impossible to resist the temptation to outdo one another.

Men also raced to keep pace with fashion during Elizabeth's reign. It is remarkable that only a short time earlier the fathers of these Elizabethan dandies, attached to the old ways, had moaned while struggling into the tight caftans that became de rigeur during Peter's reign, and demanded that their beards, which had been shaved off at the will of the austere tsar-reformer, be placed in their coffin with them when they died. Now everything had magically changed. The frivolous dandy who devoted his entire life to fashionable clothes had become the hero of various satirical works. Ivan Elagin's satire *On Petimetr and the Coquettes,* in which he castigated this type of dandy, became quite popular in the 1750s. We see the dandy at home; the room reeks—the hairdresser is waving the dandy's hair. The dandy is in low spirits, for he has acquired too dark a suntan, and in those days it was improper for a member of high society to look swarthy. The following lines (which also apply to Russia today) describe the infatuation with foreign goods:

Here he drains all the fragrance of the perfumes
Which different countries supply.
And knowing well our fondness for novelty
They laugh and for no reason charge us triple.
And if they were to bring no lipstick from France
Our Petimetr would be done for like Troy without Pallas.

It was difficult for most noblewomen to compete with Elizabeth, as her resources were unlimited. In addition to the routine customs inspections of foreign merchant vessels. Of course, most goods did not interest Elizabeth, only fancy goods, apparel, fabrics, and other luxury items for women. By law the goods would not be released for sale until the empress had personally selected the items she wanted for herself. Otherwise her wrath was terrifying.

On July 28, 1751, she wrote to Vasilii Demidov, who served in Her Imperial Majesty's Cabinet: "I have been informed that a French ship has arrived with various ladies' attire and men's hats, and for women beauty-spots and gold taffeta of various types . . . have all this and the merchant brought here immediately."[29] When it became clear that the merchant had already sold part of the cargo to other followers of fashion Elizabeth was beside herself. His actions were understandable, as the empress was stingy and it was impossible to dicker with her. Demidov received a new order: "Summon the merchant and ask why he was lying when he said that he had sent all of the lapels and collars, which I had chosen. Not only is this not all of them, but there's not a single one of those which I saw, namely scarlet-colored. There were more than twenty of them; and similar ones were on the dresses which I selected, and now I demand them, so order him to find them and not keep them for someone else. And if [any one] . . . holds them back tell him from me that he will regret it (ladies included). Whoever I see wearing them will share his penalty."[30] The tsaritsa provided names of fashion seekers who might have bought the items and demanded that the merchant immediately take everything back from them, "and if they will not give them back, then you yourself can send for them taking my order with you."[31] It is difficult to imagine a document that could better characterize Elizabeth's personality and mores.

The luxury of Elizabeth's court and continual festivities required huge expenditures. The empress could take money from the state treasury, but her courtiers had to strain their own resources to keep up. No one wanted to commit the unthinkable and show up at a masquerade in an old gown or, while impersonating shepherds and shepherdesses, come dressed in the clothing of their servants. Elizabeth's grandees aspired to the very best and most expensive Parisian goods. The nobility of the capital decorated their homes with French furniture, paintings, and splendid dinnerware. Of special importance was the outfitting of the carriage: the horses' trappings and harnesses, richly dressed coachmen, footmen standing on the footboards, preferably tall and dark-skinned. But not every nobleman could afford all this. The luxury of Elizabeth's era was on a large scale, but it lacked the sophistication and polish characteristic of the high nobility of the Russian empire beginning with the reign of Catherine the Great, who wrote ironically of Elizabeth's time: "It is not rare to see coming from an immense courtyard full of mire and foulness of all sort that belongs to a hovel made of rotten wood, a lady covered with jewels and superbly dressed, in a magnificent carriage, pulled by six old nags, shabbily harnessed, and badly combed valets, wearing a very pretty livery that they dishonor with the awkwardness of their comportment."[32]

The most wealthy of the grandees made it a rule to have an "open table," which meant they had to treat the empress and her extensive retinue to fine food at the drop of a hat should they appear unannounced. Vast sums were spent on this. "Feeling sorry" for her diamond-studded retinue, the empress ordered that their salaries be paid them a year in advance so that they could afford to dress for the next festivity. They still did not have enough money. One of the richest men of the time, Chancellor Mikhail Vorontsov, owner of hundreds of serfs, factories, and shops, incessantly begged the empress to pay him his earnings in the form of landed estates, and then, having obtained them, he immediately turned around and asked the state to buy the lands back from him. He needed money, money, and more money. In one of his requests the chancellor wrote sadly that he was obliged to buy and build new palaces, to provide himself with carriages and servants, whom he must dress in new livery, not to mention the expenditures for illuminations and fireworks. With a sigh "the poor man" concluded: "My post forces me to head a ministerial and not a philosophical life,"[33] apparently presuming that only philosophers secluded from the world's hustle and bustle could afford to live in poverty. When Count Peter Shuvalov, the richest of Elizabeth's officials, died, his estate was valued at the astronomical sum of 588,000 rubles. But even this was not enough to pay off Shuvalov's debts, which amounted to 680,000 rubles. That is what Elizabeth's extravagance led to.

From all that has been said before, one can see that the empress's personality was not as pleasant as her outward appearance. The majority of palace guests were not able, as we are, to peek behind the scenes of the never ending celebration, although many realized that Elizabeth was not all charm and grace.

In 1735 Lady Rondeau wrote of her impressions after meeting the tsarevna: "She has an affability and sweetness of behaviour that insensibly inspired love and respect. In public she has an unaffected gaiety, and a certain air of giddiness, that seem entirely to posses her whole mind; but in private, I have heard her talk in such a strain of good sense and steady reasoning, that I am persuaded the other behaviour is a feint . . ."[34]

Favier revealed more of the truth, having had the opportunity to observe the empress very late in her life: "Through her kindness and humaneness one can frequently see her pride, arrogance, sometimes even cruelty, but most of all her suspiciousness. Being highly jealous of her great status and supreme power, she is easily frightened by all that might threaten to lessen or divide that power. On more than one occasion she proved to be extremely ticklish concerning this point. To make up for it Empress Elizabeth has mastered perfectly the art of pretension. The secret corners of her heart often remain inaccessible even for the oldest and most experienced courtiers, with whom she is never more cordial than when she is stripping them of rank and favor."[35]

Those who lived day in and day out with the empress had no illusions. They saw how mean, intolerant, petty, and crude Elizabeth could be. Relatives, courtiers, and servants suffered more than a little from her naggings and suspicions. Having personal relations with the empress was harder than walking over ice in high-heeled dance shoes. Catherine II recalled that speaking in her majesty's presence was a no less difficult task than knowing the exact time of her dinner hour. There were numerous subjects of conversation that Elizabeth did not like. For instance, one must not mention the king of Prussia, nor Voltaire, nor illnesses, nor the deceased (she had even issued an order forbidding funeral processions to pass by the Winter Palace or along adjacent streets), nor beautiful women, nor French manners, nor science. All of these topics of conversation displeased the empress. In addition she was very superstitious, and it was unwise to contradict her beliefs. When she harbored grudges against someone, she had a tendency to distort everything he said, and since those around her knowingly turned her against very many people, no one could be sure that she did not have anything against him. As a result, conversation was a tricky matter. It frequently happened that the empress threw down her napkin in vexation and left the room.

The empress's anger was frightening, and she would let it rain on her retinue just as soon as the gilded doors had closed behind the last guest. Her beautiful features would become monstrously distorted, her face would turn crimson as she began to scream shrilly and hideously: "she reprimanded me importunately, and with anger and fury . . . I saw the instant when she was going to hit me, at least I feared it: I knew that she beat her women, her retinue, and even the horsemen sometimes in her rage . . ."[36]

She had apparently inherited many personality traits from her father, an unbalanced, difficult, impulsive, and impetuous man. This charming beauty, who had always demonstrated in her decrees a natural maternal magnanimity, unwaveringly sent a pregnant woman to the torture chamber and wrote a directive in this regard to the head of the Secret Chancery in the same curt, severe, and cruelly businesslike tones that her father had once used when writing to his chief of political investigations. It is obvious that she possessed her father's intolerance and nervous energy. Just like Peter, she sang in the church choir not only because she liked it, but also because she could not wait for the church service to end. At church she continually moved from place to place and even left the service unable to sit through the whole liturgy.

Also like her father, Elizabeth was always on the move and liked to take long trips. She especially liked fast winter rides in a comfortable carriage with heating and a chamber-pot. She covered the distance from St. Petersburg to Moscow (715 versts) in just forty-eight hours—unheard of speed for that time. This was achieved by changing horses every twenty to thirty versts along the smooth winter road. However, sometimes the empress rode unhurriedly, staying in palaces especially built for her along the route. From St. Petersburg to Moscow there were twenty-five of them—on an average one every twenty-five versts. And in each one preparations were made to receive a most fastidious mistress, who had to have only the best, the tastiest, and the most pleasant of everything. One gets the impression that the majority of these trips were void of purpose, not to mention state necessity. This was simply a movement through space dictated by fancy, an inexplicable desire for a change of scene.

We do not want to portray Elizabeth as a villain in an angelic mask. This is not the case. Elizabeth was not a deep, contemplative person—her own mirrored reflection suited her just fine; she was not tormented by noble passions. In life, just as in travel, she was motivated by whim, but was completely natural in her whimsical ways. She was often gay, seldom gloomy, more good than evil, almost always frivolous, sometimes angry, but fast to cool down. Elizabeth never had the kind of upbringing that would cultivate or refine her character. In advising his government to invite the twelve-year-old Elizabeth to France to become the fiancée of Louis XV, the French envoy Campredon admitted that she lacked a proper upbringing, while expressing the hope that with her flexible personality she would imbibe the manners and customs of the country that would become her second fatherland.

The engagement to Louis XV did not work out, and the wild creature grew in accordance with the dictates of her own nature. The Petersburg nobility disliked the empress, insulted by the spectacle of her rides in the company of erstwhile laundresses and footmen. They criticized her for her fondness of English beer. But like her father, Elizabeth did not strive to show or prove anything to anyone. Life was merrier, easier, and pleasanter that way.

Simple behavior—typical for Elizabeth—served her well when she made her way to power. The Guards loved their godmother, who never snubbed them and was always kind and accessible to them, which always makes a ruler popular. But the nobility perceived the tsarevna's and subsequently the empress's affable behavior as proof of her low birth. In their own circles high officials and their wives, who themselves could not boast of any particular virtues, condemned Elizabeth's frivolity and her plebeian habits. The empress had acquired this style of behavior during her childhood as she grew up in the home of her great father, who lived simply and modestly, like a Dutch burgher. But like Peter's, so Elizabeth's lifestyle was not at variance with the banal truth that the ruler's democratic ways in everyday life do not imply democracy in his or her rule.

When, in accordance with the tradition of her ancestors, the empress set out on a pilgrimage on foot, this was no hypocrisy either. She did indeed believe sincerely and superstitiously in God. But what a hike it was! Elizabeth's differed from the journey of other pilgrims along the fifty-verst road from Moscow to the Trinity–St. Sergius Monastery, one of the holiest of places in Russia. The long trek by foot to the monastery of the fourteenth-century Russian saint Sergius of Radonezh was rough; it purified believers and prepared them for an encounter with the holy shrine. Elizabeth, on her part, surrounded by her splendid retinue, favorites, and dance partners, drove to just outside the Moscow city gates onto the Trinity Road and walked five to ten versts, enjoying the natural surroundings and pleasant conversation.

And then at the tsaritsa's command tents appeared in the empty fields as if by magic, and in them Elizabeth could enjoy all the conveniences and forms of amusement conceivable at that time. The tsaritsa relaxed for several days, entertaining herself with horseback riding and hunting, and then moved on toward the monastery. At times she got in a carriage and drove off to rest in Moscow and then a week or so later she returned to the place where she had left off previously and walked along the road to the next planned stop. Such pilgrimages could continue for weeks and even months. And it would be a mistake to accuse the God-fearing tsaritsa of sanctimoniousness or hypocrisy. She was simply more comfortable like this; such was her whim.

Nevertheless, the life that in truth so resembled a perennial feast had its somber side. Contemporaries noted that the empress often suddenly left the palace by carriage late at night in order to sleep somewhere else. And we can say almost with certainty that it was not fancy but fear which drove the empress from one palace to another. Throughout the twenty years of her reign, since the night when she broke into Anna Leopol'dovna's palace, Elizabeth knew no rest. She feared a night coup, the sound of soldiers boots outside her bedroom door.

Elizabeth's genuine passion for changing and redecorating interiors was connected to her fear of assassination. Catherine II testified that the empress never left the palace for a walk or to go to the theater without ordering that something be changed in the arrangement of furniture or objects in the room. Most frequently her bed was moved from room to room. The empress rarely slept in the same place twice in a row, and she had no bedroom. Catherine's observations confirm the opinion of the artist Aleksandr Benois, who after studying the plans and inventory of the huge palace at Tsarskoe Selo, in which everything was taken into account and well thought out, came to the conclusion that the empress had had no bedroom. Benois also explained this as a result of her fear of a night coup. We believe that in ordering her bed moved, or in leaving suddenly to stay the night in another palace, the superstitious empress feared not only a coup, but the evil eye and witchcraft as well, especially after a frog bone wrapped in hair had once been found under her bed—a sure sign of a sorcerer at work.

But even more surprising is the fact that throughout her twenty-year reign, the tsaritsa did not close her eyes even once at night. She never slept at all at night! In his notes, the jeweler Posier wrote: "She never went to bed earlier than 6 A.M. and slept until midday and later; consequently Elizabeth would send for me during the night and give me whatever orders her fancy came up with. And sometimes I had to remain all night waiting for her to remember that she had summoned me. Sometimes it happened that I returned home and only a minute later was summoned by her again. She often was angry that I had not waited for her."[37]

The tsaritsa's nightly vigils were not merely whimsical. She had actual reason to fear for her life. In 1742 her chamber servant Aleksandr Turchaninov was arrested along with two of his friends from the Guards for a plot to murder Elizabeth and her close associates at night. We believe that the tsaritsa was shaken by this incident and that her hands trembled when she read the ominous part of the interrogation record of Turchaninov's accomplice Ivan Kvashnin, an ensign in the Preobrazhenskii Regiment, where he stated that after the first unsuccessful assassination attempt they reasoned: "Be things as they may [for now], but in the future the task remains, and if we do not [succeed] then others will finish it off."[38] Elizabeth paid for her desire to seize power with a lifelong fear of a night coup.

* * *

It would seem that Baroque architecture, with its whimsical volutes, fanciful curves, sensual and voluptuous luxury, was created especially for Elizabeth as a precious frame for a rare diamond. And Elizabeth spared no money for the frame. Whereas she haggled with merchants over each brooch, without as much as looking she signed gigantic building estimates which the master-architect Francesco Bartolomeo Rastrelli brought for her approval. It is to this merry genius that we are indebted for the architectural masterpieces of the Italian Baroque style in Russia, particularly in St. Petersburg. Most of his splendid works were built with extraordinary speed. However, it took him eleven years to erect the palace in the capital's suburb of Tsarskoe Selo.

Even as late as the 1730s, during Anna Ioannovna's reign, Tsarskoe Selo was a remote undeveloped suburb. In the meadow stood the small palace, which Peter the Great had presented to Catherine I and which was inherited by Elizabeth. The tsarevna had grown to love this estate, where she could hunt and spend her time merrily with friends far from Anna's court and free from spies. But living there amid thick virgin forests was dangerous. This follows from an extant letter of Elizabeth sent in 1735 from Tsarskoe Selo to her steward in St. Petersburg with the request to send her immediately gunpowder and bullets to ward off the numerous robbers who threatened to attack even the tsarevna's palace.

Everything in Tsarskoe Selo changed drastically when Elizabeth came to power. Dear to her because of the memories of her parents, it was not only her paternal home, but had the same meaning for her as Preobrazhenskoe did for Peter the Great, or Izmailovo for Anna Ioannovna. Here she had spent her happy childhood and carefree youth. Here she would hide from disgraceful old age, and here she would die. So Rastrelli was commissioned to build a new palace and not to spare either materials or money. However, despite all his talent, he could not satisfy the tastes of the empress, who forced him again and again to redo everything. And at times it was unclear just what she wanted him to do. But when the great architect finally completed his masterpiece, there was no end to the rapturous acclaim.

A magnificent view unfolded before those who made the trip from St. Petersburg to Tsarskoe Selo. They saw a huge gold mansion standing amid forests and fields, glittering against the blue sky. As Rastrelli wrote, the entire façade of the palace was built in the Italian style. The column capitals, the pediments, window casings, the pillars supporting the balconies, and statues placed on pedestals along the upper balustrade of the palace, all were covered with gilt. And hovering over all this splendor were the resplendent gold domes of the court church.

Palace at Tsarskoe Selo. From I. N. Bozherianov, "*Nevskii prospekt*." *Kul'turno-istoricheskii ocherk dvukhvekovoi zhizni Sankt-Peterburga* ("Nevskii Prospect." A Cultural and Historical Sketch of St. Petersburg at Two Hundred) (St. Petersburg, 1901–03), vol. 1, p. 128.

But the interior decoration of the palace dazzled the guests even more. Before them stretched a suite of sunlit rooms and halls that seemed to recede into a warm, golden, and mirrored eternity. Suddenly something would flash within its very depths and begin to move closer. The wave of light would ripple and grow, eventually accompanied by the rustling of fine fabrics and delicate fragrances—it was the empress approaching. This is how Aleksandr Benois describes her appearance: "From a scarcely visible but nevertheless clearly bejeweled point, she slowly turned into a distinctly outlined figure clad in rustling brocade and adorned with precious stones."[39]

And here is another version of one of Elizabeth's striking appearances which staggered her contemporary, the French diplomat Maurice Messelière: "The beauty of the rooms and their wealth are amazing; all this, however, was overshadowed by the pleasant spectacle of 400 ladies who were very beautiful and very richly dressed, and were lined up along both sides of the hall. Another cause for delight was soon added to this one: the sudden darkness that was caused by the simultaneous drawing of all curtains was chased away in that same instant by the light of 1,200 candles which were reflected on all sides in the mirrors."[40]

Messelière was referring to the 300 mirrors in gilt frames that occupied the spaces between the windows in the Grand Hall, stretching from floor to ceiling. The secret of the effect described by the French diplomat lay in the fact that all of the candles reflected not only in the mirrors but also in the smooth surface of the inlaid parquet, creating the illusion of a magical expansion of space.

"Then all at once," as Messelière recollects, "an 80-piece orchestra started up, and the ball was declared opened. Throughout the first minuets a dull but nevertheless majestic noise could be heard. Then the door was quickly opened wide, and we beheld a shining throne from which the empress was just descending and surrounded by her courtiers she proceeded into the ball room." A dead silence fell over the room and everybody heard Elizabeth's voice. The hall "was large enough: twenty couples could dance the minuet at a time, which was an extraordinary sight. The ball lasted until eleven o'clock, when the court marshal came to inform her majesty that supper was ready. Everyone entered a large, decorated hall lit by 900 candles, wherein a beautiful encrusted table stood set for 400 persons. A vocal and instrumental concert began overhead on the musicians' gallery, which continued throughout the banquet. There were dishes representing all possible national cuisines and there were French, German and Italian servants who asked their fellow countrymen among the guests what they wanted to eat."[41]

This supper apparently took place in the Picture Gallery Dining Room, the walls of which were closely hung with canvases by famous artists, mounted in narrow gilt frames, which created the illusion of one large pictorial panel. Other halls had their own distinct splendor.

Guests took special delight in the Amber Room. Its walls were decorated with panels inlaid with different kinds of amber which had been presented to Peter the Great by the Prussian king Frederick William and installed by Rastrelli in Elizabeth's palace. Today at Elizabeth's palace one can no longer see this unique masterpiece. The Germans seized Tsarskoe Selo in the autumn of 1941, dismantled and carried off the Amber Room along with many other valuable trophies. It has not been seen since. Many different versions as to its whereabouts have circulated throughout the postwar years. On several occasions there were rumors that it had resurfaced in Germany. Yet each time these hopes proved false—the original Amber Room seems lost permanently, though painstaking restoration has re-created it. It is possible that it no longer exists, just like dozens of statues and decorations from Petersburg parks and palaces that were ruthlessly destroyed by the Germans. Those who survived the Leningrad siege of 1941–1944 recall that after the war the vast fields near Peterhof and Tsarskoe Selo were covered with snow-white crushed marble—systematic hammer strokes had destroyed statues the Wehrmacht deemed to be of no use to Germany. Wanton destruction may also have been the fate of the Amber Room.

Elizabeth furnished the palace with rare furniture and Chinese porcelain. The gleaming gilt carvings, the tall sky-blue tiled stoves and the shining intricately patterned parquet floors of precious hardwoods, all were strikingly beautiful. Still full of the rich impressions of the luxurious palace, the splendid ladies, fine cuisine, and music, guests would go out for fresh air onto a spacious balcony with a hanging garden. Aleksandr Benois described it well: "On both sides, colonnades receded into the depths of the garden with their gilded capitals, decorations and statues. The entire depth of this strange hall without a ceiling was taken up by the façade of the church with its semi-bell tower, and above it glistening in the air were the gilt dome and cross. The pattern of inlaid parquetry gave way to the bright and colorful designs of curving flowerbeds; the furniture consisted of stone benches placed under cherry, apple and pear trees."[42]

After a pleasant stroll one could again immerse oneself in the fever of celebration. When twilight was setting in, the guests would all take to the windows and balconies for a fiery feast. Pyrotechnics were then a true art form, the secret of which has been lost. Allegorical figures were grouped together and, according to the idea behind the display, were lit in a specific order. White and colored sparks burning at different speeds created images strikingly beautiful and clear. Suddenly out of the darkness an orchard of fiery trees or a fiery lake would come into view and along its banks flaming animals ran, carriages moved, and in the sky above gods and birds hovered and soared. The fireworks ended with a colorful grand finale, which filled the sky with a fantastic multitude of falling stars. The entire sky would explode with hundreds of rockets firing multicolored splashes and streaks into the air. The celebration was officially over, yet the festive feeling would linger on long afterward.

Not all of the residences belonging to the nobility, or even to the empress herself, could match the comfort and splendor of the palace at Tsarskoe Selo. Catherine the Great recalled in her notes how she and her husband, Peter Fedorovich, heir to the throne, were nearly killed one night at Gostilitsy near St. Petersburg in the home of the empress's favorite Aleksei Razumovskii. Two Guards noticed that the huge house was slowly collapsing and awakened the sleeping guests in time. Catherine wrote: "We had scarcely crossed the threshold when there was a tumult all around us and a noise like that of a vessel being launched from a shipyard."[43] The sinking building crushed sixteen servants to death who were asleep on its lower floor. Fires were also common in palaces in those days, starting usually from careless servants or improperly functioning stoves. In comparison to these dangers, drafts blowing through the uncomfortable rooms, the badly scratched furniture, which was transported to wherever the empress went, the lack of even the simplest conveniences, and the abundance of vermin (cockroaches, bedbugs, rats) seemed insignificant.

* * *

The poet Gavrila Derzhavin named Elizabeth's reign the age of song. Those twenty years were indeed outstanding in the history of Russian musical culture. The empress's personal predilection and her own musical talent played a major part. There was so much music at her court that Elizabeth's reign resembled a never-ending international music festival. As we can read in the decree issued on September 10, 1749, "From this day forth music is to be heard at court every afternoon: on Mondays—dance music, on Wednesdays—Italian music, and on Tuesdays and Fridays, as per previous decree—[musical] comedies."

Italian music predominated at court. In 1742 the composer, conductor, and director Francesco Araia came to Russia from Italy with his orchestra and troupe of actors and singers and immediately set about the staging of grandiose opera performances. Opera was then the pinnacle of the theatrical and musical arts. Eighteenth-century opera differs greatly from modern opera. Solo and choral singing as well as ballet numbers alternated with recitations. Opera directors were compelled to work within the strict frames of classicism, taking plots from Greek or Roman sources and assuring that evil was always punished and that goodness prevailed. Allegorical prologues were staged before the main performances for propaganda purposes; they were designed to convince viewers that Russia had never known a better autocrat than Elizabeth Petrovna. Actors depicted on the stage such complicated figures as "The Prosperity of Russia," or "The Joy of Loyal Subjects," or finally "Striving Crowned with Rejoicing." "At the end of the opera," according to a newspaper article in *Sankt Peterburgskie Vedomosti* for 1742, "her imperial majesty showed her pleasure by a clapping of the hands, which also was done by all other viewers, while foreign gentlemen ministers testified that such a perfect and fine opera, especially as regards theater decorations, scenery and mechanisms, has never been seen before."[44]

Russia's acquaintance with Italian opera had an important effect on Russian performing arts. It was in Italian operas that the first Russian opera singers performed, among them Maksim Poltoratskii, Mikhail Berezovskii, and Stepan Rashevskii. "These young opera singers," wrote Jacob Stählin, "stunned listeners and experts with their precise phrasing, the purity with which they performed long and difficult arias, the artistic transmittal of cadence, their recitation and natural mimicry."[45] In 1758 a seven-year-old boy named Dmitrii Bortnianskii, who was to become an eminent composer, performed in the opera *Alcesta*. Russian dancers began more and more commonly to perform in ballet numbers.

Operas still remained a rare pleasure, as their staging was too complicated. Orchestral and choral concerts were more accessible. The court choir had long since recruited strong-voiced Ukrainians and was reputed for its high level of art, in which Elizabeth herself was a connoisseur. During her reign classical music went beyond the walls of the palace. Beginning in 1748, for the first time in St. Petersburg public concerts were held with open access to all except "drunks, flunkies, and debauched women," as was written in the poster announcing the first concert. Thanks to the empress's passion for music, new instruments found their place in Russian culture, such as the harp, mandolin, and guitar. Some music historians believe that Elizabeth herself was founder of the Russian romance. She herself sang several romances that were popular in the eighteenth century. She also loved Russian folk songs, which were played during the intermissions of theatrical performances and on one occasion "her imperial majesty said that the Russians are more receptive to something Russian than foreign."[46] Peter the Great's daughter had not distanced herself from her people.

The horn orchestra, an extraordinary form of art, was first practiced during Elizabeth's reign. It was invented in 1748 by the Czech hornist Johann Anton Maresh. He came to Russia and found a patron in the court's chief master of the hunt, Stepan Naryshkin. And so once in 1757 during the empress's horseback ride in the autumn fields near Moscow, she was startled by the sound of majestic music that seemed to be pouring from the heavens. Fugues by Bach could be heard in the fields. Naryshkin had prepared this surprise, a concert by a horn orchestra consisting of dozens of musicians all blowing into their huge instruments. They might not have been able to read notes, but they counted the beats and pauses in order not to miss their parts. The horn orchestra was something like a giant-size living organ. It was possible to listen to it only at a distance of some 300 to 500 meters, no closer.

However, the empress did not ride up close to the living organ and so did not see the other side of the musical miracle, just as she did not see the lives of her subjects. Very soon such orchestras would become the symbol of serfdom, the special luxury of the richest landlords, owners of thousands of slaves.

Only the dramatic theater rivaled music in popularity. Its foundations were laid during Elizabeth's reign at the military school on Vasil'evskii Island, where young noblemen were educated. The empress had loved the theater since enjoying the small opposition theater at her palace during Anna Ioannovna's reign. She sometimes exhausted her courtiers by refusing to leave the theater for hours or nearly days, demanding repetition of her favorite plays.

Of course, this theater only vaguely resembled the theater of today. Strictly bound by the dogmas of Classicism with its mandatory five acts, unities of place and time, and exalted language, it might appear to us pretentious, boring, and ridiculous. The actor's behavior, according to a contemporary textbook for the art of acting, was in no way supposed to resemble people's natural behavior. An actor was forbidden to put his hands in his pockets or form a fist, except when portraying simple folk, who were allowed to use such crude and unattractive gestures.

Here are the most important recommendations to an actor going on stage: expressing disgust, one should "turn the head to the left side, extend the arms and slightly raise them in the opposite direction as if pushing away the odious object." Expressing surprise, "one should raise both hands and place them on the upper part of the chest, palms turned toward the audience." "In great grief or sorrow it is possible and even praiseworthy and attractive to bow completely, cover the face for some time by pressing both hands or the elbow to it and in this position to mutter some words to oneself into one's elbow, even though the public might not make them out—the force of the grief will be understood by all this mumbling, which is more eloquent than words."[47]

Having read this, try to reproduce at least one such figure before your unsuspecting family members and observe the resulting effect—it will no doubt be rather strong. But do not think that audiences during Elizabeth's times would react the same way. The language of their theater was as normal for them as the language of our theater is for us, and probably ours will be just as strange for future generations.

The eighteenth-century audience, just as spectators of all times, was enthralled by the theatrical action itself. As Gogol wrote in 1842, "There the balconies and the rails of the theaters moan: everything is shaken from head to toe, all has been transformed into one feeling, into one moment, into one person, and all the people met like brothers moved by one emotional impulse."[48] That's how it was one hundred years after Elizabeth, and how it will be one hundred years after we are gone. What does it matter how sorrow is portrayed, if the entire hall freezes and cries because it believes it is real!

Shakespeare's *Hamlet* was altered beyond recognition by Sumarokov. The restless prince overthrows Claudius, marries Ophelia, and becomes the king of Denmark. But still the great monologue "To Be or Not to Be" remained and moved the eighteenth-century audience just as it did Shakespeare's contemporaries, and just as it moves us now.

And how the audience laughed at the comic heroes of Sumarokov, the first Russian to write comedies. Everyone laughed: the empress in the gilt box, the nobility in the stalls, simple folk in the gallery—it was all so familiar and so funny:

> Show me a cold-hearted clerk in the prikaz,
> A judge that doesn't understand what is written in the ukaz;
> Show me a dandy who cocks his nose
> because he's thinking of his beautiful hair,
> who, in his own opinion, was born for love
> and to win over a girl who's a fool like himself.
> Show me a proud miser inflated like a frog
> who will face the noose for a penny . . .

For Sumarokov the playwright was a critic of public vices. But his muse provided him with other motifs as well: he even ventured to instruct the empress. Thus his hero, from a drama devoted to Russian history, called on the empress to be kind and just, as her father had been, and to make sure that only worthy people surrounded her.

Elizabeth listened to all this, applauded, praised and . . . that was that. She took no heed of these admonitions, and she would have been surprised if she were told that such appeals had been addressed to her. The empress, who was always touchy about her power, was sincerely convinced that she was her great father's worthy successor, mother of her people, an excellent sovereign and benefactress. She simply did not catch Sumarokov's hints.

* * *

Having seized power, Elizabeth assumed that her task as statesman would be simple enough: she had only to eliminate the distortions and accretions the state had acquired since the death of Peter the Great and see to it that all decrees and regulations issued by Peter were precisely followed. However, the "restoration" policy conceived by Peter's daughter was a complete failure. It is impossible to restore the past, even a past so recent and so glorious, and it is likewise impossible to live by the laws of the past. Elizabeth immediately instructed the Senate to review all the laws issued after Peter's death and to nullify those that contradicted Petrine principles. The work was begun, but by 1750 only those decrees that had been issued during the first four years of the post-Petrine period (1726–1729) had been reviewed. Finally, in 1754 Peter Shuvalov, who had gained some influence by that time, took it upon himself to tell the empress and the Senate that this way was mistaken, and what had to be done was to prepare a new code of laws, for "manners and customs change with time, thus dictating the necessity to change the laws."[49]

Formally, the empress's participation in the ruling of the country was considerable—the number of decrees signed by the empress increased compared with the time of Anna Ioannovna. But early in her reign it became clear: Elizabeth had neither the strength nor the competence to cope with the heavy workload of complex decisions generated by state affairs. If Peter the Great had made no decree that would apply to the matter under consideration, if a legislative initiative was required or a new law had to be made, the empress would simply defer the decision and leave the problem alone for years. She had never been trained to perform state duties, and she had no desire whatsoever to engage in the hard and exhausting work of a statesman. No doubt she might have had some good motives, too, a desire to demonstrate her "motherly kindness" to the people, but she did not know how to go about this. Also, she had so little time, with all the dresses to try on, and performances and festivities to attend.

For this reason, after having formally abolished the Cabinet of Ministers as Anna Ioannovna had done, she entrusted individual ministers to attend to state matters informally. However, it was very difficult for them to seek an audience with the tsaritsa in order to get her signature on their documents. In 1755 Mikhail Vorontsov wrote to Elizabeth's favorite, Ivan Shuvalov: "I flattered myself with the hope of receiving through your highness her majesty's decision regarding a certain Mr. Douglas, before the court had moved to Tsarskoe Selo; and now I do not dare submit my request again for fear of angering her majesty and thereby inhibiting her amusement in such a merry and dear place; I hope, however, that [my request] will be remembered at the right time."[50] As we see, the whole problem was in choosing the right moment to get the sovereign's signature. That was no easy task, however, as one look at the tsaritsa's schedule will prove.

All her time was absorbed in concerts, theatrical performances, balls, strolls, and masquerades. According to the court record book, this is how Elizabeth spent January 1751:

January 1st—a New Year celebration, 2nd—a masquerade, 3rd—visiting Aleksandr Buturlin, 4th—Christmas Eve, 6th—a French tragedy, 7th—a French comedy, 8th—a court masquerade, 9th—a carriage ride and visit to Sumarokov, 13th—a liturgy at the church, Courtag at the Palace, 15th—a court ball, 18th—a public masquerade, 20th—Courtag, a French comedy, 22nd—a court masquerade, 24th—a Russian tragedy, 25th—a French comedy, 28th and 29th—courtiers' weddings.

Empress Elizabeth on horseback. From I. N. Bozherianov, "*Nevskii prospekt.*" *Kul'turno-istoricheskii ocherk dvukhvekovoi zhizni Sankt-Peterburga* ("Nevskii Prospect." A Cultural and Historical Sketch of St. Petersburg at Two Hundred) (St. Petersburg, 1901–03), vol. 1, p. 111.

The empress's schedules for other months and other years were similar. The reader can easily calculate that the empress devoted the majority of her time to various forms of entertainments, after which she would rest up and prepare for the next round. In a word, there was no time left to work.

However, Elizabeth's neglect of state business did not create a political situation that was acute or volatile. The state machine set in motion by Peter the Great continued its monotonous work. Thanks to eternal bureaucratic principles, this machine had survived and remained productive after its creator's death. Among Elizabeth's close associates were not only "play-mates" for her entertainment, but also truly entrepreneurial people. Elizabeth's reign became an important stage in the emancipation of the Russian nobility; many laws on the status of the nobility, formulated by Elizabeth's government, came into force later, during the reigns of Peter III and Catherine II. In the period from 1744 to 1747 a general census of the population was conducted, the first census since Peter the Great's time. After this census the people were granted a reprieve from poll-tax debts accumulated over the last seventeen years, which was seen not only as a humane gesture, but also as a reasonable political and administrative act: collecting taxes that were in arrears was a thankless task and produced little results. Timely and full payment of taxes was traditionally considered in Russia either a strange demonstration of valor or outright stupidity.

By 1750 the economic crisis that had been brought on by the strain on resources of the long Northern War of 1700–1721 was almost over. The extensive methods of management that had been imposed by Peter the Great in the course of his reforms began to yield tangible results. By the mid-eighteenth century the demand for high-quality Russian iron had reached the unprecedented level of one hundred percent of its production, which gave rise to an industrial boom and the growth of Russian industries exploiting the country's incalculable mineral wealth, unmeasured expanses of forests, deep rivers, and, most important, the free labor of Russian serfs. Commerce also began to flourish during Elizabeth's reign. Abolishment of the domestic customs, which had been in force since the sixteenth and seventeenth centuries, was an important change in economic policy. It promoted trade, and for the first time St. Petersburg was not dependent on special subsidies. Indeed it had become the country's main port city and began to bring the national treasury ever-increasing revenues in contrast to the large expenditures that the construction and development of the city had entailed.

Of the twenty years of Elizabeth's reign fifteen passed in peace. Nothing like this had happened during the entire course of the previous two centuries. What peace means to a country goes without saying. In this just as in her whole life, Peter's daughter was lucky; when the Seven Years' War broke out in 1756 (for Russia it lasted only four years), the country endured it without extreme hardship.

Elizabeth's almost complete aloofness from state affairs does not imply indifference to her role as autocrat. She maintained her position as absolute sovereign jealously and saw to it that no one tried to rule over her. The empress was inexperienced in politics; however, she was not simpleminded and gullible. Her wavering partiality and various attachments and caprices did not lead her into taking hasty or rash decisions. She would let the matter lie unresolved for some time rather than make a decision that might endanger her power—that was her principle of government, and simple as it was, it proved sound in practice.

Elizabeth's changing partiality and tastes had an effect on her government. She displayed religious intolerance when, in 1742, she stepped up her campaign against the Old Believers; the Quakers also suffered persecution, and Elizabeth ordered certain Muslim mosques and Armenian churches demolished. A decree was issued in 1742 ordering the deportation of Jews from Russia. Now, with a God-fearing maiden-tsar in power, the Orthodox Church began to nurse the hope that the institution of patriarch, abolished by Peter, would again be restored. But nothing of the kind occurred. Elizabeth never strayed from the principles of the Petrine political doctrine. Rather, she reinforced them. In her decree of February 19, 1743, for example, the empress made it once again clear to her subjects, who seemed to have forgotten themselves since the death of the severe tsar, that she was not going to tolerate any backsliding to Muscovite habits: no beards and no floor-length clothing.

* * *

For almost twenty years Elizabeth and her favorite, Count Aleksei Grigor'evich Razumovskii, lived in peace and harmony. He first came into her favor in 1731. It was then that Colonel Fedor Vishnevskii noticed Aleksei Rozum (whose name was altered to Razumovskii), a handsome and imposing Ukrainian singer with a splendid voice in the church choir in the village of Chemary near the town of Chernigov. Vishnevskii took him to join the court choir. Noticed in the choir, Rozum was invited to Elizabeth's court.

There was nothing unusual in this. Ukrainian singers were in great demand at the court and by the empress's order talented boys and young men were sought out for this purpose from all over the Ukraine. Parents were keen to send their children to St. Petersburg for the court choir—it was considered a great privilege to be at court in any capacity, and the living allowance was decent as well. Youths who did not measure up or lost their voices would return home with compensation. Others, among them Rozum, would remain in the capital.

Rozum is first mentioned in the list of Elizabeth's court attendants in late 1731 under the name of Aleksei Grigor'ev, but not as a singer or a footman, which were lower-level attendants, but rather as a chamberlain, which was a higher level of servant. This is an unmistakable indication of the particular importance which the handsome singer had acquired in the life of the tsarevna's small court. And although Razumovskii did not participate in the coup on November 25, 1741, he received from the new empress special distinctions—he became chamberlain, general, chief master of the hunt, bearer of the Order of St. Andrew, count, and owner of vast estates.

In approximately 1742 rumors began to circulate about the secret marriage of the empress to Razumovskii in the village of Perovo near Moscow. But they remained vague and unconfirmed, so dense was the shroud of mystery that surrounded an event compromising the sovereign. In 1747

Aleksei G. Razumovskii. From I. N. Bozherianov, "*Nevskii prospekt.*" *Kul'turno-istoricheskii ocherk dvukhvekovoi zhizni Sankt-Peterburga* ("Nevskii Prospect." A Cultural and Historical Sketch of St. Petersburg at Two Hundred) (St. Petersburg, 1901–03), vol. 1, p. 104.

the secretary of the Saxonian embassy Petzold wrote: "It has long been a supposition but now I know with certainty that the empress did marry her chief master of the hunt several years ago."[51] However, the diplomat provided no evidence to prove his assertion, probably for fear of entrusting it to paper.

We still have no direct evidence of this marriage. There is a strange gap, however, opposite the name of Razumovskii in the column of marital status in the register of marriages of Elizabeth's lifeguards. For every one of the three hundred lifeguards the blank has been filled in either "married" or "widower." However, the corresponding place near Razumovskii's name has been left blank. Neither has it been marked with the word "unmarried." This is not likely to have been a clerical error, for the register is strictly official and quite detailed and accurate.

Still more rumors have been generated by the story of certain Tarakanov princes—allegedly Razumovskii's and Elizabeth's children who were first kept under lock and key, and later sent abroad to receive an education. According to Aleksei Vasil'chikov, a nineteenth-century historian researching the Razumovskii family line, Razumovskii had nephews, his sister's children, whose family name was Daragan. They lived at Elizabeth's court for a long time and then were sent to be educated in Switzerland. The German press transformed them into the mysterious Tarakanovs. However, we would not insist on this version. Among Biron's children running about Anna Ioannovna's palace was a son whose mother was Empress Anna.

Razumovskii was a man of great importance at Elizabeth's court. Petzold wrote, "the influence of Razumovskii on the sovereign had so increased after their marriage that, although he does not interfere directly in state affairs, for which he has neither the inclination nor the talent, nevertheless everyone may be assured of achieving his aims if Razumovskii puts in a good word for him."[52] Razumovskii had influence over Elizabeth as far back as the 1730s, when she was still the tsarevna. Many sought his friendship even then, sent him obsequious greetings, tried through him to receive favors and help from Elizabeth.

Contemporaries paint a likable image of the favorite. Holding great power, he was reluctant to use it, neither becoming involved in the usual intrigues at court nor striving to occupy high state posts. He is described as a good-natured idler who showed little interest in anything, and never lost his people's native sense of humor, even in respect to himself and the "occasion" that made him the highest grandee in the empire. He was very attached to his clan and took good care of his numerous kinsfolk who knew no poverty thanks to their high-ranking relative.

He was especially kind to his mother, a simple Cossack woman; he had introduced her to the court and regularly sent her thoughtful letters and presents. In 1744 Elizabeth decided to go on a pilgrimage to the shrines at the Monastery of the Caves in Kiev. On her way she was to pass through Razumovskii's native land. So the favorite wrote a letter to his mother requesting that the manager of his estates, Semen Pustota, contact his numerous kinsfolk and "instruct, in my name, my brothers-in-law and uncles, and all other relatives to gather together and wait for my arrival in the village of Lemeshi and, most important, to forbid that anyone should boast in my name of the fact that they are my relatives."[53]

During Elizabeth's reign, and largely thanks to Razumovskii, the Ukraine enjoyed some relief from autocratic oppression and even reestablished the rule of the hetman. It all happened quite magically. A few years after traveling to the Chernigov region, Razumovskii managed to find a place at court for his younger brother Kirill. Kirill's career resembles the fairy tale about the shepherd who became prince. One day couriers from St. Petersburg came after the sixteen-year-old boy, who was grazing his herd, and took him on a fast carriage to the capital. First, Kirill received new clothing and then was sent abroad to travel and study. At the age of twenty he became president of the Academy of Sciences. But that was not the chief aim of the Razumovskiis. Representatives of the Ukrainian highest nobility became frequent visitors to St. Petersburg, imploring "mother" Elizabeth to reestablish the rule of the hetman in the Ukraine. And the former shepherd, who was twenty-two then, was nominated to that post of hetman.

Contemporaries who had witnessed many magical promotions at court were simply dumbfounded by this story. However, yesterday's shepherd proved to be just as simpleminded, affable, and good-natured as his brother. The history of Russian science and the history of the Academy of Sciences itself testify that Kirill Grigor'evich Razumovskii was not the worst of all presidents of the Academy of Sciences. Although he might not have been the most helpful to scientists, at least he did not interfere in work that was incomprehensible to him. And we know that such an approach has always been seen as good fortune in Russia.

Kirill G. Razumovskii. From I. N. Bozherianov, "*Nevskii prospekt.*" *Kul'turno-istoricheskii ocherk dvukhvekovoi zhizni Sankt-Peterburga* ("Nevskii Prospect." A Cultural and Historical Sketch of St. Petersburg at Two Hundred) (St. Petersburg, 1901–03), vol. 1, p. 120.

Writing in her memoirs of her youthful years at Elizabeth's court, Catherine II describes Kirill Razumovskii, who was a little bit in love with her, the wife of the heir to the Russian throne: "He was very gay and about our age. We liked him very much . . . it was known that all of the prettiest women of the court and the city snatched him up, and really he was a handsome man with an original humor, very agreeable; he was much wittier than his brother, who, on the other hand, equaled his looks, but surpassed him in generosity and charity. These two brothers were the most beloved family of favorites ever seen."[54]

* * *

Here is how Catherine II describes her first meetings with Ivan Shuvalov: ". . . I found him still in the antechamber, a book in hand, I also liked to read, so I remarked upon this; I spoke to him sometimes while hunting; this boy appeared to me to have wit and a great desire for instruction . . . He also complained sometimes of the abandonment of his parents; at this time he was eighteen years old and had a very nice face, very respectful, very polite, very attentive and appeared very naturally sweet."[55]

In the autumn of 1749 the fate of the handsome page changed dramatically: he was no longer alone, for the empress herself shared his loneliness with him. Shuvalov's chance had come. At first the forty-year-old empress's love for the twenty-two-year-old page, who had become Gentleman of the Bedchamber, seemed to many to be only a passing fancy—many young men at the court had had similar chances; however, when weeks and then months passed, it became clear that Shuvalov had ousted Count Aleksei Grigor'evich from the empress's heart as well as from the court apartments. The behavior of both, the former and current favorites, was exemplary: there were no scenes, no scandals, no slander. Razumovskii simply stepped aside, and Shuvalov did not persecute him. The empress presented Razumovskii with Anichkov Palace on Nevskii Prospekt and promoted him to the rank of field marshal-general. Razumovskii calmly received these as compensation from his former spouse and enjoyed his life to the fullest.

The liaison between Elizabeth and Shuvalov lasted twelve years to the empress's death in December 1761. One cannot help being surprised by how different the two partners were in personality and intellect. Ivan Ivanovich Shuvalov came from a noble family of modest means. He was born in 1727 and was therefore still in swaddling clothes when the tsarevna rode out hunting with her nephew Emperor Peter II in the fields near Moscow. Ivan Shuvalov came to court thanks to his cousins Peter and Aleksandr, who had been Elizabeth's close associates since the 1720s. He was not distinguished among the dazzling crowd of courtiers either for his height, build, or diamond-studded armor of orders and ornaments. He was not a warlike, dashing, or particularly courageous man.

After Elizabeth's death Peter III appointed him head of the military school, which made his friends roar with laughter. Count Ivan Chernyshev wrote to Shuvalov: "Excuse me, my dear friend, I cannot help laughing when I imagine you standing in spats and shouting: 'Present arms!'"[56] Shuvalov wrote once with sadness to his friend Voltaire: "It was necessary for me to muster all the faculties of my worn-out soul to fulfill the duties of an employment above my ambition and to enter into details which are not at all congenial to the philosophy which I would like to make my only study."[57] About a year later he wrote to his sister from abroad: "If God pleases and I remain alive, then upon returning to my Motherland I will think of nothing else but leading a quiet and carefree life; I shall retire from high society which I know fairly well; of course, it is not the ultimate prosperity of this society, which should be respected but rather that of a small group of people within it to whom I am attached either by blood or friendship. I ask God of this one thing only: believe me that neither honors nor wealth shall bring me any joy."[58] One may, of course, read these lines with some skepticism, the revelations of a retired favorite of a deceased empress. Obviously, there was no place for him at Catherine's court. But it's better to wait a little before jumping to any conclusions.

Many facts indicate that Shuvalov was an unusual favorite. He was quite modest, and did not pursue high rank and awards. Most important he did not attempt to grow rich by having his imperial lover lavish presents on him, as was the customary behavior of most favorites, in acknowledgment of their short-lived careers. In 1757 Chancellor Mikhail Vorontsov submitted a decree to Shuvalov asking him to have it signed by the empress, which would secure Ivan Ivanovich the titles of count and senator, membership in the highest governmental body, the Conference at the Imperial Court, as well as the Order of St. Andrew and ownership of a thousand serfs. Shuvalov refused to submit this decree to the empress and responded to Vorontsov as follows: "I can say that I was born without the desire to attain wealth, honors, and noble titles. And if, dear Sir, I did not succumb to these temptations throughout the years when passion and vanity possess people, then today all the more so, I see no reason to do so."[59] Remember that 1757 was the height of Shuvalov's power and therefore this confession would appear to be sincere: it is at such a time that a man often becomes weak hearing the brass trumpets of glory and smelling the incense of eulogy.

There is no doubt whatsoever that for more than ten years real power was in the hands of Ivan Shuvalov. His influence on state affairs was far greater than that of Razumovskii. He prepared imperial decrees and conducted correspondence with ministers, ambassadors, and generals. For several years he was the sole reporter to the empress, who, self-conscious about her fading beauty, did not want to see anybody and spent more and more time in the private apartments of the palace. "He intervenes in all matters though he has no special titles and occupies no special posts," Favier wrote of Shuvalov in 1761; "in a word, he enjoys all the privileges of a minister without being one."[60] With the years the mistrustful empress became more and more dependent on Shuvalov. On more than one occasion she had had the opportunity to test her young friend's honesty and decency, and he had never failed to live up to his excellent reputation of nonpartiality. In 1759 Shuvalov's friend Vorontsov asked the favorite to intercede with Elizabeth on his behalf to grant Vorontsov exclusive rights to export Russian wheat. It goes without saying that in such situations the mediator would share in the benefits of the endeavor. Shuvalov told his friend in his own subtle way that at present the state was not in need of any monopoly in wheat export, and as "it would be against my honor to act counter to the interests of the state, so you, Your Excellency, being so richly endowed with such great intelligence, will surely not insist."[61]

Moreover, Shuvalov was an intelligent and delicate man, and knew the real value of friendship with Vorontsov, another of the empress's favorites. One month before Elizabeth's death, on November 29, 1761, he wrote to Vorontsov: "I see cunning, which I do not understand, and danger, which comes from people for whom I have done only good services. My inability to continue providing these has resulted in the loss of their respect for me, which, of course, I should always have expected to happen, and I was never so naive as to think that they loved me rather than their benefit in me."[62] This reproach applied, among others, to his "true friend" Mikhail Illarionovich, who like all the other courtiers felt the empress's approaching death and began to gather around her heir, Grand Duke Peter Fedorovich.

To be sure, Shuvalov's selflessness, honesty, and devotion were the main reason for his remaining in favor so long. But there were other reasons for the empress's special fondness for him. Elizabeth had now reached the mature stage beyond which lay old age. "Young" Ivan Shuvalov provided her with the sensation of youth, joie de vivre, fresh feelings—those things that Razumovskii, who was her age, could no longer give her. In keeping her beloved by her side day and night, Elizabeth felt young once again and enjoyed the illusion of having turned back the clock.

Elagin's satire *On Petimetr and the Coquettes* was mentioned earlier. In it the satirist was sure of his target: everyone recognized Ivan Ivanovich in the capricious Petimetr, who was preoccupied with the beauty of his nails and French perfume. He was a follower of fashion and gallomaniac. According to Favier, Shuvalov "combined pleasant appearance with a purely French manner of expressing himself."[63] He was offended by Elagin's satire and requested the poet and scientist Mikhail Lomonosov to write something in rebuttal of Elagin. After much hesitation Lomonosov squeezed out a very mediocre poem. But it was probably Shuvalov's dandyism that helped him become the favorite of such a woman of fashion as the empress. He did not consider the desire to dress well and look elegant blameworthy. Taking care of his appearance and sharing the pleasures of the festive life led by the empress, he nevertheless did not forget business.

But Ivan Shuvalov is not noted in Russian history only for being Empress Elizabeth Petrovna's favorite: since his very childhood he had been deeply and sincerely devoted to culture, literature, and art. And this passion increased with the years. The dissipated life of high society gradually lost its allure, and what Shuvalov wrote to his sister in 1763 about its emptiness reflected his true feelings. He longed for a different life, for a world of harmony and quiet, music and art, calm reading, candid and serious conversations with friends. However, he had to live long in the real world of a powerful courtier and could only dream of something different.

Nevertheless, at the peak of power, in the vortex of intrigue at the restless court, he still found the time and strength to give himself up to amiable muses, and he became a great Russian patron of the arts. Shuvalov did not himself possess creative talents. Lessons in versification that he took in his youth from Lomonosov were of no help to him. He was a failure both in writing verse and in painting. But he had something that is quite rarely found in untalented people: admiration for talent untainted by envy. He was happy whenever he met genius, and he helped it to grow. Shuvalov was a true Maecenas: an attentive and appreciative listener, a connoisseur of art, a passionate collector, a generous and far-seeing man of wealth, whose aim in life was the furtherance of the arts and culture. He took true delight in assisting creative talent.

Of course, the relationship between patron and poet offered real benefits to both sides. The poet relied on the financial and moral support of the patron, while the patron enjoyed the artist's gratitude. And he could express his gratitude by immortalizing his patron in a work of art, helping him, an enthusiastic amateur, to cross the threshold of eternity.

That was the kind of relationship which brought Shuvalov and Lomonosov together; that and something else sealed their friendship, something that both believed to be eternal and invariable, namely, a faith in the infinite power of Enlightenment or, to be more precise, of the enlightened Russian intellect, which would be capable of changing everything around it for the better.

There was in Elizabeth's reign a revival of national awareness. The peasant Mikhail Lomonosov and the nobleman Ivan Shuvalov were equally inspired by the idea that, thanks to Peter the Great's reforms, Russia had at last broken its barbarian chains and become a member of the family of educated nations. One had only to work harder, be inventive for the weal and splendor of Russia, a country of unlimited natural resources, talented people, and a language capable of expressing the most subtle human emotions. In his address to schoolboys on the occasion of the opening of a new secondary school at Moscow University in 1755, Lomonosov's disciple and

Shuvalov's protégé Nikolai Popovskii said: "If you possess the desire and assiduousness, then soon you will prove that nature has endowed you with no less intellect than entire [other] nations boast of; you will convince the world that Russia has not yet joined the company of educated nations because of her late start in studying, not because of her lack of ability."[64]

In his letter to the French philosopher Helvetius, Shuvalov wrote that there were few accomplished people in Russia or, more precisely, that there were almost no such people, but the reason for this was not that the Russians cared nothing for the sciences or lacked intellect, but because education was poorly developed. Shuvalov considered the establishment of scientific and pedagogical institutions as his duty. Together with Lomonosov he developed the idea of a Russian version of Enlightenment. The purpose of education was not to destroy the old order, but to renew and reinforce it, bringing up a new generation of Russian people, who would be educated, clever, talented, but absolutely law-abiding and loyal. That is how Shuvalov viewed Enlightenment and although he admired Voltaire's creative genius, he did not share his French friend's irony, which called for destroying the old order, and he deplored Voltaire's atheism.

Thanks to Shuvalov, in 1755 the first Russian university was opened in Moscow, the first secondary schools were established, and in 1760 the Academy of Arts was founded in St. Petersburg. Moreover, Shuvalov had amassed a huge and first-rate art collection (including paintings by Rembrandt, Rubens, Van Dyck, Poussin), which became the nucleus of the world-famous Hermitage collection in St. Petersburg.

The patron spared neither strength nor money to create an intellectual milieu in Russia. He saw to the creation of laws that protected the university from the interference of ignorant secular or religious authorities. For many years he collected books for the university and the Academy of Arts. But most important, he actively sought and found talented youth.

To choose from poor but clever young men—that was his principle. In 1761 Shuvalov wrote to the Palace Chancery that the palace stoker Fedot Shubin had been enrolled in the Academy of Arts and gives cause to hope that he will become with time a skillful master in his art. That was how the outstanding Russian sculptor Fedot Ivanovich Shubin's career began. The short Shuvalov period in the history of the Academy of Arts was extremely fruitful thanks to the intellect, foresight, and thoughtfulness of its founder, who did not spare any money in hiring expensive foreign teachers, or in buying costly paintings, sculptures, books, and whatever materials were necessary to education. Shuvalov's patronage was a boon to the arts in Russia, and led to the discovery of many new talents. In the first class to graduate from the Academy of Arts were such first-rate masters as the architect Ivan Starov, the sculptor Fedor Gordeev, and the artist Anton Losenko. Without them it is impossible to imagine Russian art in the late eighteenth and early nineteenth centuries.

Lomonosov was the patron's chief adviser and friend. For Shuvalov, Lomonosov embodied the success that enlightenment would work in the Russian people. Owing to Shuvalov's insistence, and the empress seconded him, Lomonosov devoted himself to Russian history and writing verses. However, relations between the two were not simple and smooth—they were very different men. Shuvalov and Lomonosov were separated by a generation gap as well as by origin and social status. On top of that, their characters were poles apart. One was a cultured, mild, and at the same time a carefree and spoiled man; the other was testy, had an uncontrollable temper and, under the influence of alcohol, became suspicious and overreaching, constantly suffering from the stings of those who, in his opinion, were mediocrities or nonentities. Lomonosov wanted Shuvalov not only to admire his genius but also to help him execute his rather ambitious ideas at the empress's court.

But Shuvalov the courtier had his own scores to keep and his own problems to solve that the great peasant ignored and perhaps did not even understand. Thus, after opening Moscow University Lomonosov wanted, with Shuvalov's help, to establish a new university in St. Petersburg and pictured himself as its rector. Shuvalov, however, was afraid of Lomonosov's despotic tendencies, which made him at times act rashly, willfully, and unwisely. Therefore, Shuvalov was in no hurry to realize the plans they so heatedly discussed, a fact that grieved the impatient and suspicious Lomonosov.

Returning from Peterhof after his usual fruitless visit to court, Lomonosov stopped for a rest in a meadow and wrote a bitter poem addressed to a grasshopper whose life is spent jumping and singing, being free and without cares:

Whatever you see is yours, wherever you are, you are at home;
You never ask anything of anyone, you owe nothing to no one.

At times Shuvalov, a fop and *barin* (gentleman), would poke fun at Lomonosov's easily injured pride (the latter could not forget his social origin), and laughed heartily in observing the behavior of two dinner guests, Sumarokov and Lomonosov, rivals in poetry and sworn enemies in life, who found themselves in an unexpected encounter arranged by Shuvalov himself.

Upon returning home one of Shuvalov's guests wrote in his diary: "A scurvy trick played by Brigadier Sumarokov during dinner at Chamberlain Ivan Ivanovich's. A comical scene between him and Mr. Lomonosov."[65] Lomonosov interpreted the incident in a different light. He had been humiliated, he had been compared with the jester-rhymemaker Trediakovskii. So back at home Lomonosov wrote his patron an angry letter full of injured pride: "Not only do I not want to be made a fool of at the table of noble gentlemen or of any powers that be, but not even [at the table of] God Himself, Who gave me reason, unless He takes it from me Himself."[66] Ivan

Ivanovich took no offense and perhaps apologized to Lomonosov, whom he sincerely loved.

Less than a year after this incident Elizabeth died, and Shuvalov went abroad where he first lived in Paris, with Voltaire in Ferney, near Geneva, and then spent many years in Italy. When he came back to Russia, the poet had already passed away—Lomonosov died in 1765. Ivan Shuvalov fell from favor at the age of thirty-five (1762), which turned out to be the exact mid-point in his life. The next thirty-five years, until his death in 1797, Shuvalov spent just the way he had dreamed, far from vain society, in his sister's cozy palace, among his favorite paintings and books, in peace and quiet.

He remained true to himself until the very end. One of Shuvalov's guests once entered his study and found his host sitting in a soft armchair dressed in a robe, with a book by Voltaire in his hand. "Well, even though I don't like him, the rogue," Ivan Ivanovich exclaimed, "still he writes well!"[67] He was a happy man and had attained what every patron dreams of: he was immortalized by Lomonosov, who himself will live as long as the Russian language lives.

Shuvalov had seen the world, met geniuses, and spent many years in blessed Italy. He had wielded power and known esteem, love, and glory. In the second half of his life he wrote that at long last he was free, that he had managed "to make acquaintances with worthy people, this being a consolation I had not known before; all my friends, or the greater part of them, were [friends] of my welfare; now they [have become] my own."[68]

Ivan Ivanovich Shuvalov was a simple and selfless man. However, certain close relatives, his elder cousins Counts Peter and Aleksandr Shuvalov, who long ago had brought him as a shy, intelligent young man, to court, now used his kindness unceremoniously and even impudently. The older cousin, Peter, was noteworthy because of his manners and his appearance. He was a grandee to the fullest extent of its eighteenth-century meaning. According to Favier, he "roused envy by the Asian luxury in his home and by the way he lived. He was always covered with diamonds like a Mogul, and surrounded by a retinue consisting of grooms, adjutants, and orderlies."[69]

He had married well, wedding Mavra Shepeleva, who was unattractive but well-placed as a lady-in-waiting to the empress. Mavra was intelligent and quick, and knowing well the character of her mistress she subtly used her influence to obtain favors for her husband. In his notes Prince Iakov Shakhovskoi wrote about how Mavra Shuvalova, on her husband's order, had defamed Shakhovskoi in the empress's eyes. Knowing that in such cases a direct complaint never had any effect on Elizabeth, who was prone to look for an ulterior motive, Mavra resorted to cunning: while standing with one of her fellow ladies-in-waiting by a window in the palace, she started to whisper something in her ear. That was enough for the bored empress to take notice of the two ladies, approach them, and demand that she be told what they were trying to keep secret. At first Mavra refused to talk, blushed, and then, as if reluctantly and only to satisfy Elizabeth's sovereign will, flung mud at her husband's enemy.

Describing the customs at Elizabeth's court, and the morals and manners of her leading grandees, Prince Mikhail Shcherbatov called Peter Ivanovich Shuvalov a real monster, a disgusting man; at the same time noting that he was not only "ambitious but also intelligent."

Peter I. Shuvalov. From I. N. Bozherianov, "*Nevskii prospekt.*" *Kul'turno-istoricheskii ocherk dvukhvekovoi zhizni Sankt-Peterburga* ("Nevskii Prospect." A Cultural and Historical Sketch of St. Petersburg at Two Hundred) (St. Petersburg, 1901–03), vol. 1, p. 105.

Peter Shuvalov was a prominent statesman of the Elizabethan epoch, one of the pillars of her regime. He was masterful and full of drive and determination as well as a clever and broadminded thinker. His contemporaries noted that he had the ability to understand and appraise new situations and even become involved in them himself, which was very unusual for statesmen of that time. He was a prolific schemer, backing harebrained plans in every sphere of life ranging from finance to fireworks. In his vast palace in St. Petersburg, something like a "projects factory" was established and many ideas which were conceived there were later realized by him with the support of Ivan Ivanovich. But the most important measures carried out by Peter Shuvalov were reforms in economics and finance. He initiated a transition from direct per capita taxation to indirect taxation by means of increasing the prices of salt and wine. This was a new and revolutionary idea as applied to the Russian financial system. However, his reforms of the customs duty system was an even bolder measure. Shuvalov succeeded in eliminating domestic customs, which were a relic of the Middle Ages, even though other advisers of Elizabeth feared that this might result in a drop in revenues to the state treasury. The risk was real indeed, but it proved to be worth it. By eliminating the chains which bound commerce, Shuvalov increased overall turnover in trade and hence treasury revenues.

Peter Shuvalov also initiated work on a new code of laws. The results of the commission's activity, which he himself headed, were later used by Peter III's and Catherine the Great's governments. The success of Shuvalov's reforms in the army were also impressive, especially in the field of artillery, in which Russia was among the most advanced in the world. Shuvalov's howitzer cannons, which were noted for their extraordinary accuracy, immortalized his name in the history of Russian weaponry.

His accomplishments notwithstanding, Peter Shuvalov (like his brother Aleksandr) was far more renowned for embezzlement of state funds, money-grubbing, and shameless self-enrichment at the expense of the state treasury. Peter and Aleksandr Shuvalov managed to pass laws that enabled them and their close associates to appropriate the richest metallurgical plants in the Urals, from which they gathered a very large income, to enjoy unprecedented privileges, and even State financial support. They acted like highwaymen toward their competitors, who were private entrepreneurs, and managed to ruin many of them. And they enriched themselves from numerous monopolies. When Peter Shuvalov died in 1760, those who came to his funeral spent many tiring hours waiting for his body to be carried out. Catherine the Great wrote in her memoirs that some, "recalling Shuvalov's monopoly on tobacco, said that they were sprinkling [his body] with tobacco; others said that they were strewing it with salt, remembering that it was Shuvalov's idea to put an extra surcharge on salt; still others said that he was being laid into walrus blubber in recognition of his monopolies on it and cod fishing. Then they recalled, however, that one could not get cod for any money that winter and started scolding Shuvalov."[70] So Peter Ivanovich Shuvalov was taken to the cemetery at Aleksandr Nevskii Monastery accompanied by thousands of people muttering curses and damning him to hellfire. A sorry fate indeed for a statesman.

Aleksandr Ivanovich Shuvalov had always remained in the shadow of his brother, the "Mogul"; but people feared him as much as the omnipotent schemer. In 1747 he replaced the deceased Andrei Ushakov as the chief of the Secret Chancery, and remained in charge of this infamous institution until it was abolished during Peter III's reign. No one wanted to become better acquainted with Aleksandr Ivanovich's basement. His appearance was repellent owing to a nervous tic which distorted his face—the work he was doing must have been hard on him.

To be sure, he did not have a great number of serious cases to consider, as Elizabeth's reign was relatively calm and trouble-free: there were no serious conspiracies, rebellions, or large-scale revolts. Having come to power, Elizabeth swore to do away with the death penalty, and she kept her word—there were no decrees with death sentences during her reign. Of course, there were other means to persecute and torment people to death (and, in fact, these methods were employed). Still we cannot recall any other twenty-year period in the thousand-year history of Russia without a single execution.

* * *

Having mentioned Elizabeth Petrovna's almost complete aloofness from ruling the state, one small point must be clarified. There were certain matters that could, under no circumstances, be resolved without her participation. As long as she remained the autocrat and wanted to preserve her power she was compelled at least to sign all imperial edicts and maintain minimum correspondence.

Among the documents signed by Elizabeth there are some that show that she had a keen interest in at least one area of government: foreign policy. It required concentration, diligence, and talent, which the empress did not have. Nevertheless, in the whirlwind of festivities and entertainments Elizabeth did find some time to listen to reports prepared by Chancellor Aleksei Bestuzhev-Riumin or Ivan Shuvalov, and to read messages sent from Russian envoys abroad as well as excerpts from foreign newspapers. The empress's personal notes can be found on these papers. What is the explanation for this exception made by the empress, who had as a rule no aptitude for any kind of work? The explanation was quite simple: foreign policy genuinely interested Elizabeth. Diplomacy was then the trade of kings. All European countries had monarchical regimes (except, perhaps, Venice); all were ruled by emperors, kings, princes, landgraves, or dukes.

They were a large and unfriendly family of rulers, often tied by kinship but torn by conflicts and enmity. Members of the family of European royalty were constantly engaged in intrigue against each other, striving now to disrupt other countries' alliances, now to obtain new ones for themselves. The diplomatic prehistory of Elizabeth's coup is typical of those times. And one more important point: in diplomacy monarchs personified their countries, and often when referring to Austria, Prussia, or France those involved would say Maria Theresa, King Frederick, or Louis.

This was the world in which Madame Pompadour and Cardinal Fleury, Walpole, and dozens of other famous persons lived and plotted, developing a complicated balance of sympathy and antipathy, friendship and enmity in their relations. Many had never met but still felt their royal kinship. Elizabeth considered herself a full-fledged member of this family and she obviously sympathized with unattractive Maria Theresa, who had been so offended by the outrageous defiance of the Prussian king Frederick II. There can be no doubt that Russia's participation in the Seven Years' War was governed to a great extent by Elizabeth's vindictive desire to teach the arrogant and conceited Frederick, an atheist and a mason, not to behave so insolently and unceremoniously in royal society. It is obvious that Elizabeth likewise had no fondness for depraved Versailles, although she did recognize France's indisputable superiority in dressmaking.

Elizabeth enjoyed reading messages from envoys, especially those that gave a detailed description of the ups and downs of court life and the intrigues going on at the courts to which they had been appointed. In May 1745 Bestuzhev-Riumin encouraged Nikolai Korff, the Russian envoy to Copenhagen, to continue including in his messages "discussions and news, especially coming from Sweden, and concerning her imperial majesty's family and interests, as well as the family of the prince of Holstein." Bestuzhev-Riumin writes further: "Her imperial majesty reads [your messages] personally, and I assure you that her majesty is always pleased with them."[71] The empress read foreign newspapers with special curiosity. Excerpts from them were made for her so that she could keep up with the most important European rumors and scandals. The empress was carried away by the world of intrigue and gossip.

At the same time, strange as it may seem, Elizabeth demonstrated many of the inborn qualities of a good diplomat. Some foreign envoys deluded themselves by imagining the empress to be a simpleminded, naive, and gullible beauty who could be easily manipulated and with whose help one could readily achieve one's desired goal even to the detriment of Russia's interests. Those aspiring to such ends inevitably suffered a bitter disappointment. The Frenchman Lafermière wrote in 1761 that Empress Elizabeth had internalized only two qualities of the art of ruling peoples, namely, the ability to behave with dignity and to conduct one's affairs discreetly, with reticence.

Discretion is of utmost importance for a diplomat, next to intelligence, of course. Discretion helped Elizabeth on more than one occasion, saving her from taking rash actions. An example that illustrates this point is the futile effort of the handsome Marquis de la Chetardy to break the Russo-Austrian alliance and to undermine Chancellor Bestuzhev-Riumin. At first, Chetardy—an active partner in Elizabeth's coup—was seen as a hero. The Guards embraced their French comrade, and the empress called him her particular friend. Once she even took the marquis, a Catholic, on a pilgrimage to the Trinity–St. Sergius Monastery, and even, as rumor has it, permitted him more than was permissible to just any foreign envoy.

Meanwhile, Versailles remained dissatisfied with its diplomat, who sent messages regularly about his success with the Russian empress, but whose main tasks in Russia remained unachieved. On top of that, the French envoy saw that, while the empress was friendly toward him and even flirtatious, she avoided in every way possible any serious conversations or promises. Months passed one after another but the warm friendship between Elizabeth and Chetardy produced no tangible results. This enraged the marquis. According to Catherine II, ". . . [he] thus found the doors that had been open to him before closed this time, which irked him, and he wrote about it to his court without being careful either of his expressions or the persons he mentioned; he had believed that he governed both the empress and affairs, he had been mistaken; his style was bitter and caustic; he had spoken in this tone to my mother . . ."[72]

Chetardy's letters confirm Catherine's account. He wrote with vexation to Versailles that the empress was idling for days at a time, that she concerned herself primarily with changing her dresses four or five times a day, and carousing with all sorts of lowly riffraff in her apartments. This was in fact only partially true. Chetardy did not understand that the situation had changed while he was away from Russia, and having come to power, Elizabeth was aware that the empire's interests differed from those of Tsarevna Elizabeth, and that apart from love for dresses Empress Elizabeth Petrovna held certain principles that guided her actions not as queen of the ball, but as an autocrat concerned with maintaining her power and her empire.

Elizabeth's main principle was that of following the "system of Peter the Great," which entailed making the national interests of Russia the chief criterion in foreign policy. The empress had imbibed this principle in childhood, and demonstrated it by her evasion of Nolcken's and Chetardy's dogged solicitations on the eve of the coup of November 25, 1741.

Adhering to "Peter's system" meant allowing Chancellor Aleksei Petrovich Bestuzhev-Riumin, an experienced diplomat of the Petrine school, to play a leading role for much of her reign. He was also a cunning courtier of post-Petrine formation. It was he who, on observing the touching friendship between Elizabeth and Chetardy, gave orders to open and decipher the French envoy's letters (with the Academy of Sciences' help), and then later, in the summer of 1744, when enough quotes had been accumulated, all offending Elizabeth irrevocably, he seized the moment and submitted them to the sovereign. Enraged by the ingratitude of her "particular friend," she ordered Chetardy to leave the capital within twenty-four hours and never to set foot in Russia again. This was Bestuzhev-Riumin's triumph over Chetardy, who had sought to do him so much harm.

In fact, for many years Bestuzhev-Riumin had been the main topic of discussion in the diplomatic correspondence of foreign envoys at the Russian court. There is no doubt that the chancellor was corrupt and received bribes from all countries, but he performed his main work admirably: he always adhered to the single diplomatic doctrine which had been adopted as early as Peter the Great's time, orienting foreign policy toward those countries whose long-term imperial interests coincided with Russia's.

However, in 1757 the aged Bestuzhev-Riumin for the first time made several serious mistakes. First, he allowed Russia to become involved senselessly in the Seven Years' War, after which Russia long remained hostage to Austrian interests enjoying little or no benefits herself. Second, he began a dangerous court intrigue involving Grand Duke Peter Fedorovich and his wife, Grand Duchess Catherine Alekseevna. The intrigue was exposed and the chancellor was toppled from his post in 1758. He was replaced by Mikhail Vorontsov, not a very clever but an artless and reliable man, Ivan Ivanovich Shuvalov's best friend.

Vorontsov was neither the quickest nor the most cunning in the complex struggle for power. For many years, he had played minor roles, and, although he had risen to vice chancellor, he did not have much influence at court, always losing out to his more crafty boss Bestuzhev-Riumin. The latter knew about the long-standing friendship between Vorontsov and Elizabeth, for it was young Mikhail Vorontsov who played in the tsarevna's secret theatrical performances and stood on the footboard of the sledge as it took her to the Guards' barracks on the night of November 25, 1741. Therefore, Bestuzhev-Riumin sought at all costs to discredit the empress's old associate in her eyes, and in this he succeeded for years. Only in the late 1740s, when Ivan Shuvalov came on the scene, did Vorontsov come out of the shadows and enjoy again Elizabeth's benevolence. In contrast to Peter Shuvalov, Vorontsov made a good impression on his contemporaries. Favier wrote of him: "This man has good manners; he is sober, reserved, tender, affable, polite, and humane; while he may appear on the outside to be cold, he is [actually] simple and modest . . . When he has accurate knowledge of a subject, he forms a sensible opinion regarding it."[73] Ivan Shuvalov, through Vorontsov, came to exert a profound influence on Russia's foreign policy.

The last years of Elizabeth's reign were tainted by war. For several years running, the Russian army had been fighting on Prussian territory in the center of Europe. Two stunning victories were won over the Prussian forces—the first near Gross Jagersdorf in August 1757 and two years later

Aleksei P. Bestuzhev-Riumin. From I. N. Bozherianov, *"Nevskii prospekt." Kul'turno-istoricheskii ocherk dvukhvekovoi zhizni Sankt-Peterburga* ("Nevskii Prospect." A Cultural and Historical Sketch of St. Petersburg at Two Hundred) (St. Petersburg, 1901–03), vol. 1, p. 103.

near Kunersdorf. In January 1758 the Russian forces seized Königsberg, and Emmanuel Kant, then a professor at Königsberg University, together with all the city residents, swore allegiance to the new sovereign, Elizabeth Petrovna, as Russia annexed East Prussia. In 1760 the Russo-Austrian detachment captured Berlin.

Shortcomings and contradictions within the army became apparent during the war. Stealing, abuse, and incompetence were widespread. Russia suffered heavy losses. Nevertheless, its resources were virtually inexhaustible, and the skill of soldiers and officers was constantly improving with combat experience; Russian forces marched ever more resolutely toward ultimate victory in the war. Elizabeth's military leaders and diplomats handled political and tactical aspects of the war successfully. In 1758 Chancellor Vorontsov wrote to the army's commander, General Count William of Fermor, urging him to rectify the army's shortcomings and adopt anything new and useful observed in use by the enemy: "We should not feel ashamed of the fact that we were not acquainted with the effective battle formations that the enemy has introduced, but it would be inexcusable if we were to disregard these formations after having learned of their effectiveness in action. We may say with confidence that our people, being strong and law-abiding, can be likened to a very good quality substance which can take any form one may desire."[74]

It was difficult to argue with this statement. By the end of 1761 victory seemed near. But Elizabeth died, and her successor Peter III, an old admirer of Frederick II's genius, veered the ship of Russian diplomacy toward rapprochement with the Prussians.

* * *

Two scandalous criminal cases occurred during Elizabeth's reign. Both cases were heard almost simultaneously in Moscow. They were a source of trouble for the authorities and anxiety for the residents. In the late 1750s ominous rumors began to spread in the old capital about terrible things taking place in the home of the young widow Dar'ia Nikolaevna Saltykova, who lived on Sretenka. People spoke of hundreds of house-serfs tormented brutally by the lady landowner, about cruel torture and murder. Society was so alarmed by this talk that the authorities formed a commission to investigate. The commission worked for a long time, and was compelled to admit that Saltykova's brutality had caused the death "if not of a hundred people, as had been reported by informers, then of at least fifty people for certain."

It had been established that the sadist beat her house-serfs (mostly maids), using different objects and implements; she poured boiling water over them, and froze them in the snow. Following her orders, the stablemen would whip disobedient house-serfs to death. In its report, the commission attributed the enormities to the mistress's anger aroused at the sight of "carelessly washed floors and clothes."

It is obvious that Saltykova was a maniac. However, the sadist killed people not in an out-of-the-way, remote estate, but in a house standing in the center of Moscow, under the jurisdiction of Moscow police, who, it turned out, were bribed from top to bottom by Saltykova. The police readily drew up documents certifying yet another "accidental death" of one of Saltykova's house-serfs. Even the leaders of the Chief Criminal Investigation Department took bribes from the rich lady landowner. The investigation into Saltykova's crimes dragged on, and after long delays, already in Catherine the Great's reign, she was stripped of her noble title and sentenced to life imprisonment, which she served for the remaining thirty-three years of her life, showing no repentance for what she had done and cursing everyone around.

This was both unique and typical for Russia in those times. To varying degrees many landowners treated their serfs in the same cruel and barbarous way. Serfdom corrupted both the slaves and their masters. Catherine the Great wrote that during Elizabeth's reign there was not a single manor-house in Moscow without a prison and torture chamber in the basement for the slaves. The idea that the house-serfs were not human beings and that cruel treatment of them was inevitable and necessary was firmly implanted in the mind of the nobility and, according to Catherine, in the mid eighteenth-century there were hardly a dozen men in Russia who would have condemned serfdom.

Of course, Elizabeth had never given the matter any thought at all. This world with its everyday violence and humiliation seemed perfectly normal to her, and the problems of humaneness were of no concern to her. For she herself, just as her predecessor Anna Ioannovna, was a full-fledged landowner and mistress, and severe with her own disobedient servants.

The case of Van'ka Kain was no less curious; his name has become equated with a special Russian version of treachery and unscrupulousness. A serf belonging to a Moscow merchant named Peter Filat'ev, Kain had since early childhood a propensity for crime. Stealing and cheating were his natural element. After Van'ka at age eighteen had robbed his master, he fled home, and fell in with the dregs of Moscow, where he quite soon gained notoriety as a criminal.

He was fiendishly talented and inventive in the planning and execution of his thievish operations, in his ability to open tough locks, deceive vigilant watchmen, and escape from hot pursuit. Together with his closest friend, Peter Kamchatka, he had committed hundreds of crimes both in Moscow and in other cities that Kain's gang chose to include in their summer circuit. In 1741 Van'ka Kain joined the gang headed by Mikhail Zoria, whose specialty was holdups and robberies at fairs and on highways.

Van'ka didn't like this extremely dangerous and restless life, and immediately after Christmas of 1741 he came to the Investigation Office to turn himself in. In his confession he revealed the names of his accomplices, and having been provided with a detachment of soldiers, started arresting them in their various Moscow dens. In one of the caves on the bank of the Moscow River, the policemen, with Van'ka at their head, seized a fugitive soldier named Solov'ev, who had kept a record of his everyday crimes by the light of a splinter of wood. This diary has survived to our day: "On Monday evening, 70 kopecks were taken in Vsesviatskaia bathhouse . . . on Thursday—50 kopecks, and blue trousers . . . on the Stone Bridge—54 kopecks, etc."[75] Thanks to the informer's energy, dozens of criminals were arrested in the course of just a few days.

Kain's investigative zeal knew no bounds: one fine day he turned in his closest friend, Kamchatka, to the police, although Kamchatka had many times helped Kain elude the police and likely execution. As time passed Kain diversified his activities. The authorities had issued a special decree granting Kain immunity from possible prosecution; so now he continued not only to catch thieves, robbers, and fences, but he himself was robbing, blackmailing, and killing.

Kain got married and acquired a home, which he turned into a guardsroom for police soldiers and which he also used as a den with a secret tavern for gambling. It was a gathering place for criminals and prostitutes, and from here Kain departed with his soldiers to conduct raids on "gangs" and the homes of honest Muscovites. He was a man of great power, and, thanks to his excellent knowledge of the dark side of Moscow life and to his impunity, Kain became the terror of all those who lived outside of the law, for example, merchants transporting contraband, craftsmen with secret workshops, and distinguished citizens who had committed crimes in the past. Some of these people he would turn in to the authorities in order to maintain a clean record and to boost morale; others, those who he knew would keep silent, he would ruthlessly rob; still others he would magnanimously let go, having given them a good fright; still others he would even help in managing their shady business.

He entered the offices of all police chiefs by kicking the door open with his foot. Investigation Department clerks considered it an honor to drink a cup of tea with Van'ka in a tavern somewhere. They all took bribes, and received presents and a share of the profits earned by Kain. If a well-to-do person found something missing in his house he did not have to worry. He had only to call on Van'ka and the stolen goods would be found, for a price, of course. At Van'ka's orders, a large group of petty thieves and swindlers would scour every flea market and bazaar, the places used for selling stolen goods from all over Moscow.

Kain's power lasted for almost ten years. Resourceful and audacious, endowed with the traits of an actor and hoaxer, he seemed invulnerable, extricating himself with ease from any traps which had been set for him. He was a rare mix of mettle, daring, treachery, greed, and pettiness. However, women proved to be his demise, or to be more precise, his boundless appetite for love did him in. The father of one of his victims managed to receive an audience with the governor of Moscow. An inquiry was conducted, and many of Kain's other crimes came to light, whereupon Van'ka was put into prison. As before, he tried treachery to save himself and began to betray numerous accomplices, including his patrons among the police.

The government did not trust the corrupt Moscow police and appointed a special commission to investigate the Kain case. The commission uncovered a terrifying picture of numerous abuses of power, established close links between criminals and officials, and a total digregard for law. Van'ka gave a detailed description of his carefree and happy life under the patronage of Moscow officials. However, dog does not eat dog, and the officials who were mixed up in the Kain's affair got off scot-free. As for Van'ka, his imprisonment—first in jail and then in Siberia—never ended. He was not pardoned for his last treachery.

* * *

Elizabeth turned fifty in December 1759, but she looked years older. Face-creams, ointments, and powders as well as the efforts of hairdressers, tailors, and jewelers were to no avail. Old age was upon her. La Rochefoucauld's cruel remark "Old age is hell for a woman" describes Elizabeth's plight. She gazed with horror into the mirror, which did not as in Pushkin's fairy tale tell the tsaritsa: "You in all the world are the fairest and your beauty is the rarest."

Years of a fast, immoderate lifestyle, intemperance in food, drink, and recreations took its toll on the tsaritsa's health. Everyone at court was frightened by Elizabeth's sudden seizures, which came upon her at the worst places, for example, at church or during receptions. These were dead faints from which Elizabeth was slow to recover and, according to Catherine the Great, one could not even speak to her until she felt well again.

Doctors believed that the faints were the results of menopause, which was complicated by the patient's unbalanced character and hysterical fits, as well as her unwillingness to follow a healthy regimen. It was characteristic of eighteenth-century doctors to express their opinion in a vague and enigmatic way: "No doubt, the greater the number of years beyond youth, the thicker the liquids in the body and the slower their circulation, for they are scorbutic in nature." The doctors prescribed peace and quiet, enemas, bloodletting, and medicines. These things were all too disgusting for one who was used to a pleasant, noisy, and joyous life. Medicines for Elizabeth were disguised in marmalade and sweets as if she were a capricious little girl.

Everyone knew that these were the final days in the festive life of Peter the Great's jovial daughter. The word "jovial" could hardly be applied to the tsaritsa now. She secluded herself in Tsarskoe Selo, frequently refusing to see anyone. She was whimsical, gloomy, and whining. The French diplomat Lafermière wrote: "Her passion for pleasure and noisy celebrations had given way to an inclination for quiet and even solitude, but not for work. Empress Elizabeth Petrovna loathes the latter to an even greater extent than before. She detests any reminder of obligations, and her retinue often have to wait for six months at a time in order to catch the right moment to persuade the empress to sign a decree or a letter."[76]

Quite unexpectedly for herself Elizabeth realized that all was not well in her empire, that many complaints did not reach her throne but were met with rude rebuffs and retaliation by her clerks. Bitterness pervades one of Elizabeth's last manifestos: "How deep the sorrow born of love for our subjects must be when we see that many of the laws established for the bliss and prosperity of the nation are not properly executed because of our common internal enemies who prefer illegal profits to their sworn oath, duty, and honor."[77] Elizabeth demands that proper order be urgently established in the sphere of justice and any abuse of power be suppressed in every possible way. That she was ignorant of these abuses is not surprising. The lack of concern or mental sloth noted by her contemporaries characterized Elizabeth until the end of her days. The above manifesto was conceived by Shuvalov, as draft versions of it have confirmed, and the empress merely signed it.

The imperial family also had its problems. It was not large: the empress, her nephew Grand Duke Peter Fedorovich, his wife, Grand Duchess Catherine Alekseevna, and their son, Tsesarevich Paul Petrovich, who was born in 1754. "Aunt Elizabeth" and her nephew were not on good terms. After coming to power in November 1741, Elizabeth immediately summoned her fourteen-year-old nephew, Duke Charles Peter Ulrich of Holstein, to St. Petersburg, whose father, Charles Frederick, had died in 1739. Elizabeth brought him to Russia, had him baptized in the Orthodox faith with the name of Peter Fedorovich, and appointed him her heir. However, she did this not out of love for her elder sister's son, but out of tactical considerations. Living abroad, Charles Peter Ulrich, grandson of Peter I, was a threat to Elizabeth, who had usurped the throne. In Russia Peter Fedorovich was put in a golden cage.

Peter Fedorovich's manners, appearance, and behavior annoyed the empress. He was infantile and capricious, unrestrained and extravagant. As Catherine II wrote later, "their intellects and personalities differed to such an extent that they could not talk to each other for five minutes without beginning to quarrel. This is beyond any doubt."[78] Elizabeth kept the heir out of state affairs, as she had no trust in him. In 1745 he was married to the princess of Anhalt-Zerbst Sophia Fredericka Augusta (Catherine Alekseevna), the future empress Catherine the Great. As soon as Paul Petrovich was born, Elizabeth took the boy to her palace and devoted much time to him. Letters written by the empress during her later years indicate that she had a great love for this boy, was deeply and sincerely concerned about his health, education, and future. Rumor had it that Elizabeth and the Shuvalovs planned to deprive Grand Duke Peter Fedorovich of his right to the throne, deport him and his wife to Holstein, and place Paul on the throne. Initial steps had already been taken to prepare Paul for this great role in the future.

This was the scenario that frightened Catherine into starting her intrigues with Bestuzhev-Riumin and the English envoy Charles Williams, who provided Catherine with money. As we see, in less than twenty years, yet another young, ambitious woman comes on the scene supported by a foreign diplomat with a well-stuffed purse. And again there are intrigue, letters, negotiations, and an exchange of significant smiles at balls. But Elizabeth acted more decisively than Anna Leopol'dovna. The conspiracy was nipped in the bud, and only by greatly taxing her willpower did Catherine manage to withstand Elizabeth's personal interrogation and not give herself away. Of course, after this the empress had still less to trust in the grand-ducal pair.

The empress spent the entire autumn of 1761 in Tsarskoe Selo and avoided meeting anyone with the exception of Ivan Ivanovich Shuvalov, who was with her constantly. We know very little about Elizabeth's last days—Shuvalov did not talk about them to anyone. Elizabeth, whose piety and superstitiousness had increased over the years, was near despair. She must have been frightened by a sudden violent thunderstorm that passed over the palace late that autumn, a very unusual time for such weather, on the threshold of winter. No one could recall such a storm. Perhaps Elizabeth saw evil omens in the thunderbolts and bare trees, which looked deathlike in the flashes of lightning. She lived in panic fear of death. Lafermière wrote in May 1761: "Her health becoming worse and worse with each passing day, there is little hope that she will live long. But no one more meticulously conceals this from her than she conceals it from herself. Nobody has ever feared death as much as she does. The word is never spoken in her presence. She cannot stand the very thought of death. Anything which might remind her of death has been removed."[79]

However, the end was approaching inexorably. Stricken by the blind fear of death, Elizabeth refused to take any treatments or even to follow the mildest regime. The Danish envoy Haksthaus wrote about the empress's ill health in the autumn of 1761: "Her legs are covered with boils to such an extent that she cannot possibly stand on her feet. She had frequent fits culminating in faints."[80]

The end came on a great holiday—Christmas 1761. When death came for the empress, she was dressed in festive clothing for the holiday. Just the day before she had said good-bye in a low faint voice to Peter Fedorovich and his wife.

The funeral was held in the new year of 1762. Everything was typical of an imperial funeral—large crowds, beautiful displays, the pomp and panoply of state, and people collapsing from exhaustion. The eccentric behavior of the new emperor Peter III during the funeral threw off the procession and ceremony. First he was walking very slowly, then started galloping or running. In contrast, Elizabeth lay unconcerned in the coffin. And even there, according to Catherine the Great, she remained the coquette she had been all her life. "The sovereign lay in the coffin dressed in a silver lace-sleeved gown with the Imperial Crown on her head; its lower edge bore the inscription: *The most pious, the most autocratic, the Great Sovereign Empress Elizabeth Petrovna, born December 18, 1709, ascended the throne November 25, 1741, died December 25, 1761.*"[81] Another witness, Haksthaus, wrote to his government that the crown cost ten thousand rubles and that it would go with the sovereign to the grave.

CHAPTER 5

The Sovereign of the North
(Catherine the Great)

O n September 23, 1785, the French envoy Louis Philippe d'Agusseau Comte de Ségur was walking fast through the Winter Palace halls heading for his first audience with Catherine the Great. He was in agitation and tried in vain to recollect the words of the official welcoming speech he was to deliver before the empress. Let's follow the count in order to be there by the time the audience begins.

Having passed through several rooms he found himself in front of a closed door: "all of a sudden the door to the room containing the empress was opened. She was richly dressed and standing up, hand resting on a column; her majestic air, the dignity of her demeanor, the pride of her regard, her rather theatrical pose, in taking me by surprise, succeeded in making an indelible impression," as Ségur recollected later.[1]

Many people had a similar experience when they encountered the empress for the first time. Statesmen, diplomats, military leaders would grow pale and feel embarrassed the moment they saw her. The famous French writer Denis Diderot simply went rigid, and Baron Melchior Grimm, Catherine's old correspondent, became muddled and confused when he first met her in 1774.

No wonder the visitors were overwhelmed when they found themselves standing before this unusually dazzling woman, whose fame had rung throughout the world and whose majestic appearance shining amid the splendor of the Winter Palace was in full accord with this fame. However, after a minute or two, the quiet, cordial, even sweet tone of her voice would change the entire atmosphere. All embarrassment and constraint vanished, and before

Grand Duchess Catherine Alekseevna. From I. N. Bozherianov, "*Nevskii prospekt.*" *Kul'turno-istoricheskii ocherk dvukhvekovoi zhizni Sankt-Peterburga* ("Nevskii Prospect." A Cultural and Historical Sketch of St. Petersburg at Two Hundred) (St. Petersburg, 1901–03), vol. 1, p. 159.

long Catherine's visitors felt like new friends at ease with her. The empress's simplicity, combined with an inherent sense of dignity, immediately impressed her interlocutor. This contradicted certain opinions circulating about Catherine the Great as a kind of Semiramis of the North! In 1787, she wrote to Grimm: "The prince of Ligne confessed to me that on his first trip he expected, upon seeing me, to see a large woman, as stiff as a post, who only spoke in proclamations and demanded to be always admired, and that he was very relieved to have been mistaken and to find a being with whom one could speak and who liked to have a chat."[2]

After some time had passed, the visitor, having had a closer look at Catherine, would notice that she was far from being beautiful. Chancellor Mikhail Vorontsov's secretary, Jean-Louis Favier, spoke rather severely of our heroine at age thirty-five: "It would be wrong to say that she is a dazzling beauty: her waist is fairly long, slim, but not flexible; she has a noble carriage, but her gait is affected and not graceful; her breast is narrow, her face is long, especially her chin; she has a continual smile on her lips, but her mouth is flat and indented; her nose has a slight hook; her eyes are small but her look is vivacious and pleasant; her face has pockmarks. She is rather more beauteous than ugly, but one is not likely to take fancy to her."[3]

The English diplomat John Hobart, the second Earl of Buckingham, had another opinion of her. He did not see any traces of smallpox on her face because Catherine had never been ill with this disease. However, he agreed with Favier that "her features are far from being fine and regular to make up what is considered to be a true beauty." Yet in his view, she did have a special charm: "An excellent complexion, vivid and clever eyes, a pleasantly outlined mouth, and splendid chestnut-colored hair—all of these put together create an appearance which, many years ago, could not have left a man indifferent unless he was prejudiced and insensitive." Catherine was then thirty-three, a rather venerable age according to criteria of the eighteenth century. However, the count corrects himself on the spot, claiming that she had what people often like and what attracts much more than beauty: a good figure, beautiful neck and arms, and all of the parts of her body formed gracefully so that both feminine and masculine attire suit her; blue eyes whose liveliness was softened by the lanquor of her gaze, sensitive but not bland. She attached little importance to costume, yet she was always dressed too well for a woman who is indifferent to her appearance.[4]

Three more decades passed, and another of Catherine's guests, the count Joachim Sternberg, wrote a note in his memorandum book, which was almost the same as that recorded by his predecessor: medium height, sturdy constitution, long face, hooked and well-outlined nose, which imparts a serious expression to her face; shining and vivid eyes, and high forehead. Count Sternberg, however, made one mistake that Catherine undoubtedly would have resented—her nose was considered to be absolute perfection. It was not only not hooked, it was absolutely straight, a Greek nose, and Catherine wrote with pride that in profile she was the very image of Alexander the Great, which is the impression one gets after examining the cameos of Catherine in the Hermitage collection.

But let us return to an audience with the empress. Listening to her speak in exquisite French, the guests would conclude that the empress was an intelligent woman with extensive knowledge, whose opinions on various subjects were deeply founded and original. Prince Charles Henri Nassau-Siegen, who accompanied Catherine during her trip to the Crimea in 1787, wrote with unrestrained wonder: "Indeed, I admire her, and my admiration grows with each passing day, the simplicity of her manners can hardly be imagined. Her talk is charming and when it deals with serious matters, her astute opinions indicate her broad knowledge and correct reasoning. She would make the most attractive private person."[5]

And when she started laughing merrily at her interlocutor's joke, replying in the same tone, it became clear that Catherine also possessed a subtle sense of humor, and her gay and infectious laughter revealed an easy disposition and an optimistic nature full of joie de vivre.

That is the way it was. Catherine considered optimism or joviality, as they called it in those days, to be one of her primary virtues. "One must be jovial," she wrote to Mrs. Bielke, one of her mother's girlfriends, in 1766. "This alone helps and endures to overcome all things. I know that from my own experience: I have had to endure and overcome quite a lot in my life, but I laughed when I could, and I swear to you that even now when I have so many difficulties in my present position, when I have a chance I gladly play blindman's bluff with my son and often without him."[6] This was not due solely to her nature; Catherine was convinced that human genius manifests itself in optimism. When she learned that Frederick II was a jovial person, she remarked that this feature undoubtedly sprung from a feeling of superiority, and had there ever been a great man who was not noted for his joviality, and who did not have an inexhaustible supply of it? Catherine's own supply did seem to have no end. Only months before her death she wrote to Grimm that she felt well, happy, and as light as a bird.

And so it was with regret that Ségur bid farewell to the charming sovereign and left the Throne Room. Certain visitors, however, whom the empress bestowed with kindness, simply went into rapture: Diderot clung to her by the hands, while Grimm asked her to install him in her study as a pet pug. We, dear readers, not wishing to disturb Catherine, shall follow Ségur out of Catherine's study and retire to the archives and libraries trying to find out more in detail about the sovereign Catherine the Great.

* * *

She did not like to celebrate her birthdays. "Each time [I have a birthday] I receive as a gift one more year, something which I would willingly pass up. To tell the truth, it would be a charming thing to have an empress who was only fifteen years old her whole life."[7] And she tried all ways to avoid congratulations and festivities that mark the day some people for some reason consider to be the main day in the year. For Catherine it was an ordinary

Empress Catherine. From I. N. Bozherianov, "*Nevskii prospekt.*" *Kul'turno-istoricheskii ocherk dvukhvekovoi zhizni Sankt-Peterburga* ("Nevskii Prospect." A Cultural and Historical Sketch of St. Petersburg at Two Hundred) (St. Petersburg, 1901–03), vol. 1, p. 179.

day of labor and recollections. The first version of her memoirs she opens with the words: "I was born 21/22 April/May 1729 (that makes forty-two years to this day) at Stettin in Pomerania."[8]

We can imagine how these lines were written. April 21, 1771, was Catherine's birthday; she woke up as usual early in the morning, lit the wood laid the previous evening in the fireplace, drank a cup of very strong coffee, and sat down at her secretaire, on which blank sheets of paper were waiting for her. That's how hundreds of the empress's days actually began, birthdays being no exception.

Sophia Augusta Fredericka—such was the name Catherine had received at her Lutheran christening—was descended from the old, albeit poor, princely family of the Anhalt-Zerbst rulers. That was the line of her father,

Prince Christian Augustus. As to the pedigree of her mother, Duchess Johanna Elizabeth, her origin was nobler still, for the duke's family of Holstein-Gottorp, from which our heroine's mother had descended, was among the most distinguished families in Germany, and Catherine's uncle, Adolf Frederick, ruled as king of Sweden during the years 1751–1771.

When the princess Sophia, or Fike as they called her at home, was born, her father was the commander of the Prussian regiment quartered in Stettin (nowadays Szczecin, Poland). He held the rank of general, and thanks largely to the marital success of his daughter, he later became field marshal and governor at Frederick II's order. The fact that he was not sitting on the throne in his tiny Zerbst, but was in the service of the Prussian king, was not unusual in Germany at that time. The ruling German nobility were much poorer than their Russian counterparts, like Sheremetev or Saltykov, for example, and therefore they were compelled to serve with a variety of powerful sovereigns—French, Prussian, and even Russian (thus, for instance, the sovereign prince of Hesse-Homburg became a Russian field marshal). The father of the future Catherine also chose this way when he was very young, for his small domain could not bring in enough profit to maintain a family. Therefore, we will leave it upon the conscience of the taleteller [Hans Christian] Andersen, who wrote touching stories about a poor king answering a knock at the castle doors with candle in hand to let in a passing swineherd.

Fike was born in a Stettin castle which has survived to our day. "I resided and was raised in the wing of the castle, when one entered the castle's grand courtyard on the left; I occupied the three vaulted rooms up above, next to the chapel in the corner; the clock was next to my bedchamber; it is there that Mademoiselle Cardel indoctrinated me and Monsieur Wagner taught me the Brüfungen; that is also the place from which I would frolic down the whole wing to go to my mother's rooms, which were at the other end, two or three times a day. Now, I do not see anything very interesting in all of that, unless you believe that the locale is good or is conducive to making passable empresses."[9] Historians have every reason to think so!

Fike's childhood was typical of that of any eighteenth-century child, for children were not considered priceless treasures by their parents as they are in our days, and nobody seemed to worry much if a child (especially a girl)— as a rule, one out of many in a family—fell sick and died. "The Lord giveth, and the Lord taketh away." A child's fate depended wholly on its natural strength. In 1777, while pondering the future of her newborn grandson Aleksandr, Catherine whispered jokingly: "Ladies, some nature, a bit of nature, and experience."[10]

The angels had supplied Fike with more than enough "nature," and this helped the girl survive in conditions that were horrible from the present-day point of view. At the age of seven she had a terrible cough, fever, and pains in her side. The girl suffered for three weeks, after which time she seemed to have recovered: "when they started to dress me I had, during this time, contracted almost a Z-shaped figure, my right shoulder had become higher than the left, my spine was in zigzags and my left side slumped."[11] The local "doctor," who in addition to being a bonebreaker was also a bonesetter, recommended massaging the shoulder with saliva as well as wearing a corset, with which the girl did not part for several years.

Nature notwithstanding, Fike was also extremely lucky: she was not bitten by the typhus louse, and she did not die of spotted fever at the age of thirteen like her younger brother; inept nurses did not drop her on the floor at the age of one-and-a-half as was again the case with her brother, and she did not have her thigh dislocated as her brother did, who as the result of a fall walked with a severe limp until his early death. We should also note that she would never have become the Russian empress had she lost her eye in childhood from an accidental prick with the scissors; the point of the scissors pierced through the eyelid but miraculously missed the eyeball. Likewise, she did not lose her sight as a result of chronic avitaminosis (scrofula), which covered her body from head to foot with a layer of scab on and off during her childhood. "When it came to my head, they cut off my hair, powdered my head and made me wear a bonnet. When it came to my hands, they put gloves on me that I was not to take off until the scabs fell off."[12]

In this family there was no intimacy between parents and children. Her father, an old man, was preoccupied with his business affairs and existed somewhere far away as the supreme authority in the family. He was rarely seen by the children. Catherine's mother, Johanna Elizabeth, had been given away in marriage to the forty-two-year-old Christian Augustus when she was fourteen years old. She was a carefree woman keen on intrigues and the amusements of high society. Children were not her primary concern (according to Catherine's recollections, her mother did not like displays of affection). It is interesting that later, when the thirty-two-year-old Johanna Elizabeth came to Russia with her fourteen-year-old daughter, who was betrothed to the grand duke Peter, she behaved as if the trip had been organized for her alone and was jealous of her own daughter, who was the focus of attention at the Russian court.

In contrast to her dutiful husband, the duchess had always traveled, paying long visits to her numerous relatives who lived in different cities in Germany. She often took Fike and her younger brother, Friederick Augustus, with her. So from early childhood the girl grew accustomed to new places, adapting quickly to unfamiliar situations, and easily making friends with people. All this proved useful to her in later life.

We should mention one more specific feature of the principality where "fair empresses were made": Catherine lived in the Protestant part of Germany, which was more developed than other parts of the country. The French Huguenots had been coming there in great numbers since the late seventeenth century, fleeing from the terror of Catholic repression. Thus, French culture and education had taken deep roots in northern Germany and

Prussia. Such was the atmosphere in which the family of the future Catherine lived. We should consider Louis XVI's opinion, who argued with Claude Carloman de Ruhlière, one of the first historiographers of Catherine the Great. Ruhlière alleged that Catherine's early life was permeated with the spirit of the barracks. Nothing of the sort!—exclaimed the king. The author was simply unfamiliar with the style of domestic and court life in small German principalities whose courtiers spoke exquisite French.

Whatever the case may be, Fike had absorbed the French language together with the milk of her wet-nurse, and it was a powerful driving force behind intellectual development during the eighteenth century. When she was grown up, Catherine often thought of her governess, Elizabeth (Babette) Cardel, a French immigrant. Babette was a person of rare kindness and charm, endowed with an elevated spirit, a fair intellect, and a noble heart. She was a patient, gentle, gay, just, and consistent person. In a letter dated 1775 Catherine wrote of her already long-deceased tutor that Babette had been very well educated and could recite by heart many excerpts from various comedies and tragedies.

Fike, a lively and impressionable child, drank in all of these, and knew La Fontaine's tales as well as she knew the Bible, for she was to learn entire verses from it by heart. But it is important to stress that neither in Fike's family, nor in the community of Protestant Germany, was there any trace of the religious fanaticism that so often spoiled children's souls in those days. We will return to Catherine's religious outlook later. Here suffice it to mention that it would have been impossible in the Catholic part of Germany to imagine a little princess discussing with her confessor the absurdity of the ancient Greek writers condemned to hell for the sole reason that they had been born before Christ and knew nothing of his edifying doctrines.

Fike took a particular liking to books. Babette had found a perfect method to cultivate this habit; she would read something interesting to the girl aloud but on the condition that the girl behaved herself well at her lessons; if Babette was displeased with Fike's progress in her studies she would read silently to herself, which made the girl very unhappy. Probably, at this very time in Kiel, the young Duke of Holstein, Charles Peter Ulrich, almost the same age as Fike, his future wife, was being beaten by his tutor, Count Otton Brümmer, who frequently deprived him of his dinner, tying him up instead to the leg of the table, or often made the duke kneel down on his bare knees on dried peas, which made the duke's feet swell. This might be one of the reasons that Peter III and Catherine were such very different people.

Of course, Fike's domestic education was fragmented and by no means systematic. But no one really intended to make an educated lady out of her. As soon as it became clear that Fike would survive into adulthood, another destiny was assigned for her. At the prime age of fourteen or fifteen Princess Sophia would become the wife of a prince or a king. That was an established order in the world in which she lived. So preparations began for her future marriage while she was still very young: manners, languages, needlework, dances, and singing. These were the primary subjects she was to master, even though Fike proved to be absolutely unfit for singing, since she didn't have a good ear for music. However, the rest were quite sufficient for her to make a good wife for some king or royal heir. So Fike looked expectantly forward to meeting her future husband."I knew only to obey, and it was up to my mother to have me married."[13]

From a very early age she knew that she would marry not a man of her own choosing, but a descendant of a royal blood, one to whom fate and parents would give her away in marriage, and whom she, as an honest and respectable girl, would have to love, of course, and bear successors to. Then everything would be all right. Was it her fault that these dreams never came true?

And at last, the long-awaited day came, which sealed the princess's fate. This is how Catherine described that day: "The first of January 1744 we were at the table, when a large packet of letters was brought to my father; the latter, after having opened the first envelope, gave to my mother several letters addressed to her. I was next to her and I recognized the handwriting of the field marshal of the court of the Duke of Holstein, then the grand duke of Russia . . . My mother opened the letter and I saw these words: 'with the princess, her oldest daughter.' I took it as said; I guessed the rest, and found out that I had guessed correctly."[14]

Yes, the letter spoke of precisely what the girl had been waiting for: on behalf of the empress Elizabeth, Count Brümmer was inviting Johanna Elizabeth and her daughter to visit Russia under the pretext of thanking Her Highness for all the favors that she had bestowed on their family. As soon as dinner was over, Catherine recalled, her father and mother closed themselves in their room and a great fuss began all over the house. This went on for three days.

In her memoirs Catherine writes that she made her mother relate to her the contents of the letter in great detail and convinced her parents to agree to go to Russia. There is some doubt that it happened just like that. It is well known that Johanna Elizabeth had been blazing a trail to Russia for some time. She had sent Empress Elizabeth flattering congratulations and a portrait of Elizabeth's elder sister, Anna Petrovna, the Duchess of Holstein. Moreover, it was likewise no accident that Duke Augustus of Holstein, Johanna Elizabeth's brother, had personally delivered to St. Petersburg in March 1743 a portrait of Princess Sophia painted by the artist Antoine Pesne, which has survived to our days. In it we see an oblong face with a fresh complexion, a small mouth and heavy chin. The artist made no attempt to embellish nature. However, the tilt of the head and the bold and attentive look lacking any trace of a smile do reveal the princess's personality and character.

However, it is not likely that it was because of this very portrait that Empress Elizabeth had decided in favor of Fike. Similar advertisement for potential brides had always been a matter of course, and one would think that ugly or ill-tempered princesses had never existed. The empress had her own plans which had nothing to do with aesthetics. She had quite long been looking for a fiancée for her successor among the European crowned families and other distinguished families. Among the potential candidates were a princess from a French royal family and one of the Polish king's daughters, the beautiful Maria Anna, but Empress Elizabeth had selected Fike, for she satisfied two of the most important criteria: first, she was a Protestant, which meant she could more easily convert to the Orthodox faith; and second, she had descended from a noble, albeit insignificant, family. Therefore, neither her relations nor her retinue would draw any attention or arouse envy on the part of Russian courtiers. These were the reasons she gave to Vice Chancellor Aleksei Bestuzhev-Riumin to justify her selection.

Absence of influential relatives was, in our opinion, the main advantage of the princess from Zerbst. Elizabeth did not want any special party to appear in the court who would gather around the successor to the throne and his wife with a clan of foreign crowns supporting it. However, one powerful person made an attempt to jump secretly into the carriage that was taking Fike on January 10, 1744, away from Zerbst and out of Germany for good. This person was Frederick II, the Prussian king. As soon as he had learned about Brümmer's letter, he wrote a letter to Johanna Elizabeth informing her that it was his idea to marry the Russian successor to her elder daughter, and that it was he who had given orders to make efforts to this end in deepest secret, even without the knowledge of the girl's parents (!), and that despite many difficulties he had finally succeeded. Empress Elizabeth's invitation had at last arrived. Using this trick, Frederick proceeded to reap where he had not sown.

When Fike, accompanied by her parents, arrived in Berlin on her way to Russia, a reception was given in her honor. None of the dozens of princesses born in the many German provinces was ever given so grand a reception. Princess Sophia was surprised when she learned that at the dinner she was to be seated next to Frederick II himself. She became confused and was about to leave but the king insisted that she stay. He was exceptionally considerate and polite, and spent the whole evening talking only with Fike. Frederick's gallantry is explainable: one could not think of a better way to influence the position of Russia than via the wife of the successor to the throne, who might later become the empress. Now we shall trace Fike's path and fate after she had bid farewell to her father. In contrast to Fike's mother, he had not been invited by Empress Elizabeth to St. Petersburg.

At parting, Christian Augustus gave his daughter an instructive note in which he entreated her to preserve her Lutheran faith and to obey God, the empress and her future husband. Christian Augustus advised her to avoid court intrigues and state affairs, to keep her accounts accurate, to avoid card games with big stakes, not to make friends with anybody, and to always be reserved toward other people. Regardless of how much Fike loved her father, she did not in fact follow a single one of his recommendations. Her life changed drastically when Princess Sophia Augusta Fredericka set foot in the Russian Empire.

It happened on January 26 (on February 6 according to the Gregorian calendar), 1744, in the city of Riga. This is both a memorable and significant date: the great empire met its future great empress. And that meeting was magnificent: volleys of triumphal salutes, drum rolls, a luxurious carriage, the highest Livonian officials dressed in parade uniforms, majestic apartments; later, a marvelous snow caravel—a gigantic sleigh trimmed with silver and sable fur, and drawn by ten horses; and finally, an honor guard.

Johanna Elizabeth took notice of the brave young cuirassiers who were led by an adroit captain showing off before the spectators. She described this episode in a letter which she sent home. She might even have asked the name of that brilliant captain, but forgot it the very moment she heard it; for that name meant nothing to her, or to Fike, or to anyone else for that matter. However, to us this name does have significance. The twenty-four-year-old captain, head of the honor guard of the future empress, was none other than Baron Carl Friedrich Hieronymus von Münchhausen. Yes, that unsurpassed "king of liars." Well, was he really such a liar after all?

Probably, many years later, while sitting among his friends, a glass of beer in his hand, in his quiet native Bodenwerden, he narrated his incredible stories about Russia, a country of fierce wolves and severe snowstorms that covered houses with snow up to their roofs and churches up to the crosses of their domes. One of his stories might open with the following words: "When I was the head of the Honor Guard of Catherine the Great and helped her lie down in the gigantic sleigh trimmed from top to bottom with silver galloons and precious sable fur, and drawn by ten snow-white, swan-like, horses." While listening to these stories his guests probably laughed themselves silly. It never occurred to them that all that could have been the truth: the wolves, snowstorms days long that covered the Russian villages with snow to the roof tops, the empress (albeit the future one), and the sleigh edged with sable fur and silver trim with ten or even sixteen horses harnessed one after another.

Of course, Münchhausen, as always, fibbed a little. It was not him but the chamberlain Semen Naryshkin who helped Fike to lie down in the sleigh (it was impossible to travel otherwise). Catherine recollects: ". . . to teach me to get up in the sleigh, they said to me: 'one must step over [enjamber], so step over.' This word, which I had never before heard pronounced, made me laugh so much on the way that I could not remember it without bursting into laughter."[15]

Princess Sophia remained Fike—a girl, gay and easily amused. Without fear or any doubts she drove at full speed in the sleigh along the smooth winter road to St. Petersburg and was, probably, thinking about the future, since youth is more disposed to dream than to recollect. Riding beside her was her mother, the duchess Johanna Elizabeth. Though she was an experienced woman who had seen much in her time, still the changes that had taken place recently turned her head.

The long and agonizing way from Berlin to Königsberg and Memel through impassable mud, the nights spent in bug-infested inns, highway-robbers, and the ice-cold wind from the sea—all these things miraculously vanished when they reached the Russian border. Attention, respect, richly laid tables, warm sable coats from the tsarina's own shoulders, a light frost on the smooth road, and the rollicking whoops and calls of the coachmen.

The sleigh covered the distance between Narva and St. Petersburg in just twenty-four hours. The capital welcomed the mother and daughter by a cannon salute from the bastions of the Sts. Peter and Paul Fortress. High officials, courtiers, and ladies-in-waiting appointed by the empress met them. Excellent apartments were prepared in the Winter Palace. Unfortunately, Elizabeth Petrovna herself was out of St. Petersburg: the Russian court had moved to the old capital. Nevertheless, the duchess and her daughter were given a lavish, royal welcome, which caused great envy among their German provincial relatives when Johanna Elizabeth triumphantly informed them of the event.

A reception was held in honor of the important guests and an elephant show was arranged. The merry Russian Shrovetide with its show-booths, swings, pancakes, gigantic snow mountains, and screaming, shouting, and singing filled the busy streets of the capital, which had nothing in common with the small quiet German cities they had left. It was another world—smart, motley, and utterly new to the girl.

Then came a swift journey to Moscow. Sixteen horses were harnessed to the sleigh and, as Johanna Elizabeth wrote to her husband, they flew rather than rode the entire distance (fifty versts per three hours was a great speed in those days). On February 9, both mother and daughter were already in the Annenhof Palace on the Iauza River in Moscow, where they were cordially greeted by Empress Elizabeth. They had already met the grand duke when he came running out and, without so much as inviting them to take off their coats, began chattering away with Fike as if she were an old acquaintance of his. That was actually the case, for the two had already met in Germany in 1739.

And now the bride-show began. The German guests were examined from head to foot, as the mother wrote, though presumably it was the daughter who was the true focus of attention. And everybody liked her. "The empress is delighted," wrote Jacob Stählin, Grand Duke Peter's teacher, in his memoirs describing Elizabeth's first impression of her meeting with Princess

Sophia. Johanna Elizabeth wrote to her husband that Fike had passed inspection with flying colors: the empress is affectionate and the grand duke loves her. And when in early March Fike suddenly fell gravely ill, the empress cut short her pilgrimage to the Trinity Monastery and hurried back to Moscow. Catherine recollects that when she finally regained consciousness she found herself in the empress's arms. The grand duke was equally distressed by Fike's illness for they had already become friends. There were no doubts after that episode: clearly Fike's bridal candidacy had been endorsed by imperial will.

Up to this point various court factions had argued bitterly over the question of the grand duke's fiancée. Vice Chancellor Aleksei Bestuzhev-Riumin, a politician greatly respected by the empress, feared an increase in Prussia's influence over Russian policy that might result from a marriage between the grand duke and the princess of Zerbst. One had every reason to harbor such misgivings. Following Frederick II's instructions, Johanna Elizabeth plunged into Russian politics, without even familiarizing herself with life in Moscow. She became friends with the French envoy Marquis de la Chetardy, his friend and Elizabeth's doctor, Count Jean Herman Lestocq, the heir's ober-hoffmarshal Count Otton Brümmer, and the Prussian envoy Baron Axel Mardefeld. Frederick informed the latter that he was expecting that the duchess of Zerbst would help him to settle his problems. All these people were choice enemies of the vice-chancellor and his political strategy—which was anti-French and anti-Prussian—and seemed to have been only waiting for the old sly fox to be thrown down from the political Olympus. Johanna Elizabeth's intrigues against Bestuzhev-Riumin as well as her silly and jealous attitude toward her daughter could not pass unnoticed by Elizabeth Petrovna, who was first displeased and then angered. It is no coincidence that immediately after Peter's and Catherine's marriage the empress sent Johanna Elizabeth abroad and never again allowed her to visit Russia or correspond with her daughter.

Fike did not take part in intrigues: her life path increasingly diverged from that of her mother, though Johanna Elizabeth tried, from force of habit, to keep her daughter under control. However, the duchess met with growing resistance on the part of the empress, who seemed to have admitted Fike into her small family and was defending her interests. Having found herself in the fantastic surroundings of Elizabeth's court Fike plunged headlong into the perpetual feast that the empress had arranged for herself and other people around her.

Catherine wrote in her memoirs: "I loved to dance so much that in the morning, from seven o'clock to nine o'clock, I danced under the pretext of taking ballet lessons from Landai, who was both the court's and the city's dancing master; then, at four o'clock in the afternoon, Landai returned once more and I danced under the pretext of practicing until six; then I dressed for the masquerade, where I once again danced for part of the night."[16] The

girl had entered that fascinating and brief period of life when tedious studies were over and the hated routine was gone, when boring restrictions had
somehow been lifted, and at last the longed-for adulthood had arrived, as
yet without the tiresome responsibilities that were to come later—for now
just the thrill of newfound freedom was sufficient; one could dance till one
dropped, wear any clothes one chose, spend hours making any hairdos one
liked; in fact, one didn't have to go to bed at all at night!

Spending nights with the young countess Maria Rumiantseva in her
bedchamber, Princess Sophia enjoyed a free-for-all: the girls jumped, danced,
and romped all night long and went to bed only toward morning. And when
the grand duke's fiancée was assigned eight chambermaids she was beside
herself with joy. They were all lively young girls and together in the evenings
they would raise a terrible din. Blindman's bluff was their favorite game. Fike
learned to play the harpsichord from Araia, a precentor of the empress's Italian choir. The princess later recalled that when Araia came "he played, and
I gamboled around the room: in the evenings the cover of my harpsichord
became of great use to us, because we put mattresses on the backs of couches
and on these mattresses the harpsichord cover, and that served us as a moun-
tain from which we would slide down."[17]

All this company, including the grand duke's fiancée, would bed down
for the night right on the floor, and the girls would conduct noisy discussions about the differences between the sexes. "I believe that for the most
part we were of the greatest innocence; for myself, I can swear that even
though I was sixteen years old, I was completely ignorant of what the difference consisted of; I did more: I promised the ladies to question my mother
about this the next day; this being said, we went to sleep. The next day, truly,
I asked my mother several questions for which she scolded me. Shortly afterward I had another caprice. I had the forelocks of my hair shortened, because I wanted them curled, and I urged that this troop of females should
do the same; many among them showed repugnance to this idea; others
cried, saying that they would be like tufted birds, but finally I succeeded in
convincing them to have their forelocks curled."[18]

By that time Fike had received a new name: in the summer of 1744 she
had converted to the Orthodox faith and had become Grand Duchess
Ekaterina (Catherine) Alekseevna. Her preparation for that event had been
going on a long time: she had been studying Russian, but she had paid the
greatest attention to learning by heart words to the Symbol of Faith: "I
believe in one God, the Father Almighty, Creator of Heaven and Earth . . ."
On June 28, 1744, the solemn baptism was held inside the Dormition Cathedral of the Moscow Kremlin, in the presence of the empress, the court
and the higher clergy. Fike-Catherine performed well. Soon after, Johanna
Elizabeth reported to her husband that their daughter had read the Symbol
of Faith in Russian without missing a single word in a clear, steady voice and
with such good pronunciation that she surprised all those present at the

ceremony, causing them to weep with emotion. Not even Catherine's envious mother could conceal her admiration for the nobility and grace displayed by the royal heir's future wife.

On the very next morning the long-awaited engagement ceremony took place. Grand Duke Peter Fedorovich and Grand Duchess Catherine Alekseevna were officially declared bride and groom. The whole country rejoiced in the event. A royal present was prepared for the public on this festive day: six roasted oxen stuffed with roasted poultry, and bread and wine in inconceivable amounts. Scenes of food giveaways for the masses have always been abhorrent. The last of these events occurred at Khodynka in 1896—and resulted in multiple deaths during the coronation of the last Russian tsar, Nicholas II.

The French diplomat Marie-Daniel de Corberon described a similar feeding during the reign of Catherine II, remarking that there was a large square in front of the palace which held up to thirty thousand people. A platform of logs with several steps was erected in the middle of the square. On the platform they placed a roasted ox covered with a red cloth. The people stood around, their voracious eagerness being restrained by the police. This picture resembled French hunting dogs lying in wait for their part of the deer. On this same square, there were fountains on both sides of the platform from which wine and kvass streamed. The first cannon shot put people on the alert. And it was only after the second shot that the police stepped aside and all the mob rushed forward. At that moment the people were like barbarians or cattle. There was one more additional incentive besides gluttony. The people seized the bull by the horns and tore the head off. The man who could bring the head to the palace would receive a reward of one hundred rubles for adroitness and strength. They maim, mutilate, and trample each other, as everyone wants to gain notoriety. Three hundred wretched men carried off this horrible trophy.[19]

However, we should keep in mind that Corberon himself came from a country where in the spring of 1770 more than one thousand people were trampled in a mad rush for the free meal provided in celebration of Louis XVI and Maria Antoinette's wedding. It must have been no less terrible to watch than the scene which the Frenchman observed in Russia.

However, this time there were no prizes, and even the wine fountains stood idle. This was due to the crowd, which at the first signal shot broke through the police cordon and tore the bulls to pieces in a disgraceful fight.

As the wedding day drew nearer, the bride felt increasing sadness and, as she recalled in her old age, she cried often without knowing the reason. Catherine's tears were not the tears of an ordinary bride who was saying good-bye to her carefree maidenly life. Her dreams of a dashing prince whom she would marry and love were soon dispelled. The destined prince was there, all right, but she could neither love him nor open her heart to him. This was no requirement as far as he was concerned and he would not even have understood the problem, for at seventeen he was still a capricious and ill-mannered child.

There was an explanation for this. Charles Peter Ulrich—the son of Peter the Great's daughter, Anna, and Charles Frederick, the Duke of Holstein—was born in Kiel in February 1728. Shortly after his birth his mother died of consumption. His father did not concern himself with problems of child-rearing and turned over this duty instead to Count Brümmer, who became the boy's tutor. One could hardly think of a worse teacher for the young prince, for he ridiculed the boy, beat him and taught him very little indeed.

With his drab character, Peter's father had influence over his son only in one sense: he trained the boy in military drills from a very early age, which the boy absorbed readily and, paradoxically, this later became a curse for the future generations of the Romanovs: they just went mad at the sight of a drill ground, the lined-up toes, and manual of arms. As a matter of fact, it was usual to entrust the general officers or even soldiers with supervising the education of princes. It was believed that this category of people, who toiled their whole lives in the army, knew the secret of turning sickly and delicate young men into great military leaders. As such, the Holstein officers who, following the duke's order, were to instruct seven-year-old Peter, taught him the things they knew best: service regulations, manual of arms, marching drills, discipline, and order.

Of course, one could not expect that those people should be familiar with studies of the Aristotelian or Copernican systems, and their tastes, jokes, and needs were quite primitive. Frederick the Great had a natural love for the military life, with its linear tactics and indispensable drills, though this did not prevent him from becoming educated, witty and a distinguished politician as well. However, the drill ground, camp, and ideally straight regimental forma-tions had played a special, exaggerated role in the life and biography of the future Russian emperor Peter III. His love of military affairs revealed a basic weakness rather than a strength, becoming an escape from the real world, which he found complicated and unfriendly. But that came later, in Russia. The foundations of such a worldview were laid during his childhood when drum rolls in the city streets or trooping the color in the palace yard caused the boy to abandon all his lessons and stand by the window in awesome wonder of marching soldiers. His father died in 1739 when Peter was eleven years old. A weak, sickly and puny child, the boy had become Duke of Holstein. Fike met her future husband as one of her relatives, for Peter was her second cousin.

The scheme of the filial relations looked like this: during the late seven-teenth century the Holstein-Gottorp ducal family was developing along two lines founded by brothers. The elder brother, Duke Frederick II, was killed at war in 1702. He was succeeded at the throne by his son, Charles Frederick, the husband of Tsarevna Anna Petrovna and the father of Charles Peter Ulrich, the future Peter III. Frederick II of Holstein's younger brother,

Christian Augustus, became the father of Johanna Elizabeth, and Fike's grandfather. Johanna Elizabeth had a brother, Adolf Frederick, the Bishop of Lübeck, who then—in 1739—was regent for Charles Peter Ulrich, the very young Duke of Holstein. It was in her uncle's palace that ten-year-old Fike met eleven-year-old Peter.

Young Fike paid no attention to the boy. Instead, she reveled in the rare opportunity of freedom to run around the castle and to cook a magic milk-soup with the housemaids. She had noticed, however, that her second cousin envied the freedom she was enjoying in the castle, for he was surrounded by numerous tutors who checked his every move.

When Empress Elizabeth Petrovna came to power in November 1741, she immediately took notice of her nephew. She was governed not only by family relations but by political reasons as well. According to the will of his grandmother, Catherine I, Peter the Great's grandson had more right to the Russian throne than did Elizabeth herself; therefore, he had better be kept under supervision. So in early 1742 Peter was brought to Russia, christened in an Orthodox church, given the name of Peter Fedorovich, and declared successor to the Russian throne.

His intellect, upbringing, and interests created a grim impression on all of the people around him. Elizabeth worried about her nephew's infantilism, capriciousness, hot temper, and his lack of manners. In May 1746, Bestuzhev-Riumin ordered Chief Hofmarshal of the grand duke's court to take every step possible to prevent Peter from playing and joking with footmen and servants. In addition, they were to see to it that the heir behaved himself properly in church and "was prevented from doing or saying indecent things, and playing pranks on servants, such as pouring [substances] on their clothes and faces, and other similar acts of mockery and humiliation."[20] Bear in mind that we are talking not about a cheeky teenage terror, but about an eighteen-year-old man who, by that time, was already married.

During the first months of Fike's life in Russia, she and Peter became friends. However, it was not the kind of friendship that develops into love. "He then was sixteen years old; he was handsome enough before the small-pox, but very small and very childish; he spoke to me of toys and soldiers, which occupied him from morning until evening. I listened to him out of politeness and complaisance and often I yawned without him guessing why, but I did not leave him, and he also believed that it was necessary to talk to me, and as he only spoke of what he liked, he amused himself very much in talking to me for long hours. Many people took this for true affection, especially those who hoped for our marriage; but never did we speak together the language of tenderness: it was not for me to begin it, modesty would have forbidden me if I had felt it, and the natural pride of my soul was sufficient to hinder me from making the first steps; as for him, he did not realize a thing, which, to tell the truth, did not dispose me favorably towards him; girls, however well raised they may be, like sweet and tender speech, above all from those from whom they can hear it without blushing."[21] Peter did not need a wife, but as Catherine wrote in her memoirs, he needed "a confidant in his childishness." And she became that for Peter, but that was all.

They were married on August 21, 1745, and Fike became the wife of the heir to the Russian throne. On their first wedding night, Catherine spent many hours lying in bed waiting for her husband, but the meeting did not promise nuptial harmony. As Catherine described it, after a heavy supper, Peter came into the bedroom and lay down in bed, remarking that it would amuse the servant to see them in bed together. He promptly fell asleep and slept peacefully until the next day. The situation remained unchanged for the next nine years.[22]

Fike was as unfortunate in love as she was in family life, though according to the constitution of her character she seemed to have been born for happiness. With sadness she wrote to Mrs. Bielke in 1767: "there is nothing as bad as having a child-husband. I know what one is worth, and I am one of those women who believes that it is always the husband's fault if he is not loved, for truthfully, I would have loved mine very much, if it could have been done, and if he had had the kindness to want it."[23]

She returned to this theme later in her memoirs: "I would have loved my new husband very well if he had wanted it or could have been lovable . . . but such is the temperament of my heart that it would have belonged entirely and without restrictions to a husband who would have loved only me, and with whom I would not at all have had to be apprehensive about the antics that I had to endure with this one; I always regarded jealousy, doubts and distrust, and all that comes from these, as the greatest of misfortunes, and I have always been persuaded that it depends on a husband to be loved by his wife if the latter has a good heart and a sweet character; the complaisance and good manners of her husband will win her heart."[24]

And these are not empty words. Several years before Catherine wrote them, Earl John Hobart had noted that the empress, by nature, was a very loving woman. It was enough to look at her to see that she was capable of love and that her love would bring happiness to a worthy admirer.

For many years her husband remained an overgrown child. When Elizabeth decided to arrange the marriage of her sixteen-year-old nephew, Doctor Lestocq advised the empress not to do so before Peter had reached the age of twenty-five—so backward was the heir both physically and mentally. Catherine describes how, for several years of their married life, Peter would bring toys into the bedchamber and right into bed, playing with dolls for hours and often involving his chamber woman in this childish pastime. But the duke's backwardness was not the only point. Catherine was a proud and arrogant woman, with a sense of dignity; that was apparent from the first meeting with her. Most of all, such women fear insult or even ambivalence.

Catherine recollected that during the very first days of her life with her husband, "I made a cruel reflection on him . . . I said to myself: if you love this man, you will be the most unhappy creature that has ever been on this earth; with the character that you have, you will want it to be returned; this man hardly even looks at you, he speaks only, or almost only, of dolls, and he pays more attention to any other woman than you; you are too proud to make a fuss about it, so then proceed with caution, if you please, in your tenderness toward this gentleman; think of yourself, madame. This first impression, poured in a heart of wax, remained with me, and this reflection has never left my head; but I was careful not to breathe a word of this firm resolution in which I found myself to never love without restriction someone from whom I would not be repaid in kind."[25] This confession is filled with a dry rationalism, very unusual for such a youthful age. That was the reverse side of tender Fike, that egotistic prudence, which always gives birth to ambition.

As the reader may remember, Fike's father advised his daughter to honor God, the empress, and her husband. Catherine had this advice transformed into a formula: "1) please the grand duke, 2) please the empress, 3) please the nation. I would have wanted to fulfill all three points, and if I did not succeed, it is either that those whom I sought to please were not disposed to it, or that providence did not wish it; because truthfully I neglected nothing to arrive at these ends: complaisance, submission, respect, desire to please, desire to do good, sincere attachment, all was constantly employed by me from 1744 to 1761. I confess that while I despaired of succeeding in the first point, I redoubled my cares to fulfill the two last ones; I thought I had succeeded in the second more than once, and the third point was a success in all its extents and without any restrictions at any time, and consequently I believed that I had fulfilled my goal rather well."[26]

It was apparent that the first problem was beyond solution. It often happens over the years that the contradictions of family life lessen, spouses draw closer together and even acquire subtle similarity. This couple's family life produced the opposite effect. In a formal portrait painted early in their marriage, the spouses are depicted standing awkwardly hand in hand, two long-nosed teen-agers bearing a great resemblance to one another whom fate had brought together. Later portraits show how they changed, becoming strikingly dissimilar, two estranged people with little in common, each one having since gone his or her own way.

From games with wooden soldiers and living servants Peter had graduated to incessant real war games, which substituted for real life. He had established a large Holstein army unit and during the summers he would conduct maneuvers, marches, parades, and troop the colors in the vicinity of Oranienbaum. He had turned into a real military man who breathed no other air but that of soldiers' barracks. He was the heir to the Russian throne, he was the Duke of Holstein who had been temporarily brought, for reasons unknown, to a foreign country with a terrible climate, a dismal capital, muddy towns, a pagan church, idiotic steam baths, which he refused to visit, an arrogant and servile nobility, an extravagant aunt, the empress, with whom he had never established intimacy. He endured with great difficulty all that was connected with her name, silently hated her, and desperately feared her.

Seeking to preserve his own self he incorporated various methods of defense. In youth it was through lying and in maturity it was through coarseness, self-isolation within the circle of his servants and soldiers of the Holstein army, idealization of his dear and great Holstein, and a boundless love for Frederick the Great. But all of these were ludicrously exaggerated: the lies and the coarseness, and the military games with both live and toy soldiers. Ludicrous was his patriotism as well, and his love for his idol from Potsdam. In fact the grand duke's whole appearance was ludicrous—narrow-shouldered and lean, dressed in a very tight Prussian uniform, with an enormous sword by his side, and gigantic jackboots on his feet.

When we read Catherine's memoirs we see Peter with her eyes. We hear the yelps of dogs he tortured, the screeching of a fiddle, noise and clamor. At times he would burst into his wife's apartments, reeking of tobacco, dogs, and wine, and wake her up just to tell her some scabrous story, or to relate the charms of the princess of Courland or a pleasant chat he had had with a lady he was currently chasing. Just as in the first months of her life in Russia, Catherine pretended to listen to him attentively, yawning discreetly, and waited until he had finished with his revelations which, of course, brought her no special pleasure.

They were absolutely different people, each speaking a language unknown to the other. Catherine writes that it was especially difficult for her to partake in detailed conversations of military matters, which gave him pleasure to talk about while she tried as hard as she could to conceal from him that she was tired and bored to tears. "I loved to read; he read also, but what did he read? Stories of highway robbers or novels which were not at all to my taste. Finally, never did spirits resemble each other less than ours; there was no rapport in our tastes, and our ways of thinking and envisaging things were so different that we would never have agreed on anything if I did not for the most part seek to be agreeable so as not to directly oppose him . . ."[27] And at last when he would take his leave, reading even the most boring of books seemed to her a most pleasant pastime.

Besides, Peter repeatedly demonstrated his own cowardice to Catherine; he was unable to defend the interests of their small family from the constant and unceremonious intrusions of strangers—Elizabeth's special messengers and informers. On more than one occasion the empress started to scold Catherine and the grand duke would join her and start scolding his wife, too, just to please his aunt. The year 1758 turned out to be a most difficult one for Catherine: suspected together with the chancellor Bestuzhev-Riumin in a conspiracy, she was interrogated by Elizabeth in person in the presence of the chief of the Secret Chancery, Count Aleksandr Shuvalov and the grand duke, the latter not only showing his doubts about his wife's defense but doing everything possible to direct the empress's rage at Catherine. Eventually, his actions roused the indignation of Elizabeth herself.

And there were also many occasions when the grand duchess, while sitting at the table next to her drunken husband, burned with shame for his grimaces, crudeness, and behavior in public, which was unworthy of the heir to the throne. All this obviously impeded the establishment of intimacy between them. But we should keep in mind that the above opinions are based on Catherine's personal memoirs. We see her husband, whom she hates, through her eyes. It would be wrong to say that Peter was absolutely indifferent to his wife. She cannot conceal this fact in her memoirs. When Catherine was suspected of taking a fancy to the handsome manservant of her bedchamber, Andrei Chernyshev, the following touching scene took place between the spouses: after dinner Catherine was lying on the couch reading a book. Peter came in, "he went straight to the window; I got up and went to join him. I asked him what was wrong and if he was mad at me. He was troubled and said to me after a moment of silence; 'I would like for you to love me as much as you love Czernischew.'"[28]

Like Catherine he felt alone at the court, and there were spies everywhere watching every step he made. When Kramer and Rumberg, two chamberlains who were dear to him and had been the most trustful and closest people he had known since his childhood, were dismissed from service and sent away from him, then, according to Catherine, Peter, "not being able to unburden his heart to anyone, turned to me in his distress. He often came to my bedchamber; he knew, or rather felt, that I was the only person with whom he could speak without a crime being made of the smallest thing he said; I saw his situation and I pitied him . . ."[29]

However, they failed to build a bridge of confidence and tender intimacy. It was as if he did not see a woman in her, taking her, at best, as a fellow-sufferer, while at the same time she was keeping a severe vow that cold reason had prompted her to make.

The grand duchess, the future empress, was a genius at conversation. She could charm and win over to her side all sorts of people. She possessed a kind of magnetic charm that attracted not only people but also animals. One contemporary recollects that dogs used to run to her from the whole district to be petted; they would find ways into the palace and would enter the empress's apartments in order to lie down at her feet; monkeys and birds trusted her alone.

A husband is not a monkey, of course, but for some reason Catherine's charm had no effect on him. Their family problems were caused, perhaps, not only by Peter's callousness and infantilism, and not only by Catherine's pride and extremely high demands of her partner, but also by the somewhat cold and sober calculations she had made during the earliest days of her marriage. This was apparent from the very beginning, and confirmed in her memoirs when she writes about those cruel thoughts that came to her mind during the first days of their life together: she was urging herself then to think about her own well-being.

In another place in her memoirs she blurts out: "The Grand Duke had given much attention to me during my illness, which he continued when I was better; I appeared to please him; I cannot say that he pleased me, nor that he displeased me; I knew only to obey and that it was up to my mother to have me married, but in truth I believe that the Russian crown pleased me more than his person."[30] She did not strive for unity, either; and she viewed herself as Peter's rival. The ambition that flared up very early in the princess of Zerbst and the Russian grand duchess prevented them from coming together.

The second task in her plan of conquering Russia—that is, to enjoy the favor of the empress—was also difficult to carry out. At first, Elizabeth was well disposed toward the girl from Zerbst, writing her affectionate letters and calling Catherine "my dear niece." Then changes occurred. The empress did not like the intrigues Princess Johanna Elizabeth organized at the Russian court, and she did not like the fact that Catherine had been involved in these intrigues. Moreover, with time the empress's antipathy toward her nephew began to extend to his wife: associating with the grand-ducal pair began to oppress her. For her part, Catherine realized soon enough that the luster of Elizabeth's court concealed dirty intrigues, envy, and hatred, and that the divinely beautiful empress could transform at will into a very real witch who was capable of releasing her fury at the drop of a hat, abusing and harassing the people around her with trivial carpings, although they had done nothing wrong, just to take pleasure in giving her relatives, officials, and servants a dressing-down. But most important, the empress was very hard to please—there was no limit to her whims and suspicions. Catherine lived next to Elizabeth for eighteen years, and that period was a sheer test of nerves, a school of endurance. Recollecting with sadness the years of her youth, Catherine wrote in her memoirs that the empress scolded her frequently and was rude to her often without any particular reason, offering her neither attention nor tenderness.

The whole life of the grand duchess was strictly regulated: days for feast and days to have a bath; a place for a sofa in the room and time to have a stroll; they refused to give her paper and ink and sent ladies-in-waiting over to tell her what dress she was to put on and what dress to take off. Although the empress lived in a room quite literally adjacent to that of the young couple, she did not see them for months at a time. However, she constantly gave them to understand that she never took her critical eye off them: it was her custom to send courtiers or even servants over to reprimand Catherine and Peter, often crudely, for their delinquencies of which she had learned

Catherine's mother, Johanna Elizabeth of Anhalt-Zerbst. From I. N. Bozherianov, "*Nevskii prospekt.*" *Kul'turno-istoricheskii ocherk dvukhvekovoi zhizni Sankt-Peterburga* ("Nevskii Prospect." A Cultural and Historical Sketch of St. Petersburg at Two Hundred) (St. Petersburg, 1901–03), vol. 1, p. 116.

from her spies. Catherine was even deprived of the right to correspond with her relatives, and she only signed the messages written on her behalf by the College of Foreign Affairs.

When Catherine's father died in 1747, the empress had sent a court lady to her with an order to stop weeping, for the prince of Anhalt-Zerbst was not a king, so his death was not that serious. The young woman had only to establish close relations with housemaids, servants, or court ladies, and they were immediately dismissed from court. This was done deliberately as Catherine was not allowed to make friends with anyone, be it man or woman. That was what distressed the grand duchess most of all, being a sociable and open person. Therefore, the bitter experience of being deprived of those she had become close to taught Catherine the art of concealing her affections.

She had neither the support nor the defense of her husband, and was lonely among Elizabeth's courtiers. She despised them and considered them frivolous, ignorant, and envious weavers of intrigue. However, living this life Catherine had learned much: she had accustomed herself to being sly, patient, and reticent. She had mastered the great art of a politician: the ability to control herself and to repress her feelings. A courtier wrote about Catherine that she seemed to be made of a fire that could ignite at the smallest spark, yet she was capable of regulating that fire with perfect control.

It took years and great effort for the grand duchess to win a living space for herself. She considered it to be a great victory to have the right to be left alone in her bedchamber, where she could read to her heart's content without anybody disturbing her. At first, Catherine started to read out of boredom and loneliness; but then she got accustomed to this kind of pastime, and reading became her passion and salvation; it was a whetstone that the future empress used to hone her mind. She was seen with a book in hand from the early morning till late at night, and she was very unhappy when she had to put it aside at dinner time, or to take a stroll or entertain guests.

Catherine was a voracious reader. At first she read everything indiscriminately. Very long, insipid French novels about shepherds and shepherdesses soon ceased to satisfy her, and she turned to more serious literature. It should be kept in mind that many people who came to know Catherine foretold her bright future and advised her to think about her education if she wanted to succeed. Among these were the court physician Jean-Herman Lestocq, the Prussian envoy Axel Mardefeld, and the count Hennings-Adolf Güllenborg from Sweden. The count's advice fueled Catherine's ambition and urged her to perfect her mind by reading books, which was the only type of university available in her situation. *Les lettres de Mme de Sévigné,* emotional, vivid, and witty confessions of an eighteenth-century French aristocrat, made an indelible impression on Catherine. Historical books from Tacitus to *Histoire générale d'Allemagne* by *le père* Barre accustomed her to a historical analysis of life and politics.

This time it was not just entertainment or escape from boredom but hard intellectual work, and Catherine had to deliberately exert herself: perusing one volume a week, she thus completed all the ten large volumes by Barre. It was with the same zeal and industry that Catherine took to studying the gigantic *Dictionnaires historique et critique* by Pierre Bayle, a compendium of diverse bits of knowledge on history, philosophy, religion, and philology rendered in an original and critical fashion, to which she gave an entire four years of her life. For many years, King Henry IV of France, the beau ideal of politician, statesman, and sovereign, became her hero. Many years later she would write to Voltaire that she dreamed of meeting King Henry in the other world, and I believe these two would have had something to talk about: as conversationalists they are really worthy of each other. One could also imagine Montesquieu and Voltaire, two other idols of Catherine's youth, joining their company as it was they who gave a powerful impetus to the intellectual growth of the future empress as statesman and lawmaker.

She would later confess to a lack of originality as a thinker. Moreover, writing at the decline of life, in 1791, she had the following to say: ". . . I never believed that I had a creative spirit; I met many people in this world, in whom I saw with neither envy nor jealousy much more wit than in myself."[31] One must respect this remarkable woman who could, at the peak of her worldwide fame, make such a confession. Even if, admittedly, she had some reason to say so, the whole variety of new and profound ideas on society, state, law, morals, and religion contained in works by Montesquieu and Voltaire, from which Catherine was drawing, helped her to stay all her life at a very high intellectual level far surpassing that of many of her contemporaries and even those who came in her wake.

Just as it is nowadays, there were then a great number of men whose very lives were based on a commonplace yet not irrelevant motto, "Books are a source of knowledge," and they were far more well-read than Catherine. Reading is, however, not enough to make one a personality and sovereign of her caliber: all this gigantic literary material had to be converted into the energy, rationale, audacity, and prudence of a politician, into an ability to think along broad lines, to ride a half pace ahead of events, lest they crush you like a high wave and drag you away into obscurity. Catherine proved capable of turning the material of books into ideas of her own.

For all this, she was far from being a bluestocking. After becoming a grand duchess, Catherine for the first time took up riding, in which she, almost at once, achieved a remarkable success (she even invented a saddle after her own fashion), and her riding was greatly admired by Elizabeth Petrovna, who was an excellent rider herself. Catherine was keen on hunting and fond of long walks in the forest and, generally, all kinds of movement: dancing and costume balls were a joy to her. Being truly feminine, she knew what's what in dress and decoration and more than once appeared at a court ball so dashingly attired that even the empress—who as we have seen was herself a woman of fashion and fine taste—looked on with envy. Catherine liked dressing up and it is truly remarkable that, when recalling those far-off days in her memoirs, she would plunge into minutest details describing the cut and color of her "victorious" dresses as well as those of Elizabeth and other ladies at court.

On September 20, 1754, that is, nine years after her wedding, Catherine gave birth to a boy, who was christened Paul. His parentage immediately gave rise to many rumors, the most tenacious of which was that it was Sergei Vasil'evich Saltykov, chamberlain of Peter III's court, rather than Grand Duke Peter Fedorovich, who sired the future emperor Paul I. The fact that the parents of the heir to the throne remained without an offspring for so long a time—nine years—was undoubtedly the cause of much concern for Elizabeth, who wished to see the continuation of Peter the Great's line.

Moreover, the empress remembered only too well that imprisoned in Kholmogory were Emperor Ivan Antonovich, whom she had dethroned, and his two brothers, Peter and Aleksei, and two sisters, Catherine and Elizabeth. Seeing that after a lapse of about nine months the marriage gave no issue, which the empire so badly needed, Elizabeth appointed her cousin Maria Choglokova as a new chief stewardess of the court to the grand duchess, prescribing her to keep a good watch over Catherine.

In fact, Choglokova received an instruction whose purport was, despite its being written in a flowery style, as clear as a day: this marriage was to bring forth an issue and the chief stewardess's duty was to see to it that Catherine behaved in a way conducive to conception and childbearing. Viewed as a matter of state and dynastic interests, this decision seems neither an act of cynicism nor a brute violation of man's intimate life, being motivated, as it was, solely by the reasons of state expediency and convenience. This surely accounts for so strict a routine and a constant observation under which Catherine remained. Incidentally, following Paul's birth, this routine was greatly slackened and the grand duchess obtained the freedom that she could not dream of before.

The instruction being issued and put into effect, the grand duke would not spend a single night outside his wife's bedchamber—he was also under constant observation—yet months and years passed by without issue. Elizabeth went as far as forbidding Catherine to use the man's saddle for fear that it might thwart her chances of conceiving a child. Yet all was in vain. The reader must have rightly guessed that Catherine had her own, rather stern attitude toward her union with Peter; yet dynastic marriages produce children even when the spouses are totally indifferent to each other. Sources make obscure hints to some physical defect of Peter's, which was fairly easily eliminated surgically after a lapse of some years. Besides, Peter was prodigiously inexperienced in matters of sex. It would be more appropriate, however, to let Catherine herself elucidate the matter as she did in her *Open-Hearted Confession*, written in 1775 specially for Potemkin. The method of sexual edification applied by Choglokova to her wards was, in principle, fully warranted by the morality and higher state interests of the time. Eighteenth-century manners, especially those adopted at royal courts, were, by and large, favorable to it, being rather loose, to say the least, and Catherine herself not infrequently mentions the court intrigues going on around her. A lady having no paramour was considered unattractive. Adultery was the norm, whereas the faithful conjugal relations were rarely met with. As a heroine in a play of Sumarokov puts it indignantly, she is "not like some lowly wife who adores her husband."

There is no doubt that Catherine took a fancy to the twenty-six-year-old Sergei Vasil'evich Saltykov, who, incidentally, was married at the time, and their going their separate ways gave her "much sorrow" later. Catherine caught sight of Saltykov, "fair as day," as one may gather from her account in the *Open-Hearted Confession,* a few years following Choglokova's appointment, in 1752, as the grand duchess's chief stewardess.

The Saltykov tale as it figures in Catherine's memoirs has a romantic flavor about it, which often marks reminiscences dealing with the first, pure and exalted affection, but his declaration of love during a hunt, to be later fictionalized by the memorialist, looks more like a scene from a novel: "Serge Soltikof waited for a moment when the others were pursuing the hares and approached me to speak to me of his favorite matter; I listened to him more patiently than usual. He sketched out his plan for me: that he had arranged to envelop in a profound mystery, he said, the happiness which someone could enjoy in such a case. I did not say a word. He took advantage of my silence to persuade me that he loved me passionately, and he begged me to permit him to believe that he could hope, that at least I was not indifferent to him. I told him that he could play in his imagination without my having the power to hinder him. Finally, he compared himself to other people of the court and made me acknowledge that he was preferable to them, from which he concluded that he was favored. I laughed at what he said, but in essence I acknowledged that he pleased me well enough. After an hour and a half of conversation I told him to leave because such a long conversation could become suspect. He told me that he would not leave if I did not say to him that he was acceptable [*si je ne lui disois, qu'il étoit souffert*]; I answered him: 'Yes, yes, but leave.' He said: 'I insist upon hearing it,' and gave two kicks to his horse, and I cried out to him: 'No, no,' and then repeated to him: 'Yes, yes'. Thus we separated."[32] This meeting took place at the estate of the Choglokovs, with whom Saltykov was on close terms.

Yet no one can say with certainty that Paul's father was no one but Sergei Saltykov. Rumors circulated at the time when Catherine was the empress, reaching Tsesarevich Paul Petrovich's ears, which could not have been good for his mental equilibrium. There remains a note, written in harsh tones by the empress to the chief marshal of the court, Nikita Golitsyn, in approximately 1783, in which she forbids the chamberlain, Dmitrii Matiushkin, to ever show himself in her presence. One may assume that the anger of the empress, who put the court chamberlain into disgrace, was induced by the latter's spreading gossip about Paul's origins, which he had imprudently shared with the tsarevich himself and his consort. Catherine saw in it an attempt to make her quarrel with her son and cast suspicion on her honor. It should be noted, in passing, that D. M. Matiushkin's wife, Anna Alekseevna, née Gagarina, used to be one of the grand duchess's maids of honor and her close friend in youth. She was dismissed from court immediately after Paul's birth, which coincided with the time when Saltykov was sent abroad. By enjoining her chief marshal of the court to announce her imperial displeasure to Matiushkin in the presence of the latter's wife and at the same time stressing that she was not privy to her husband's prattle, Catherine was nonetheless aiming, in her roundabout way, at Anna Alekseevna as well, forewarning her that she should hold her tongue in check and refrain from providing her husband—fool and prattler that he was—with gossip or, shall we say, the reliable information that she had at her disposal? Also worthy of note here is an order issued by Catherine on July 25, 1762, soon after she became sovereign, appointing Saltykov envoy to Paris. On August 19 the same year, she pressed the diplomatic service, as follows: "Dispatch Sergei Saltykov as soon as possible."[33] Later, on learning of her former favorite's ill-health, the empress required that Saltykov's archives be sealed in case he died.

Paul's birth was a cause for great joy at court. No sooner had the baby been washed than Empress Elizabeth took him under her care. Grand Duke

Catherine's son, Grand Duke Pavel Petrovich. From A. V. Morozov, *Katalog moego sobraniia russkikh gravirovannykh i litografirovannykh portretov* (Catalogue of My Collection of Engraved and Lithographed Portraits), vol. 3 (Moscow, 1913), folio CCCII.

Peter Fedorovich went off to his quarters to celebrate the heir's birth in the company of his pals, and the woman recently confined stayed alone in an empty room forsaken by all and suffering from cold drafts and thirst. All her life afterward Catherine remembered these bitter first hours following her delivery, as they symbolized the general attitude to her as a woman, whose only function in life was to give birth to an heir to the throne. Her first-born son was taken away from her and she saw him for the first time only forty days later. Elizabeth took upon herself all the care of the boy, keeping even his own parents away from him.

On giving birth to a son, Catherine acquired, at last, her much-coveted freedom. Peter visited her but occasionally, having plunged into his military pursuits and drunken revelries in his friends' company and, in addition, seriously fallen for the maid of honor Elizaveta Vorontsova. As a result, the grand duchess could without impediment turn herself to fulfilling the third and, probably the most important, task of her scheme, which was "to win the love of people."

Starting in 1754–1755, Catherine was assiduously grinding away at the subtleties of political life. She comprehended fairly early the two most vital factors determining her life as politician: the first was public opinion, the second her ties among Russian society's upper crust and, more precisely, with the Guards officers. These were her two little secrets of winning the love of a great people.

The first thing to do was, in her opinion, to become Russified and the sooner, the better. On becoming the wife of the heir to the Russian throne, Catherine did all possible to be regarded as Russian. She did not find it difficult. Prior to her arrival to Russia, Fike lived and was educated in a fairly cosmopolitan German Lutheran milieu tinged with French and the spirit of the Enlightenment. The whole tenor of her family's life and their frequent journeys over Germany made it unlikely that the girl should develop any strong attachment to any particular place, in this case, her parental household. An ability to adapt herself to different surroundings and an innate resourcefulness were the qualities Fike possessed since childhood. As her memoirs reveal, she made it a rule for herself to please the people she had to rub shoulders with, studiously assimilating their ways of life and manners: "I wanted to be Russian so that the Russians would have affection for me."[34]

Later, in 1776, writing to her son's bride, Sophia-Dorothea, princess of Württemberg (the future empress Maria Fedorovna), Catherine II thus formulated her "doctrine of assimilation": when changing the place of residence, one has to be grateful to one's new motherland for being chosen in preference to other nominees. It was this kind of feeling that Catherine herself experienced. When she was speaking of "my country" neither she herself nor anyone else doubted that it was Russia she had in mind, that is, the country that she was fond of and prided herself on being sent there. A courtier said that Catherine deep in her heart was Russian, being born, as she was, for the empire of Russia. She observed all Russian customs, took part in the frolics and carols at Christmas-tide, wore Russian dresses, which she introduced at court, knew all the Russian proverbs and sayings, and even took the Russian *bania*.[35]

Of course, there were more important things than just steam baths and songs. An institution to be revered most was the Russian Orthodox Church, as only those professing Russian Orthodoxy deserved to be called Russians. This was a notion that Catherine was quick to acquire. One can imagine how much patience and willpower this woman—herself an atheist and disciple of Voltaire's—had to exercise in order to endure church services lasting hours, bowing scores of times down to the ground, leaving church premises looking thoroughly pacified amid a covey of her new compatriots. It was only on becoming the empress that she allowed herself to hear the service from her place at the gallery, playing some complex solitaire at a small discreet table, but before that, God forbid!

The result of all this was that, as Catherine's biographer, Vasilii Bil'basov, puts it, little by little, under the sway of diverse factors, circumstances, and pressures, the Fike of Zerbst was noticeably turning into the Russian Ekaterina Alekseevna. How far she had gone in the course of Russifying is well shown by her behavior in the incident with the chamberlain Shkurin. The latter, despite Catherine's interdiction, related to Choglokova some innocuous remarks made by the grand duchess. When she learned of this, Catherine went to the wardrobe room in which Shkurin used to stay and on finding him there, slapped him in the face as hard as she could, adding to this that she would have him whipped to boot. "Could that have been done by Fike of Zerbst?" Bil'basov inquires rhetorically.[36]

One should also cite here an amusing episode of 1768 that was related to the forthcoming arrival of the king of Denmark in St. Petersburg. Catherine, who was already the empress by then, ordered the governor-general of Moscow to send her a list of all Moscow beauties with a view of choosing the most dashing ones among them, who were then to be brought to the northern capital. "What for?" one would ask. Only to give Catherine the opportunity to casually remark, in reply to the Danish king's admiration of the beauty of Russian ladies, that "here in Russia, they are all like that." The Danish king's visit did not come off but the temptation to "throw dust into the foreigners' eyes" (which is still our wont) became natural to the empress.

Another important piece of truth that Catherine came to learn back in the early years of her life in Russia was that despite a certain muteness of society, there existed in Russia what was later referred to as public opinion, which only a fool would ignore. Foreigners accompanying the empress in her trips across the country could not but marvel at Catherine's piety as she heard the liturgy over and over again in all the churches along her way. They also noticed how often Her Majesty got off her carriage to have a talk with simple folks, who immediately ran up to her from all sides. Count Ségur recalls that at first the crowd would prostrate themselves before the empress's feet but then they would surround her, the peasants addressing her "Our Dear Mother" and speaking to her in a hearty way and without fear and the village women vying with each other to kiss her so that later she would have to wash herself thoroughly to take off the ceruse and rouge that the village beauties had smeared her with.

This fairly populist (to use the modern term) stance taken up by Catherine had its purpose and reason. Having neither Riurik nor, for that matter, Romanov blood in her veins and making, on June 28, 1762, short work of her husband, she needed all the popularity and love of the people she could muster. She was well aware that the tidings of her short stay in some godforsaken village or her attending the liturgy at some poor parish church would swiftly spread round the area; the light-winged rumor of the good mother-tsarina who had no qualms about descending from her ethereal heights down to her people would then fly all over the entire uezd and province. That was the reason she forbade in 1763 Adam Olsuf'ev and Nikita Panin to erect prior to her visit there a richly decorated reliquary over St. Dimitrii of Rostov's holy relics; simple folks might think that they were purposely hidden from the eyes of a foreign empress.

She had adopted this manner of doing things at an early stage, when she was only aspiring to power. The means that the grand duchess used to win society's favor may well be illustrated by what she said to Countess Rumiantseva. "Both on ceremonial occasions and at ordinary gatherings and parties I would come up to old ladies and sit down at their side . . . inquire about their health and give them a piece of advice as to what medicine to take when ill, I would listen with patience to their endless stories about the days of old and the ennui of the out times, about the foppishness of youth. I would ask their advice on this or that matter and then heartily thank them for it. I would learn the names of all their pug-dogs and lap-dogs, their parrots, and female jesters. I would know when each of those nobles' wives had her name-day. On that day my personal chamberlain would congratulate them on my behalf and present them with flowers and fruit from my greenhouses at Oranienbaum. Within less than two years, the warmest praise of my wit and heart was heard from every corner, spreading all over Russia. In this easy and harmless way, I managed to win great fame for myself so that when it came to ascending the Russian throne, I had a considerable majority at my side."[37]

Of course, what Catherine was telling here is only part of the truth: in fact, her path to power was far from easy and short. What is beyond any doubt, however, is that she always took into account the voice of public opinion, which she turned to her own advantage.

We also remember that one reason Empress Elizabeth had chosen Fike as her nephew's future spouse was that the princess of Zerbst could not and, as Elizabeth reckoned, would not gather up a party of her own in Russia.

At first, the empress's reckoning was right: Catherine devotes many pages of her memoirs to an account of her total isolation during the first few years of her married life. After the birth of her son, however, her situation gradually changed for the better as the control over the grand duchess was relaxed. Aided by her courtiers and, especially, Sergei Saltykov, who had just returned from Poland and was, in Catherine's own words, "a devil incarnate" as far as intrigue was concerned, and Lev Naryshkin, she would steal out of the palace to meet her friends, who grew in number, to frolic and talk shop. Her political views, which she never hid, were now to be reckoned with by such high-ranking officials of the Elizabeth's court as the Shuvalovs, Field Marshal Stepan Apraksin, Vice Chancellor Mikhail Vorontsov, the Razumovskiis, and also Chancellor Aleksei Bestuzhev-Riumin himself.

It was the latter who, on seeing that Catherine was a person of much intelligence and resolve, risked dragging the grand duchess into a political game of his own. When in the mid-1750s Elizabeth's health took a turn for the worse, the chancellor realized that being an implacable enemy of Prussia, he would be cashiered as soon as Peter III came to power. Sensing that here was a strong personality, he staked on Catherine, while assigning for himself the role of her preceptor and tutor. He made every effort to win the grand duchess's confidence, helping her to start a clandestine correspondence with her mother and taking under his protection the handsome dandy Stanislas Poniatowski, with whom she was having a tumultuous love affair.

What Bestuzhev-Riumin and Catherine feared most was that Elizabeth might, on her deathbed, sign her last will and testament in favor of Tsarevich Paul, appointing someone from the Shuvalov clan as regent to the infant emperor, thus barring both Peter and Catherine from the throne. Bestuzhev-Riumin prepared the draft of a manifesto under which Catherine was to ascend the throne as regent to Emperor Paul, whereas he himself was to get the posts of president of all the main colleges and commander of all the Guards regiments. On presenting his plan to Catherine, the ambitious chancellor had no idea that the woman he was dealing with was a full-fledged politician herself who needed neither instruction not patronage and that the grand duchess had long been blazing with an ambition of her own.

In September 1796, two months before her death, Catherine was writing to Baron von Grimm: "Reign or die, that is our motto; it should be engraved on our coat of arms from the beginning; at present, it is too late."[38] Here the empress does not sin against the truth: it simply slipped her mind that this motto had already figured on her invisible shield some forty years before. In her letter to the British ambassador Sir Charles Hanbury-Williams, dated August 12, 1756, the grand duchess spoke in detail of the actions she would take on the day of Empress Elizabeth's death in case the Shuvalovs attempted to elevate Paul to the throne and remove her and her husband from power. Alluding to King Adolph Frederick of Sweden, who was limited in his rights by the Riksdag, she writes as follows: "The blame will lie on my party if [they] have the upper hand. But be assured that I will not play the meek and weak role of the Swedish king: I will either reign or perish."[39]

Such was the creed of a twenty-seven-year-old woman who was aiming high. Williams was, in fact, her closest political comrade: he continually provided the grand duchess with money, and it was in him that she confided all her plans of the future takeover. Their particulars are of minor importance and interest here: what is far more valuable, however, is that her letters to Williams reveal that side of Catherine's character that is left out in her memoirs and touching narratives of her unpretentious canvassing among old ladies in St. Petersburg salons. It is here that she comes out under her new guise of a cynical, calculating, and audacious woman who will stop at nothing in her pursuit of power and who is ambitious in the extreme. Reading these letters, one recalls the mock confession she made to Duke de Ligne on observing her marble bust in the Hermitage. She stated that she could not pass it without feeling the bile rise in her throat, its expression having something brazen in it, something which the daubers and carvers call the lofty mien.[40] It is the same brazen face that lurks behind the grand duchess's letters to the British ambassador. On the other hand, can one lacking it achieve anything in politics?

The debut of Catherine the plotter was a disastrous flop: Elizabeth recovered, the plot of Bestuzhev-Riumin and Catherine was exposed, and although the investigators failed to dig up anything illuminating on the old chancellor's and young enterprising lady's projects (fortunately for himself and Catherine, Bestuzhev-Riumin managed to destroy their correspondence), things got unpleasant for both of them. In the spring of 1758, Bestuzhev was relieved of his post and exiled to his village; Field Marshal Apraksin, who sympathized with the conspirators, died during the interrogation in August 1758; Poniatowski and Williams were banished from the country, and Poniatowski's intimate, Ivan Elagin, was sent off to Kazan' province. Peter turned his back on his wife once and for all, avoiding her as if she were plague-stricken.

"Our poor grand duchess is in despair," "things are in a bad way with the grand duchess"—these were the phrases recurring most regularly in reports of western diplomats with regard to Catherine after Bestuzhev-Riumin's downfall. For months on end she remained in isolation, which was tantamount to house arrest, writing frantic letters to the empress, asking for an audience which would "give me the ineffable joy to behold the visage of Your Imperial Majesty." Elizabeth, however, remained mute to her entreaties. Feeling utterly desperate, Catherine feigned dying and even received last rites from her confessor. The trick worked and the audience, devised as a kind of unrecorded interrogation, did take place. Mobilizing all her wit and willpower, Catherine managed to vindicate herself in the eyes of her august interrogator: she melted the empress's heart by begging Elizabeth to send her back to her mother in Germany, since it was clear to her that here in Russia she was not being trusted and was kept as a criminal. This was a shrewd move and Elizabeth fell for it: in May 1759, the grand duchess was allowed to go out. That episode prompted Elizabeth to conclude that her nephew was a fool and his wife a very clever woman.

Having escaped permanent damage, Catherine had to go through parting with Stanislas, who was obliged to leave Russia. "This impatient man," as she refers to him in one of her letters of 1758 to Ivan Elagin, who had by that time been banished to the country, "left me a month ago already and my boredom and grief are great [although] I hope for his return."[41] However, months went by and a year passed and then another one but Stanislas Poniatowski had not returned and seemingly made no attempts to do so.

Meanwhile, to live one's life in obscurity, surrounded by foes and strangers, was a heavy burden, indeed. Little by little, however, Catherine's distress ebbs away, her ennui vanishing into thin air when in 1760 she gets a new favorite, this time the handsome soldier and dashing daredevil Grigorii Grigor'evich Orlov. This twenty-five-year-old artillery captain, who had just returned from the war in Prussia, was one of five brothers Orlov, who were famed for their feats on the battlefield and successes among St. Petersburg ladies.

Orlov turned out to be a godsend for Catherine: behind his broad-shouldered back one could safely hide oneself from all misfortunes of life. This was a happy match, as Orlov, being a real gallant, would go through fire and water for his lover's sake. What really mattered was that here was not a court Lovelace and rake like Saltykov, nor a foreigner like Poniatowski, whom Russians regarded as an alien, but a native Russian. Here was an officer befriended by all St. Petersburg and enjoying the company of a multitude of people, all his boon companions and fellow servicemen, who loved him as a kind and generous fellow, for he was generous indeed, having at his disposal the moneys of the Ordnance Corps, which he spent, to be sure, not only on making new artillery wagons.

Empress Elizabeth passed away at two o'clock in the afternoon on December 25, 1761. She gave them no surprises on her deathbed, peacefully bidding her last farewell to Catherine and Peter and asking them to take good care of their infant son. Without much ado, the grand duke was crowned emperor and the grand duchess became empress. However, Catherine's worries over the future did not disappear. As the French diplomat Breteuil notes in his memoirs, while the majority grieved at heart for Elizabeth, they felt fear and timidity rather than affection toward the new emperor.

Little has changed in Peter Fedorovich's life since our last meeting with him. He is a grown-up man now and no longer plays with dolls, and rather than disciplining his valets, he drills youths of the Cadet Corps and men of the regiment brought over to him from Holstein. He has taken to drink-

Grand Duke Peter Fedorovich. From I. N. Bozherianov, "*Nevskii prospekt.*" *Kul'turno-istoricheskii ocherk dvukh vekovoi zhizni Sankt-Peterburga* ("Nevskii Prospect." A Cultural and Historical Sketch of St. Petersburg at Two Hundred) (St. Petersburg, 1901–03), vol. 1, p. 108.

ing, which he now does in the open, and he plays his fiddle often. His behavior in society was so outlandish that all the diplomats said with one accord: "Such an emperor will not sit on the throne for long."

Back in 1747, when Peter was only nineteen, the Prussian envoy Finkelstein prophetically wrote to King Frederick II that the Russian people hated the grand duke so much that he risked losing the crown even when it came over to him the legitimate way, following the death of the empress. When, in 1761, Peter was thirty-three years of age, the Frenchman

Lafermière wrote that the grand duke was a remarkable product of the forces of nature and the first impressions of childhood who, though he was thirteen when he was taken from Germany and handed to the Russians, who brought him up in the traditions of their religion and the morals of their empire, he never ceased to be a German to the marrow of the bone. Never had a titled heir enjoyed so little affection from his people. Now and then Peter's too blatant liking for the Germans wounded the self-esteem of the Russians. Not being very pious, Peter also failed to win the confidence of the clergy.[42]

Lafermière summed up Peter in a nutshell, and we may only add to it some particulars, such as how, to Russia's detriment, the new emperor made peace with Frederick II; how, in Holstein's interests, he started preparations for a war with Denmark; how he publicly scorned the liturgy and never crossed himself in church; how he kept for himself a retinue of Germans, walked around clad in the Prussian uniform, and introduced the strictest discipline coupled with incessant drills, which although indispensable in the army, were quite burdensome for Catherine's Guards. The list could go on. Inflexible and stubborn, he pushed his way through no matter what, regardless of the grumbling going on behind his back and advice given to him by his idol Frederick II and other well-wishers.

The British envoy Robert Keyth once could not contain himself, remarking to Countess Bruce, while watching Peter III, that the emperor had gone completely mad: one simply does not behave as he does. However, Peter was neither a madman nor a fool nor a rascal, and he spilled no one's blood. He looked absurd and queer on the Russian throne, like someone who got there by mistake. Ungovernable and eccentric, he was unable, on assuming unlimited power, to handle events in a rational way, to be a politician and perceive himself as the autocrat of All Russias.

Peter III's life is dramatic in that he had the precarious fate to reign in a precarious country. Had he stayed in Holstein, he would probably have lived a long life and died an exemplary duke much bereaved by his subjects. Instead, it fell to his lot to come to Russia, where he had the offensive nickname "foreigner" stuck to him, meaning that here was a Russophobe, a lover of military drills, a petty tyrant, and a fool. If it is true that every man is a master of his fate, then Peter had obviously bungled his and one had to agree with Catherine's writing that Peter III himself was his own worst enemy—so irrational were all his actions.

Now let's return to Catherine. Those five weeks during which the populace bid their farewell to the late empress were spent by Catherine in full mourning at the side of her coffin. She would not depart from the deceased for a single day and even the strong odor of decay would not scare her off. To be sure, it was not grief that made Catherine return to that darkened funerary room each morning. We know that her relations with Elizabeth had been quite strained and that it was the grand duchess who so imprudently

Emperor Peter III. From A. G. Brikner, *Istoriia Ekateriny Vtoroi* (History of Catherine II) (St. Petersburg, 1885), p. 107.

repeated in her letter to Williams the words Poniatowski had addressed to the empress: "Oh, that log of a woman! She simply drives us mad! Would she die at last!" Her gesture here meant something else. She was clever enough to realize that her prolonged grief would not be left unnoticed, gaining her some favor, all the more so as nearby was her august consort horsing around and prattling with her maids of honor and mocking and mimicking the clergymen.

At the same time, however, her clinging to Elizabeth's coffin meant that she was in mortal fear to part with her past and face all the trials and tribulations awaiting her outside the walls of the mourning room. Everybody noted that there was no mention of the empress's name in the manifesto on Peter III's accession, that he openly humiliated his royal spouse in public, and that she, who was full of ideas, learning, and ambitious thoughts and intentions, possessed not a shadow of real power.

The British envoy Keyth wrote to London in March 1762 that the empress's influence was slight: not only was she disregarded in matters of state, but in private affairs, too, it would be useless to hope for success, relying on her mediation. The French ambassador Breteuil followed suit, noting that the empress's plight was desperate. She was held in utter contempt as the emperor redoubled his attention to the Vorontsova maid, appointing her Stewardess of the Household. Vorontsova now resided at court and enjoyed everyone's esteem. Why it would be hard to say, for she was not noted for her wit and her features were repugnant. She looked, in Breteuil's opinion, like some scullery maid of the lowliest kind.[43]

Well, tastes differ—after all, we do not know what Breteuil's wife looked like! What is beyond any doubt, however, is that Peter's attachment to Elizabeth Romanovna Vorontsova was strong. In fact, it posed a serious threat to Catherine: Elizabeth Vorontsova was backed by all the Vorontsov kinsmen, who, with her uncle, Chancellor Mikhail Illarionovich Vorontsov, wielded much influence at court. Peter not only made no bones about his liaison with her but he also repeatedly voiced his intention to leave his loathsome wife. Rumors of a neat cell being prepared in the Schlüsselburg Fortress near the one to which Ivan Antonovich was confined spread around the capital. In her letter of June 1762 to Baron Osten, Catherine herself stated that the Vorontsovs had made plans to shut her up in the cloister and put their relative on the throne at Peter's side.

In 1766, a folk ballad was recorded in Moscow narrating of a tsarina who goes weeping from loneliness and when taking a walk in a grove is more afraid of her own husband than of all the wolves and brigands: "He walks in the open with his favorite maid of honor, Elizabeth Vorontsova, they walk hand in hand, thinking of how to do away with the tsarina."

On top of these difficulties Catherine faced another one: pregnancy. On April 11, 1762, she gave birth to a boy—Orlov's son (future count Aleksandr Grigor'evich Bobrinskii)—and the newborn was immediately snatched away from the palace to the house of the empress's valet, Shkurin.

Recurring to Breteuil's report, one cannot but notice that it ends on a fairly optimistic note. He thought that the empress, whose personal pluck and ardor impressed him, would sooner or later make up her mind to take some drastic measures. He knew she had friends who, while doing their best to console her, would stop at nothing, would she but ask them.[44]

And, indeed, Catherine's friends kept pressing her to stop sitting idle but, benefiting from the all-around hatred of Peter, overthrow him, immuring in a dungeon, and herself take up the reins of government, ruling as empress or regent during the minority of her son. The situation as it developed at the early summer of 1762 was much conducive to it: indignation was running especially high in the army and the Guards, who were soon to embark and sail off to the war with Denmark, as it was the wish of the Russian emperor, intent on revenging himself for the annexation, in 1702, of a part of the Duchy of Holstein. The war was just as unpopular as the Prussian-cut uniforms that the soldiers were now wearing. Catherine knew that she was not alone and that her loyal friends would not waver—one had only to look at the Orlov brothers to get evidence of this. She also discussed her version of a coup d'état with Count Kirill Razumovskii—influential dignitary and patron of the Izmailovskii regiment and with the heir's tutor, Count Nikita Panin. Both were ready to back her up. However, as is often the case with such undertakings, it was not easy to pluck one's courage and bring oneself to such a desperate business as a coup d'état without an impulse so powerful that it allowed no alternative, no retreat.

The incident that served as a spur took place at a ceremonial dinner held on June 9, 1762, when Peter, enraged for some reason at his wife, shouted "*folle*" at her across the table, with all the nobles, generals, and diplomats present witnessing the affront. It was obvious that Peter, despite his living all these years side by side with Catherine, was unable to comprehend that one could not openly insult a woman of her kind with impunity. From that day on, Catherine paid more heed to those who advised her to act decisively and promptly.

It was now June and all the court had moved out of town. Catherine settled in Peterhof while Peter resided in his much beloved Oranienbaum, which the empress visited June 19, seeing the emperor alive for the last time: she attended a comedy piece being performed at a small stage of the Oranienbaum Palace in which Peter participated by playing his fiddle. We shall never know what Catherine's thoughts were on that occasion. Perhaps, while watching her imperial spouse fiddle amid the orchestra players, she varied Emperor Nero's last words and said to herself: "What a musician is being wasted!" After the performance Catherine went back to Peterhof. She was ready for her revolution and only waited for a signal from the Orlovs.

On June 28, the eve of his name-day (as June 29 is the holy feast devoted to St. Peter and St. Paul), Peter, accompanied by Chancellor Vorontsov, Field Marshal Burkhard Christopher von Münnich—the Prussian envoy whom Peter had by that time rescued from exile—the Vorontsova maid, and other ladies and gentlemen of the court, set off to Peterhof to attend a reception in Monplaisir Palace. Arriving at Peterhof, the emperor and his entourage found Monplaisir Palace, residence of the empress, empty, Catherine, to their surprise, having left in secret for St. Petersburg at five in the morning. Feeling something amiss, the ladies started wailing.

Frederick II related to Count Ségur on the coup d'état of June 28, 1762: "Their conspiracy was mad and badly plotted; Peter III's lack of courage, despite the advice of the brave Münnich, caused him to lose; he let himself be dethroned like a child being sent to bed."[45] The Prussian king added, however, that ". . . *neither the honor nor the crime of this revolution* can be justly credited to the empress; she was a young, weak, isolated foreigner, on the eve of being repudiated, locked up. The Orloffs did everything; . . . Catherine was not yet able to lead anything: she threw herself in the arms of those who wanted to save her."[46]

Much of what the great king said rings true. The Orlov brothers, being the rowdies, boozers, and braggarts that they were, make a truly farcical sight as a pack of plotters. Trying to win the favor of the Dear Mother, they acted so ineptly that the ministers of Peter learned of Grigorii Orlov's seditious campaigning and appointed to him a spy, Peter III's aide-de-camp Stepan Perfiliev, who was to wheedle out of Orlov all his evil designs.

Yet it would be appropriate, without ever questioning Frederick the Great's astuteness and life experience, to remark here that Russia and Germany are very different in many respects and that coup d'états in Russia are almost invariably slated for success. Was the plot devised by Elizabeth Petrovna in 1741 or the one against Biron in the fall of 1740 hatched better? All revolutions are foolhardy, the designs of revolutionaries alogical and seemingly unfeasible, being, as they are, at odds with reality; yet they often score successes, at any rate in Russia. In fact, the glorious revolution of June 28 was prepared not so much through the effort of the gallant brothers Orlov, who championed Catherine's cause by carousing with their fellow officers of the Guards and handing out money to their company men for a glass of vodka to be drunk toasting the empress's health and their "Dear Mother's kindness," as by Peter III himself, whose foolish policy so alienated his men and officers that everybody was seething with discontent and one needed only to strike a match for a revolt to flare up. Meanwhile, the emperor was grossly ignorant of what was going on, living in utter complacency with himself.

In reply to Frederick II's warnings of Catherine's ambitious intents and a plot being hatched by the Guards, Peter wrote: "As to Your worries about my personal safety, I beg You not to take it too much to heart: my men refer to me as their 'Father'; in their own words, they prefer to obey a man rather than a woman. I go on foot unescorted along St. Petersburg streets: if anyone had planned anything evil against me, they would have carried out their intents long ago. However, I do no harm to anyone and put all my hopes on God only. Protected by Him, I have no fear."[47] Most probably, Peter had not learned the Russian version of the proverb "Rely on God but do not yourself slip up."

The situation on the eve of the flare-up may well be illustrated by an episode with an unnamed corporal of the Preobrazhenskii Regiment, which, in fact, set the stage for the overthrow. The corporal, probably for fear of missing the historic event, passed from one officer to another, asking them the same question: "When shall we start overthrowing the emperor?" The lieutenant Izmailov, while sending the man about his business, did, nevertheless, for the sake of his own safety, report him to his company commander, who informed his superiors. The word got out that the day before the corporal had inquired the same thing of Captain Peter Passek, who, likewise, put him off but, unlike the martinet Izmailov, did not report him to his commanding officer. This was a serious crime in Russia. Passek was arrested and taken into custody at his regiment's quarters. Passek was the Orlovs' closest friend and boon companion, hence, a fellow plotter, and on learning of his arrest the Orlovs started to rush about the capital, sending frantic messages around: "Passek is arrested! The plot is exposed! We'll all perish, one must act immediately!"[48] As Grigorii Orlov was excused from the job— he was busy treating to liquor his eavesdropper Stepan Perfiliev—the "revolutionary committee" was made up of his younger brothers Aleksei (Alekhan) and Fedor.

Fedor Orlov went to see Kirill Razumovskii, to whom he said that his brother Aleksei was about to set off to Peterhof for Catherine, whom he intended to fetch to the Izmailovskii Regiment, where there were many officers well disposed to the empress. On hearing this, Razumovskii, rather than starting to run about his study in confusion, as he knew the Orlovs' worth, only nodded several times in reply to Fedor's impassioned speech and sent him out on his errand. As soon as the latter left, however, Razumovskii, acting now as president of the Academy of Sciences, gave orders to get the academy's press ready to start printing, at first call, the manifesto on the accession of Catherine II. It may be inferred that the crafty statesman had no doubts as to the success of this undertaking.

"It is time to get up, everything is ready to proclaim you!"[49] were the historic words with which Aleksei Orlov greeted Catherine, who was suddenly wakened in her Monplaisir Palace early in the morning on June 28. She promptly got up and having dressed herself, got into the coach, accompanied by her maid of honor, Catherine Shargorodskaia. Orlov got up on the coach-box, and the horses started at a gallop . . . Frederick II guessed right: Catherine did not stand at the head of the plot—there was no need for that—she had her own role to play in it and she played it to perfection. Her role was simple: she was called upon by the people who were infuriated by Peter III's way of reigning, and she answered their call.

This was, in essence, the content of a notice issued by the College of Foreign Affairs to envoys accredited at the Russian court: "Her Imperial Highness, [acting] in accordance with the unanimous wish and persistent requests of Her loyal subjects and true patriots of the Empire," acceded to the throne.[50] All the same, one must give Catherine credit for showing much courage.

Her self-control, willpower, and composure were qualities that always came to her aid at crucial moments of her life. She remained calm when during a trip to the south her carriage horses suddenly bolted downhill; another time Catherine surprised everybody by staying calmly in her cabin, rather than rushing on deck, when her yacht collided with another vessel at night. Said Catherine, explaining the reason for her tranquillity: "If it is a case of danger, I shall be of no help, only getting in everybody's way; if one must think of rescue, you will, no doubt, tell me about it."[51]

She was in the same mood when, on June 28, 1762, the horses, their mouths foaming, were tearing her coach at full speed along the dusty road to St. Petersburg. Catherine raced toward her destiny with the serenity of an optimistic fatalist: there is no way back, the horses gallop on, her loyal men will not leave her in the lurch, what will be will be, or, in the Russian saying, *Bog ne vydast, svin'ia ne s'est!* Legend has it that she was laughing all the way through, making fun of her maid of honor, Catherine Shargorodskaia, over some indispensable article of toilet, which she had left at the Monplaisir in the haste of departure.

Alekhan was a master of a coach: it took him but an hour and a half to fetch the empress from Peterhof to the Red Inn at Avtovo, where he solicitously passed her, like some precious trophy, over to his brother Grigorii, who, after outdrinking the spy Perfiliev, was waiting for them in the company of Prince Fedor Bariatinskii. It was an open barouche into which they sat Catherine. In fact, this worthless, timeworn carriage became Catherine's chariot of glory.

On reaching the settlement of the Izmailovskii Regiment, the barouche was surrounded by the regiment's men thunderously shouting the good health to their "mother." The regiment's chaplain used the occasion for putting the officers and men under oath to the empress whereupon the Izmailovskii men, led by their commander Count Razumovskii, headed in the carriage's wake for the barracks of the Semenovskii Regiment only to see the rejoiced Semenovskii men running toward them to greet their "mother." Soon, they were joined by the men of the Preobrazhenskii Regiment, who begged to excuse their latecoming: they were busy tying up some insubordinate officers.

When they moved out onto Nevskii Prospekt, the capital's main thoroughfare, the empress was greeted by the Horse Guards standing in full formation, with their armor and arms shining in the sun and their standard unfurled. Everybody was shouting "Hurray," and people were running to the barouche from everywhere: the coup was turning into a triumphal procession: a parade of victors. For a short while, Catherine made a stop at the Kazan' Cathedral to attend service, then moved on. There was a lot of tipsy excitement around as innkeepers served out drinks free without a word of protest to all those "true sons of the fatherland." The number of "true sons" was growing with every minute and soon the Nevskii was thronged with people. Catherine's carriage crept forward. At last, the Winter Palace came in sight, where all the state officials and courtiers had already gathered to swear allegiance to their new sovereign. The enthusiasm of the soldiers ran so high that in no time carts loaded with the military outfit issued in Elizabeth's time and rejected by Peter III were fetched to the Palace Square, where they, the ladies notwithstanding, started changing, tearing off and throwing down on the ground their much-detested Prussian uniforms.

After a short rest and council with trusted persons, it was decided to finish the job with a decree to the senate on Catherine's decision to set off on a march with her army for Oranienbaum, where her enemy, the now former emperor Peter III, and his Holsteiners were quartered. It is difficult to cite a similar instance in history of a war waged by a wife against her husband. Catherine changed into the green uniform of the Preobrazhenskii Regiment, looking smart in her cocked three-cornered hat, with a sword at her side,

Empress Catherine II. From A. G. Brikner, *Istoriia Ekateriny Vtoroi* (History of Catherine II) (St. Petersburg, 1885), p. 132.

which the expeditious one-eyed young sergeant Grigorii Potemkin promptly handed her as she sat in the saddle of an excellent horse, which she could ride like no one else.

They set off from St. Petersburg at ten in the evening. It was warm, and the sun was still in the sky. They probably made quite a sight: the glitter of arms, the Guards regiments drawn up in battle array with their standards waving, crowds of people lining the streets and, riding ahead of all on a high horse with a sword in her hand, was a dazzling amazon of an empress.

It was two o'clock in the afternoon when Peter III and his retinue arrived at Peterhof, which coincided with the time when Catherine opened the council of her higher officials to settle the issue of the fate of the emperor. At three in the afternoon, Peter learned of the unrest in the Preobrazhenskii Regiment from Lieutenant Bernhorst, arriving from the capital. One cannot say that, on learning the news, Peter behaved like a little child: on the contrary, he promptly sent an order to Kronstadt for three thousand of his troops to be immediately dispatched to Peterhof; the same order was received by the non-Guards regiments (Astrakhanskii and Ingermanlandskii) quartered at the capital: these were ordered to urgently march to Oranienbaum. Had Peter's orders been obeyed, Catherine's raid in the company of her merry Guards may have ended not so triumphantly as it began. Münnich proposed that the emperor arrive at St. Petersburg in person, where his formidable appearance would alone quench the riot in much the same way as Peter the Great's had in his time thwarted the designs of the strel'tsy-musketeers. Alas, Peter the Great's grandson was but a pitiful shadow of his mighty grandfather. Weak-willed and cowardly, he panicked, rushing about and revoking the orders he had just given, which only added to the confusion. There was still a chance for him to escape: either to Livonia or to Narva, where his regiments, ready to move off to Denmark, were stationed, or else abroad. He could have sailed off to Finland or Sweden. Peter did none of these things, however, partly because he was almost at once cut off from the outside world. Messengers and envoys sent by him to different destinations were simply not coming back (being either held by Catherine's supporters or deserting on their own to the victorious party) and thus the emperor was unable to get a clear idea of what was going on in St. Petersburg.

Catherine proved to be more agile than her consort. She immediately sent orders that all means possible be used to halt Peter's escape. As a result, Peter lost time: embarking a galley, he approached the Kronstadt harbor only to see its entrance blocked and the midshipman on duty, Mikhail Kozhukhov, when ordered by the emperor to let him, Peter III, through into the harbor, shouted in reply that now there was no Peter III: there was only Catherine II. This could only mean that Catherine's emissaries had got to Kronstadt before Peter's men. The exit into the open sea was also blocked by a man of war.

It was at that point that Peter, his spirits flagging, abandoned any further attempts to fight Catherine. Having returned to Oranienbaum, he started to act in precisely the way that was later immortalized by Frederick II, that is, he did allow himself to be overthrown like a little child who is ordered to go to bed.

When in the morning on June 29 the troops reached Strel'na, Catherine received a letter from Peter in which he begged his wife's pardon for all his wrongs and promised to put things right. Catherine made no reply and the march continued. At Peterhof, Peter's messenger passed the empress a second note, scribbled in pencil, in which Peter promised to abdicate in exchange for a modest pension, the Holstein throne, and the maid of honor Vorontsova. That was the price that Peter the Great's grandson set for the Russian empire. Cheap did he hold his grandfather's legacy, very cheap indeed!

This time Catherine replied, demanding that he confirm his abdication in writing. By lunchtime, Grigorii Orlov delivered from Oranienbaum to Peterhof Peter III's abdication, written in his own hand, and then the former emperor himself, in Vorontsova's company. At Peterhof, these two were immediately separated, this time forever. Later the same day, Aleksei Orlov, Captain Peter Passek, and Prince Fedor Bariatinskii snatched Peter away to Ropsha. It was intended that the prisoner stay there for a few days before going over to Schlüsselburg, where his "chambers" were being prepared for him. To preclude the possibility of two former emperors being simultaneously confined on the same little island, it was decided that its original captive, Ivan Antonovich, be immediately moved to the northern fortress of Kexholm.

The regiments were ordered back to the capital, and Sunday, June 30, was turned into the day of all-around feasting and drunken revelry. The empress would not join in the merrymaking, however. She racked her brains, devising the way to bring the whole country under her heel: one had to think of the future. Her biggest worry was Peter III himself—future lifelong prisoner and hence martyr (a case in point was Ivan Antonovich, whose suffering for the "true" Orthodox faith had become a byword). It was impossible to make a bargain with Peter, as his infantile capricious behavior clearly showed that here was a man who had no real grasp of the situation. Even the letters that he sent his wife on the June 29 are written in an unsteady child's hand.

The first of these has the following lines: "Your Majesty. If you do not absolutely want to kill a man who is already unhappy enough, then have pity on me and leave me my only consolation, Elizabeth Romanovna. Doing so would be one of the greatest works of charity of your reign. As to the rest, if your majesty would like to see me for an instant, that will be the height of my desires. Your very humble servant, Peter."[52]

Following this note was another one: "I would also beg of you to allow me, who has complied with your will in everything, to go to foreign lands together with those of whom I had previously asked your majesty, and I put hopes on your magnanimity in that you will not leave me without subsistence."[53]

His reiterating the request to return to him his sweetheart, whom the empress found most detestable, and to let him leave with her for Holstein, supplying them with "subsistence," suggests that no matter how sorry we feel for Peter as a human being, his naiveté should here bear another name. In fact, he was unable to grasp that Catherine was usurping the authority of the legal emperor, Peter the Great's grandson, to boot, nor could he foresee the consequences, both at home and overseas, of his emigration to Holstein. Even the recent example of Ivan Antonovich, whom Elizabeth never released from solitary confinement and whose only fault was becoming emperor at the age of one, did not come to his mind.

On June 30, another letter from Peter reached Catherine. In it, he showed himself vexed at the situation: his apartment is too small and he cannot stroll about it, which, as one knows, he is so fond of doing. Besides, the officer on duty remains in the room when the captive answers a call of nature. He ended the letter, as follows: "Your Majesty may be assured that I will neither deliberate nor do anything that may harm Your person and Your reign."[54] No, Catherine could not trust such a weakling as was Peter. She had to think up what to do next.

We have no proof to assert that Catherine gave a secret order to kill Peter. There is every reason to think, however, that the tragedy might have been averted, had she so wished. This may be evidenced by the letters written by Aleksei Orlov from Ropsha on July 2 and 6. In the letter of July 2, he has the following to say: "Our Dear Mother, Merciful Empress, we wish Your Majesty to enjoy good health for countless years to come. At the moment, we are . . . all well. Only the one who is with us [that is, their prisoner Peter—E.A.] is taken badly ill: he was seized, for no reason at all, by some colic and I fear lest he might die this very night. And I fear more lest he might get over it." Further on, Alekhan thus elucidates the danger of the former emperor's recovery: "First danger is that he talks nonsense all the time and we get no fun out of it at all. Another danger is that he is really dangerous for all of us as he makes comments sometimes as though wishing to acquire his former state."[55]

This was, in fact, the root of the future tragedy. Peter was guarded by men who were directly implicated in the plot that deposed him. Aleksei Orlov masterminded the whole affair. It was only natural that these men should be much concerned about dodging the heavy responsibility. It is only through committing a new crime—murdering the former emperor—that they could manage to unburden themselves, and Catherine, being as clever as she was, could not but see this. Orlov's letter of July 2, that is, four days before the murder, is as plain as a pikestaff in this respect, yet the empress made no response, neither did she replace the jailers, leaving everything as it was.

Now, a few words about Peter's health. In fact, starting from June 30, he did feel unwell, which was probably a kind of nervous breakdown. However, the doctors arriving on July 3 and July 4 testified to an improvement in the patient's health.

On July 6, Alekhan sent Catherine another two letters. The first of these runs as follows: "Our Dear Mother, Merciful Empress. Don't know how to begin. I fear Your Majesty's anger, fear that You might think of us something fearsome, and lest we should inadvertently become the cause of the death of the evildoer to Your Majesty, and all Russia, and also the law of ours. And now, in addition, that valet Maslov appointed to him has also been taken ill. And he [that is, Peter—E.A.] himself is so bad that I don't think he should last till the evening as he is now almost fully unconscious, of which all of our men here know, begging God to take him off our hands as soon as possible. As for this Maslov valet and the officer dispatched to You, they may report to Your Majesty what his state now is, in case You . . . may have doubts on that account."[56]

It is clear that the showdown is imminent: Peter III's valet Maslov, who "was taken ill" in the morning, yet was, nevertheless, brought to St. Petersburg to corroborate the news of his master's sudden and grave illness. It is also suspicious that Orlov, who was not much of a medic, should take upon himself diagnosing the patient, stating that he "will not last till the evening." This "diagnosis" sounds more like the sentence.

This is exactly what happened, in fact: at about six o'clock the same evening came Orlov's lachrymose letter: "Dear Mother, Merciful Empress. How can I explain, how describe what has occurred? You will not believe Your devoted servant but before God I am telling You the truth. Dear Mother! I am ready to meet my death but I myself do not know how this misfortune came about. We are lost if You do not forgive us. Dear Mother— he is gone! But it was none of our desire, for how should we have dared to raise our hand against our sovereign? But, Majesty, this misfortune has occurred. We were drunk, and so was he. He started to quarrel with Prince Fedor [Bariatinskii—E.A.] during dinner; no sooner had we hurried to part them than he was no more. We cannot even remember what we did, but all of us, down to the last man, are wholly guilty and deserve to die for it. Have mercy on me if only for love of my brother [that is, her favorite, Grigorii— E.A.]! I have confessed my sin and there is nothing more to seek. Forgive, or have me put to death, the soonest. My life is a burden to me: we have offended You and we are damned for all eternity."[57]

So the murder has been committed, although no one knows the exact circumstances. It is no accident that Orlov asked the empress not to launch an investigation on account of his having "confessed his sin." No investigation was ever carried out. If it was, one would have to somehow explain the inconsistencies cropping up in Orlov's two letters of July 6, the first of these telling of Peter being mortally ill and "almost fully unconscious," whereas the second one narrating of this seemingly hopelessly sick man drinking with his jailers, as if nothing had happened, and starting a wrangle and later a fight with Bariatinskii. Catherine was perfectly aware of all these non sequiturs but, being on an entirely different plane of thinking, she was mainly concerned about the final outcome, which was plain enough: Peter was dead, hence, there was no problem any longer.

It was officially announced that the former emperor had died a natural death of "hemorrhaged colics."[58] The credulous French ambassador Mercy d'Argenteau described the goings-on at Ropsha as a kind of Rabelaisian tale, namely, that the deposed emperor had allegedly been so immoderate in eating and drink, when in Ropsha, that he got the acutest stomach gripes. Notwithstanding these, he kept on drinking, and an inordinate amount of food and all kinds of hot drinks consumed caused a hemorrhage, of which he died twenty-four hours later. In a word, he perished from gluttony!

Ropsha has survived till the present day. The park stands neglected and overgrown. Crumbling and deserted is the wreck of a palace—the damned place of crime. And here are the names of those who committed it, thus damning their immortal souls: Count Aleksei Grigor'evich Orlov and Prince Fedor Sergeevich Bariatinskii. Both are surely the murderers. But Orlov does make a point in his letter, stressing that "All are guilty, down to the last man," and this is worthy of note.[59] We know how Peter III's son, Emperor Paul I, was assassinated in 1801: all his assassins rushed at him like a pack of wolves, each dealing a blow of his own so that no one would stay unsullied, and which of the blows proved fatal is not for us to say.

Historians have the names of the rest of the Ropsha pack. They are the physician Karl Fedorovich Kruse, the corporal Grigorii Aleksandrovich Potemkin, the founder of the Russian theater Fedor Grigor'evich Volkov . . . fourteen persons, all in all. But no, not all! Justice calls for another name to be added: Catherine II.

* * *

When in 1763, on the eve of Catherine's coronation, the court jeweler Jeremia Posier made her a big imperial crown (now preserved in the Moscow Armory as a precious symbol of Imperial Russia), it proved to be quite heavy, weighing five pounds in all. However, Catherine was satisfied with it, adding that she would somehow manage to hold it on her head during four or five hours of ceremony. And, indeed, she did manage to hold this "heavy thing" and not only during the four or five hours of the coronation ceremony, which took place at the Dormition Cathedral of the Moscow Kremlin, but for the thirty-four years of her reign that followed.[60]

How heavy the imperial crown was she sensed in full on the very first day of ruling, when she had to decide her husband's destiny. This, as all other days, months, and years of her reign, demonstrated to her that there was quite a distance between being the grand duchess, who may be ambitious and conceited but has no power at all, and being the empress, endowed with immeasurable authority. Covering it overnight on June 28, 1762, Catherine realized that her actions in the future would have to be different from what she had imagined they would be perusing Montesquieu and Madam de Sevigné.

The world of a man risen to top power changes accordingly, and the outlook of a ruler is determined by criteria differing from those of an ordinary man: the wish to retain power, considerations of political expediency, the sense of great responsibility for a dynasty, the fate of an empire and a nation, and by many other circumstances which matter so little to the ordinary man. "Le terrible métier," thus would Catherine phrase it in a letter dated early 1763 to her correspondent, Madam Jeoffrin. Somewhat later, she would say to Ségur that in the eyes of even the most self-critical monarchs, politics is rarely subject to moral laws, as their actions are governed by gain.

In the first months and years of her rule, Catherine's position was vulnerable. And there was good reason for this: she had staged a coup d'état, deposing the legal emperor, who was the absolutely legitimate heir of his aunt Empress Elizabeth both in accordance with her last will and testament and as the next descendant in the male line. "Meeting halfway the wishes of people," Catherine did in fact become the captive of this people and more exactly, of her closest retinue and the Guards. Writes Catherine in the fall of 1762 to Poniatowski in Poland: "It behooves me to be very cautious, as the least important man of the Guards can, on seeing me, say to himself: 'This is my doing.'"[61]

As to those standing higher in rank, they were aware of her debt to them and claimed the interest. Even the huge grants of landed estates and rewards failed to satiate the most avaricious and impudent among the supporters of her takeover. This is what Breteuil wrote at the end of 1762: "It is interesting to observe, on the days of court receptions, how the empress does all she can to please her subjects, with what ease most of these comport themselves, how persistent they are in speaking to her about their businesses, in relating their projects to her . . . She accepts this all with a remarkable modesty and grace. I wonder what it all costs her and to what extent she finds this kind of behavior as binding for her as she goes by it."[62] Further on, he related a hot dispute Catherine had with Aleksei Bestuzhev-Riumin, who had returned from exile. At the end of it, Catherine came up to Breteuil and asked whether he had ever seen a hare being chased by hounds. When he replied in the affirmative, she remarked: "You must admit that something of the kind is being done to me, too, as I am being chased and hunted down everywhere despite every effort on my part to evade such talks, which are not always based on common sense and fair convictions."[63] Later, she added that she had to rule over people who are impossible to satisfy.

It was far from easy to extricate oneself from the drunken embraces of her fellow plotters, as the empress and her heroes were now firmly tied together by a common destiny. Besides, it was for the first time since 1741

that the Guards felt their power and right to elevate one monarch and depose another. There was yet another reason that the empress relied on them
so heavily: at the beginning, she had no other support but the Guards.
Breteuil noted perspicaciously that the fear of losing all that she had managed to gain so far showed itself so plainly in all that the empress did that
every more or less influential man at court felt entitled to show his clout in
her presence. Catherine did not despair, though. In much the same way as
she had done in Elizabeth's times, she began, following the 1762 takeover,
to wage a struggle for her freedom or, rather, for her real and unrestrained
autocracy. In doing so, she had to make sure that no one was offended, least
of all, driven away: she had to be cunning, patient, and persevering.

Breteuil, who kept a close watch on Catherine during the first months of
her reign, speaks of a whole gamut of feelings that she experienced then. One
of these was a sensation of utter bliss that she showed at the very notion that
she was *empress*. Once, at a court rout, she repeated scores of times the phrase
"Such a huge and powerful empire as mine," standing quite unabashed under the mocking glance of the French ambassador.[64] She spoke at length of
her former ambitious plans, all of which had felicitously come true at the
moment.

At the same time, notes the ambassador, the empress had her moments
of weakness and indecision, which generally were not in her nature. Of
course, taking her first actions as ruler, Catherine had no experience in this
walk of life and was only beginning to discover the hidden levers of Big
Politics. Being a woman of keen mind, however, she grasped the magnitude
of problems she would have to tackle and her soul cringed at them with fear
and confusion: Will she be strong enough to endure all, to hold out, not to
fail? One had only to make a few steps along the edge of an enormous map
of the country spread on the floor to see all those areas from which, as one
of Nikolai Gogol's characters put it, "you may ride a galloping horse for three
years without ever reaching any other county"—so large was Russia!

A woman of lively imagination, Catherine stood breathless, beholding
these boundless wastes, this cosmos, this yawning chasm. Later on, however,
getting used to the heights to which destiny had elevated her, she regained
her composure, although years afterward she would confess to Potemkin:
"Russia is great as it is and whatever I do is but a drop in the ocean."[65] At
the beginning, she was rather scared and, while priding herself on her good
fortune and the delights of her new position, once confided to Breteuil that
her life was full of apprehension, depriving her of peace of mind. "The very
thought of being the empress makes her head go round; notwithstanding
this, however, she is confused and restless."[66]

Catherine's political notes, compiled not later than the summer of 1761,
that is, about a year before she ascended the throne, make curious reading.
They may with confidence be compared to a political daydreaming entertained by a man who, while being well read, is utterly ignorant in the mat-

ters of real politics, whose deepest wish is to do good and only good while on the throne, that is, to do away with despotism in Russia, to free the serfs from bondage, and so on and so forth. "Freedom, soul of everything, without you all is dead," is the phrase that begins one of her sketches. "I desire to have obedience to laws but not slavery; I strive for a common goal—to make [all people] happy—but not self-will, eccentricity, or cruelty, which are incompatible with that goal." "The power without the trust of people is void." "It is necessary that the people should be indebted to You, not to Your favorites." "I wish to introduce the order when one tells me the truth instead of flattery." "It is contrary to the Christian faith and justice to make people slaves. They are all born free."[67] One can come across a number of such unrealized maxims in her notes.

The situation in real life, however, turned out to be more complicated, more contradictory, and meaner than anything one could read about in books by Western European philosophers, Catherine's teachers. She almost immediately abandoned the idea of implementing any but modest political reforms. When Catherine began her reign, she received a project drafted by Nikita Panin on the creation of a state council and senate reform. The project aimed at creating a supreme representative body in Russia. Approving it at first, Catherine soon reversed her decision, directing all the efforts of her reformers not at political changes but administrative ones that would improve the mechanism of autocratic rule. And here she became a great reformer. In the same way as her predecessors and, later, her descendants, Catherine zealously guarded the inviolacy of autocracy. The autocracy must have the support of the gentry, which must be granted ever new privileges—this was her doctrine from the very start of her reign. This was, in fact, a direct and natural continuation of the course pursued by Catherine's predecessors, who had evidently read neither Voltaire nor Montesquieu.

In early July 1762 Field Marshal Münnich was joking gloomily about having to live with three sovereigns at one time: one sitting in Ropsha, another in Schlüsselburg, and the third in the Winter Palace. On July 6, the field marshal got a degree of relief, with only two emperors left. He was more accustomed to this situation, having lived with two sovereigns for the past twenty-one years. The existence of Ivan Antonovich, the emperor-in-prison, did not bring joy either to Elizabeth Petrovna, Peter III, or Catherine. Rumors were circulating throughout the country about "poor Ivanushka" who was allegedly suffering for the "true faith"; there was a lot of talk about his right to the throne as decreed by Anna Ioannovna. During the very first year of Catherine's reign several plots were uncovered: their organizers expressed sympathy to Ivan Antonovich, and even proposed that as heir to the Romanov family he should marry the empress. Numerous anonymous letters, found in the streets of St. Petersburg, also expressed empathy with the imprisoned "Ivanushka." Prompted by anxiety and curiosity, the empress visited Schlüsselburg in the summer of 1762, where she met with Ivan

Antonovich, the Russian "iron mask." In her manifesto of August 17, 1764, announcing Ivan VI's death, the empress described her visit to Schlüsselburg, and noted that she had paid it with the sole intent of seeing the prince, and "learning of his emotional traits so as to ensure a quiet life for him, one commensurate with his nature and upbringing." However, the empress's original intentions fell short of their goal: it became clear to her that nothing could help the poor fellow, who had lost his senses, and therefore it would be better for him to stay where he was—in the fortress casemate. Catherine further writes that before she left Schlüsselburg she had seen to it that the prisoner had a reliable guard "which would not allow villains to use him to their end or . . . to instigate a revolt." When there came an attempt to liberate Ivan Antonovich by one Morovich, as recounted earlier, the two guard officers, Vlas'ev and Chekin, "had made the extreme decision," namely, that of killing Prince Ivan.[68]

There is no mention, however, that the guards had acted in accordance with Catherine's secret instructions, which bound them to "kill the prisoner rather than let anyone take him alive" should an attempt be made to free Ivan Antonovich.[69] It was also of no small importance that Catherine, though struck with a humane impulse to ease the noble prisoner's life, did not do anything at all, but left him in the same terrible conditions of incarceration in the damp, dark room under the surveillance of the crude guard, forbidding them even to call in a doctor in case Ivan Antonovich fell ill. A prisoner of such high rank might expect better treatment.

We believe that Ivan Antonovich was a sane, mentally healthy person. One gets the distinct impression that the tragedy that took place on the night of July 4 to 5, 1764, had been prepared in advance by a skilled director who had delegated the roles and guided the action throughout the performance. Or at least the circumstances took such a fatal turn that no other result would have been possible. Yet it took a long time before the leading performer made his appearance—a nervous, ill-fated, ambitious young man who planned to restore justice and to get back the money and estates his ancestors had been deprived of. When he appealed to his influential fellow countryman, the hetman Kirill Razumovskii, the latter gave him advice instead of money: "You are a young man, so make your own way in life; try to do as other people have done, try to catch fortune by the tail and you'll become a big man just like the others."[70] The way in which other people had accomplished this he had seen with his own eyes on June 28, 1762, the day of Catherine's quick and almost bloodless revolution. In a word, Mirovich was the type of man who could be easily drawn into such a shady enterprise. Some historians say openly that that is exactly what Catherine did. Although there is no concrete evidence to prove it, many witnesses said that Mirovich, being a very nervous man, was unusually calm before the execution as if he were sure that he would be granted mercy at the last moment. No mercy came, however. Two more circumstances are worthy of note. First, letters have survived that

Count Nikita Panin, who was commissioned by the empress to investigate the case, wrote to Vlas'ev and Chekin. In the letter of August 10, 1763, he thus responds to the urgent request of the guards to be released from their tiresome work: "Have yet a little more patience and I assure you that your service will not be forgotten; I also assure you that your mission will end shortly, and you will be duly rewarded."[71] In the letter of December 28, 1763, Panin sends one thousand rubles for each of them (an enormous sum of money in those days), and entreats the two guards again to keep patience: "You will be relieved of your duties before the first summer months are over."[72] Just what Nikita Ivanovich meant when he referred to relieving the guards of their mission in the near future we cannot say.

Second, the empress explicitly forbade the torture of Mirovich while he was under investigation—a usual procedure in cases involving crimes against the state. Neither did Catherine allow Mirovich's brother to be brought into the investigation. Officials from the Political Investigation Department had always summoned the accused's relatives following the laws governing the procedures for investigating state crimes. One may consider this either as evidence of the empress's humaneness or her unwillingness to have Mirovich and others give undesirable testimony under torture.

Panin and Catherine reacted to the tragedy in Schlüsselburg with a notable want of dolor. Breaking this news to the empress, Panin wrote that everything had turned out "happily, with God's miraculous providence." Catherine responded likewise: providence had obviously shown her a sign of favor by having brought this enterprise to an end. But Catherine followed the rule "God helps those who help themselves."[73]

However, we should be cautious with our suspicions: it really could have happened that the stars had shifted into positions favorable for Catherine, thus allowing two of her rivals forever to be united with their forefathers, one having died in Ropsha of "hemorrhoidal colic" and the other having been killed when some daredevil made an impossible attempt to free the secret prisoner.

* * *

Catherine had to work diligently in order to win the epithet *great* as she did in history. And she had to work even harder to overcome the monotonous drudgery of dull daily affairs. There had been no other so persistent a person to sit on Russia's throne since Peter the Great. "I get up at six o'clock sharp"—Catherine told Mrs. Geoffrin about her daily routine in 1764—"I read and write alone till eight; then different ministers come to read their reports to me. Those who want to see me enter my room in turn one after another. And all this ends at eleven or later. Then I dress myself. On Sundays and holidays I attend the liturgy; on other days I go to the reception hall, which is usually filled with many people who come to see me. Having talked to them for half an hour or three quarters of an hour, I sit at the table.

When I leave the table, the intolerable General [I. I. Betskoi—E.A.] comes to read me his admonitions: he takes the book and I take my work [knitting—E.A.]. Our reading, if it is not interrupted by letters or other hindrances, could last till half past five o'clock. Then I go to the theater and start to play, or chat with whomever I happen to meet until supper, which ends before eleven o'clock. Then I go to bed and the next day it begins all over again exactly as before."[74]

Catherine does not mention here that when she woke up in the morning she drank a cup of strong Turkish coffee (one pound per five cups!) with thick cream, and that she usually devoted the morning hours to her most serious work, that is, writing memoranda and editing laws and various state documents, while after dinner she spent time "scrawling letters" to numerous addresses abroad.

We should also add here that in the morning Catherine usually worked with her secretaries, each of which had his own day to report. After 11 A.M., while the empress was being dressed and was having her hair done, she listened to the reports delivered by the procurator-general of the senate and the chief of the city police. The latter informed her in detail about public sentiments and the most important rumors and gossip circulating in the city. There were many matters to attend to, and they came in a continual stream. "I work like a dog," the empress wrote in 1788.[75]

As earlier, she never spent a single day without reading a book, thus continuing the home university of her youth. On December 7, 1779, commenting on Georges Louis Buffon's *Histoire Naturelle,* which she had just read, Catherine wrote to Grimm: "Monsieur, this book has given a lot to think about." And further: "The Emp[ress], visibly, according to you still the same, has become extremely solitary for some time now; she does not have a moment to herself; she spins like a top while standing still; twenty-four hours is too short; she writes and reads a lot, never has time for anything, works ceaselessly, less, however, than she would like; an enormous confusion occupies three desks." Catherine went on to complain that she had not a minute to herself and that twenty-four hours were not enough for her. She wrote and read always in a rush and was working without rest and still not as much as she wanted to. Stacks of written material took up three shelves.[76]

The empress's capacity for work, a rather rare quality peculiar to rulers of those times, evoked everyone's respect. Frederick II spoke enviously of this trait, considering Catherine a living example with which to rebuke idle monarchs; and he generously ranked her among the great people of her time. Every educated person in Russia had read Gavrila Derzhavin's poem "Felicia," which was devoted to Catherine. The poet admired the empress's untiring work for the benefit of the country.

Like many great people, Catherine was a graphomaniac. There is no disparaging implication here. I just want to emphasize Catherine's all consuming desire to pour out her thoughts on paper, to work with a pen in hand. "It is that I have never seen a new quill without smiling at it and without having felt a keen temptation to use it." And, ". . . the demon of scribbling possesses me, I sense it."[77]

Anyone who writes will understand and appreciate the empress's feelings. The experience of creative joy is indescribable as you acquire the power to soar over your writing, to express your thoughts smoothly and clearly, when ideas gush one after another in a torrent, and a pile of paper used keeps growing, to both your horror and delight. This is when you do not have enough time, ". . . nothing is finished, much is cleared up, many things only half so, one matter threads another's needle, immense materials are collected on all sides and ready to be implemented."[78]

Following the famous *Nakaz,* or *Instruction,* which she prepared for the Legislative Commission of 1767, lawmaking had become Catherine's passion. She jokingly called it "legislomanie," attacks of which seized the empress regularly, keeping her riveted to her desk and causing her to exclaim, "Oh, the poor woman! she will die of it, or she will finish it."[79] In her letters to foreign friends Catherine described often and in great detail how much she worked, how she wondrously "scribbled" and "scratched" her manifestos and decrees.

These letters are full of self-aggrandizement, immoderate bragging, and an insatiable thirst for praise. Yet they corroborate something truly astonishing. The extant documents from Catherine II's office, as well as from other institutions dating to the second half of the eighteenth century, prove the unequivocal capacity of the empress for work; once she had decided not only to reform the state machine but also to single-handedly develop a new code of laws that she titled "our legislative establishment." In drafting new laws, she worked very hard for "an integral body of laws," and hundreds of Catherine's original manuscripts, bound in gigantic volumes, indicate that the tsarina alone did the work of an entire legislative commission. And this labor continued till the end of her days. During her reign, Catherine wrote almost ten thousand letters and signed fourteen thousand five hundred acts and decrees! And there need be no doubt about her having read every paper she signed.

Although the empress was an industrious person and came to know the ins and outs of state affairs quickly, the first years of her reign were, as mentioned earlier, very difficult. When in the autumn of 1762 Chancellor Bestuzhev-Riumin, who had returned from exile, suggested that Catherine assume the title of "The Mother of the Fatherland," she replied that it was still too early to do so because such a step would be interpreted as a manifestation of vanity at court. It was not that Catherine feared the reputation of being conceited; it was clear to her that the title of "The Mother of the Fatherland" would provoke nothing but mockery and laughter. At one of the receptions held in late 1762 Catherine told the French envoy, while pointing at her group of courtiers, that it would take them years to grow accustomed to her. One more thing should be noted here: she set a five-year term for herself, at the expiration of which people could tell what kind of a sovereign she was. She needed that time to establish order and to see what fruits her work would yield.

Catherine had calculated the term of probation very precisely, for the year 1767 was indeed the year of her triumph: the first session of the Commission on Writing a New Legislative Code was held in late July. Similar commissions existed during the reigns of Peter the Great and Elizabeth, but none of them was accompanied by such a loud, propagandist campaign. Previous committees had held quiet sessions, talked with local representatives, written and supplemented existing laws, as well as debated new ones. During Catherine's reign the procedure changed. More than 570 people—some dressed quite exotically—came to Moscow from all over the country, making a striking sight: it was the first time since the *zemskie sobory* of the seventeenth century that all the "Land," all of Russia, had gathered in the capital. According to time-honored tradition, the opening ceremony took place in the Faceted Chamber of the Moscow Kremlin, and was in itself a magnificent event. Equally magnificent was Catherine's verbose *Nakaz* to the delegates, which was full of proud, elevated, and even seditious—for those days—political notions such as the equality of all citizens, freedom under the protection of laws, the rights of individuals, and so forth. The commission worked with a spirit of solidarity and seriousness, which spoke of the joint intentions of both the authorities and delegates to reform the country.

Catherine's *Nakaz* was a rather mediocre compilation (mostly from the *Spirit of the Laws* by Montesquieu) of the principles of a preferable state structure, delegates' impassioned speeches merely created the illusion of parliamentary freedom, and their many months of work yielded insignificant results. Nevertheless, the commission and its initiator became the objects of talk within the country and later throughout the world.

Foreigners noted that the commission's activity enhanced the Russians' pride in their country and people. In fact, now that our empire has collapsed, we, the Russians, feel keenly what the national humiliation or triumph, shame or glory, may mean in the history of a people. The Russians saw the commission's activity as the civil triumph and glory of Russia. Naturally, all this was associated with Catherine, whose *Nakaz* the delegates listened to with tears in their eyes.

The Russian empress's reputation as "a republican," an ardent patroness of freedom, equality, and enlightenment in Europe, was confirmed when the *Nakaz* was banned in Paris. One could hardly think of better publicity for Catherine, for it gave her cause for many years to assert that there was no other country in the world that had more freedom than her empire—it would occur to no one in Russia to ban the *Nakaz*. And indeed only a madman would have suggested banning one of the autocrat's writings in Russia!

By the end of 1768 the commission had become obsolete. The novelty of plenary sessions was lost; the delegates' committees ceased to produce real results; the endless discussions proved fruitless. Catherine realized that there was a gigantic gap between the "fantastic" thoughts of her *Nakaz* about the equality, rights, and freedom and the real lives of slaves and masters, corrupted judges, malicious bosses, and ordinary people deprived of civil rights; it would take years of persistent work to make the slightest changes for the better in Russia. So Catherine dissolved the commission on the pretext that war had broken out with the Turks. The commission had played its role in consolidating her power.

This war was akin to the Nakaz or the establishment of the commission on laws: a favorable outcome was needed now to keep Catherine basking in glory. It is a known fact that the war was started by the Turks. Yet few know with what rejoicing Catherine embraced the idea of war. We should note, however, that in those days people did not think of war as a catastrophe; on the contrary, war was often regarded as a sure means of helping to consolidate a country's position and relieve the tension in a long-idle army craving ranks, trophies, and feats of heroism. War served as an instrument to ease the pressure of internal problems in the country, which apparently could not be solved because of external enemies. Besides all that, the sovereign needed to be seen as a glorious victor.

It is not incongruous, therefore, that on December 20, 1768, Catherine wrote excitedly to Count Ivan Chernyshev: "Having done away with the peace treaty, I find that I have relieved myself of a heavy load that weighed on my mind. Thousands of tricks, thousands of conditions, and thousands of small stupid things were required to appease the Turks' cries. Now I am calm, I can do anything, and Russia, as you know, can do a lot and sometimes Catherine II also imagines all kinds of Spanish castles. And now there is nothing to restrain her; and now they have aroused the sleeping cat and it has dashed at the mice, and now just wait and see; and now they will talk about us, and now we will raise a din such as no one had ever expected from us!"[80] The letter is disjointed and lacks style, but the sentiments here are clear and direct: at last, the time has come to show our strength. Let the arrogant Versailles and hypocritical London hear about us; let Frederick scratch his head while looking at our victories. This will force certain people in Russia to bite their tongues as well. We need victories not only in the peaceful realm of lawmaking and establishing wise institutions, but on the battlefield, too. Forward!

And although they were not immediate, victories did come. The bland military action of 1769 was succeeded by the fiery campaign of 1770, wherein General Peter Rumiantsev defeated the Turks at Riabaia Moghila, then at the river Larga, and finally near Kagul. The Turks suffered heavy losses, the superiority of the Russian army was overwhelming. One month earlier, a Russian fleet under Aleksei Orlov sailed from the Baltic to the

Mediterranean Sea and defeated the Turks in the Strait of Chios, then—on the night of June 26—the Turkish fleet was trapped and burned in the Bay of Chesme. For the first time Russian ships entered the Aegean Sea and blocked the Dardanelles.

In the years that followed, the Russian commander Aleksandr Vasil'evich Suvorov displayed his brilliant talent: in 1773 he defeated the Turks near Turtukai, and in 1774 near Kozluji. In that same year, the Treaty of Kuchuk Kainarji was signed. It was the most advantageous peace treaty in the long history of Russo-Turkish wars. Now Russian ships could not only sail on the Black Sea but also pass through the Straits. Russia gained the much-suffered-for port of Azov, consolidated its position in the strait of Kerch, and, what was most important, established its protectorate over Moldavia and Wallachia. As to the Crimean khanate, it declared its independence from the Ottoman Empire, which amounted to dependence on Russia. Emperor Peter the Great's dream had come true, as had Catherine's sovereign will, which she had declared as early as 1769. The Russian border now reached the waters of the Black Sea. At last ships flying Russia's flag sailed there freely, in accordance with the Treaty of Kuchuk Kainarji.

* * *

Victories are achieved by people, and one must admit that Catherine's reign saw the appearance of many talented statesmen, political and military figures, artists, and writers. A monument of Catherine II stands in St. Petersburg today. It shows the empress, her head raised high, looking off into the distance, with nine of her most famous associates seated in a row at her feet: Generalissimo Aleksandr Suvorov, Field Marshal Peter Rumiantsev, Prince Grigorii Potemkin, Count Aleksei Orlov, Princess Ekaterina Dashkova, President of the Russian Academy of Sciences Ivan Betskoi, the fellow enthusiast of the Enlightenment Admiral Vasilii Chichagov, Vice Chancellor Aleksandr Bezborodko, and the poet Gavrila Derzhavin. A dozen more celebrities could have been placed in this row, among them the historian Prince Mikhail Shcherbatov, Admiral Fedor Ushakov, the statesman Nikita Panin, the architect Vasilii Bazhenov, the poet Mikhail Kheraskov, and numerous other worthy people.

There can be no doubt that these gifted people rose to fame thanks to Catherine. She possessed the rare ability to choose the right people and invest them with her confidence, thus making them obliged and grateful to her. Many times Catherine attempted to explain how she did this. Not all that was spoken or written by her on this subject is true, yet the fact remains that the empress went through history literally surrounded by a host of talented people, which certainly cannot be said of the reigns of her grandchildren, for example.

Catherine never complained of a lack of intelligent people. "In my opinion, no country has a scarcity of men; it is not a matter of looking, it is a

Ivan I. Betskoi. From A. V. Morozov, *Katalog moego sobraniia russkikh gravirovannykh i litografirovannykh portretov* (Catalogue of My Collection of Engraved and Lithographed Portraits), vol. 1 (Moscow, 1912), folio LXXIX.

matter of using all that you have at hand. It has been said of us continually that we have a scarcity of men; nevertheless, everything gets done. Peter I had many who knew neither how to read nor how to write; well, did things not go well then? Ergo, there is not a scarcity of men: there is a multitude."[81]

But we had better not take too much to heart this particular claim of Catherine's—the empress merely made it look easy to select necessary people. The empress would invite prospective officials into her elite circle in the

Hermitage, and closely scrutinized their merits in a casual setting, parting forever with fools and obvious scoundrels. "Study people," she warned her descendants in her memoirs; "try to use them without trusting in them indiscriminately; search for true talent, even if it is at the world's end: usually it is modest and hidden away somewhere on the periphery. Valor never shows off in a crowd, never strives for recognition, never displays greed, and never advertises itself."[82]

Catherine had the talent of making people like her, capturing their interest, winning them over to her cause, turning once hostile or neutral people into her faithful servants, reliable associates, and good friends. Manifestations of this rare capacity can be found in historical documents. In 1771, she wrote to the field marshal Count Vasilii Dolgorukov, who had just captured the city of Kerch: "I can see in your letters your personal love for and attachment to me, and this in turn prompts me to think of something pleasant which I could now do for you." Along with this kind letter Catherine sent the field marshal an elegant snuff-box with her own portrait on it, and a "request that it be ever with you, for I am sending it to you as a keepsake from the innermost depths of my heart."[83]

Very likely, the old soldier's heart could not help but melt at such display of endearment on the part of the sovereign. The same can be said of the French envoy, Count Ségur, who, despite his deep sympathy for Catherine, was unable to check the anti-Russian policies of Versailles, which had been on the increase throughout the 1780s. Ségur recollects that once at the theater performance he was sitting close to the empress thinking gloomily about unpleasant news he had received from France: "I was thus absorbed, when all of a sudden I heard a voice very close to my ear; it was that of the empress, who, having leaned towards me, said quietly, 'Why are you sad? What are these dark ideas good for? What are you doing? Consider that in all of this you have nothing to reproach yourself for.'"[84]

Some time ago Mademoiselle Cardel had repeatedly taught little Fike that if one use the words "dear sir" often enough, one's tongue will not wither and fall out, and that showing politeness and respect to people is the primary quality of a kind person. And Catherine had imbibed these lessons well enough. This accounts for her fury when she discovered that her courtiers had been beating their servants, as well as for her habit of using her left hand to pinch tobacco from the snuff-box so that guests who were customarily allowed to kiss her right hand would not be offended by the smell of tobacco.

It would not be irrelevant to recall an incident between Catherine and Admiral Chichagov, who won a big victory over the Swedes. Catherine wanted to meet the hero, although people around her tried to talk her out of it. The admiral was not a man of fashion; moreover, he was a foul-mouthed person. Yet the empress insisted on the meeting. When it finally took place the admiral was asked to recount the story of his victory over the Swedish squadron. At first he was embarrassed and spoke awkwardly. But gradually he became excited, forgot himself, and addressed several choice expletives at his enemy. Then having realized what he had done, he fell down on his knees before Catherine asking for her mercy, and she replied simply as if nothing had happened: "It's all right, Vasilii Iakovlevich! Please proceed. I don't understand your naval terms anyway."[85]

Catherine usually got to know people and won their hearts during personal, confidential conversations. She had the ability to listen to another person, not merely wait for a pause in his speech in order to start to talk about herself, about things dear to her. I have already mentioned that the tsarina was a person with whom one felt easy and comfortable talking. Baron Grimm recollected: "The empress had one rare talent which no other person I knew possessed in such capacity: she always managed to grasp her interlocutor's idea and therefore she never picked at inaccuracies of exaggerated boldness and, of course, she never took offense at these. One had to have seen her lovely head, this combination of genius and grace, to understand what thoughts crowded and collided therein, flowing, so to say, one after another like the clear streams of a waterfall."[86]

Some principles of the empress's attitude to people can be gleaned from her letter to Field Marshal Peter Saltykov, then the governor-general of Moscow, who was the very leader who had defeated Frederick II in the battle near Kunersdorf in 1759. Saltykov was to meet an important foreign guest— Prince Heinrich, Frederick II's brother, who was expected to visit the old capital in November 1770. In this letter Catherine not only shows a deep knowledge of people, but also advises her high-placed servant as to how he should treat the guest and what he should do to please him: "I should tell you one more thing: at first sight Prince Heinrich appears to be an extremely cold person, but you should disregard this coldness, for it will thaw. He is bright and clever, and he knows that the Field Marshal–General may be jolly and amiable too when he wants to . . . Try to see to it that the Prince is not bored. He is very well-mannered and fond of acquiring new knowledge. Make all the necessary arrangements for him to see every notable thing. And finally, Mr. Field Marshal, I hope you would tell everyone that politeness and thoughtfulness never do one any harm and those who have these qualities command respect of themselves rather than show respect to other people. My wish is that when the Prince returns home he can say: 'The Russians are not only victorious, they are also polite.' You know how I love my Fatherland, I want our people to be famous for both their military and their civil virtues, and excel other nations in every respect."[87]

We do not know how the rather crude Saltykov used Catherine's advice, but having read this letter one can say for sure that the empress was a clever and delicate woman. No matter what different kinds of people she was dealing with she invariably sought profit both for herself and for Russia. She never demanded the impossible from people and often repeated her favorite proverb: "Live and let live." Catherine knew how to take from people what they could give: ". . . because this or that one is close-minded, still the master is not."[88] Once she was told that a message had arrived at the Senate from a provincial *voivode* about an incredible event, or so it appeared to the ignorant official, namely, a solar eclipse, and that it had been suggested that this ignoramus be removed from his post. The empress refused to do so saying: "Supposing he is a kind man and a good judge? Send him a calendar instead."[89]

An official who enjoyed the empress's confidence could count on her complete support. Catherine had formulated this idea at length in her instructions to the new procurator-general, Prince Aleksandr Viazemskii, in 1764: "Rely on God and me, and when I find your behavior pleasing to me, I will never betray you."[90] In her relations with people Catherine was neither sentimental nor too kind and indulgent, which could be a detriment to herself and to her cause. She was full of the spirit of rationalism, and warm recollections and friendly relations could never stop the empress's rage when she saw idleness, injustice, deception or unworthiness in the behavior of her high officials.

For quite some time Catherine had been on friendly terms with the Count Iakov Sievers, the governor of Novgorod and Pskov. The empress was often pleased with him and expressed her attitude in a letter: "I have read your report to the Senate from cover to cover, and I am sure they do not receive reports of this type very often; it's you all over: very reasonable, imbued with the spirit of order and even the sincere kindness of my Governor, and a pleasure to read."[91] An official could hardly count on receiving higher praise from the empress. The letter was written in the 1760s. In the late 1770s Sievers conducted himself very unworthily: when divorcing his wife he took the children from her by force, made scandalous scenes over the property, and ignored the decision of the arbitrator and even Catherine's exhortations.

At first she tried to bring him to reason by appealing to him with kindness: "Mister Sievers! The spirit of justice, impartiality, and moderation displayed by you during the performance of your public duties has won my confidence. You know it better than anyone else how much I abhor violence. In any circumstances I prefer gentleness and moderation to the extreme [measures]. Stop as soon as possible and without further squabbling all these altercations for which both sides are usually to blame . . . Return my Governor, the one I have known for fifteen years."[92]

But Sievers had already taken the bit between his teeth, and the empress changed her tone: "It is really painful and sorrowful to see how a man can change in several weeks' time . . . You've been ruining your good name. You've been ruining my good opinion of you. You have disregarded my advice . . . Spite has seized your soul to such an extent that it has completely erased all nobleness and generosity from your actions; it blinds you to such an extent that it makes you commit violence before my eyes. I leave it to you to judge how offended I am and how people will regard a man who acts like that."

Then she proceeds: "Those insulting complaints which you have brought against the arbitrators are nothing but your own partiality showing in all this matter. The judges can be blamed only for assuaging the dictatorial tone of your despotic claims. I am warning you that I do not like this tone, either. On pain of disgrace before me, I forbid you to demonstrate further violence either here, in my capital, or in any other place. I order you to leave for your province to soothe your boiling anger and I spare you the trouble of answering this letter."[93]

That was a disgrace, a severance of relations, but he was a businesslike man, so let him work! In 1770, when Catherine caught Count Sergei Vasil'evich Gagarin in a lie—he had submitted a false petition to the College of Justice—she wrote to him in an angry tone: "Count Sergei Vasil'evich, I cannot interfere in this matter openly, as it has been handed over for lawful dispersal of justice. However, your Excellency, just between us, where is Count Sergei Vasil'evich's conscience? The truth alone has compelled me to write to you, for I see that justice may become obscured by other passions. If I were not the empress, I would have been the primary witness against you. All the best."[94]

In her above-cited letter about an alleged lack of qualified people in Russia, she reveals the essence of that which she considers to be of particular importance for those who work with people: "One merely has to force them to do what is required to be done, and once there is such a driving force, everything will go all right. What does your coachman do when you are sitting in a closed carriage? If one has good intentions, all the roads will be open for him."[95] People should be given work that is familiar to them and that they can do well, and matters will pan out—that is what the empress is saying here.

In another letter to Grimm she is straightforward: ". . . I have always felt in me a very strong penchant for letting myself be led by people who know more than I do, provided only that they do not make me feel they have the desire or pretension to do so, for then I flee as fast as I can."[96] Probably, Catherine's main merit as a leader is revealed in this ability to use people, and to be the driving force. However, not only in that.

Catherine was talented, conscientious, and well aware of her merits. She was not afraid of having competitors and realized that the light of somebody else's talents would not darken but only increase her own brilliance. She wrote in one of her letters to Grimm: "Oh, as to that, if someone believes that the merits of others scare me, they are very wrong; on the contrary, I would like to have only heroes around me, and I have done all that I could to make into such all those in whom I glimpsed the least vocation for it."[97]

In 1783, Grigorii Orlov and Nikita Panin, two of her closest associates since her rise to power, died almost simultaneously. While grieving over their

deaths, Catherine wrote to Grimm: "These two men, continually of conflict-
ing opinions, not at all liking each other . . . I spent many years with these
two counselors dangling at my ears, and nevertheless things went along, and
went along very briskly. I often had to do as Sire Alexander with the Gordian
knot, and then the opinions would be reunited. The one's boldness of spirit
and the other's mitigated prudence and your very humble servant doing the
quick gallop between them gave grace and elegance to modest, unpretentious things. You will say to me: How to make do at present? To this I will
answer you: 'As we can.' Each country furnishes the people necessary for
things, and as everything in the world is human, thus human beings are able
to cope [*und da Alleß in der Welt menschlich ist, so können denn Menschen
auch damit fertigwerben*]."[98] She could talk like this because by that time
Potemkin's talent had reached its peak.

* * *

In the early 1770s the empress's personal life became clouded by a serious
crisis. Her relations with Grigorii Orlov, which had started before the coup
of 1762, became a burden to her. Yet at first it had been so nice. It seemed
that Catherine had at last found her happiness: she had a real man, a knight
by her side—a courageous, strong, beautiful, and loyal defender and conqueror, who had proved his worth in such a dangerous affair as the coup of
June 28.

There is no need to enumerate titles, decorations, and ranks as well as the
amount of money and number of estates and houses received by Orlov exclusively for his loyalty and masculine beauty—because the list would be
endless (by the way, Gatchina and Ropsha were among those gifts). All roads
leading to the glory of a great statesman or military leader were open before this minion of fortune. However, he chose neither of these two opportunities, and led the life of a debauchee and rowdy as he did when he was
Guards captain, though he received the titles of count and, later, prince and
was wearing a general's uniform complete with decorations.

Catherine and Orlov had lived under one roof for a long time—about
eleven years, up to 1773. Some authors believe that apart from the well-
known Count Bobrinskii, the empress had conceived from Orlov two more
sons and several daughters. Around 1763 persistent rumors circulated in the
capital about Orlov's and Catherine's intention to get married in a church.
These rumors are not unfounded. The empress was crazy about her hero,
and he was persistent and impatient. However, in the end common sense
prevailed along with apprehensions for imperial power, which would have
inevitably been discredited by the sovereign's marriage to a common subject, especially to one so ill respected. Catherine could not disregard public
opinion, which she had always considered very attentively. However, this did
not prevent Grigorii from ruling at the palace for no less than ten years until his power came to an end.

Grigorii G. Orlov. From I. N. Bozherianov, "*Nevskii prospekt.*" *Kul'turno-istoricheskii ocherk dvukhvekovoi zhizni Sankt-Peterburga* ("Nevskii Prospect." A Cultural and Historical Sketch of St. Petersburg at Two Hundred) (St. Petersburg, 1901–03), vol. 1, p. 181.

This is what Catherine wrote about Orlov in her *Open-Hearted Confession* to Potemkin: "This man would have stayed forever, if only he did not feel bored. I learned about it [his unfaithfulness—E.A.] on the very day of his departure from Tsarskoe Selo for the Congress [Orlov headed the delegation to the Russo-Turkish peace negotiations held in Focsani in the summer of 1772—E.A.], and I came to the conclusion, when I learned about it, that I would not be able to have any confidence in him any more—this thought tormented me terribly and forced me to make a choice [she refers to Aleksandr Vasil'chikov—E.A.], which caused me to grieve more than I can tell up to this very month . . . and every caress brought tears into my eyes, so I think I have not cried so much my whole life as I have during the last year and a half. At first I thought that I would get used to it, but with time it became worse . . . Then a heroic knight came along." That was Potemkin, to whom the *Open-Hearted Confession* was addressed.

Catherine had good reason to cry: the breakup with Orlov proved to be a long and agonizing process for her. Prince Grigorii's companions tried to persuade him to give up the "mother-tsaritsa," but without success. His ostentatious resignation and readiness to surrender to fate would be quickly succeeded by drinking-bouts and drunken brawls, fits of rage and violent scandals. All this made the empress fear for herself—so furious and unpredictable at times was the behavior of the onetime favorite. Then would follow a period of calm with both parties competing in generosity: she presenting him with the Marble Palace on the Neva River, and he sending his gifts in return—among them the huge Nadir-Shakh's diamond, known nowadays as the Orlov diamond, one of the most valuable treasures in Russia. Orlov would begin his escapades again, shocking high society and the court. In the autumn of 1772, Catherine wrote to Voltaire that the only thing she wanted was a mutual peace. Catherine was looking for peace, for she had made her ultimate decision, which was to leave Orlov.

There were several reasons for parting with Orlov, one of which was the unfaithfulness which Catherine had mentioned in her *Confession*. In May 1773 the empress told the diplomat Durand in an offended tone that Orlov was no more fastidious in his love affairs than he was about food. A Kalmyk, a Finnish woman, or an extremely elegant lady were all the same to him—"that was the nature of this Russian muzhik." Of course, drinking-bouts and constant love affairs on Grigorii's part offended Catherine as a woman and discredited her as the empress—the mistress of this regular of brothels and fellow of lowlifes.

But another reason for the breakup is equally important: Orlov caused her to live with the memory of the events that took place in June and July of 1762; he stood before her eyes as a recollection of their common sin and more than once had even speculated on it. Of course, Catherine was grateful to Grigorii and his brothers for everything they had done for her, but, as we know, there is a limit to human gratitude, and Catherine had already reached it.

In the spring of 1773 she told Durand that she remembered well her obligation to the Orlovs and would never forget their service, yet her decision to part with Grigorii was final: "I have suffered for eleven years, and I want, at last, to live the way I see fit and absolutely independently. As to the prince, he can do whatever he wants: he can travel or stay in Russia, drink and hunt; he can occupy the posts he once held and be in charge of state affairs again. He was born a Russian muzhik and he will remain one until he dies . . . He is interested only in trifles. Though he may be engaged in serious matters at times, yet it is all done without any system; while talking about serious things, he lapses into contradictions, and his views indicate that he is still young in his soul, lacks education, craves glory which he does not adequately understand; he is indiscriminate in taste, and often demonstrates aimless activity motivated by ordinary whim."[99]

Such a crushing opinion of the intellectual and business talents of her former lover, whom she had adored at the beginning of their life together, reveals one thing: they had been using their time differently and approached their parting as different people. Grigorii carelessly passed away the years, only occasionally imitating some kind of serious activity (Catherine gave him the appropriate nickname of the "flaming idler"). The empress had become a prominent state figure in European terms thanks to her talent, perseverance, patience, and ability to learn; and her reputation as an enlightened sovereign, an experienced and subtle politician, continued to spread. She worked hard and next to her, on the canapé, snored the drunk artillery-captain, just as he had ten years earlier. Of course, she realized that Orlov's origin differed from hers. During the first months of her reign when she introduced Grigorii to foreign diplomats and travelers, the empress, as if apologizing to her refined guests for her choice, praised the brilliant intellect and abilities of her new favorite, hoping for future improvement. Her belief in the power of reason and enlightenment was enormous. Count Beckinghemshire wrote: "At the initial stage of Grigorii Orlov's rise, the empress used to say that she herself would teach him good manners and educate him. She succeeded in teaching him to think and to reason, but to think and to reason in the wrong way, for nature had provided him with only that light which blinds, and not with [the light] which shows the way."[100]

Whether the pedagogical method was inadequate or the pupil slow to learn, we will never know; but the fact is that Orlov failed to become a great state figure. This reveals the third reason for their severance: Catherine got tired of Orlov's loafing. She needed a trustworthy associate, a helpmate in bearing the great burden of state affairs, which was taking its toll on her. In the spring of 1774 the English chargé d'affaires Gunning wrote that Catherine's former courtesy and indulgence had vanished, difficulties in conducting her duties affected her health and mood, the Turkish war weighed heavily, there were many problems and much dissatisfaction in society, and she needed a helpmate. And along came Potemkin, who took the burden of the world of state affairs onto his own broad shoulders.

Even after Potemkin had established himself in the foreground, still Orlov did not hurry to retreat into the shadows, and every time he was pushed away from the "matushka" he would loiter somewhere nearby, causing Potemkin to bite his nails with vexation. Of course, by that time Catherine had enough power to exile Grigorii from the capital, but she could not bring herself to do it, that was the point. For her, parting with Orlov was dictated not by antipathy or hatred, but primarily by state necessity, by fate. The good-for-nothing remained nevertheless dear to her heart, for they lived so long and close together, and she had borne him children conceived in moments of passionate love. All that cannot be so easily forgotten and thrown out of the heart! And so Catherine did not take her eyes off her ne'er-do-well prince until the end of his days.

When in the spring of 1776 Orlov was suddenly taken gravely ill, the empress, despite Potemkin's great displeasure, abandoned all her affairs and hurried to Orlov's bedside. That impulse was, probably, stronger than all her calm cool reason, more powerful than the pedagogical doctrine she had developed over many years for taming her own temperament. So when the forty-three-year-old Orlov, having recovered, surprised everybody, including the empress, by marrying Katen'ka Zinov'eva for love, a nineteen-year-old lady-in-waiting and his cousin, Catherine was not happy at all. She had thought that all his life Grigorii would drown his eternal and one and only love for her in wine, while she would pacify him and make him happy with an occasional unexpected visit. But it did not turn out that way.

The newlyweds left for Europe and lived there happily. But news soon came from abroad at first of a serious and later fatal illness of the Princess Orlova and how the Prince refused to leave his beloved wife's bedside. In 1782 she passed away quietly in her husband's arms in Switzerland; then it became known that Grigorii Grigor'evich was being taken back to Russia and that he had lost his mind with grief. When Catherine came to see him, Orlov was already unable to recognize anybody. He, "the most handsome man in the North," was reduced to a slobbering child. In April 1783 the illness killed Orlov; he died and was buried in his country estate, which bore the pleasant name of *Otrada* (delight; comfort).

* * *

Grigorii Aleksandrovich Potemkin had only one thing in common with Orlov: he too often used to lie on the sofa for hours at a time; in other respects he differed greatly from the retired favorite. Those who met Potemkin point to his keen intellect, phenomenal memory, outstanding abilities, imperiousness, and wide range of thought. It is impossible to say exactly at what point his rise began.

Up to 1773–1774 his life was full of vague zigzags and turns, which often obscure him from view. Potemkin was born into a noble Smolensk family in 1739 and hence he was ten years younger than Catherine. He left his parent's house early, studied at Moscow University for some time, but then abandoned the temple of the sciences to start military service in the Cavalry Guards, and was among those who distinguished themselves during Catherine's coup. In one of her letters to Poniatowski, Catherine characterized Potemkin as a brave, clever, and energetic officer. Potemkin was also among the killers in Ropsha, was decorated, and then unexpectedly for many was appointed assistant chief-procurator of the synod. We must give him his due, however—the future field marshal had always taken an interest in theology and church history, and was very knowledgeable in this field.

Yet venomous tongues asserted that Potemkin's real distinction was not his erudition or his eye lost in peacetime under mysterious circumstances, but his singular ability to imitate the voices and manners of high-ranking officials, which had cleared the way for him into the intimate circle surrounding Catherine, for she was a woman with a well-developed sense of humor. But Potemkin's career proper dates from March 1, 1774, when the empress promoted him to the rank of adjutant-general. And on July 14 of the same year Catherine wrote to Grimm that he was "*un des plus grands, des plus drôles et des plus amusants originaux de ce siècle de fer.*"[101]

It would be a mistake to think that Catherine welcomed him chiefly for his witty escapades. Potemkin was not a jester, and he did not like to play this role at court. In 1769, then a Guards lieutenant, he volunteered to battle the Turks, intending, probably, to change his jester image and role as a self-taught theologian into something more worthy of his talents and thus to win the empress's favor. And he succeeded in this to the fullest. He made a quick career in the war, distinguishing himself as a brave cavalry general during the battles near Focsani, Larga, Kagul, and Cilistria, and soon was honored with the praise of Catherine, who corresponded with him secretly.

In 1774 the zealous lieutenant-general was recalled to St. Petersburg. It took some time for Catherine to become close friends with Potemkin. She wrote in the *Open-Hearted Confession*: ". . . we asked him to come here by letter, but with such hidden intention as to avoid taking blind steps upon his arrival, and ascertain first whether he has that inclination . . . the one which I desire." Potemkin did have that inclination and rose quickly to the top.

Relations between Catherine and Potemkin remain vague. According to P. I. Bartenev, the publisher of the *Russian Archives*, they were secretly married in St. Petersburg either in the autumn of 1774 or in January 1775. They celebrated their honeymoon in the late spring or early summer of 1775, spending it near Moscow. It was then that Catherine bought the estate they both liked so much.

The *Open-Hearted Confession*, addressed to Potemkin and concluding with assurances of love and loyalty, was written during that period. However, this does not fit logically with what was to follow. As early as 1776 Peter Zavadovskii, a high-ranking official, appears at Catherine's court and becomes her new favorite. In 1777 he was replaced by Zorich, who became the empress's lover only for a short time. Potemkin is apparently untroubled by all this and, according to one diplomat, lives in bliss.

Moreover, everybody was certain that the line of young favorites who found themselves in the "matushka's" bedchamber underwent scrupulous examination by the Most Serene Prince Tavricheskii (of Tauride), for that was Potemkin's last title. He picked out the most dull-witted young men who could thus constitute no danger to him, nevertheless keeping them under surveillance through his agents. Grigorii Aleksandrovich was not to be outdone by Catherine, traveling himself with a small harem, which consisted of sleazy girls and others' wives, the latter fearlessly writing inviting messages to their lover.

One gets the impression that a short period of unclouded love between the empress and her favorite was followed by a series of quarrels and mutual displeasure, which ended with the drawing up of a peculiar "contract on cooperation," wherein both parties agreed to give free rein to the other. This is evident from the extant correspondence between Catherine and Potemkin, which is peppered with greetings from some new "Sashen'ka" or "baby."

Of some interest to us is Catherine's letter to Potemkin, who had intended to win the heart of one lady by appointing her husband inspector-general. When that fact became known to Catherine she protested most decisively against such an arrangement, warning him that it was a futile and foolish pursuit.[102] One can hardly say that this letter was written by a woman who was tormented by unfaithfulness or suffering from fits of jealousy. We can see that she is concerned by the practical and the negative effect Potemkin's affair might have on the army and other matters. These values became key in the relations between the empress and her favorite in the years to come. Catherine had formulated this simply and clearly in a letter to Potemkin in 1787, summing up their relationship with the words, you serve me, I am grateful, and that's that.

The Austrian emperor Joseph II, who knew Catherine and Potemkin very well, remarked that he was more than useful, actually indispensable.[103] That was precisely so—as if Joseph had read all of the empress's letters to Potemkin during the 1780s. They are full of constant care and worries about the prince's health, and the main refrain throughout the many years of correspondence is "Guard your health, I and Russia need it." "You are not an insignificant private person who can live the way you like and do whatever you like. You belong to the State and you belong to me. You must, and I order you to take care of your health. I have to insist on it, for the wealth, protection, and glory of the Empire are entrusted to you and to perform your duties you must be sound both in body and in soul."[104] That is what the empress wrote in 1787, and not for the first or the last time.

Catherine's letters to Potemkin constitute an interesting record of their age and of human relations. At first these were notes to her beloved, whom she jokingly calls "giaour, cossack, Muscovite"; later, as the years go by their relations change, and the empress's letters turn into messages addressed by

Grigorii A. Potemkin. From the journal *Russkaia starina* (Russia of Old)
(St. Petersburg, 1875), tip-in plate.

an assiduous landlady to her benevolent landlord, "dad," "daddy," "papa."
The coarse, joking style of these letters reveals her absolute trust in the addressee and lack of epistolary embellishment and tender words. Rather they
are full of business, requests, instructions, and orders.

The letters of the 1780s show that more important and more serious
matters than love bound Potemkin and Catherine together. It took all of their
combined strength to pull the heavy load of state affairs uphill and he,
Potemkin, bore the brunt of the burden—without him they would be stuck.
Nothing else can compare in importance, and so the "matushka's,"
"landlady's" gratitude for "daddy's" efforts in performing his duties knows

no bounds: "There is no affectionate word, my friend, which I would not like to tell you. You are a wonder in that you captured Bendery without losing a single man."[105] And yet another refrain: "Don't worry, I shall not forget you," in the sense that she does not believe his enemies, his credit is reliable and there is no need to worry about the future.

Some readers may ask whether Potemkin's role was really so great within the Russian power system that the empress so strongly clung to him. Yes, throughout a fifteen-year period—from the mid-1770s till his death in 1791, Potemkin was the essential man in Catherine's government. That her reign was so successful and victorious must to a large degree be credited to His Highness. However, we will deal with this later, for now it would be appropriate to say a few words about Potemkin's personality.

There can be no doubt—he was no ordinary man. "About seven o'clock in the evening his sleigh stopped in front of the governor's house," recalls one traveler about Potemkin's visit to Mogilev, "and a tall, handsome, one-eyed man stepped out. He was dressed in a gown, and his long uncombed hair, which hung disheveled over his face and shoulders, proved that this man could not care in the least about his appearance. As he dismounted the sleigh all those present saw that in addition to his messy dress he had forgotten to put on that article of apparel which is considered to be integral to any suit; he managed to do without it throughout his entire stay in Mogilev, even when he met with ladies."[106]

The fact that the key article of men's dress was missing from Potemkin's suit was neither evidence of his peculiar absent-mindedness nor an act of disrespect to Mogilev society. He received envoys and courtiers and distinguished foreigners without his trousers on. Prince de Ligne calmed down the Poles who had taken offense at Potemkin: "The empress should not be deprived of your friendship for the reason that while receiving many of you in Elizavetgrad Prince Potemkin came out to meet you without his trousers on. Those who know the prince understand that such action on his part should be interpreted as a sign of confidence."[107]

Let us take another excerpt from the memoirs of a witness from Mogilev: "Five-feet-and-ten-inches tall, that handsome brunette was then about fifty years old. His face has a rather gentle expression, but when sitting at the table he looks absent-mindedly at people around him as if thinking of something unpleasant at the same time; he would lower his head on his hand, supporting his lower jaw, and continue observing all that was going on around with his single eye, then the squeezed lower part of his face would give him an ugly, beastly expression."[108]

His Highness made a dubious impression on many people. Prince de Ligne, who had seen him near besieged Ochakov, gave probably the most vivid albeit somewhat fictitious description of Potemkin: "I see here an army commander who seems lazy and works ceaselessly, who has no other desk than his knees, no other comb than his fingers, always abed and sleeping neither day nor night . . . worried when faced with danger, gay when he is in the middle of it; sad in his pleasures, unhappy by dint of being happy, blasé about everything, getting disgusted easily, morose, inconsistent; a serious philosopher, an able minister, or a child of ten. With one hand he signals to the women who please him, and with the other he makes the sign of the cross."[109]

Count Ségur's account confirms the words of de Ligne: "for maybe never has anyone seen, in a court, in a council and in a camp, a courtier who is more ostentatious and more uncivilized, a minister who is more enterprising and less hard-working, a general who is more audacious and more indecisive; his whole person offered the most original ensemble, by its inconceivable mixture of greatness and pettiness, laziness and activity, audacity and timidity, ambition and lack of concern . . . a man such as could be made rich and powerful, but whom it was impossible to make happy . . . Bored with what he possessed, envious of all that he could not obtain, desiring all and disgusted with all."[110]

Too much time has passed and too little evidence is available to help us understand the contradictions in Potemkin's personality. Traditions of the hedonistic eighteenth century, his early life, his original psychological type, and the long years of boundless power, which corrupts even the humblest of people—all these and probably many other factors had contributed to Potemkin's particular extravagant behavior and shocking habits. However, in all fairness we must admit that Grigorii Aleksandrovich Potemkin went down in Russian history not as an eccentric without pantaloons but as a large-scale imperial leader on a par with Peter the Great himself.

* * *

The Kuchuk Kainarji Peace Treaty was not a long-lasting one. The Russian Empire had only reached the edge of the Black Sea and the Crimean peninsula; this blessed crossroads of the northern Black Sea region had become somewhat of a no man's land, for the Turks had already lost power over it, but Russia's influence had not yet been fully established. In St. Petersburg, it seemed inconceivable that the Crimea could be independent, and, therefore, Catherine was most displeased when in 1774 the throne of the khanate was taken by Davlet-Geray, advocate of Crimean independence.

Catherine's course of action proceeded from traditional imperial policy: in the autumn of 1776, the Russian forces crossed Perekop and seized the peninsula, bringing with them the "right" khan, Shagin-Geraym, whom Catherine had kept in Poltava waiting until the appropriate moment arose. Supported by friendly bayonets, he mounted the throne in 1777, and these same bayonets were used to suppress the uprising of his new subjects. In 1779, the Turks were reluctantly forced to recognize this Russian version of Crimean independence, which meant an actual domination of Russia over the peninsula.

And at this point Potemkin came into the scene wielding, as a favorite, almost unlimited power. But the lot of the tsarina's favorite looks sweet only at a distance. Although Potemkin was engaged in numerous court intrigues, which was perhaps inevitable in his situation, in fact, he felt thoroughly bored. His energy, ambition, and hunger for glory required other deeds and other scales. He found these on the shores of the Black Sea as Peter the Great had gained fame on the shores of the Baltic Sea. Here, on the vast territory of the virgin steppes, far away from the court camarilla, jealousy, and spies, he could unfurl the breadth and strength of his nature.

Catherine wholeheartedly supported Potemkin's striving. As empress, she was interested in developing Russia's southern expanse bordering on Poland. There, in the south, boundless opportunities opened up for the empire. The country's future lay there. Catherine understood Potemkin as a man as well, as her letter to Grimm written in 1777 suggests: "I even like uncultivated countries; believe me, these are the best."[111] Novorossiia, the name given to the northern Black Sea region, was a virgin area. It was the richest country, an area for testing any, even the most fantastic projects, thanks to the backing of the "matushka" and Russia's manpower and material resources, which had never been duly measured and calculated.

Potemkin started with strengthening his power. He became governor-general of Novorossiia and the adjacent provinces. He dismissed Count Peter Rumiantsev and Prince A. D. Prozorovskii from the administrative management and military leadership in the south of the country. Count Nikita Panin also had to step aside, providing the favorite with space at the wheel of foreign policy. Soon Potemkin had become a peculiar vice emperor of the southern part of the empire. He was given complete freedom, and he took full advantage of it. Military achievements, crowned with Suvorov's brilliant victories, combined well with rapid administrative, economic, and naval advances in that region.

All this resembled the time of Peter the Great—if we consider the scope, great scale, unjustified haste, and inevitable sacrifice. Cities were built in the bare steppe, which were given sonorous Greek names: Kherson, Sevastopol', Melitopol', Odessa. Tens of thousands of peasants were driven together for construction of fortresses, canals, and embankments. They erected factories, opened shipyards, and planted forests. Streams of Russian and Ukrainian settlers and German colonists set off for Novorossiia, opening up the black earth zone of the southern steppe. In a short span of time the Black Sea fleet was built practically from scratch and immediately started to defeat the Turks.

According to Potemkin's intentions, the new region was to have a splendid capital, Ekaterinoslav on the Dnieper River (now Dnepropetrovsk), which was to be as great as St. Petersburg. He planned to build a big cathedral there—higher than St. Peter's in the Vatican—a theater, a university, museums, a commodities exchange, greenhouses, gardens, and parks. Wolfgang Amadeus Mozart was to conduct the orchestra in the theater: the Russian

envoy in Vienna was already negotiating with Mozart the terms of his en-
rollment in Russian service. And if Mozart and Potemkin had not died almost at the same time in 1791, they would certainly have met and become
friends, for His Highness was a subtle music lover, having not only a harem
to accompany him during his journeys but also a group of fine musicians,
and he knew the worth of musical talent.

Potemkin's initiative extended to the army as well. Thanks to his reforms,
the army was transformed and could now fight in the hot southern regions;
never before had the Russian soldiers fought under these conditions. The
field marshal was an advocate of new tactics and strategies that had passed
muster in battles. He encouraged initiative in soldiers and independent decision making in officers. Several generations of Russian soldiers spoke well
of Potemkin, who replaced the tight German-style uniform with a light and
comfortable outfit designed for the climate in each particular theater of war.
He did away with braids and powder, which had been pure torture for the
soldiers.

The decree Potemkin issued on that matter is written with lightness and
aphoristic character reminiscent of Suvorov's commands: "To wave hair, to
use powder, and to wear plaits—is that what soldiers should do? They have
no chamberlains. What then are their curls for? Everybody should agree that
it is more useful to wash one's head and comb one's hair than to burden
oneself with powder, fat, flour, hairpins, and plaits. The soldier's dress must
be simple—he must be ready when he gets up."[112]

All of Potemkin's numerous whims and fantastic plans were implemented
without delay. In 1787 he could already show the empress, who came to visit
the south, his achievements, which many people associate, for some reason,
with the notorious "Potemkin villages," though both Kherson and
Sevastopol', the cities Potemkin showed off, were not decorations but serious beginnings from the very first days of their existence; the same can be
said about the Black Sea fleet. In all fairness we should cite the words of the
Austrian emperor Joseph II, who accompanied Catherine on her journey to
the south, and who referred first of all to the cost of the work done: "As
for the rest, all appears easy when one lavishes money and men's lives. We
could not try in Germany or France what is risked here without obstacles."[113]

But Potemkin felt quite constrained even amid the vast expanses of New
Russia. His only live eye vigilantly searched through the mist over the Black
Sea, looking for the minaret towers of Istanbul, which from the fifteenth
century to the days of Ataturk was persistently referred to as Constantinople
in Russia. It was mainly through Potemkin's agency that the so-called Greek
Project, specifying the expulsion of the Turks from the Bosporus and the
restoration of the former Byzantine empire, came into being. This was, in
essence, the old-time idea of launching a crusade against the "Hagarians"
to despoil them of Constantinople and the main holy relic of Orthodox
world, the Hagia Sophia.

This blend of state and religious ambitions, which was coined into the Cross-onto-St. Sophia formula in the nineteenth century, had stirred many minds but it was Catherine, backed, as she was, by the Russian military triumphs on the northern shores of the Black Sea, who came closest to its realization. The idea of the Greek Project was suggested to the empress by none other than Voltaire himself. It was he who, back in 1769, pounded his bone-dry fist on the desk in his snug study at Ferney, calling Catherine to drive the Turks out of Europe and turn Constantinople into the capital of Russia.

When in April 1779 a second grandson was born to the empress, he was christened Constantine. The boy's name was chosen by Catherine herself, who jokingly announced that she wished to invite the Sultan Abd-El-Hamid as his godfather. A Greek wet-nurse was assigned to the child and a medal showing the Hagia Sophia on the reverse was issued in honor of the Tsarevich's birth. A Greek cadet corps was founded at the same time.

In 1787, high-ranking foreign guests arriving in Kherson together with the empress were amazed to see a magnificent triumphal arch with a legend "Here is the way to Byzantium" running across it. Of course, the empress realized it would be far from easy to achieve such imperial ambitions. In October 1789, she said, referring to the ten-year-old boy: "Constantine is a good lad; in thirty years, he will travel from Sevastopol' to Tsar'grad. We are now clipping the Turks' wings so by then they will have been clipped up and this will be much better for him."[114] In other words, Catherine envisaged the Greek Project to have materialized by the 1820s. It is remarkable that in the summer of 1829 the Russian troops of Catherine's other grandson, Emperor Nicholas I, bivouacked at Edirne (Adrianople), on the threshold of Istanbul. But then, it was a different situation.

The Greek Project, emerging from the general idea of expelling the Turks from the Bosporus, was gradually fleshed out with specific geopolitical issues, which were mainly brought up by Potemkin. In her letters to Joseph II of Austria, whom Catherine tried, in vain, to pull into this scheme, she described how it would be carried out. The breakup of the Ottoman Empire implied dividing one part of it between the Russians and the Austrians. The other part was to become the basis for creating two states anew: Byzantium proper, with its capital at Constantinople, its throne occupied by Constantine III (Constantine I, called the Great, was the founder of the Byzantine Empire; the last emperor of the Eastern Empire, perishing in 1453 during the siege of Constantinople by the Ottoman Turks, was Constantine II, Paleologus), and a Kingdom of Dacia, which was to be set up on the territories of Turkey's possessions in the northern Black Sea region (Moldavia, Wallachia, and Bessarabia). A new dynasty was to be created for the Dacian throne. Although Catherine did not go into details as to who would sit on it, for many a courtier it was an open secret as one could clearly see thrusting out behind this ambitious undertaking the ass's ears of the Serenissimus prince Potemkin. There was yet another variant in the offing, just in case: it was proposed that a kingdom of Albania would be created in place of Turkey's Asian possessions (that is, in the Caucasus and Cis-Caspian lands), whose throne would accommodate Potemkin just as well.

In her letters to Joseph, Catherine emphasized (although no one would take it seriously at the time) that the newly formed states would be wholly independent of Russia. The empress herself had but very hazy ideas of what course Russian geopolitics would take in the case of Russia's military triumphs in the south. Here is what she wrote to Grimm in 1795, that is, not long before death: "in Russian history, the possessors of the north of the empire easily became the masters of this empire's south. Without the north, the power of those who held the south remained weak and sluggish. But the north could very well do without the south or the southern provinces."[115]

Clearly discernible here is the Eurocentric view of world politics, widespread in the past (and nowadays), according to which only the Europeans—inhabitants of the north—are capable of creating a civilization and culture and that their migration to the south, that is, lands settled by the great masses of the "barbarian" Asian and African peoples, is as natural as it is inevitable. The white men, northerners, are to rule the south, the east, and, eventually, all the world.

Proceeding from this notion was another idea, namely, that the true capital of the Russian Empire was yet to be found and that, in all probability, it was not for her to fix its vicinity. She does not elucidate the exact whereabouts of the "real capital"—this task is relegated to her successors—but recalling, apropos, a recent war with Sweden, when there was a real threat of St. Petersburg's capture by the enemy, she speaks of the danger of locating the capital at the empire's frontiers and of the necessity to move it over in the direction of the all-out imperial advancement to the south.

The tsarina was carried away by her dream of imperial expansion. Filled with enthusiasm over the military successes of the Russian army, Catherine could, without boasting too much, write to Grimm: "Victories are something that we are accustomed to." Looking at the empress, the calm and sensible Joseph II told the French ambassador at Sevastopol': "I am doing what I can here . . . but, you see it yourself, this woman is exalted."[116]

Joseph saw the crux of the problem fairly well; he looked at it as a member of a large, yet unfriendly and envious, community of European states. The Austrian emperor did not doubt that the violation of a status quo in such an important and strategic area as the straits would cost Russia dearly. The fairy tales about independence from Russia of newly formed Greek and Dacian kingdoms might well be told to little Constantine when he was rocking in a cradle, but neither England nor France nor, for that matter, any other state having its own strategic interests at the Bosporus would, under any circumstances, allow Russia to radically strengthen its position in the area one-sidedly. Austria also found it quite unprofitable to have

Russia and its satellites as its neighbors. Joseph put it in a nutshell when he said: "For Vienna, at any rate, it is safer to have neighbors in turbans than in fur hats."

And there was reason in what he said. Much water had flowed under the bridge since the heroic deeds performed by James Sobieski and Prince Eugène de Savoie—the Turks themselves had changed a lot so that now one could well bargain with them. All the same, the wet blanket thrown on the Greek Project by Joseph helped but little to cool off the fervor of its begetters and only Potemkin's sudden death in the fall of 1791 undermined the entire scheme of advancement to the Bosporus. Incidentally, one of the versions of Catherine's last will had the following words written in her hand: "My intention is to elevate Constantine Pavlovich to the throne of the Greek Eastern empire."

* * *

Catherine II was the most Russian-minded empress in the history of Russia. It will not be a gross exaggeration to assert that the former Princess Sophia Augusta Frederica had become the first Russian nationalist. It is not hard to comprehend whence it all sprang: one can find interwoven here both the sincere love for the country and gratitude to that country which had made her a great ruler and which had become her second homeland, bringing her everlasting glory ("I wish and desire only the good to the country to which God has brought me. Its glory makes me glorious as well").[117] Every visitor to the country who allowed himself any ill-natured judgment of Russia was immediately put into the category of Catherine's personal enemies, and there was no invective with which she would not denigrate him on his departure!

Herein lies the admiration of the Russian people, which was like a stone wall behind which one felt safe despite all the scrapes at home: "The Russian people is unique in the whole world. God vested it with qualities lacking in other peoples."[118] One should not disregard the psychological quirks of a patriotism fostered in a foreigner who passionately strove to be accepted by the Russians as their own and who achieved this goal with tremendous success: "I believe that there are few countries in which foreigners have more ease in being accepted than in Russia."[119]

And how fond Catherine was of the Russian language! She spoke it with a slight German accent, which she retained till the end of her life, but her speech was rich in idiom and variety of expression. In the history of Russian literature, she occupies her own, albeit modest, niche: the empress was the author of a dozen or so theatrical pieces. She was, in fact, the first to undertake a translation of the *Iliad* into Russian. The Russian proverbs cropping up in Catherine's letters are always to the point, and sound natural. She was also fairly well versed in the colloquial utterance of the day, and possessed a rich stock of billingsgate, as one may well infer from her letters.

The tsarina also loved various nicknames and sobriquets. One cannot but laugh reading her letters from the days of the war with Sweden (1788–1791) in which she introduced a comical homophone "Sidor Ermolaevich" for the Swedish naval commander, the Duke of Södermanland, and called the Prussian envoy a "Buttoned-Up Prick," because he was a pedant and a bore. The empress was firmly convinced (and she wrote it to Voltaire) that the Russian language is richer in idiom than the French and is capable of giving utterance to the most intricate and subtle matters of politics and law.

Yet the main line of her professed "consanguinity" with Russia was connected with the empire and the dynasty. Catherine looked upon herself not just as Peter III's widow but, rather, as a member of the Romanov House. If ever she mentioned her "late grandmother," it would be entirely wrong to presume that she had Albertina Frederica of the Baden-Durlach in mind. Far from it! She meant Catherine I. The same is true when one comes across the expression "my forbears." These are the Romanovs, rather than the dukes and princes of Holstein and Anhalt-Zerbst. She felt herself to be a link in this genealogical succession and it was here, among her late husband's Russian progenitors, that she asserted her roots.

Count Ségur recalls the empress as she appeared at the Field of Poltava, where Potemkin staged a grandiose dramatization of the great battle of 1709: "Joy and glory shone in Catherine's eyes; one could have believed that Peter the Great's blood flowed in her veins."[120] No wonder that she refused to maintain relations with her German kith and kin: she even denied entry into Russia to her own brother, who would, no doubt, be only too ready to taste the rich Russian *kulebiaka* pie.

She wrote in one of the drafts of her testament: "For the sake of the empire's welfare . . . I advise you to exclude from state affairs and councils . . . the princes of Württemberg [brothers of Paul's wife, Maria Fedorovna—E.A.] and have to do with them as little as possible." Frederick could not even have pictured in a bad dream that the same timid princess of Zerbst who sat at his table in 1744, modesty incarnate, whom he had reckoned he would use for his political ends, would, years afterward, soothe Potemkin in her letter to him with the following casual remark: "Spit on the Prussian [bastards]: we will repay their mean trick in kind!"[121]

Catherine's imperial way of thinking sprang from her unshakable faith in the intrinsic superiority of Russians not only over other Slavic peoples but the rest of mankind as well. As a diligent student of philology and history, she drew the conclusion—whose veracity she never put to question—that, first, the Norse God Odin came from the Don area and, hence, was a Slav; second, that the Scythians were also of Slavic origin, being beautiful in appearance and honest and humane in nature; third, that in earlier times the Slavs (that is, Russians) had inhabited the entire earth; and, last, that it was directly from ancient Rus' that the British had borrowed their much-vaunted institutions, and so on and so forth.

Well, if the Britons rated so low in her opinion, what could be said of the
Ukrainians, Poles, and other nationalities! In her instruction to the procurator-general A. Viazemskii, issued in 1764, she stated categorically: "Little
Russia, Livland, and Finland shall be russified in the easiest way possible so
that they would not look like wolves in the wood."[122] In her instruction to
P. A. Rumiantsev on the governing of Ukraine she clarified what the easiest
way would be: first, the limitation of freedom of movement for peasants and,
later, the expansion of serfdom over them, which is exactly what was successfully achieved in subsequent years. It was under Catherine that the title
of hetman was abolished and the formerly freeborn Cossack Ukraine turned
into an ordinary Russian *guberniia* with its own serfs and landowners. In
1771, the empress also issued an order setting up the notorious Pale of Settlement for Jews.

And yet no nation was more detestable for Catherine than the Poles. There
was something unnatural in her hatred, coming, as it did, from the otherwise kindly ruler. On the other hand, we have already spoken of the difference existing between state and private ethics. Catherine the empress hated
the Polish Lithuanian Commonwealth for its people's love of freedom, the
proud dignity of its nobles, and the democratic traditions that her autocratic
mind found utterly unacceptable.

The tragedy that the Polish Lithuanian Commonwealth went through in
the eighteenth century was seen by the empress as the consequence of the
Poles' inability to lead an independent existence, and a manifestation of their
innate corruptibility. Prompted by some inner and unpremeditated dictates
of self-censorship, I, being a Russian and well remembering those icy mountains of hatred and mutual injuries that have been steadily building up in
Russo-Polish relations for the last three centuries, somehow cannot bring
myself to quote those shameful lines written about the Poles that come from
the hand of this intelligent, refined, and otherwise fairly sensible woman.
Instead, I will point out, with regret, that in the dramatic plight of the Polish Lithuanian Commonwealth, torn asunder by the three black eagles of
Russia, Austria, and Prussia, and in the persistence and brutality with which
this was done during the partitions of 1772, 1776, and 1793, Russia's role
was most disreputable and shameful. Catherine's imperial stance was dictated
not only by some general geopolitical considerations and the good of the
empire but also by that peculiar aversion that the empress had for the Poles.
What was the sum total and the outcome of all of this is only too familiar:
the insurrections, Suvorov over the downtrodden Warsaw, blood, hatred, and
blood again.

It is true that the empress's rage against some particular nation would
abate as soon as it became a part of the Russian Empire. It was her firm belief
that the Poles should rejoice at the loss of their independence, for they should
take it as the first step toward their own prosperity. And how cross Catherine
was at the two French diplomat-fops who, during her stay in the Crimea,

spied in Bakhchisarai on the Tartar women taking off their yashmaks. "Messieurs, this joke is in very bad taste and sets a very bad example. You are in the midst of a people conquered by my arms; I want their laws, their religion, their morals and their prejudices to be respected."[123]

* * *

The theme "Catherine and Men of Enlightenment" could well serve as a subject of a separate book—so numerous are the letters Catherine exchanged with Diderot, Voltaire, and d'Alembert, so remarkable and versatile are the contents of these letters. The correspondence started soon after Catherine's accession to the Russian throne, one of her first addressees being none other than the great Voltaire. In the French historian Alfred Rambaud's view, at the beginning of this correspondence Catherine was like a young girl brought up within the four walls of a boarding school who, on having read in secret some poet's verse, falls in love with the author, making him the idol of her fancies until one day she, all of a sudden, gets an opportunity to write to the hero of her dreams.

And indeed, the empress's first letters are both ingenious and openhearted. Catherine prides herself on her lucky chance of corresponding with the inimitable Voltaire and takes delight in receiving his replies. And afterward, too, until the very death of Voltaire in 1778, she sticks to the style worked out in the early years of her epistolary friendship with this genius, regularly sending off to Ferney her letters written in a tone of a humble obedience by a modest pupil of his, seeking the approval of the great Teacher and Patriarch. She values his opinion higher than anything else in the world, asserting that it was him who became the formative influence on her personality.

When the sage of Ferney died, the empress seemed utterly grief-stricken: ". . . and all of a sudden I felt an overwhelming despondency and a great contempt for all things of this world . . . I wanted to scream."[124] It was in this vein that she wrote to Grimm, asking him to purchase for her a hundred copies of a new edition of Voltaire's works: "I want them to set an example; I want them to be studied, learned by heart, to nourish spirits; they will form citizens, geniuses, heroes and authors; they will develop one hundred thousand talents, which would otherwise be lost in a night of darkness, of ignorance, etc."[125] No better epitaph could have been devised! And it is precisely a public response that this disciple of Voltaire's had in mind, as Grimm made no secret of Catherine's epistles.

Scholars researching Catherine's correspondence with Voltaire express a remarkable unanimity of opinion, pointing to the purely pragmatic aims of the empress: she was striving for public recognition in Europe, which was a matter of extreme importance for Catherine. Like no one else before her on the Russian throne, she set great store by public opinion both inside the country and beyond its borders. In this sense, Catherine's correspondence with the *philosophes* was tantamount to her embraces with village women, whom she encountered on her way from St. Petersburg to Moscow. Both added to her popularity, which, being a usurper of the throne of the legitimate tsar, she was badly in need of. Anything that undermined her popularity incensed the empress.

Count Ségur noticed, to his surprise, a marked change that occurred on such occasions in the otherwise tolerant, intelligent, and even-hearted Catherine: she would eagerly relate all the false rumors about her ambition that circulated around Europe, she would read out epigrams aimed at her and some amusing bits of gossip regarding the decline of Russia's finances and the empress's health. She would pay heed to every spiteful story spread about her by the "political windbags," as she herself called them, and would do everything possible to neutralize it either by making a statement in European papers through some of her men of straw or by writing a letter to those of her addressees whose talkativeness she did not doubt. And here Catherine would lash at her adversaries without mincing words: they were all "scum," "scoundrels," "rogues," and "beasts." And what instructions would our "philosophe enthroned" issue on failing to silence this or that book publisher, author, or newspaperman! "Order all our ministers," wrote Catherine to the College of Foreign Affairs in 1763 on receiving a French book relating the story of Peter III's deposition, "to zealously search out for the author and have him punished, to have everything confiscated . . . and to forbid the book's entry into Russia."[126]

Once, the empress got much vexed with an article appearing in one of the British newspapers. In her resolution made upon A. P. Vorontsov's report about it, Catherine indicated four ways of dealing with the author: "1) To take the author out of the way and give him a sound thrashing; or 2) to wean him from writing with money; or 3) to do him in; or 4) to rebut him in writing. In any case, he evidently has nothing to do at [our] court. So it is up to you to choose one of these."[127]

Catherine's correspondence with Voltaire was a blessing to her: Europe had no better authority than the incorruptible Voltaire, who pledged no allegiance to any power and challenged all and sundry with his caustic wit. When rebuked by the Metropolitan Platon for her correspondence with this impious atheist, Catherine replied as follows: "Can anything be more innocent than an epistolary intercourse with an octogenarian who strives in his writings, well known all over Europe, to glorify Russia, to abase her foes, to keep in check his compatriots, always ready to pour forth everywhere their venomous hatred of Russia and whom he did, not once, manage to hold back from doing it? From this point of view, I believe that my letters written to an atheist have done no damage to either the church or our motherland."[128]

Catherine and Voltaire had much in common: their atheism, their cynical attitude to faith and church, their animosity toward the Bourbons, Jews, Poles, and Turks; the last, in the opinion of both, had no place in Europe.

And, indeed, what right to existence has the people who could not make head nor tail of the French language, queried Voltaire, and his pupil would share her patriarch's doubts. It is patent fact, however, that both knew well the worth of their mutual confidences, puns, and confessions, which would become known overnight by all the reading public in Europe. For both of them it was a kind of game, in which neither of the players lost.

It is important to underscore here that this game was a paper one, by correspondence only. When Voltaire decided to "shake up his old bones" and set off to St. Petersburg, Catherine was firmly against it. And it was not the hardships of the journey on the teacher's weak health of which Catherine was so touchingly solicitous, but rather her unwillingness to make a personal acquaintance with a man who was famed for his cunning perspicacity and who, seemingly, read everyone like an open book. She had no wish to have such a keen observer nearby, preferring to give the Ferney hermit news of her own concoction. Sending him off cheerful letters describing her triumphs in war and peace, she would fib a bit occasionally, exaggerating the number of trophies seized by her army or underrating the scale of her defeats but this was also part of the game she was playing with Voltaire and we shall never know for sure whether he did not take it with a pinch of salt.

It could well be, however, that, looking at it from his far-off Ferney, Voltaire may have believed Catherine's tales à la Münchhausen, to wit, that there was no villager in Russia who would not eat chicken meat, which he would prefer to that of turkey. Catherine deemed it superfluous to invite Voltaire to see for himself the veracity of her intimations to him, all the more so as she had already had the experience of communicating with another observant French *philosophe*. This was Denis Diderot. The latter, on arriving at St. Petersburg in 1775, showed himself to be a rhapsodic, garrulous, and credulous man. The empress sensed her superiority over this simpleton, and easily cleared up all his "tricky" queries regarding serfdom and autocracy in Russia, leading him completely astray. Yet this *philosophe*, whom she thought to have twisted around her little finger, picked at her famous *Nakaz* (Instruction to the Legislative Commission), which naturally incurred her displeasure.

As to the impressions made on her by Diderot's philosophical concepts, they were most unfavorable. "I conversed with him often and at length, but with more curiosity than gain. If I had believed him, all would have been upset in my empire; legislation, administration, politics, finances, I would have overturned everything for the sake of impractical theories."[129] This is what she said to Diderot himself: "In all of your plans for reform you forget the difference between our two positions: *you* work only on paper, which tolerates everything, is uniform and supple, posing no obstacles either to your imagination or to your quill; while *I*, a poor empress, work on human skin, which is more irritable and ticklish."[130]

Another time, she made fun of the jurist Mercier de la Rivère who, tempted by the empress's invitation, arrived in Russia with the intention of rebuilding this savage country in accordance with his own plans. Rewarding him at his true worth and having a good laugh at him, Catherine sent him off about his business.

It should be admitted that her attitude toward arts and sciences was far from simple. On the one hand, she spoke at length of the good of knowledge and science, and unhesitatingly put herself in the hands of the famous physician of the time, Baron Dimsdale, who inoculated the empress and heir against smallpox in the fall of 1768; on the other hand, she firmly held that all doctors were quacks: in fact, she was known to have coined the popular dictum "Doctors are all fools." Her treatment of medicine was typically Russian in that she superstitiously set it at naught, relying herself exclusively on self-treatment. And it was not by her trust in science that she was driven to vaccination, either—far from that! Catherine was an adventurer by nature. She once said that were she born a man, she would, no doubt, have died young as she would wager her head to win a stake. It was the same kind of resolve here: the hullabaloo made of the Russian empress's vaccination all over Europe was worth taking a risk of falling ill with smallpox. She could then casually write to Grimm about Louis XV's death of smallpox in 1774: "I am still of the opinion that it is shameful for a king of France who lived in the eighteenth century to die of smallpox; it is barbaric."[131] So, if all of this was in any way related to science, it is but the science of politics, of which she was an unquestionable master.

As to the rest, Catherine regarded science and philosophy as quite useless. "For all of that it must be confessed that these philosophers are a peculiar class of people: they come into the world, I think, to put dots on the i's and to make obscure and doubtful all that which one had been persuaded of, like the fact that two and two make four."[132] For all this, however, she was fond of speculating about the "philosophic conduct," to whose precepts she strove to adhere all her life. As one may gather from her letters, what she meant by the "philosophic conduct" boiled down to stoicism, indifference to danger, concealing one's real feelings and holding in check one's passions, contempt of unnecessary comfort, disdain of authority and of one's own health: in a word, the ideal propounded by Diogenes.

The great empress suffered from two complexes, which came out particularly well in her correspondence with the *philosophes* and talks with the erudite. The impact of the first—"dropout complex"—can be seen fairly distinctly in her judgment of the *philosophes,* whom she calls the "bizarre folk." Once, getting back into her carriage after her talk with peasants and their wives, which gave her much satisfaction, Catherine said to Count Ségur with aplomb: "More is learned, she said to me one day, in speaking to ignorant people about their own affairs than in addressing scholars, who have only theories, and who are ashamed to have no answer, so they respond with ridiculous assertions on things about which they have no definitive knowledge. How I pity them, these poor scholars! They never dare pronounce these four words: 'I do not know,' which are so useful for us ignorant people and which sometimes stop us from making dangerous decisions; because, when doubting, it is better to do nothing than to do the wrong thing."[133] Of course, the empress's words have a true ring about them and even nowadays one can come across such scholars. Yet at all times, science would be dead but for those who dared to doubt and put conventional wisdom to the rigorous test of facts.

One must say that in her contempt for science Catherine was far from being alone: at that time of infatuation with man's natural estate and Rousseau's philosophy, science was often seen as shackling man's vitality. "Instruction," pontifically wrote Catherine in 1779, "often quenches [man's] innate quickness of mind."[134] This liking for platitudes, coupled with her evident intellectual superiority over many men of her circle, including scholars, and her much inflated self-esteem, all made Catherine's pronouncements sound too categorical at times and, alas, not always very intelligent. "I respect your knowledge, but I like ignorance better, I want to know only what is necessary to conduct *my little household*."[135] "Her little household" playfully referred to here is nothing but the Russian empire proper, which she governed—allegedly, better than anyone else—without ever being a Sorbonist or Oxonian. "And I, who have never been a student and who have not been to Paris at all, have neither science nor wit, and consequently I do not at all know what must be learned, nor even what can be learned, and where to receive all of this if it is not in your countries."[136] Here one can hear an undisguised irony aimed by the "unlearned" but great empress at the windbag scholars, to whom she mockingly takes off her hat, fishing, obviously, for a compliment on her wit and achievements. Self-humiliation is greater than self-pride.

It is remarkable that the above quotation exposes another fairly amusing side of the empress, her "provincial woman's complex." Paris, the world's intellectual capital and arbiter of every conceivable and inconceivable fad and fashion, never left the empress's mind at rest. She strove to outstrip France, Paris, Versailles, in everything. The "provincial woman's complex" shows itself quite plainly in her playful quip, aimed at Ségur during her journey to the south: ". . . your beautiful ladies, your elegant and knowledgeable Parisians, pity you quite a bit for traveling in bear country, to the home of the Barbarians, with a boorish tsarina."[137]

She has the same in mind when writing to Madam Jeoffrin: "It surprises me that you regard me as witty. I had always been told that only those who visited Paris could be considered witty in your country." But this is all coquetry: our "provincial" was sure that she would beat all Parisian ladies, both learned and unlearned, together with their gallants even if the odds were a hundred to one in their favor. "Paris ladies would soon wilt if they happened to lead such a hectic life as mine. But as you see, I am as free-and-easy as a bird," she wrote by way of commenting to Mme. Jeoffrin.[138]

The empress's correspondence with this estimable lady—matron of a celebrated salon in Paris—comes in much the same way as her letter of many years earlier to Baron von Grimm, in which she reveals another trait of her character: Catherine strove not only for European fame but also for simple friendship and sympathy. At the start of her correspondence with Mme. Jeoffrin, she wrote: "I want to repeat once again that I do not wish any kowtowing: this is not the way between friends. If I have won your sympathies, please, do not treat me as if I were some shah of Persia."[139]

Further on, she throws light on what has always been a curse of rulers—the isolation and lack of understanding on the part of people surrounding her, who do not follow solely the dictates of their hearts: "Believe me, there is nothing more unpleasant than high rank. When I enter a room, everyone present there turns to stone and takes a submissive pose as if seeing the Gorgon's head. Sometimes, it drives me mad, and I start screaming at them like an eagle at other birds. I must confess, however, that this leads nowhere: the more I scream at them, the more constrained they become . . . Whereas, if you came to my room, I would simply say to you: 'Sit down, please and let's have a chat.' You would take a chair in front of me, I would sit opposite and we would talk at odd moments of this and that: I am quite good at it."[140]

Many years afterward she would write of her loneliness to Prince de Ligne, elaborating the theme: "We, sovereigns, may at times be quite unbearable in society. When I enter a room . . . ,"[141] and then repeating word for word the contents of her letter to Mme. Jeoffrin written some twenty years earlier. It is clear that this feeling, this thought of hers, got deep into Catherine's heart, so frequently does it crop up in her reminiscences.

We shall slightly digress here as to remind our readers of the colossal role that letter-writing played in eighteenth-century European culture. The epistolary form of literary works enjoyed wide currency at the time: readers of the day cried over letters exchanged by pitiful lovers and admired the terse style of military leaders and the profundity of philosophers. In those days, of course, the tempo of life was incomparably quieter. Brief as it was against our span of seventy or eighty years, life was nonetheless not so helter-skelter but more measured and subdued.

The eighteenth-century man lived in a world in which the rhythms of life were created by early waking at sunrise, the chimes of the town clock, and the days on which the mail arrived and left the town. To get ready for that day, one had, without undue haste, to light up a fresh candle and, after carefully sharpening the pen and smoothing out a thick yellowish piece of paper, to start one's regular letter to one's far-off addressee who was, likewise, looking forward to the mail day, when he would receive greetings and news from afar. It was inconceivable, insulting, and unworthy to leave letters unanswered.

Catherine, being the product of her age, was possessed of all these feelings in full. Of course—and we would like to say it again—her letters often had purely pragmatic aims; of course, she cheated and fibbed, making political capital, and read her own epistles, looking at them through the eyes of a bystander, as if over her own shoulder. But at the same time, she remained an affable, sociable woman who wanted to receive not only official reports but also, from time to time, an affectionate letter from some boon companion of hers, to whom she would write of life's trivia, with whom she would be pleased to share, as her equal, her thoughts or just chat. Long ago, she had decided that since no such confidant could be found among a crowd of court adulators, she would find one among distant correspondents. Catherine assigned this role to Baron von Grimm, the writer and publisher of a literary bulletin about life in France, which he dispatched to every European state.

Though neither an original thinker, serious scientist, or even witty conversationalist, Grimm was known for his exactitude in business matters and his blind adoration of the Russian empress. Both qualities perfectly suited Catherine, as the former made Grimm a punctilious correspondent and the latter ruled out even a shadow of ridicule or double entendre in his answers to the indiscreet intimations that the empress occasionally made to him. In March 1778, Catherine wrote to Grimm that she had a pile of unanswered letters lying at her writing desk, including those to Frederick II, Voltaire, and the king of Sweden; she was somehow disinclined to reach for these: "but as they do not amuse me, because to them it is necessary to write, and with you I chatter, but never write . . . I prefer to amuse myself and to let my hand, my quill and my head go freely where it pleases them to go. Let us go then!"[142] At some other time she wrote to him: "I am taking up the quill again. Let us ramble on for a bit."[143]

Catherine's correspondence with the *philosophes* was a boon to her. They introduced her to the intellectual cream of European society, brought fame to her state affairs, causing a tide of praise addressed to the "brightest star of the north" as she was dubbed by Voltaire. Few of her contemporaries noticed Rulhiére's (sober) judgment of her, drowned as it was in the flow of exalted eulogizing: "The overblown flattery pampered her [vanity] as people surrounding her instilled in her [mind] a false notion of a genuine greatness and of the means used to make people happy. The philosophers of our time, whose opinion she required as a kind of good advice, instilled in her egotism, which is harmful for any man and not only the sovereign. They made her strive only for being talked about, they taught her to rejoice at any praise uttered, with which she was showered by all and sundry, and to make herself the focus of everyone's attention, without caring much what the state's plight's will be after her death."[144] There are, no doubt, an extremely small number of people in world history who passed unscathed the hardest trial of being extolled to the skies. Unfortunately, Catherine must be excluded from this small circle of the truly great.

* * *

Catherine appreciated at its true worth a gratifying solecism made by Prince Ligne when he wrote, aiming to flatter, "Catherine le grand," which sounded almost like "Peter the Great." Comparing herself to Russia's great reformer, Catherine saw almost no difference between herself and Peter, and in some respects felt she was even superior to him. She also jealously and not impartially "kept count" of her strong points on the European and world scene, pondering on her advantages over Maria Theresa and cherishing a dream to eclipse even the sumptuous glory of Louis XIV. And what jealousy lurked behind those mutually honey-tongued compliments that Catherine continually exchanged with Frederick the Great of Prussia, who was her inveterate contestant at the battlefield of fame. Reflecting on all this, one ponders over those pages of Count Ségur's memoirs, in which he remarks that a person attaining to such fame as Catherine did should apparently be indifferent to the pricks of envy, ridicule, and spite. Not Catherine! In much the same way as her teacher Voltaire, it was with much acerbity and nervousness that she responded to any doubt, however slight, voiced in regard of her numerous merits.

This conceited quest for fame was in her blood ever since those young days when she had uttered her famous phrase "To reign or to die!"[145] In her letters to correspondents abroad she is inclined to boast. "My soldiers go to the fight with barbarians as if it were a wedding," thus she described to her friends a most fatiguing war against the Turks.[146] As years went by, her attitude to herself was less and less mingled with humor, and she rendered her patronage to any outward expression of "Catherine-philia," as she herself called it, more and more becoming a sucker for flattery, no matter how mean and fulsome. "Flatter her" was the advice given to the new British envoy by Potemkin, who knew his "goodhearted mother" only too well. "This is the only means to gain whatever you wish from her. And in this way people achieve everything. Do not try to sound clever—she will not listen to you. Rather, appeal to her feelings and passions. Do not offer her the treasures, or the British fleet: she has no desire for these. What she really needs are praise and compliments. Give her what she herself desires and she will repay to you by giving you all the forces of her state."[147] Count Ségur, too, wrote that one could lead the empress astray by playing on her love for fame.

Of course, this is a bit simplifying: no compliments would induce Catherine to give Britain "all the forces of her state." From the first to the last day of Catherine's reign her own fame and that of Russia constituted a single whole. In 1761, she wrote of Russia: "Its glory brings fame to me, too."[148] There is no doubt that she would have taken Russia's abasement in the same way, that is, as her own disgrace. Once, traveling across the south in a carriage that she shared with some foreign envoys, she overheard through her nap their talk on the then vital issue: whether the British king George III would feel more at ease if he put up with the loss of his fourteen overseas provinces in America, which were becoming an independent state. Wakened up with a jolt, Catherine said, without mincing her words, that had she been in George's shoes, she would rather have put a bullet through her head.

Unlike many rulers of the day, Catherine was not possessed with a mania for world domination. Conquering the Bosporus was the limit of her desires, and even here she was fully aware of all the difficulties involved in realizing her Greek Project. Nor was she eager to support the Russian trailblazers of the American continent and in her reply to a request made by the merchant Ivan Golikov, who asked for aid to his company for pursuing trade with the "barbarous peoples" of North America, she remarked, not without wit, as follows: "Our imperial aid is now directed at our activities in the south, for which reason both the barbarous American peoples and the trade with these are left to their own lot."[149] It was something of the kind that she inscribed on a draft of a campaign to conquer India: "There are enough lands and possessions in Russia for us to have no need to set off for conquests in India."[150] She also had a clear idea of things that were beyond the grasp of many of her fellow seekers of fame. Thus, she was not pleased at all with the idea of seeing a monument erected to her own person or a historical treatise compiled about her in the panegyrical tones by some court historian. What is the good of these: contemporaries are incapable of judging the true worth of a statesman living in their own time.

Catherine, grown wise with life experience and the knowledge of history, distinguished well between the cheap and precarious renown of the moment and great and abiding fame. Moreover, she even knew how to achieve the badge of immortality. She was sure that no victory, edifice, peace treaty, or monument in the whole world could vie in longevity with the quiet voice of a genius. "Would you like me to tell you what I think about this Chechen peace that you laud so highly and about the glory which, according to you, the peacemakers deserve? Throughout my life I have not attached glory to what is most extolled: each person extols or does not, according to his interests. It is not that: the glory that pleases me is that which is often the least lauded; it is that which produces good not only in the present, but also in the future, for races of men and countless benefits; it is this that even the scholarly will search for, lantern in hand, and will stumble over without understanding anything if they lack the genius for development; ah, monsieur!

a bushel of such glory effaces, in my eyes, the small glories about which people would like to speak to me. My motto: work in silence, doing good to produce good, letting all the rest frolic about."[151]

Now the reader will see why, on waking up at dawn, the tsarina would immediately hurry to her writing desk and start working on her code of laws: she was consumed with a passionate ambition to attain to the immortal glory of great lawgivers: Lycurgus, Solon, Justinian, Iaroslav the Wise, and Peter the Great. It is with this in view that she assiduously compiled her "Catherine Code" in the mornings . . .

To do her justice, this was the province in which she was largely successful. Catherine's fate proved that willpower and ambition may become no less a crucial factor in history than scores of gunships and thousands of soldiers. The fame that Catherine the empress did create for herself became her weapon and force, which was just as formidable as that warship that bore the name *Catherine's Glory* (it should be noted, in passing, that the empress requested Prince Potemkin to have the ship renamed lest the Turks, on capturing it by chance, would rejoice at possessing Catherine's fame). As the French diplomat Corberon pointed out in his report, the fame that the empress had built up for herself, her resolute character, her talents, and personal luck may well be placed on a par with the cunning of politicians and the bravery of experienced generals.

Nowadays, some two hundred years later, when a large number of fame-seekers have to some extent put Catherine in the shade, we may nevertheless state with certainty that the empress went down in history as an outstanding statesperson and that her reign may rightly be reckoned as a time of grand reforms and significant legislative acts. Of course, one may rejoin here that it was not particularly difficult to be a great reformer in a country as rich as Russia was then. The Austrian emperor once put it this way. "The empress is the only sovereign in Europe who is really rich; she spends a lot, everywhere, and owes nothing: her currency is worth what she wants it to be worth; if the whim took her, she could make money out of leather."[152]

As we know only too well, however, even a fabulously rich country could be brought to the brink of ruin by a dim-witted ruler. Catherine was far from dim-witted. The goals she faced were quite realistic: the strengthening of autocracy and the carrying out of urgent military, administrative, and estate reforms. These she carried out as parts of a single whole, proceeding from one general principle: boosting to the maximum the development and perfection of that "orderly" state whose foundations were laid by Peter the Great. The *Statute on Provinces* of 1775, forming the basis of a new administrative order, was the end product of Catherine's work of many years, of which she was greatly pleased to inform Grimm. And, indeed, this was one of the most significant reforms of the eighteenth century.

Of great importance for the destinies of the Russian nobility was the *Charter on Rights, Liberties, and Privileges to the Genteel Russian Nobility,* issued in 1785. From that time onward, the Russian nobility prayed to God for their "Mother-Tsarina." The Charter confirmed some exclusive privileges of the nobles: it freed them from compulsory service, poll-tax, billeting *(postoi)*, and corporal punishment; it ensured their right to own land and serfs, and their right to set up noble assemblies that had their own administrative bodies. The same year, 1785, saw the issue of another fundamental law, the *Charter on Rights and Privileges to Towns of the Russian Empire,* which granted townsfolk some important rights of urban self-government.

It was these main legislative documents which, coupled with the unpublished Granting Charter *(Zhalovannaia gramota)* to state peasants, constituted an integrated code of laws. Catherine's legislature far outlasted the empress, becoming, along with the main Petrine laws, the basis of Russian statehood for years to come. It was, properly speaking, this kind of summing up of her reign that the ambitious lawgiving tsarina probably hoped that the future historian would make.

The ideological framework of Catherine's reign rested on the foundation laid in his time by Peter the Great. Aptly applying the ideas of Enlightenment, Catherine only slightly refurbished Peter's old-fashioned autocracy, changing it into her "enlightened absolutism." The general ideas of this social order, termed "absolutism with a human face" by the historian A. B. Kamenskii, ensured the unlimited power of the state, which takes good care of its subjects who obey it without demur. Accordingly, the monarch, occupying the top of the social ladder, possessed vast authority. Proceeding from the lofty idea of attaining the common good, that is, "the well-being of subjects and the glory of the Fatherland" (as stated by Catherine), the sovereign reckoned himself fully entitled to regulate the life of the state's subjects, create and abolish social estates, determine their status as sole bearers of rights. Reading of enlightened absolutism and its human face, one should not think that the terms used here are tinged with irony. Compared with the reigns of Peter the Great and Anna Ioannovna, the age of Catherine was indeed humanitarian and tolerant. Nor can Catherine the person be likened to her predecessors, especially the nearest ones. There were also certain principles of governing which the empress reckoned essential for Russia. One of these now goes under the term "legitimacy." When defining it, Catherine wrote as follows: "It is only the force of law that has unlimited power, whereas the man who wishes to rule despotically becomes a slave."[153]

In Catherine's mind, this principle got well along with that of autocracy which, in her view, was to remain inviolate because it was of vital importance for Russia. Such a vast country as Russia could not exist without the institution of autocracy. Given the republican form of government, the country would simply collapse under the weight of inevitable internecine feuds; it would be incapable of withstanding the attacks of its rapacious neighbors. Catherine reckoned all other arguments as extraneous. Since she was well aware of the vulnerability of her position, she often referred to herself, both orally and in writing, as a woman with the heart of a republican, who was, alas, obliged to rule as an autocrat. What was to be done, then? This was a contradiction that could not be resolved.

For all this, she cannot be called a diehard monarchist. In her note on the steps to be taken for the restoration of the king's rule in France, she avoids sticking to a rigid stand of reinstating the absolutism of Louis XIV's reign. Life goes on and one has to take into account the changes going on in people's minds and morals: "It behooves one not to turn a deaf ear to the common voice of people." Further on follows a thought that gives credit to Catherine's political astuteness and subtlety: "Parliaments are great machines that can be very useful when one knows how to govern them and give them wise regulations. As there is an infinity of families and people attached to parliaments, it appears that it would be wise to align as many people and opinions as possible on the side of sustaining the monarchy... The cry of freedom can be satisfied in the same way by good and wise laws."[154]

The French Revolution, which was unfolding before Catherine's eyes, showed the world the power of ochlocracy at its basest, manifested, as it were, in excesses of adventurers and rascals. In Russia, that is, the country in which the populace was, in Catherine's view, "restive by nature, ungrateful and full of tattlers," and, in addition, had never had democratic institutions of any kind, only a madman could allow something like this to happen. Catherine, who had a great love for Russia, would never agree to that, even being a thrice-republican at heart! "If the monarch is an evil, this evil is unavoidable, without which there is no order, nor quietude," thus unambiguously did Catherine make her point once, according to Dashkova.[155]

The issue of serfdom, acute as it was, got tackled in a similar way. There is no doubt that Catherine was opposed to serfdom as such, but again, it was only at heart. Of course, serfdom often manifested itself in a most hideous way: the Saltykova case (see Chapter 4) was on everyone's lips. Count Ségur had a personal encounter with serfdom in one of its most unusual manifestations. While having a walk in the Crimea, he came face-to-face with a woman strikingly resembling his wife, who was in St. Petersburg at the time. On learning this, Potemkin, wishing to please the Frenchman, told him that he would give him this woman as a present. Ségur prudently refused the offer, saying that it would offend his wife's sense of propriety. The European mind was shocked by the very fact that such a deal could be possible. Should the enlightened empress have broached the subject of freeing the peasants, however, she would immediately have been ostracized (as she herself rightly presumed in her *Memoirs*).

This was the order the destruction of which in Catherine's age seemed to be fraught with danger for, first and foremost, the empress herself. The wild outburst of a grandiose uprising launched by Emel'ian Pugachev in 1773 clearly showed that freedom was perceived by huge masses of the Russian population not as equality, order, and responsibility but, rather, as bloody anarchy accompanied by massacres and outrages on the old and infirm, women and children, by ravages of churches and pillages of defenseless villages and towns, and by highway robberies. It is small wonder that serfdom, with its patriarchal relationship between the landowner and his bondsmen, was regarded as a necessary restraint on the wild passions of the lower classes. It was also held to be the backbone of the country's economy and the well-being of the nobles. An ingenuous question—where would they, that is, the nobles, get their servants if the peasants were all emancipated, which was put by the writer Aleksandr Sumarokov—did not seem then so naive, to say nothing of the unsophisticated queries made by landowners about the source of corvée *(barshchina)* or money dues *(obrok)*.

The only hope that remained, therefore, was that change would take an evolutionary course: that laws would gradually improve; moral principles would mollify the harshness of the system; enlightenment would affect both the peasants and the gentry alike, as it was the latter who often headed bands of their serfs turned highwaymen. "Common sense, good order, complete serenity, and humaneness," were the words inscribed on Catherine's banner. Of course, one may declare my observations naive but this is not so. Despite the bloody crushing of the Pugachev revolt (had the authorities any other way out?), Catherine's reign was a fairly tranquil one. She is credited with saying those sagacious words that "unless we agree to lessen the severity and to alleviate the unbearable lot of [our serf] humankind, they will, sooner or later, take their freedom themselves against our will."[156]

In reply to the senate's proposal to have the whole village executed for the murder of their landowner by the peasants, the empress appended the following resolution: "One may prophesy that if entire villages are exterminated in revenge for the life of one landlord, the revolt of all of our serf villages will follow."[157] The humaneness of the empress was a household word. If one hears all the stories told about it, one may get an impression that the empress had to abstain from her usual walks in her beloved park at Tsarskoe Selo, for awaiting her behind every bush would be a petitioner with a complaint in his hand. Be that as it may, it was forbidden to hold back letters that came by post addressed to Catherine, and she read them all through that she might later give the necessary instructions to her government officials.

An extant note written by Catherine in April 1763 to Olsuf'iev runs as follows: "I hear that Lomonosov is in dire straits. Try to settle this with the Hetman [Kirill Razumovskii, President of the Academy of Sciences—E.A.] and see whether he can get a pension for him and then let me know the outcome."[158] Catherine often declared her intolerance of violence in any form. In the spring of 1771, she wrote to the Palace Department: "Although, at the start of our reign, we already prohibited to have any of our liveried servants, no matter what his rank is, beaten at our court by anyone or with anything, we are greatly surprised to learn that despite that injunction of ours, our will has not been obeyed and this evil custom of beating valets has been resumed at our court. We, despising all cruelties borne from or invented by ignorance, hereby interdict, once and for all, under the threat of our wrath, that our servants, whatever their rank at court, be beaten by anyone or with anything."[159] Catherine learned to rule Russia fairly soon. Apart from her knack of dealing with men (which we have already mentioned), the empress laid down a few principles for herself that were crucial in her work as ruler.

Here are some of these: "My will, having been expressed but once, remains unchanged. Thus, everything is settled once and for all and each day is like the one before. Everyone knows what to expect and has nothing to worry about in vain." "Great deeds are always achieved with modest means." "One must do things in such a way that people should think they themselves want it to be done this way." "It is necessary to have the wolf's teeth and the fox's tail."[160]

It is in her note on the restoration of monarchy in France that her principles are stated most explicitly, whereby she taught a good lesson to the ill-starred emigré princes of the blood: "In such a critical affair . . . one must set one's mind firmly on one's object, wanting it passionately and communicating one's own persuasion to others and acting accordingly without hesitating once the resolution is made, then showing the greatest calm during the tumult and never appearing either upset or worried about the upshot."[161]

Of course, politics is a fairly complicated and rather dirty business. And Catherine could not have come out of it unstained. There are many documents testifying to the empress's violating, in the name of goals wide of humanism, many a good principle that she professed and trusted in earnest. Declaring her tolerance of freedom of expression on the part of her subjects, she opened and inspected correspondence on a large scale and punished any offense therein detected. During her reign, the gag-rule was practiced in a variety of ways. In 1766, for instance, the empress sent a secret order to the governor-general of Moscow in which she advised him that "someone going under the name of Prince Aleksandr Vasil'evich Khovanskoi never misses an opportunity of interpreting all my enterprises and deeds as a most villainous impudence, imparting to them an aspect which is contrary to all my intents."[162] Catherine requested him to pass the word to Khovanskoi that in case he continued what is, in our age, referred to as the "slanderous fabrications," he would "get himself transferred to a place where even a raven would not be able to find his bones."

The *Tainaia ekspeditsia* (Office of the Political Police), which superseded the awe-inspiring Secret Chancery, although operating in a less ostensible fashion, was nonetheless quite efficient. One may state with certainty that neither Voltaire nor Mme. Jeoffrin, for that matter, had an inkling of the existence of a secret order issued by their enlightened correspondent under which the commandant of the Dinaburg fortress was in 1769 enjoined to have a certain Il'ia Alekseev immured in a dungeon, leaving only a narrow opening, which was blocked up for the night with an iron shudder.

Nor was it ever divulged to them what was the end of the Tarakanova impostor, who posed herself as Elizabeth Petrovna's daughter and eventually perished in the dungeons of the Peter and Paul Fortress. In a manner that has since become so characteristic of the rulers of our country would Catherine sign orders to ban the utterance of the name of a certain Metel'ka—a ringleader of insurgent peasants—and to change the name, in the aftermath of the Pugachev revolt, of Iaik River (as if to punish it for the revolt) to Ural River and of Pugachev's native village of Zimoveiskaia to Potemkinskaia. The job of an informer and a spy was also much rewarded, which is in the nature of things in Russia.

* * *

Potemkin's sudden death in the fall of 1791 only came not as a blow to Catherine's private life but was also a landmark of her reign, for from this time on she alone had to carry the entire burden of ruling the country. It so happened that Potemkin's demise coincided in time with a process that no politician, however astute and able, can escape when his authority, having passed through periods of rise and flowering, enters, one day, into that of decay and ruin. No matter how intelligent and far-seeing, the empress also had moments when her power of reasoning, her will, and sense of propriety began to fail her. The later years of Catherine's reign saw a shameful ascendancy at court of the brothers Platon and Valerian Zubov. The story of their slipping into favor started long before . . . their births.

Count Ségur—a keen and perceptive observer—recalls: ". . . this extraordinary woman offered, in her character, a surprising mélange of the strength of our sex and the weakness of her own; time had aged her features, but her heart and her ego were still youthful; the one and the other were thus acutely wounded."[163] It was 1789, the year when the empress entered the sixtieth year of her life. To her surprise, she discovered that her favorite Sasha—thirty-year-old Aleksandr Matveevich Dmitriev-Mamonov—was not so devoted to her as she was led to believe. Mamonov's unfaithfulness terribly upset the empress: tears, hysterics, heart-to-heart talks, and reproaches followed one another. What was the crux of the matter? Why should the empress cry her eyes out and grieve so much when such young men were legion?

Here, we touch on a very subtle matter, risking to tear it up inadvertently with a coarse move. It seems to me that all her life Catherine was very unhappy in matters pertaining to love. Her family life was bereft of love from the very beginning, her affairs with Saltykov, Poniatowski, Orlov, and Potemkin all failed for various reasons, bringing her only sorrow in the end. But Catherine could not exist without love and this was the source of her personal drama and the cause of her so many abortive love affairs. She confided to the effect in her *Open-Hearted Confession:* "The trouble is that *my heart wishes not to stay without love, even if only for an hour.*"[164] One cannot but recall here the lines written by the poet Aleksandr Pushkin: "And is my heart afire again and loving as it cannot help loving."

At a certain time in her life, Catherine realized that no man had so far come into this world who would be capable of satisfying her discriminating taste. If this is so, she reckoned, then such a man should be created, appropriately brought up, and taught to rightly feel and love. This was well in line with the very idea of the enlightened "remodeling" of human nature done with the aid of knowledge, kindness, and liberty. She had already had some experience of this kind before, although her pedagogical experiment had then largely failed: so inflexible and unresponsive was the nature of Catherine's first pupil, Grigorii Orlov.

The new disciple who appeared in her life in 1778, Ivan Korsakov, earned the affectionate sobriquet "Pyrrhus," and the empress was head over heels in love with him. "When Pyrrhus takes up a violin, the dogs listen to him; when he sings, the birds come to hear him, like Orpheus. Never did Pyrrhus make any gesture, any movement which was not either noble or graceful; he shines like the sun, he spreads his brilliance around him; all of that is not at all effeminate, but virile and as you would like someone to be; in a word, he is Pyrrhus, king of Epirus, all is harmony . . ."[165] The "King of Epirus" was soon dismissed: he lacked that flexibility and responsiveness the tsarina found in her new choice, Aleksandr Lanskoi. Handsome and young (twenty-four years old), he seemed to Catherine to be ideally suited for her "pedagogy of heart." She was delighted with this young guardsman, who was as splendid as Joseph of the Scriptures. I shall not dwell here on Lanskoi's true merits—as I believe they were little more than modest. There is no doubt about one of these, however: Lanskoi proved to be a perfect time-server and, being a real gigolo, he did his best to please the empress. Now, to her great delight, he would bound and hop like a goat (*"il sautera comme un daim"*) on receiving a message from Buffon, whom Catherine adored; now he would immediately start filling in the gaps in his education to be in the know on things she fancied.

And Catherine, too, was perfectly happy: gone was the oppressive feeling of loneliness, as there appeared a kindred soul who seemed open to the sensations and thoughts that animated her refined, gentle, and fervid heart. In June 1782 she wrote to Grimm: ". . . a young man, whatever delicacy he may have, becomes infatuated easily, and especially a passionate soul like his." Citing Aleksei Orlov as saying, ". . . you will see what man she will make out of him!", Catherine adds, "He started by gobbling down the poets and poetry in one winter; several historians in another; novels bore us; we are taken with Algarotti and company. Without having studied, we will know countless things, and we are pleased only in the best and most educated company; besides all of that, we build and we sow, we are beneficent, gay, honest and full of tenderness."[166]

In December the same year, she asked Grimm to procure for Lanskoi a painting by the artist Greuze, assuring him that "these already beautiful colors will become even more vivacious, and the eyes, which anyhow resemble two torches, will throw sparks."[167] At some other time, she advised the baron that General Lanskoi had almost swooned on learning that Grimm had failed to purchase a collection of cameos that was commissioned from him. This idyll was short-lived, however, lasting a little more than two years: on June 25, 1784, Lanskoi died of scarlet fever.

Plunged into despair, Catherine wrote to Grimm, ". . . my happiness is gone: I myself thought I would die of the irreparable loss that I just suffered, eight days ago, of my best friend. I had hoped that he would become the support of my old age: he applied himself to advantage; he had acquired all of my tastes; this was a young man whom I nurtured, who was grateful, sweet and honest, who shared my pains when I had them and who rejoiced in my joys . . ."[168] Her dream of having a kindred soul at her side broke down again.

Catherine's grief was so deep that on burying her sweetheart in the garden at Tsarskoe Selo, she wept bitter tears for days on end, sitting at his urn and, to quote one Dr. Weikart, fell prey to some "misanthropic fantasies" so that she even seriously contemplated taking the veil and immuring herself at her Pella manor-house, which was being speedily erected on the bank of the Neva in a wooded and inhospitable countryside.

These plans of Catherine's were heard with displeasure by Potemkin, who gathered that the "Mother had got into one of her whims," forgetting her more important matters. The "Serenissimus" hurried back to St. Petersburg, where he extracted the woebegone empress from her hermitage, and quickly got her a replacement to Lanskoi, who, incidentally, had from the very beginning been Potemkin's creature. This time it was the above-mentioned Aleksandr Mamonov, nicknamed "Red Caftan," who became Catherine's new disciple. And her letter of January 2, 1787, to Grimm has a familiar ring: ". . . Monsieur Red Caftan is no more than an ordinary person; he sparkles with wit without ever pursuing it; he tells stories perfectly well and is of a rare gaiety; finally, he is full of pleasures, honesty, courtesy and cleverness; in a word, he is very humble and unpretentious . . ."[169] In her letter of April 2 the same year, Catherine continues: "This Red Caftan is, moreover, so amiable, so witty, so gay, so handsome, so complaisant, such good company that you will do very well to love him without knowing him. Besides all of this he loves music passionately . . ."[170]

Little wonder that her new Sasha got particularly enamored of the cameos and medals that the empress was so fond of so that it took Catherine some pains to drag him out of the room in which she kept them. (He would probably have felt quite content, dozing there amid the boxes while Catherine was not around.) And no doubt the empress feared that her "Red Caftan" would go mad with delight on hearing of the purchase of the cameo collection commissioned by her.

In mid-1789, however, it came out that it was not only the cameos but also a young Princess Shcherbatova that the "Red Caftan" was keen on. Catherine acted magnanimously, arranging an excellent wedding for the young couple although she herself was terribly pained by it and could not calm down for quite a while, regularly passing to Potemkin the gossip of how badly the newlyweds got along. Potemkin was also chagrined by this turn of events, albeit for a different reason: the unfaithful Mamonov let him down as patron by "leaving his place in a most infamous fashion." No sooner had Potemkin found a decent replacement, than Catherine, all by herself, acquired a new beau in the person of the guards cornet Platon Aleksandrovich Zubov. It was with the latter in mind that she made the following remark: "By educating young men, I also do a lot of good for the state."

Meanwhile, the opposite was closer to the truth as each new favorite of Catherine's did the state a lot of damage, for the empress never skimped in making presents and grants, and was not in the habit of taking them back after taking on a new favorite. Here is a rough estimate of expenses that she made for Lanskoi, who, owing to his early death, had not got all to which he was entitled by his peculiar status: one hundred thousand rubles for his wardrobe, a collection of medals and books, residence in the palace, board for twenty men at the cost of three hundred thousand rubles. All of his re- lations were duly promoted and received awards, and the rank of general- in-chief or general-fieldmarshal with the allowance to match was, one may say, almost in his pocket. During the three years of their liaison he received from Catherine seven million rubles, not counting presents, two houses in St. Petersburg, a house at Tsarskoe Selo and, in addition, the buttons for his ceremonial caftan, which cost eighty thousand rubles. All the above fig- ures should be added up and multiplied by at least seven, that is, roughly the number of Catherine's disciples.

Platon Zubov was a twenty-two-year-old loafer who quickly wormed him- self into the aging empress's favor so that she soon began to mention him as her novice in her letters to Potemkin. On August 5, 1789, Catherine ad- vised Potemkin something that is of interest here, namely, that Platon had a young brother, eighteen-year-old Valerian, who "is here on guard, in place of him; he is still quite a child and a beautiful kid; he is a lieutenant in the Horse Guards: help us to make a man out of him . . . I am well and cheer- ful again, like a fly in spring . . ."[171] This suggests that Platon's younger brother was also a prospective disciple. A week later, Catherine sent Potemkin by dispatch a story relating to one of the brothers (it is not clear which of them figures in it; in my view, it is Platon): "I am very pleased, my friend, to hear that you are happy with me and my little novice; he is such a sweet child, really: not stupid, having a kind heart, and hopefully, not to be easily spoilt. Today, he has composed, with a stroke of the pen, a pretty nice letter to you, in which he pictures himself the way he was created by nature."[172]

On August 24, she sent Potemkin the following message: "I am fairly pleased with his and his brother's conduct: both are quite innocent souls and sincerely attached to me; the elder is not stupid, the younger an interesting child."[173] From a letter of September 6, it becomes clear that the "child" did get spoilt with astonishing speed: "Shall we put our child in command of a hussar escort? Write to me what you think of it . . . Our child is only nineteen, in case you do not know. But I am terribly fond of this child and he is attached to me, too, and cries like a baby when barred from seeing me."[174]

However, as soon as September 17, events took another turn: "I have let our child, Valerian Aleksandrovich, out to the army at a rank of lieutenant-colonel and he is eager to leave for Your dispositions, to which he is about to set off."[175] The cause of the "child's" urgent trip is fairly prosaic—the elder brother got jealous of the younger one and probably not without reason. From that time, the "darkie" and "playboy" Platon remained in the palace all by himself.

What was the matter with Catherine, then? To be sure, age and unfavorable physical changes must have had their effect on the empress's psychological makeup, but this is not the point. More important here was that her soul, ever young and craving for love and heartiness, was playing a sly trick on her. A curious incident took place at the Hermitage Theater in the fall of 1779. In April that year, Catherine had "celebrated" at her writing desk her fiftieth birthday, which is a painful landmark in the life of any woman. On that day, October 12, she was there together with her court, watching a play by Molière. The heroine made the following remark: "That a woman of thirty may fall in love is just as well. But at fifty? This is intolerable!" The reaction of the empress, sitting in a separate box, was as swift as it was absurd. No sooner had the words been uttered than Catherine jumped to her feet, saying, "The thing is stupid and dull!"[176] and hastened out of the auditorium. The performance was interrupted. Later, the episode was reported, without comment, by the French chargé d'affaires Corberon. The words on stage unexpectedly struck home, hurting the innermost feelings of the fifty-year-old empress, who could not face imminent old age and the aching void in her heart. The "kids" came in handy not as such; rather, as we can clearly see it from the bits of above-cited correspondence, in the empress's mind, they were all merged in some abstract image endowed with some spurious merits, that is to say, the merits that she wanted to see and develop in them, that she needed herself for bolstering her feeling of youth and unfading love. These men were like flowers put in a vase: regularly changed, they preserved the invigorating aroma of spring. However, the law of nature is inexorable:

everything is good at its season and one cannot hold back the spring nor stop the onset of old age.

* * *

"From the former duck's nest, now St. Petersburg," were the words that Catherine prefixed in her letter to Grimm of October 25, 1777. She could rightly take pride in the town that she had grown to regard as her native one. In all the years of her reign, Catherine spared neither trouble nor expense embellishing St. Petersburg. Her accession to the throne coincided with a new style in art, classicism, which superseded baroque. The baroque style, with its volutes, capricious meanders, allegories, and sumptuous decorative finish, suited well the whimsical temperament of Empress Elizabeth, who left us the Winter Palace, the palaces at Tsarskoe Selo and Peterhof, and the Smol'ny Convent, all designed and built by the amiable master of the baroque Francesco Bartolomeo Rastrelli. The aesthetic of Catherine II, on the other hand, was more in line with the lucid, harmonious, coherent, and noble style of classicism. Rationality, simplicity, and naturalness became the guiding principles of architecture.

Catherine poured ridicule on churches symbolizing the preceding age, which "only the devil knows whence they came with all their imbecilic and ugly allegories, overblown to the enormous size as if in an effort to bring up something utterly nonsensical."[177] She also wrote of her detestation of fountains, which "torture" water, making it flow in an unnatural fashion.

As always, it was in the realm of architecture that the new aesthetics found fullest expression. One may write volumes on the subject—so rich is Russian architecture of the latter half of the eighteenth century in architects, buildings, and ideas, which, although not always original, were altogether grand and costly. Two brilliant architects, Vasilii Bazhenov and Matvei Kazakov, embodied the Moscow trend in architectural classicism of the time. The Tsaritsyn Palace near Moscow and the famous Pashkov Mansion in the center of Moscow are Bazhenov's masterpieces. Kazakov exercised his talent reconstructing the senate building of the Kremlin; he is also credited with designing Moscow University, the Petrovskii Palace, and the Assembly of the Nobility with its sublime Hall of Columns.

Moscow's neoclassical edifices were not decisive in determining its architectural skyline of the city. The buildings erected by Bazhenov's and Kazakov's counterparts in St. Petersburg, however, changed the aspect of the northern capital so that by the late eighteenth century the town looked entirely new. It is that same town with the latter-day additions to it created by the geniuses of Carlo Rossi, Adrian Zakharov, Auguste de Montferrand, and others that has come down to our days. Catherine disliked Moscow for, as she put it, its tiresome crowds and stench. How much livelier St. Petersburg—"this real Mrs. Grundy, this capital of mine!" She thus gave a special committee on masonry construction, headed by Aleksei Kvasov, a free hand and unlimited funds. The committee worked out a plan of reconstruction of the capital's center, which boiled down to rebuilding the streets so that "all the houses standing in one street should range along uninterruptedly and be of one height." Such ideas came directly from the concept of the well-ordered police state of the Petrine age. Thanks to the geniuses of its master-architects, however, the rebuilding scheme did not turn the city's center into a dull drilling square surrounded by rows of army barracks.

The recognized doyen of the architectural guild at the time was Aleksandr Filippovich Kokorinov. He was in charge of erecting the building of the Academy of Arts on the Neva Embankment. His assistant was Jean-Battiste Michael Vallin de la Mothe, who started his career winning a victory over the famed Rastrelli by designing Gostinyi Dvor (Trading Arcade) in the neoclassical style rather than baroque, as was the intent of Russia's chief architect during Elizabeth's reign. This Frenchman was also the author of the Small Hermitage (1764–1767) and the New Holland complex (1770–1779). Talented, too, were Catherine's other architects: Antonio Rinaldi, who designed the Chinese Pavilion and the Toboggan Hill in Oranienbaum, and also the palace in Gatchina and the Marble Palace in St. Petersburg; Ivan Starov, the designer and builder of the Tauride Palace (1783–1789) and Trinity Cathedral at the Aleksandr Nevskii Lavra; Nikolai L'vov, who designed the building of the Central Post Office.

One cannot leave out here the great Giacomo Quarenghi, who was active mainly in the 1780s and 1790s. His numerous buildings at Tsarskoe Selo, his Hermitage Theater, Academy of Sciences, Assignatsionnyi (Banknote) Bank on Sadovaia Street in St. Petersburg are all masterpieces of the neoclassical style. Add to it the Cameron Gallery and the Pavlovsk Palace by Charles Cameron, the Rumiantsev Obelisk by Vincenzo Brenna, the Public Library by Egor Sokolov, and one gets an idea of the buildings that transformed St. Petersburg into the epitome of classicism.

Running the risk of turning this chapter into a mere catalogue, I cannot leave out Iuri Matveevich Velten, who was the author of the exquisite Chesme Church and the famous ornamental iron fence of the Summer Gardens (1773–1784). Velten is credited with facing with granite the Neva and its tributaries and canals. As a result, the marshy banks of Glukhaia River turned into the gracious bends of Catherine Canal and the Fontanka River glittered through the interstices of wrought iron railings. And finally, in 1782, the renowned statue *The Bronze Horseman,* by Etienne-Maurice Falconet, was installed and has become a quintessentially St. Petersburg work of art.

Catherine's reign was not only the time of erecting magnificent architectural ensembles: the empress had a real fondness for nature and countryside. She thoroughly detested Peterhof and not only because of the nasty memories of the summer of 1762 but also, as she herself put it, for its ostentatious architecture and the bogus beauty of its fountains and allegorical sculpture. How much better was Tsarskoe Selo with its park, the quiet waters of its ponds, and the murmur of trees.

The second half of the eighteenth century saw the emergence of the Russian country estate in the form that we are familiar with from nineteenth-century works of fiction. The large and unwieldy farmstead, which differed little from the log-huts of peasants, came to be replaced with the manor-house of the nobles, with its elegant porches, pilasters, and columns built in the neoclassical style. Set on a hill, it would be surrounded by a decorative garden or park, laid out so artfully as to become part of landscape. Reflecting itself in still waters of a pond or quiet river, the manor-house looked welcoming, and evoked a feeling of harmony and peace, demonstrating man's ability to render his constructions compatible with nature. It is no wonder that such country estates became favored by thousands of gentry, who would hurry to their "nests," looking impatiently out of their carriages to catch sight, at a distance, of the whitewashed columns of their dear manor-house, the lattice-work of a bower in the park, and the church cupola floating up above the tree crowns.

Yet it was undoubtedly the Hermitage that became the most illustrious landmark of Catherine's age. The French idea of an abode secluded in the quiet of woods, a kind of temple for meditations and friendly communion, "regardless of rank," was transformed in Russia into that of a luxurious palace, which Catherine erected next to the tsar's residence, the Winter Palace (today both form part of the State Hermitage Museum). No sooner did one step over the threshold of the Hermitage than one entered a new and fanciful world—the realm of beauty—made up of rare books, paintings, sculpture, music and singing, amity, equality, and mutual affinity. Catherine, who was notoriously ignorant about art and music, nevertheless spared no money for decorating her beloved Hermitage. By her own reckoning, there were by 1790 almost four thousand paintings, thirty-eight thousand books, and twenty thousand engravings and carved stones assembled in the Hermitage. Listing all the famous painters represented there would alone take quite a few pages. A visitor strolling along the gallery decorated with exact replicas of the Raphael Loggias would feel transported to Renaissance Italy. Under the glass ceiling of the Winter Garden, a place of everlasting summer, one is turned into a different being: relaxed, lively, and as natural as birds singing merrily. The rules of conduct in the Hermitage were as strict as those of Peter's austere soirées. Those who committed a gaffe were made to drink a glass of water rather than an enormous cup of the "Great Eagle"—as in Peter the Great's time—or to read through a whole chapter of a most boring poem, "Telemachiade" by Vasilii Trediakovskii, which was a punishment harsh enough but not as ruinous to one's health.

Thus, besides being a kind of fairyland and museum at once, the Hermitage was a meeting-place of people specially invited there to share in the

Новой **ЕГО ИМПЕРАТОРСКАГО** *Le Nouveau Palais d'hyver*
ВЕЛИЧЕСТВА *Зимней Домъ къ de SA MAI.IMP. du côté de la grand*
Луг. place nomée la prairie.

The New Winter Palace. From I. N. Bozherianov, "*Nevskii prospekt.*"
Kul'turno-istoricheskii ocherk dvukhvekovoi zhizni Sankt-Peterburga
("Nevskii Prospect." A Cultural and Historical Sketch of St. Petersburg
at Two Hundred) (St. Petersburg, 1901–03), vol. 1, p. 175.

empress's leisure. Strictly speaking, there were three kinds of Hermitage
gatherings in accordance with the number of persons admitted: big, medium,
and small. It was everyone's dream to get to the most intimate of these—
the small one. It was a decent pastime, which had none of the debauchery
of the "All-Drunken Synod" of Peter the Great's time or the mean squabbles
between buffoons of the reign of Anna Ioannovna. Admittance was given
only to the select few, and many a courtier would give everything to have a
chance to play blindman's bluff or forfeits with Catherine in person or sing
together with her favorite Russian songs, to say nothing of the happiness of
dancing a circle dance next to the empress herself, who would be clad in a
Russian sarafan-frock of a flowery design.

It is known that an official would rarely be appointed to a key post without his first being invited to the Hermitage for inspection. Placed here in
an informal, natural setting, the candidate, no matter how hard he tried to
puff himself up, was easily seen through, and if he was a fool, it came out
soon enough. In the 1780s and 1790s, the gatherings at the Hermitage
became merry and boisterous: Catherine's grandsons and, later, granddaughters were part of the affair.

Throughout our story, the name of the empress's son, Paul, has been mentioned only in connection with some mystery surrounding his origin. This

and some other reasons strained relations between mother and son. They had their spells of mutual sympathy but these were short-lived, giving way to ice-age periods of estrangement. Following her accession, Catherine and her eight-year-old son became inseparable, the empress taking him with her everywhere and feeling much concerned over his health as the boy did grow up weak and sickly. Later on, however, when Catherine plunged into her state affairs and private problems, she lost touch with the youth, who got friendly with his governor, Count Nikita Ivanovich Panin, who, while being Catherine's close ally, did not rank himself among the great admirers of her talents and character. It was this attitude to Catherine that Panin handed down to Paul, who saw his mother through his tutor's eyes and censured, either from the inexperience of youth or out of sanctimony inculcated in him by Panin, her "transgressions."

As recorded by many contemporary writers, Catherine and her son were so alienated from each other that the tsarevich even feared for his life. The Frenchman Sabatier wrote in April 1770 that Paul was afraid of his mother.

In the fall of 1773, the nineteen-year old tsarevich was married to Wilhelmina, princess of Hesse-Darmstadt, who, on her coming to Russia, was given the name of Nataliia Alekseevna. The daughter-in-law proved to be quite unworthy of the lot chosen for her by Catherine. She turned a deaf ear to the advice, well familiar to us from our earlier chapters, on the love of one's own husband and people, on the trust of one's mother-in-law, and did everything to the contrary. Meanwhile, Catherine regarded her own experience of naturalizing in Russia as the perfect model for emulation and the only possible way to be taken by the newly arrived young German.

In 1776, Nataliia died in childbirth. She expired in a terrible agony, leaving her young husband in inconsolable grief. Catherine devised a cruel and disreputable way to cure the grieving son of his distress: she let him read the love correspondence that the deceased had had with Paul's closest friend and companion, Count Andrei Razumovskii. The therapy worked: his anguish did disappear but it must have been traumatic for the young Paul to go through.

Paul's second bride was also searched out for him by Catherine and also came from Germany. This was Princess Sophia Dorothea of Württemberg, who went down in Russian history as the empress Maria Fedorovna, and was the mother of the emperors Aleksandr I and Nicholas I and eight other children. The wedding, celebrated in the fall of 1776, was a joyous occasion for Catherine. It awakened in her, as it were, her long-forgotten motherly feelings for her son. Mingled with it was another thing: she was enamored of this movingly youthful couple. There remains quite a few of the empress's letters addressed to them, in which she shows herself unusually affectionate and tender to the newlyweds. "My dear son!" she writes in one of these, "Yesterday I came here [Tsarskoe Selo—E.A.] and I am well. It is quite desolate here without you and I feel deprived of my best enjoyment in just the same way as

Tsarskoe Selo is bereft of its embellishment when you are not here." The empress's letters, written to them when they were abroad, are lavish with praise of Maria: her daughter-in-law is a nymph, a rose, a lily. Later on, however, the rift, ever present in the relationship between mother and son, appeared again and began to grow wider and wider until it became a gulf.

One may surmise that a major cause of the breach between mother and son becoming final and irrevocable was an otherwise felicitous event: on December 12, 1777, the young couple had their firstborn child, Aleksandr. To the distress of his parents, however, the child was immediately snatched away from them by his grandmother to be placed and brought up in her palace in St. Petersburg, away from his father and mother, whose residence was in the far-off Gatchina. History repeated itself: Paul's grandaunt Elizabeth had taken him away from Catherine and Peter Fedorovich. Aleksandr's lot was also that of his brother Constantine, born on April 27, 1779. That it was planned to make Constantine the emperor of Byzantium has been mentioned above. A different lot was intended for Aleksandr.

The "grandma" never parted with her grandchildren for long, and when setting off for the Crimea she was much distressed to learn of their illnesses, as she intended to take the boys with her. With the birth of Aleksandr and Constantine, Catherine seemed to have become completely oblivious of her son and daughter-in-law, who were taken notice of only as obstacles to her enjoyment of the grandchildren. On June 1, 1785, Catherine informed Grimm in her letter from Peterhof, "*J'attends cet après-diner mes petits fils, que je fais venir ici; die schwere Bagage wird erst den 26 ankommen.*"[178] The "heavy luggage" here was, in fact, the children's parents, whom Catherine regarded as a heavy and unnecessary burden.

The tsarevich was irritated and offended by many things going on around him: odious rumors about his origin, numerous love affairs of his mother whose "disciples" were as often as not a few years his junior, and, last but not least, continual humiliations that he suffered from his mother's "nightly masters." The disgrace and insults that he had to endure from the Zubov brothers were especially tormenting. And what were his prospects? In the mid-1790s, Paul was past forty! The relatively short span of life of eighteenth-century man meant he may never get to reign, and there was nothing he, the tsarevich, heir, the tsar's legitimate son, could do.

In the beginning, he longed to apply himself to work for the public good, his head full of noble, lofty, but vague ideas and plans for the country's reconstruction based on the principles of common good, equality, and justice. These ambitious dreams of the youth were inculcated by Count Nikita Panin, with whom Paul zealously argued his projects. However, Catherine kept a vigilant eye on her son; she always treated him as a potential adversary well regarded by the people who traditionally look with discontent upon the ruler holding power at the moment. For this reason, the empress did not allow her son to take up any weighty military or civic matters of the day. When he asked her to make him a member of the Council of State, he met with a flat refusal, which Catherine explained on the pretext that the opinions voiced at the council may differ from those of the tsarina and, seen in that light, the tsarevich's participation may create some unnecessary legal problems. One cannot claim that Paul's time was spent in idleness. Yet as years went by, his aspirations began to wither, and he gradually sank deeper and deeper into the abyss of trivia of the military-cum-administrative cares of his Gatchina "appanage" (granted to him on Orlov's death), which became his own domain, household, and haven, where he hid from the hostile environment created by his mother. Paul felt hostility increase as Aleksandr, who was his grandmother's favorite grew up.

The upbringing of Aleksandr and Constantine went according to a blueprint made up by the empress herself. When Catherine was compiling this program, her mind was on Paul: a weak and sickly child, spoiled by the corruptive "womanish" treatment in the stifling atmosphere of Elizabeth Petrovna's apartments, which made him an apathetic, nervous, and jealous good-for-nothing. Aleksandr was destined to be his opposite: hardy and accustomed to sleeping, lightly clad, in the open air, this young Spartan would easily divide his time between useful physical activities and serious studies under the coaching of an experienced and well-educated tutor. The duty of Aleksandr's tutorship was entrusted to the French republican Laharpe.

When nowadays, at the beginning of the twenty-first century, one reads through the *Instructions on the Upbringing of Grandchildren,* written by Catherine in the spring of 1783, one marvels at the depth of her knowledge of child psychology and her purposeful pedagogical effort to implant in the children robust, humanitarian, and everlasting principles.

Here are some extracts from the *Instructions:* "To forbid and discourage Their Highnesses from inflicting any harm on themselves and any other human; hence, it should be proscribed that anyone be beaten or scolded in their presence and they should not be allowed to beat up, pinch, or scold a man or beast or to hurt anyone in any other way. It should not be allowed that Their Highnesses torture or kill innocent animals, such as birds, butterflies, flies, dogs, cats, or others or that they damage anything on purpose, but they should get accustomed to taking care of a dog, bird, squirrel, or any other pet at their disposal and to working for the benefits of these down to the potted flowers, which they should water . . . Both the children themselves and the people surrounding them should be forbidden to lie and cheat and even, when joking, one should never lie but aim at turning them away from lying . . . Lying should be exposed to them as something dishonest and entailing contempt and mistrust of all people . . . One should take care that all talk and stories and rumors aiming at diminishing the love for good and virtue and amplifying vice be avoided . . . The chief merit of instructing children is in teaching them to love their neighbor (do not do to anyone what you do not want done to yourself), as well as in the general goodwill toward mankind, in the benevolent attitude to men of all walks of life, in the gentle and tolerant treatment of all and sundry, in continual good-temperedness, in frankness and nobleness of heart, in striving to get rid of one's impulsiveness, empty fears, cowardice, and suspiciousness."[179]

The boys' life now centered around their grandmother, who supervised their learning the alphabet and their outdoor games, walks, and journeys. It was Aleksandr, however, who gave Catherine the greatest pleasure. Time and again she returns in her letters to the beauty of his spirit and body, calling him the "consolation of our heart." Gradually, many people began to see through this blind attachment of the grandmother's. Paul and his supporters were especially concerned when Catherine married sixteen-year-old Aleksandr to the fourteen-year-old princess Louise of Baden (who, on being baptized under the Orthodox rite, became Elizaveta Alekseevna). This seemed to confirm the rumors of the empress's intention to bypass her unloved son and bequeath the throne straight to the grandson, who had now become the head of a family of his own and a full-grown man. Although no testament to the effect has come down to us, the haze of rumors engendered by the possibility that Catherine wanted to circumvent Paul in favor of Aleksandr is so thick that even nowadays, looking at this from afar, we are still palpably aware of its reality. Incidentally, apart from the rumors about Paul's destroying the testament, there is circumstantial evidence pointing to Catherine's intention to pass the crown to her elder grandson.

In August 1792, she was writing to Grimm, probably continuing their previous postal discourse, as follows: "Listen, I do not like hasty coronations; Solomon said: 'there is a time for everything.' My Aleksandr will be married, and with time crowned with all the ceremonies, solemnities and public festivities possible; he will go through this with splendor, magnificence and grandeur; oh, how he will be happy and how people will be happy with him!"[180] All this was being related to Europe's loudest mouthpiece in a tone as if Tsarevich Paul had long "gone the way of all flesh." In September 1791, Catherine wrote to her friend that if the French Revolution spread all over Europe there would emerge a tyrant who would enslave Europe, ". . . but it will not be in my time, nor, I hope, in that of Monsieur Aleksandr."[181] Was it implied that Paul's reign had been skipped over?

It is natural that Paul's destiny occupied her thoughts. The evidence of this is Catherine's own note on the tragic conflict between Peter the Great and his son, Tsarevich Aleksei, whom his father had disinherited. At first glance, there is nothing personal in it—just an observation of the historical event in question. But then, how firmly is Catherine convinced of the rectitude of Peter's action, what passion and hatred color her characterization of the wretched tsarevitch, which sounds as if she herself were mortally insulted by him? And, above all, one can clearly see the pug-nosed face of Grand Duke Paul coming through the blurred image of Aleksei: "One should agree that unhappy is that parent who finds himself compelled, for the sake of saving the common cause, to disinherit his own offspring. Here clash together or are combined the power of the autocrat and that of the parent. Therefore, I deem it that Peter's wisdom is here unquestionable for he had the loftiest reasons for dethroning his ungrateful, disobedient, and incapable son. The latter was filled with hatred for his father, with malice and singular jealousy, searching out specks of evil in a basketful of good of his father's deeds and actions, hearkening to grovelers and turning a deaf ear to the truth, and he could be pleased only by abusing and reviling his most glorious sire. Whereas he himself was but an idler, coward, double-dealer, infirm of purpose, unfriendly, timid, a drunkard, hot-tempered, stubborn, a hypocrite, ignorant, weak in mind and body."[182] And Catherine was not in haste in her actions, for whither was she to hurry? There was so much to do and so much time ahead, all in good time . . .

In the mid-1790s, however, old age was not only at the threshold of her house but had even crossed it. Despite her optimism, joie de vivre, and never-ending quest for love, Catherine felt new times coming on, which she herself was not destined to see. The eighteenth century, shaken to the roots by the terror of the bloody revolution in France, was nearing its end; passing away with it were, one after another, its outstanding men, who gained it its glory. The year of 1786 saw the death of Frederick the Great, Catherine's main opponent in world politics, and without him, without the constant subtle *ruse de guerre* with this "Herod," as the empress called him, she felt the world empty. In 1790, Catherine's longtime friend Emperor Joseph II of Austria ended his days; in 1791, it was Potemkin's turn . . . On March 15, 1792, King Gustavus III of Sweden was assassinated at a costume-ball in Stockholm.

Catherine's relationship with the latter was ambivalent. In 1788, Gustavus declared war on his relative, the Russian empress. The moment was fairly propitious for the Swedes: the Russian army was disposed in the south and, in order to defend the capital, Catherine had to muster manpower and even contemplated putting the townsfolk under arms. Catherine, who was left in the capital on her own, that is, without Potemkin and Suvorov but only with a bunch of witless generals, got so alarmed that she even lost weight and had to have all her dresses altered. And there was good reason for that, too: a real war was knocking at the French windows of her Winter Palace with its constant cannonade of a naval battle being waged for days on end at the nearby island of Goghland, while the west wind brought down to the town the clouds of thick gunpowder smoke, which prompted the empress to say in her letter to Potemkin that she, too, had had a chance to "smell the gunpowder." Afterward, following the Russian victory, the royal friendship was restored and Gustavus was rehabilitated in Catherine's eyes owing to his consistently anti-French policies. "The two of us," said Catherine once to her secretary, "often see it in our mind's eye that we drift along the Seine in our

Catherine II, Paul I, Aleksander I. From the journal *Russkaia starina* (Russia of Old) (St. Petersburg, 1883), tip-in plate.

gunboats."[183] Alas, these dreams were not destined to come true: in 1792, Gustavus was treacherously stabbed dead in the bustle of a court gala.

It was the events of 1793, however, that came as the most terrible blow. The unfortunate Louis XVI of France was, to the consternation of all monarchical Europe, guillotined in the Place de Revolution. Some time later, the revolutionaries committed a new atrocity by putting to death Queen Marie Antoinette.

There were also changes in Catherine's own milieu. She saw that there appeared more and more new faces among her retinue, and some totally unknown young men fluttered before her eyes at the balls and gala occasions in the Hermitage, which would plunge her into a melancholy mood.

Only the ancient Grimm now remained to share in the empress's low spirits and it was to him that she wrote on February 11, 1794: "I have two things to tell you: the first is that the day before yesterday, Thursday, February 9, marks fifty years that I arrived in Moscow with my mother on a Thursday, February 9, and consequently here I am with fifty years passed here, in Russia, and of these fifty years I have reigned for thirty-two of them, by the grace of God. The second thing is that yesterday there were three marriages in the court. You can well understand that it was the third or fourth generation that I have seen here, and I think that here in St. Petersburg there are not ten people alive who remember my own arrival. First of all, there is Betski, blind, decrepit and more than rambling, who asks young people, did you know Peter I? There is the countess Matuchkine, who at seventy-eight years old danced at the weddings yesterday. There is the grand cupbearer Narichkine, whom I found as a gentleman of the bedchamber in the court, and his wife. There is the grand squire, his brother: he still denies this fact, because it makes him too old. There is the grand chamberlain Schouvalof, who almost never leaves the house because of his decrepitude. There is an old chamber woman here who is senile. Those, approximately, are my contemporaries; that is strange: the rest of them could be my children or grandchildren. Here I am, very old. I know the fifth or sixth generation of some families. These are great proofs of old age, and maybe even this anecdote confirms it, but what to do? and in spite of this like a child of five I madly love seeing blind man's bluff and all possible children's games being played. The young people and my grandsons and granddaughters say that I must be there for gaiety to reign as they wish, and that they are more bold and at their ease when I am there than without me."[184]

It is hardly likely that the children had by then learned to tell lies as ingratiatingly as the grownups, nor could they easily be duped with sham gaiety, either: it was simply the fact that the youthful heart of aged Fike opened up to them and they were so pleased with her that they wished their charming blue-eyed grandmother never to leave their noisy company . . .

But, alas, she was pressed with urgent matters awaiting her in her study and her secretaries would also be waiting with their reports. The news from France was particularly bad: there was bloodshed and violence there that resembled the religious wars of the Dark Ages or, perhaps, presaged the advent of a new Iron Age of ours. Such a fierce confrontation was unheard of in the illustrious eighteenth century, whose men would even refrain from using the merciless and destructive term "enemy" (with which we have become so familiar in our days), preferring a more discreet term "military adversary," the latter being a kind of antonym of "ally." Catherine followed the developments in France with great concern. As they had no direct impact on Russia, she failed at the beginning to grasp the sinister pattern of events developing in Paris since 1789. The tsarina was even content with the summoning of the States General, which, as she reckoned, would at last put an end to the extravagant spending of the Bourbons, who obviously lived far beyond their means. Later on, however, the lack of coherence in the events unfolding there made it clear that the greatest power of Europe had fallen prey to the bloody plague of revolution. France was speedily descending into terror and civil war.

On the whole, Catherine was quite reluctant to accuse her friends, the men of the French Enlightenment, for what was going on there, but their ideas had inspired Robespierre and Danton. On December 5, 1793, she wrote to Baron Grimm: ". . . the French philosophers who are believed to have laid the ground for the French revolution might have been mistaken in only one thing, which is that they believed they were preaching to people who had a good heart and convictions and consistency, and instead of this the prosecutors, lawyers and all the scoundrels covered themselves in these principles and, under this cloak that they soon shook off, performed all of the most execrable, horrible deeds of villainy ever committed, and this Parisian rabble, subjugated by the most atrocious crimes, dares to call itself free, all while it has never experienced a crueler or more absurd tyranny. At present, it is famine and plague that will restore its reason, and when the king's murderers have perished at each other's hands, then there may be more hope of seeing another order of things rise up."[185]

While supporting morally and financially the French emigré princes of the blood (on a mutually beneficial basis), the empress made no secret of her firm belief that the corrupt Versailles was itself to blame for the opening of Pandora's box (just as, in his time, Peter III was the perpetrator of his own ruin). It may be stated with certainty that this accusation only reveals the old-time animus of a thriving provincial toward the misfortunes befalling the capital of the world; nowadays, we know for sure that the Bourbons, who were unable to learn their lesson properly, threw the grenade ready to explode right under their own sofa and with their foolish policies brought the country to the verge of catastrophe.

Catherine had no illusions on that account ("no cure has as yet been devised for stupidity, and reason and common sense cannot be inoculated like some vaccine against smallpox"). She believed that the former absolutism of France had been done away with, that one had to put up with the existence of parliament, to grant certain freedoms to citizens, in a word, to learn to live in a new France. This, in itself, did not mean, however, that the Russian reigning autocrat had resigned herself to what was being done there. She never identified the law-abiding and responsible folk with the mob of vagabonds and unruly lower orders, being firmly convinced that, on passing through the inevitable stage of self-destruction and rule of the spirit of unbridledness, France would eventually return to the idea of monarchy. On January 13, 1791, she wrote to Grimm, saying that a new Caesar would come and "put down this den of vice," adding to it in another letter to him, written on April 22: "Do You know what will become of France if one succeeds in making it a republic? Everybody there will crave for the monarchic rule! Believe me, no one is so keen on the court life as republicans."[186] It is a great pity that the empress did not live to see December 5, 1804—the day Napoleon I was crowned—her prophecy coming true only thirteen years afterward! Besides, she held that the revolutionary contagion would spread all over Europe and that a new Tamerlane or Genghis Khan would come to swallow it up whereupon it would be Russia's turn to save the whole world.

It is certain that the tsarina had never read the predictions of Nostradamus, having only her own experience, intuition, and power of reason to go by. There is a ring of triumph in the words that Catherine uttered in reply to Potemkin's praise of her intrepid resolution: "The Russian empress, who has sixteen thousand miles of land behind her back, troops that have been victorious throughout the century, commanders of great military prowess, and officers and men courageous and loyal, cannot, without feeling her dignity abased, help displaying 'intrepid resolution.'"

The events in France were instrumental in leading Catherine to one important resolution: one must do everything to check the penetration of revolutionary contagion into Russia. It was for this reason that this period of Catherine's reign saw the tightening of censorship in Russia, a crackdown on the activities of a fairly innocuous Moscow publisher of masonic treatises, Nikolai Novikov, which largely won him, unlike other unsuppressed publishers, fame as an important Russian educator. Aleksandr Radishchev, who was competent as the chief of St. Petersburg Customs but rather mediocre as a writer, fell prey, as is often the case in Russia, to a smear campaign, and was exiled to Siberia. Trembling with fear were the Masons themselves, whose pursuits had always been despised by the rationalist-minded empress and whose mysteries she put to relentless ridicule. Previously her attitude to criticism aimed at her was fairly tolerant, but now she saw in it the rocking of foundations. She gave a sound dressing-down to the then-president of the Academy of Sciences, Princess Dashkova, for issuing at her academic press the play *Vadim* by Ia. B. Kniazhnin, written on the subject of the republican period in the history of Novgorod. Dashkova, like the empress herself, had not read the play before printing. "You must agree," exclaimed Catherine resentfully, "that this is all very unpleasant . . . I am being prevented from doing good, which I have been doing as much as I can both for private persons and the country in general; can it be that they want to start the same kind of horrible things as we see being done in France?"[187] One has to remember, however, that it was 1793 and that in France the National Convention had just drafted draconian bills against speculators; the queen, Marie Antoinette, was estranged from her son and a hideous trial was being launched against her, the prosecutors accusing her of an incestuous tie with her child. So one can well see the point the empress was making: a child burnt will dread the fire. In Paris, too, everything had started with plays and proclamations.

Empress Catherine the Great. From I. N. Bozherianov, *"Nevskii prospekt."*
Kul'turno-istoricheskii ocherk dvukhvekovoi zhizni Sankt-Peterburga ("Nevskii
Prospect." A Cultural and Historical Sketch of St. Petersburg at Two Hun-
dred) (St. Petersburg, 1901–03), vol. 1, p. 176.

What, then, was the situation inside the country? There were surely no
grounds for panicking or even worrying. Things took their normal course.
Having defeated the Turks, Swedes, and Poles, Russia enjoyed its time of
peace. With Potemkin gone, however, its policies lost their former élan and
coherence and everything went, in many ways, through the force of inertia.
It was now Platon Zubov who was in charge of everything. He had some
education and spouted queer words but, essentially, was empty and worthless, although trying vainly to assume a puffed-up and pompous air in an
effort to look like Potemkin. The other favorite, Valerian Zubov, persuaded

the empress, who had previously never lacked common sense in these matters, to send him at the head of an army on a march to India, which was an absolutely fantastic idea and had no prospects whatsoever; on his way there, he lost a great number of Russian soldiers, who perished storming the Cis-Caspian strongholds, but he never reached India.

That Platon Zubov could climb to the top was seen by many as the main evidence of the regime's degradation and decay. Here is what Catherine's contemporary writes of that last favorite of hers: "As Her Majesty's strength, ability to work and genius were declining, he was acquiring more power and riches. Each morning, crowds of sycophants besieged the doors of his apartments, filling the anteroom and reception hall. Old venerable generals and courtiers saw nothing shameful in kowtowing to his most despicable valet. The same servants were often seen kicking generals and officers away from the doors at which they gathered in clusters, obstructing movement. Sprawled in the armchairs in brazenly careless dress sat this young man picking his nose and staring at the ceiling in a nonchalant way, a puffed-up and lifeless expression on his face, in complete disregard of the people around him. He either amused himself, watching the antics of his monkey jumping over the heads of those mean lickspittles or talked to his jester, while all these venerable courtiers—Dolgorukiis, Golitsyns, Saltykovs, under whose command he used to serve as a sergeant—and the rest stood waiting when he would vouchsafe to turn his eyes down on them so that they could bow down and kiss his feet."[188] Of all the minions of fortune living at the time of Catherine II, none was so debile both physically and spiritually as Zubov. What a distance from the aspirations of young Catherine, dreaming, as she did, of her reign as the time of truth, lawfulness, justice, and mercy. The tsarina herself simply would not see or know about it all, and if she did occasionally, what would she not forgive her "child," or her "darkie"—I am utterly confused now as to which endearment Catherine used for which brother.

The years went by, and Catherine began to think of death. She would often try, albeit in a romantic and bookish way, to picture her last hour. Now she would will to have herself buried in Tsarskoe Selo near the Lanskoi urn, now at the Donskoi Monastery in Moscow, now near Strel'na, and, by all means, clad in white and with a gold wreath on her head. She composed a lengthy epitaph for herself, from which one may gather that modesty was not her forte. She also dreamt that her dying ceremony would be unusual: beautiful and elevated. "When my hour strikes," she wrote, "let only the battle-hardened hearts and cheerful faces be around when I breathe my last." As it tuned out, however, her death was neither glamorous nor ceremonial but rather the contrary.[189]

Shortly before she died, that is, in the fall of 1796, two events occurred that had an adverse effect on her health. In September, a terrible scandal broke out, which was unheard of at Catherine's court: the uncouth actions of Platon Zubov and Count Morkov wrecked the marriage of the empress's granddaughter, the charming Grand Duchess Aleksandra Pavlovna and the youthful King Gustavus IV of Sweden. The rupture occurred on the very eve of the wedding ceremony when the empress, the bride, and the whole court waited, in vain, for several hours, all gathered in the Throne Room, for the arrival of the Swedish king. On hearing the news, Catherine was so stupefied that, in the words of a contemporary, she remained with her mouth agape with astonishment and outrage for a few minutes, whereupon she hit Morkov twice with her stick and, throwing down her mantle, left the hall in fury. After this incident, the empress fell ill and no wonder: she had never in her life been so humiliated.

The second event was of an ominous nature. Once, during the night, a terrible thunderstorm broke out (the tsarina had by then moved to her beloved Tsarskoe Selo), and this was strange as it was late autumn outside. Looking at the bare trees of the park, groaning at the ghostly flashes of lightning under the torrents of heavy rain, which was of no use at this time of the year either for the people or the earth, Catherine remembered that long ago, in the late fall of 1761, the same kind of storm had thundered over Tsarskoe Selo and then it was Empress Elizabeth's turn to die. As witnessed by a contemporary, this omen greatly frightened Catherine, who, it was known, had always been a brave and even foolhardy woman.

Death stalked Catherine in the Winter Palace at nine o'clock in the morning on Wednesday, November 5, 1796, in a narrow passage leading from the study to her dressing room. Having worked at her writing desk in the study, as was her wont, the tsarina went out to change. The chamberlain Zotov found the empress lying unconscious on the floor in a semirecumbent position as, the place being narrow and the door closed, she did not fall right on the ground. He called the valets, and these strong men could barely drag the tsarina out and carry her over to her bedroom. They were unable to lift her up onto her bed—so heavy was Catherine, who grew to be very stout at the end of her days—so they simply put the choking empress onto the morocco mattress spread on the floor. The doctor was sent for immediately. Prince Zubov, who was the first to be notified, lost his head completely: he even prevented the doctor-on-duty from bleeding the empress. This would not have helped, though; the diagnosis made by Catherine's personal physician, Dr. Rogerson, was decisive: "The stroke proceeded to the head and was lethal."

Speaking in modern terms, Catherine had cerebral thrombosis. Modern medicine can save such a patient, but in November 1796, medicine was, indeed, helpless. She lived till 7 A.M. the next day without ever regaining consciousness, then the agony started. A whole epoch came to its close in Russian history . . .

The empress did not die the way she wished, surrounded by her good friends and courageous companions. Instead, she was lying on the floor, with her disheveled maids of honor weeping loudly nearby; meanwhile, running to and fro past the expiring body of the great ruler, their iron-shod boots busily rattling on the floor, were the new emperor, Paul Petrovich, and his Gatchina retainers: they were ransacking the cabinets, shelves, and secretaire. Their time had come.

Notes

CHAPTER 1

1. According to modern medical historians, Peter the Great died of prostate adenoma or stricture of the urethra resulting from an inflammatory process in the urethra.

2. J. J. Campredon, "Doneseniia frantsuzskogo poslannika v Rossii vo Frantsiiu," in *Sbornik imperatorskogo russkogo istoricheskogo obshchestva* (SIRIO), vol. 52 (St. Petersburg, 1886), p. 436.

3. H. F. Bassewitz, *Zapiski pri Petre Velikom* (St. Petersburg, 1886), p. 173.

4. Ibid., p. 180.

5. SIRIO, vol. 58, p. 23.

6. N. A. Belozerskaia, "Proiskhozhdenie Ekateriny Pervoi," in *Istoricheskyi vestnik*, vol. 87 (1902), pp. 56–80.

7. N. G. Ustrialov, *Istoriia tsarstvovaniia Petra Velikogo*, vol. 4 (St. Petersburg, 1863), pp. 139–140.

8. *Zhurnal, ili Podennaia zapiska Petra Velikogo* (St. Petersburg, 1777), pp. 43–44.

9. C. de Bruin, *Puteshestvie cherez Moskoviiu* (Moscow, 1883), p. 99.

10. "Donoshenie d'iachka Vasiliia Fedorova," in *Chteniia Obshchestva istorii i drevnostei rossiiskikh*, bk. 2 (1860), p. 21.

11. G. V. Esipov, *Tsaritsa Evdokiia Fedorovna* (Moscow, 1863), pp. 9–10. Evdokia died in 1731. The last years of her life, which coincided with the accession to power of her grandson Peter II and Anna Ioannovna, were relatively peaceful and comfortable. Surrounded by her retinue, she lived in the Novodevichii Monastery near Moscow. Lady Rondeau, the wife of the English Envoy to Russia, saw her

shortly before her death and even talked to the former Tsaritsa. In a letter to her girlfriend in England she wrote: "She has not forgotten her refined manners and conduct. Although she is aged now and quite stout, traces of beauty still remain in her features. Her face expresses importance and tranquillity together with gentleness, her eyes being unusually bright." *Russkaia starina,* vol. 11 (1874), p. 357.

12. *Russkaia starina,* vol. 5 (1872), pp. 805–806.

13. G. V. Esipov, "Zhizneopisanie kniazia A.D. Menshikova," in *Russkii arkhiv,* bk. 2 (1875), pp. 241–242.

14. *Pis'ma russkikh gosudarei i drugikh osob tsarskogo semeistva,* vol. 4 (Moscow, 1862), pp. 1.

15. *Arkhiv S.-Peterburgskogo filiala Instituta rossiiskoi istorii Rossiskoi akademii nauk* (SPFIRI), fund 270, file 114, p. 103.

16. *Pis'ma russkikh gosudarei,* p. 14.

17. Ibid.

18. Ibid., p. 22.

19. E. V. Anisimov, *Zhenshchiny na rossiiskom prestole* (St. Petersburg, 1997), p. 24.

20. *Zakonodatel'nye akty Petra I,* compiled by N. A. Voskresensky, vol. 1 (Moscow and Leningrad, 1945), pp. 179–180.

21. A. F. Bychkov, "O svad'be imperatora Petra Velikogo s Ekaterinoi Alexeevnoi," in *Drevniia i novaia Rossiia,* vol. 1 (1877), p. 324.

22. SIRIO, vol. 61, p. 145.

23. Petr Velikii, *Vospominaniia: Dnevnikovye zapisi. Anekdoty* (Paris, Moscow, and New York, 1993), p. 157.

24. Bassewitz, *Zapiski pri Petre Velikom,* p. 27.

25. *Pis'ma russkikh gosudarei,* p. 159.

26. Ibid., p. 70.

27. Ibid., p. 166.

28. Ibid., p. 76.

29. Ibid., p. 51.

30. N. G. Ustrialov, *Istoriia tsarstvovaniia Petra Velikogo,* vol. 6, pp. 346–348.

31. Ibid., pp. 497–498.

32. *Pis'ma russkikh gosudarei,* p. 51.

33. E. V. Anisimov, *Vremia petrovskikh reform* (Leningrad, 1989), p. 459.

34. F. W. Bergholtz, *Dnevnik kamer-iunkera,* pt. 4 (Moscow, 1860), p. 59.

35. SIRIO, vol. 52, p. 220.

36. Bassewitz, *Zapiski pri Petre Velikom,* p. 27.

37. *Pis'ma russkikh gosudarei,* p. 112.

38. Ibid., p. 43.

39. Ibid., p. 96.

40. Ibid., p. 45.

41. Ibid., p. 23.

42. Ibid., p. 97.

43. Ibid., p. 83.

44. Ibid., p. 84.

45. Ibid., p. 146.

46. SIRIO, vol. 66, p. 80.

47. Ibid., vol. 52, p. 359.

48. Bergholtz, *Dnevnik kamer-iunkera,* pt. 4, p. 118.

49. Velikii, *Vospominaniia,* p. 231.

50. E. V. Anisimov, *Rossiia bez Petra* (St. Petersburg, 1994), p. 61.

51. SIRIO, vol. 55, p. 350.

52. SIRIO, vol. 58, p. 104.

53. *Russkii arkhiv,* vol. 1 (1871), p. 514.

54. Anisimov, *Rossiia bez Petra,* p. 78.

55. "Kniga prikhodno-raskhodnykh komnatnykh deneg," in *Russkii arkhiv,* vol. 1 (1871), pp. 514–567.

56. Anisimov, *Zhenshchiny,* p. 58.

57. Ibid.

58. SIRIO, vol. 64, p. 481.

59. Ibid., vol. 66, pp. 83–84.

60. Ibid., p. 75.

61. Ibid., vol. 64, p. 548.

CHAPTER 2

1. SIRIO, vol. 5, p. 351.

2. D. A. Korsakov, *Votsarenie imperatritsy Anny Ioannovny* (Kazan', 1880), pp. 71–72.

3. Ibid.

4. Bergholtz, *Dnevnik kamer-iunkera,* pt. 3, p. 33.

5. Izdanie M. Mikhailova, *Sbornik istoricheskikh materialov i dokumentov, otnosiashchikhsia k novoi russkoi istorii XVIII i XIX veka* (St. Petersburg, 1873), pp. 10–11.

6. Korsakov, *Votsarenie imperatritsy Anny Ioannovny,* pp. 17–18.

7. Ibid., p. 19.

8. I. G. Korb, *Dnevnik puteshestviia v Moskoviiu* (St. Petersburg, 1906), p. 16.

9. Ibid.

10. *Pis'ma russkikh gosudarei,* pp. 41–42.

11. G. K. Kotoshikhin, *O Rossii v tsarstvovanie Alekseia Mikhailovicha* (St. Petersburg, 1906), p. 12.

12. M. I. Semevskii, *Tsaritsa Praskoviia* (Moscow, 1989), p. 41.

13. F. H. Weber, "Zapiski o Petre Velikom i ego preobrazovaniiakh," in *Russkii arkhiv,* vol. 4 (1872), pp. 1684–1688.

14. Semevskii, *Tsaritsa Praskoviia,* p. 46.

15. *Pis'ma russkikh gosudarei,* pp. 68–69.

16. T. Golikov, *Deianiia Petra Velikogo,* vol. 9 (Moscow, 1898), p. 529.

17. Semevskii, *Tsaritsa Praskoviia,* pp. 68–69.

18. *Pis'ma russkikh gosudarei,* p. 42.

19. S. M. Solov'ev, *Istoriia Rossii s drevneishikh vremen,* vol. 19 (Moscow, 1993), pp. 39–40.

20. Ibid., p. 37.

21. P. Shchebal'skii, "Kniaz' Menshikov i graf Morits Saksonskii v Kurliandii, 1726–1727," in *Russkii Vestnik,* vol. 25 (1860), p. 17.

22. M. M. Shcherbatov, *O povrezhdenii nravov v Rossii* (Moscow, 1983), p. 47.

23. *Pis'ma russkikh gosudarei,* pp. 211, 218.

24. Ibid., pp. 218–219.

25. Solov'ev, *Istoriia Rossii,* vol. 19, p. 131.

26. Ibid., pp. 132–133.

27. Ibid., pp. 131–132.

28. *Pis'ma russkikh gosudarei,* pp. 243–244, 253–254.

29. *Sbornik istoricheskikh materialov i dokumentov,* pp. 12–15.

30. Feofan Prokopovich, "O smerti Petra Vtorogo i o vosshestvii na prestol gosudaryni imperatritsy Anny Ioannovny," in *Moskovsky Vestnik,* pt. 1 (Moscow, 1830), p. 52.

31. Korsakov, *Votsarenie imperatritsy Anny Ioannovny,* p. 70.

32. *Chteniia Obschestva istorii i drevnostei rossiiskikh,* pt. 3 (1863), pp. 28–29.

33. Korsakov, *Votsarenie imperatritsy Anny Ioannovny,* p. 277.

34. Ibid., p. 274.

35. Ibid.

36. Ibid.

37. Anisimov, *Zhenshchiny,* p. 97.

38. *Bezvremen'e i vremenshchiki. Vospominanie ob epoche dvortsovykh perevorotov 1720s–1760s* (Leningrad, 1991), pp. 165, 262.

39. Duc de Liria, *Zapiski duka Lirriskoga* (Moscow, 1845), p. 114.

40. Anisimov, *Rossiia bez Petra,* p. 272.

41. Anisimov, *Zhenshchiny,* pp. 99–100.

42. Ibid., p. 100.

43. "Kniga zapisnaia," in *Chteniia obshestva istorii i drevnostei rossiiskikh,* vol. 1 (1878), 33, p. 11.

44. Ibid., p. 3.

45. Ibid., p. 124.

46. Ibid., p. 177.

47. Ibid., p. 134.

48. Korsakov, *Votsarenie imperatritsy Anny Ioannovny,* p. 274.

49. "Kniga zapisnaia," p. 200.

50. Ibid., p. 210.

51. Ibid., pp. 100–101.

52. Ibid, pp. 210–211.

53. I. E. Zabelin, *Domashnii byt russkikh tsarei v XVI–XVIII stoletiiakh* (Moscow, 1872), pp. 416–417.

54. Ibid.

55. "Kniga zapisnaia," p. 177.

56. Ibid.

57. Ibid., pp. 100–101.

58. Ibid., p. 135.

59. Anisimov, *Rossiia bez Petra,* p. 385.

60. *Bezvremen'e i vremenshchiki,* pp. 161–163.

61. Ibid., pp. 58–60.

62. Ibid., p. 60.

63. SIRIO, vol. 33, p. 475.

64. *Bezvremen'e i vremenshchiki,* pp. 58–60.

65. SIRIO, vol. 33, p. 502.

66. Ibid., vol. 124, pp. 159–160.

67. Anisimov, *Rossiia bez Petra,* p. 285.

68. Ibid., p. 284.

69. SIRIO, vol. 124, pp. 159–160.

70. "Kniga zapisnaia," p. 42.

71. P. Shakhovskoi, *Zapiski* (St. Petersburg, 1872), p. 17.

72. SIRIO, vol. 104, p. 510.

73. Korsakov, *Votsarenie imperatritsy Anny Ioannovny,* p. 155.

74. SIRIO, vol. 33, p. 466.

75. Ibid., p. 502.

76. Ibid., p. 483.

77. Korsakov, *Votsarenie imperatritsy Anny Ioannovny,* p. 83.

78. Solov'ev, *Istoriia Rossii,* vol. 20, pp. 345, 332.

79. Ibid., pp. 467–468.

80. N. N. Repin, *Vneshniaia torgovlia Rossii cherez Arkhangel'sk i Peterburg v 1700-nachale 60kh godov XVIII veka* (Leningrad, 1985), p. 523.

81. Anisimov, *Rossiia bez Petra,* p. 383.

82. *Bezvremen'e i vremenshchiki,* p. 269.

83. Ibid., p. 260.

84. Ibid., p. 272.

85. Anisimov, *Rossiia bez Petra,* p. 167.

86. G. V. Esipov, *Liudi starogo veka* (St. Petersburg, 1880), pp. 370–376.

87. Ibid., p. 376.

88. Anisimov, *Zhenshchiny,* pp. 141–142.

89. SIRIO, vol. 85, p. 24.

CHAPTER 3

1. Solov'ev, *Istoriia Rossii,* vol. 17, pp. 46–47.

2. *Zhurnal, ili podennaia zapiska Petra Velikogo,* pt. 2 (St. Petersburg, 1777), p. 100.

3. Bergholtz, *Dnevnik kamer-iunkera,* pt. 2, p. 206.

4. Liria de, "Pis'ma o Rossii," in *Osmnadtsatyi vek,* bk. 2 (Moscow, 1864), p. 100.

5. N. A. Voskresenskii, *Zakonodatel'nye akty Petra I* (Moscow and Leningrad, 1945), p. 162.

6. Perepiska: see *Pis'ma russkikh gosudarei,* vol. 2, pp. 35, 40.

7. Ibid., p. 40.

8. Ibid.

9. Ibid.

10. Ibid., p. 48.

11. Ibid., p. 50.

12. Ibid., p. 60.

13. Ibid., pp. 60–61.

14. Ibid., p. 62.

15. Ibid.

16. Bergholtz, *Dnevnik kamer-iunkera*, pt. 2, p. 206.

17. Ibid., p. 30.

18. Ibid., p. 240.

19. Ibid.

20. Ibid.

21. Rondeau, *Letters from a Lady Who Resided Some Years in Russia, to Her Friend in England* (London, 1777), pp. 205–206.

22. Ibid.

23. E. J. Biron, "Obstoiatel'stva, prigotovivshie opalu," in *Vremia,* vol. 6 (1861), p. 100.

24. Ibid.

25. SIRIO, vol. 75, p. 450.

26. Rondeau, *Letters,* p. 249.

27. Ibid., p. 206.

28. Ibid., pp. 205–206.

29. SIRIO, vol. 85, p. 162.

30. Anisimov, *Zhenshchiny,* p. 160.

31. Ibid., p. 163.

32. SIRIO, vol. 85, p. 236.

33. Ch. H. Manstein, *Zapiski o Rossii* (St. Petersburg, 1875), p. 198.

34. Ibid., pp. 361–362.

35. Ibid.

36. Ibid., pp. 199–200.

37. Ibid., pp. 203–204.

38. SIRIO, vol. 6, p. 100.

39. Ibid.

40. *Münnich Ebauch pour donner,* pp. 139–140.

41. Ibid.

42. Manstein, *Zapiski o Rossii,* p. 424.

43. SIRIO, vol. 85, p. 244.

44. E. Belov, "Otnoshenie Fridrikha II do vstupleniia ego na prestol k russkomu dvoru s 1737 po 1740 god," in DNP, vol. 2 (1875), p. 54.

45. P. Pekarskii, *Markiz de la Shetardi v Rossii. 1740–1742* (St. Petersburg, 1862), p. 416; SIRIO, vol. 96, pp. 629–630.

46. Ibid.

47. M. A. Korf, *Braunshveigskoe semeistvo* (Moskva 1993), pp. 108–109.

48. Ibid.

49. Ibid., p. 113.

50. Ibid., p. 120.

51. G. Brickner, "Imperator Ioann Antonovich i ego rodstvenniki," in *Russkii vestnik,* no. 9 (1874), p. 515.

52. E. V. Anisimov, *Elizaveta Petrovna* (Moscow, 1999), p. 76.

53. Brickner, "Imperator Ioann," p. 523.

54. Korf, *Braunshveigskoe semeistvo,* p. 109.

55. SIRIO, vol. 12, pp. 73–74.

56. "Priikliucheniia posadskogo cheloveka Ivana Subareva," in *Istoricheskie bumagi K. A. Arsen'eva* (St. Petersburg, 1875), pp. 375–376.

57. E. Kovalevskii, *Graf Bludov i ego vremia* (St. Petersburg, 1866), p. 229.

58. Ibid., p. 229.

59. Ibid.

60. Korf, *Braunshveigskoe semeistvo,* pp. 198–199.

61. Ibid.

62. Brickner, "Imperator Ioann," p. 526.

63. "Manifest imperatritsy Yekateriny II ob umershchvlenii printsa Ioanna Antonovicha," in *Chteniia Obshchestva istorii i drevnostei rossiiskikh pri Moskovskom universitete,* vol. 1 (1861), p. 183.

64. Brickner, "Imperator Ioann," p. 534.

65. Korff, *Braunshveigskoe semeistvo,* pp. 380–381.

66. Ibid.

67. Ibid., pp. 382–383.

68. Ibid., p. 382.

69. Ibid.

70. Ibid.

71. *Russkaia starina,* vol. 24 (1879), p. 542.

72. Ibid., pp. 411–412.

CHAPTER 4

1. Shakhovskoi, *Zapiski,* p. 30.

2. Ch. H. Manstein, *Memoires sur la Russie* (Leipzig, 1771), p. 415.

3. Pekarskii, *Markiz de la Shetardi v Rossii,* p. 264.

4. SIRIO, vol. 92, pp. 231–232.

5. "Kniaginia Angalt-Zerbstkaia Anna-Elizaveta, mat' Yekateriny Vtoroi," in *Russkii arkhiv,* vol. 2 (1904), p. 465.

6. SIRIO, vol. 92, pp. 228, 247.

7. V. V. Pochetnaia, *Petrovskaia tema v oratorskoi proze nachala 1770-kh godov, XVIII vek,* Sbornik statei (Leningrad, 1974), p. 334.

8. P. N. Petrov, *Tsarevna Anna Petrovna* (St. Petersburg, 1871), p. 54.

9. E. V. Anisimov, *Rossia v seredine XVIII veka. Bor'ba za nasledie Petra* (Moscow, 1986), p. 13.

10. *Pis'ma russkikh gosudarei,* vol. 1 (1861), p. 14.

11. SIRIO, vol. 49, pp. 324—325.

12. Rondeau, *Letters,* p. 26.

13. Liria, "Pis'ma o Rossii," pp. 118–119.

14. "Pis'ma k gosudarine tsarevne El. Mavry Shepelevoi," in *Chteniia Obshchestva istorii i drevnostei rossiiskikh,* vol. 2 (1864), pp. 67–72.

15. Rondeau, *Letters,* p. 83.

16. "Izlozhenie vin grafov Ostermana, Minikha, Golovkina i drugikh," in *Istoricheskie bumagi, sobrannye K.E. Arsen'evym* (St. Petersburg, 1872), p. 231.

17. Ibid.

18. A. N. Benois, *Tsarskoe Selo v tsarstvovanie imperatritsy Elizavety Petrovny* (St. Petersburg, 1910), p. 22.

19. Anisimov, *Elizaveta Petrovna,* p. 63.

20. "Cherty is zhizni Elizavety Petrovny," in *Russkii arkhiv,* vol. 1 (1865), pp. 329–330.

21. A. P. Sumarokov, *Polnoe sobranie vsekh sochinenii*, vol. 2 (Moscow, 1771), p. 18.

22. Liria, "Pis'ma o Rossii," pp. 34, 115.

23. Ekaterina II, *Mémoires*, vol. 1, p. 40.

24. J. L. Favier, "Zapiski," in *Istoricheskii vestnik*, vol. 29 (1887), p. 189.

25. Ibid.

26. *Kamer-fur'erskie zhurnaly 1750–1752*, p. 22.

27. Ibid., p. 10.

28. J. Stählin, "Zapiski o Petre Tret'em," in *Chteniia Obshchestva Istorii i drevnostei rossiiskikh*, bk. 4 (1866), p. 100.

29. *Russkii arkhiv*, vol. 16, pt. 1 (1878), pp. 10–15.

30. Ibid., p. 14.

31. Ibid.

32. Ekaterina II, *Mémoires*, vol. 1, p. 169.

33. *Arkhiv kniazia F. A. Vorontsova*, vol. 2 (Moscow, 1871), p. 617.

34. Rondeau, *Letters*, p. 106.

35. Favier, *Zapiski*, p. 385.

36. Ekaterina II, *Mémoires*, vol. 1, pp. 85–86.

37. I. Posier, "Zapiski pridvornogo brillianthshchika Poz'e o prebyvanii ego v Rossii," in *Russkaia starina*, vol. 1 (1870), p. 76.

38. Anisimov, *Rossiia v seredine XVIII veka*, p. 159.

39. A. N. Benois, *Tsarskoe Selo v tsarstvovanie imperatritsy Elizavety Petrovny* (St. Petersburg, 1910), pp. 59, 130–131, 141.

40. M. de la Messeliere, "Zapiski," in *Russkii arkhiv*, bk. 12 (1874), p. 970.

41. Ibid., p. 971.

42. Benois, *Tsarskoe Selo*, p. 145.

43. Ekaterina II, *Mémoires*, vol. 1, p. 255.

44. Anisimov, *Rossiia v seredine XVIII veka*, pp. 73–174.

45. J. Stählin, *Muzyka i balet v Rossii XVIII v.* (Moscow, 1935), p. 58.

46. Ibid.

47. F. Langa, "Rassuzhdenie o stsenicheskoi igre," in *Starinnyi spektakl' v Rossii* (Leningrad, 1918), pp. 141–174.

48. N. V. Gogol, *Sobranie sochinenii*, vol. 3 (Moscow, 1952), p. 8.

49. Anisimov, *Rossiia v seredine XVIII veka*, p. 49.

50. P. P. Cherkasov, *Dvuglavyi orel i korolevskie lilii* (Moscow, 1995), pp. 86–87.

51. SIRIO, vol. 6, p. 616.

52. Ibid., p. 618.

53. A. A. Vasil'chikov, *Semeistvo Razumovskikh*, vol. 1 (St. Petersburg, 1880), pp. 47–48.

54. Ekaterina II, *Mémoires*, vol. 1, p. 272.

55. Ibid., pp. 106–107.

56. Pis'mak Shuvalovu, *Russkii arkhiv*, vol. 2 (1864), p. 1844.

57. *Novye teksty perepiski Vol'tera* (Leningrad, 1970), p. 62.

58. "Pis'ma Shuvalova k sestre ego rodnoi P.I. Golitsynoi," in *Moskvitianin*, vol. 5 (1845), p. 140.

59. "Pis'ma I. I. Shuvalova k grafu M. I. Vorontsovu," in *Russkii arkhiv*, bk. 7 (1870), p. 1396.

60. Favier, *Zapiski*, p. 392.

61. *Arkhiv Vorontsovykh*, vol. 6, p. 290.

62. Ibid., p. 299.

63. Favier, *Zapiski*, p. 392.

64. *Iz proizvedenii russkikh myslitelei vtoroi poloviny XVIII veka* (Moscow, 1952), p. 92.

65. I. F. Timkovskii, "Zapiski," in *Ruskii arkhiv*, bk. 6 (1874), pp. 1455–1456.

66. M. V. Lomonosov, *Polnoe sobranie sochinenii*, vol. 10, p. 546.

67. *Arkhiv Vorontsovykh*, vol. 6, p. 287.

68. Ibid.

69. Favier, *Zapiski*, p. 394.

70. Ekaterina II, *Zapiski* (St. Petersburg, 1907), pp. 531–532.

71. SIRIO, vol. 52, p. 100.

72. Ekaterina II, *Mémoires*, vol. 1, pp. 47–48.

73. Favier, *Zapiski*, p. 389.

74. *Arkhiv Vorontsovykh*, vol. 6, pp. 353–354.

75. G. V. Esipov, "Van'ka Kain," in *Osmnadtsatyi vek*, bk. 3 (Moscow, 1869), pp. 280–342.

76. F.-H. Lafermière, "Russkii dvor v 1761 godu," in *Russkaia starina*, vol. 22 (1879), p. 194.

77. *Polnoe sobranie zakonov Rossiiskoi imperii*, vol. 14, no. 10650 (St. Petersburg, 1838).

78. *Russkii arkhiv*, vol. 2 (1878), p. 386.

79. Lafermière, "Russkii," pp. 194–195.

80. *Russkii arkhiv*, vol. 7 (1907), p. 348.

81. V. A. Bil'basov, *Istoriia Ekateriny II*, vol. 2 (Berlin, 1900), p. 453.

CHAPTER 5

1. Comte De Sègur, *Mémoires ou souvenirs et anecdotes*, vol. 2. (Paris, 1826), p. 223.

2. SIRIO, vol. 23, p. 432.

3. *Istoricheskii vestnik*, vol. 29 (1887), p. 100.

4. Ibid., p. 226.

5. *Russkii arkhiv*, vol. 3 (1878), p. 153.

6. SIRIO, vol. 10, p. 103.

7. Ibid., vol. 23, p. 1.

8. Ekaterina II, *Mémoires*, vol. 1, p. 5.

9. SIRIO, vol. 23, p. 51.

10. Ibid., p. 72.

11. Ekaterina II, *Mémoires*, vol. 1, p. 8.

12. Ibid.

13. Ibid., p. 45.

14. Ibid., p. 30.

15. Ibid., pp. 36–37.
16. Ibid., p. 55.
17. Ibid., pp. 62–63.
18. Ibid., pp. 66–67.
19. *Russkii arkhiv*, vol. 16 (1888), p. 5.
20. *Arkhiv kniazia F. A. Vorontsova*, vol. 2, pp. 104–111.
21. Ekaterina II, *Mémoires*, vol. 1, p. 45.
22. Ibid., p. 86.
23. SIRIO, vol. 10, p. 164.
24. Ekaterina II, *Mémoires*, vol. 1, p. 75.
25. Ibid., p. 75.
26. Ibid., p. 58.
27. Ibid., p. 102.
28. Ibid., p. 86.
29. Ibid., p. 101.
30. Ibid., p. 45.
31. SIRIO, vol. 42, p. 166.
32. Ekaterina II, *Mémoires*, vol. 1, pp. 314–315.
33. *Russkii arkhiv*, vol. 7 (1912), p. 321.
34. Ekaterina II, *Mémoires*, vol. 1, p. 60.
35. P. S. Sumarokov, "Cherty Ekateriny Velikoi," in *Russkii arkhiv*, vol. 11 (1870), p. 2082.
36. V. A. Bil'basov, *Ekaterina Vtoraia*, vol. 1 (St. Petersburg, 1890), p. 231.
37. *Russkii arkhiv*, vol. 3 (1873), pp. 336–337.
38. SIRIO, vol. 23, p. 694.
39. *Russkii arkhiv*, vol. 228 (March 1909), p. 25.
40. SIRIO, vol. 13, p. 97.
41. Ibid., vol. 7, p. 79.
42. *Istoricheskii vestnik*, vol. 29, p. 389.
43. "Iz diplomaticheskoi perepiski o Rossii XVIII veka," in *Russkaia starina*, vol. 84 (1895), pp. 110, 115.
44. Ibid., p. 119.
45. Sègur, *Mémoires*, vol. 2, p. 138.
46. Ibid.
47. "Iz diplomaticheskoi perepiski," p. 117.
48. V. A. Bil'basov, *Istoriia Ekateriny Vtoroi* (London, 1895), p. 20.
49. Ibid., p. 21.
50. Ibid., p. 85.
51. *Russkii arkhiv*, vol. 2 (1907), p. 193.
52. Ibid., p. 22.
53. Ibid.
54. Ibid.
55. Ibid., p. 24.
56. Ibid., p. 25.
57. Ibid.
58. Korf M. Braunshveigskoe semeistvo, (Moscow, 1993), p. 215.
59. *Russkii arkhiv*, vol. 5 (1911), p. 25.

60. "Zapiski pridvornogo brilliantshchika Poz'e o prebyvanii ego v Rossii," in *Russkaia starina,* vol. 1 (1870), pp. 112–113.

61. *Russkii arkhiv,* vol. 12 (1909), p. 396.

62. *Russkaia starina,* vol. 85 (1896), p. 127.

63. "Iz diplomaticheskoi perepiski," p. 127.

64. Ibid.

65. SIRIO, vol. 27, p. 180.

66. "Iz diplomaticheskoi perepiski," p. 127.

67. SIRIO, vol. 7, p. 83.

68. "Manifest imperatritsy," pp. 183–185.

69. Korff, *Braunshveigskoe semeistvo,* p. 230.

70. Bil'basov, *Ekaterina Vtoraia,* vol. 2, pp. 320–321.

71. Ibid.

72. Ibid.

73. SIRIO, vol. 7, pp. 365–366.

74. N. Grigorovich, "Kantsler kniaz Bezborodko," in *Russkii arkhiv,* vol. 1 (1877), p. 23.

75. *Russkaia starina,* vol. 77 (1893), p. 516.

76. SIRIO, vol. 23, p. 166.

77. From the letters of 1770s. SIRIO, vol. 23, p. 58.

78. Letter to Grimm of December 7, 1779. SIRIO, vol. 23, p. 166.

79. "Pis'ma Ekateriny Vtoroi r baronu Grimmu," in *Russkii arkhiv,* vol. 2 (1878), p. 61.

80. "Sobstvennoruchnye pis'ma imperatritsy Ekateriny II-i r grafu Ivanu Grigor'evichu Chernyshovu," in *Russkii arkhiv,* vol. 1 (1871), p. 1324.

81. SIRIO, vol. 23, pp. 607–608.

82. "Nravstvennye idealy Ekateriny II," in *Russkii arkhiv,* vol. 1 (1863), p. 380.

83. "Pis'mo imperatritsy Ekateriny II-i kniaziu Dolgorukomu-Krymskomu ot 17 iiulia 1771 goda," in *Russkii arkhiv,* vol. 1 (1871), pp. 1348–1350.

84. Sègur, *Mémoires,* vol. 3, pp. 307–308.

85. *Russkaia starina,* vol. 10 (1871), p. 775.

86. SIRIO, vol. 2, p. 333.

87. "Pis'ma imperatritsy Ekateriny Velikoi k feld'marshalu Petru Semenovichu Saltykovu. 1762–1771," in *Russkii arkhiv,* vol. 3 (1886), p. 87.

88. SIRIO, vol. 23, p. 608.

89. *Russkii arkhiv,* vol. 2 (1907), p. 192.

90. SIRIO, vol. 7, p. 345.

91. "Pis'ma Ekateriny II-i k grafu Ya. E. Siversu," in *Russkii arkhiv,* vol. 1 (1870), p. 1422.

92. Ibid., pp. 1435–1436.

93. Ibid.

94. "Imperatritsa Ekaterina II. Sobstvennoruchnye poveleniia, pis'ma i zametki. 1770–1792," in *Russkaia starina,* vol. 14 (1875), pp. 444–445.

95. SIRIO, vol. 23, p. 56.

96. Ibid.

97. SIRIO, p. 255.

98. Ibid., p. 275.

99. "Iz diplomaticheskoi perepiski o Rossii XVIII veka," in *Russkaia starina*, vol. 86 (1898), pp. 1772–1773.

100. "Graf Dzhon Bekingkhemshir pri dvore Ekateriny II (1762–1765)," in *Russkaia starina*, vol. 3 (1902), p. 650.

101. SIRIO, vol. 23, p. 4.

102. "Zapisochka Ekateriny II-i k kniaziu Potemkinu," in *Russkii arkhiv*, vol. 3 (1875), pp. 253–254.

103. Sègur, *Mémoires*, vol. 3, p. 246.

104. "Ekaterina i Potemkin. Podlinnaia ikh perepiska," in *Russkaia starina*, vol. 16 (1876), pp. 241, 244.

105. SIRIO, vol. 42, p. 13.

106. "Puteshestvennik, videvshii G. Potemkina," in *Russkaia starina*, vol. 22 (1878), p. 332.

107. Sègur, *Mémoires*, vol. 3, p. 433.

108. "Puteshestvennik," p. 332.

109. Sègur, *Mémoires*, vol. 3, pp. 344–345.

110. Ibid., vol. 2, pp. 260, 263–264.

111. SIRIO, vol. 23, p. 70.

112. A. G. Brikner, *Potemkin* (St. Petersburg, 1891), pp. 65–66.

113. *Russkii arkhiv*, vol. 3 (1907), p. 246.

114. Ibid., vol. 3 (1878), p. 77.

115. SIRIO, vol. 23, p. 648.

116. Sègur, *Mémoires*, vol. 3, pp. 210–211.

117. SIRIO, vol. 7, p. 83.

118. *Russkii arkhiv*, vol. 11 (1870), p. 2082.

119. SIRIO, vol. 42, p. 172.

120. Sègur, *Mémoires*, vol. 3, p. 223.

121. *Russkaia starina*, vol. 17 (1876), p. 638.

122. SIRIO, vol. 7, pp. 345–346.

123. Sègur, *Mémoires*, vol. 3, p. 192.

124. SIRIO, vol. 23, p. 93.

125. Ibid. pp. 104–105.

126. *Russkii arkhiv*, no. 7 (1912), p. 329.

127. Ibid.

128. Ibid., no. 7 (1877), p. 292.

129. Sègur, *Mémoires*, vol. 3, p. 42.

130. Ibid., pp. 42–43.

131. SIRIO, vol. 23, p. 3.

132. Ibid., p. 17.

133. Sègur, *Mémoires*, vol. 3, pp. 37, 38.

134. *Russkii arkhiv*, no. 3 (1878), p. 15.

135. Sègur, *Mémoires*, vol. 3, p. 23.

136. *Russkii arkhiv*, vol. 3, p. 16.

137. Sègur, *Mémoires*, vol. 3, p. 23.

138. "Pis'ma imperatritsy Ekateriny II k gospozhe Jeoffrin," in SIRIO, vol. 1, p. 260.

139. Ibid.

140. *Russkii arkhiv*, vol. 7 (1877), p. 284.

141. SIRIO, vol. 27, pp. 189, 394.

142. *Russkii arkhiv*, vol. 3 (1878), p. 46.

143. SIRIO, vol. 23, p. 83.

144. "Dva pis'ma o Rossii i ob Ekaterine Velikoi (Iz bumag gospodina Rulhièra," in *Arkhiv kn. F. A. Vorontsova*, vol. 25 (Moscow, 1882), p. 442.

145. *Russkii arkhiv*, vol. 228 (1909), p. 25.

146. SIRIO, vol. 10, p. 353.

147. Valishevsky, *Roman odnoi imperatritsy. Ekaterina Vtoraia* (Moscow, 1908), p. 77.

148. SIRIO, vol. 10, p. 358.

149. *Russkii arkhiv*, vol. 4 (1864), p. 401.

150. SIRIO, vol. 10, pp. 358, 383.

151. *Russkii arkhiv*, vol. 3 (1878), p. 61.

152. Sègur, *Mémoires*, vol. 3, p. 211.

153. SIRIO, vol. 7, p. 6; *Russkaia starina*, vol. 88 (1896), p. 428.

154. *Russkii arkhiv*, vol. 3 (1866), p. 406.

155. *Russkii arkhiv*, vol. 2 (1884), p. 270.

156. *Russkaia starina*, vol. 87 (1896), p. 255.

157. Ibid., vol. 88, p. 255.

158. *Russkii arkhiv*, vol. 1 (1863), p. 418.

159. Ibid., vol. 1 (1878), p. 139.

160. SIRIO, vol. 7, p. 382.

161. *Russkii arkhiv*, no. 3 (1866), p. 422.

162. Ibid., no. 3 (1886), pp. 51–52.

163. Sègur, *Mémoires*, vol. 3, p. 495.

164. *Russkii arkhiv*, vol. 5 (1911), p. 107.

165. Ibid., vol. 1 (1878), p. 55.

166. SIRIO, vol. 23, pp. 244–245.

167. Ibid., p. 264.

168. Ibid., pp. 316–317.

169. Ibid., p. 392.

170. Ibid., p. 398.

171. *Russkaia starina*, vol. 17 (1876), p. 34.

172. Ibid., p. 34.

173. SIRIO, vol. 42, p. 28.

174. Ibid., p. 35.

175. Ibid., p. 38.

176. Ibid.

177. *Russkii arkhiv*, vol. 3 (1878), p. 16.

178. Ibid., p. 57.

179. SIRIO, vol. 27, pp. 301–303.

180. Ibid., vol. 23, p. 574.

181. Ibid., p. 555.

182. *Russkaia starina*, vol. 108 (1901), p. 79.

183. *Russkaia starina*, vol. 18 (1877), p. 412.

184. *Russkii arkhiv*, vol. 3 (1873), p. 209; SIRIO, vol. 23, pp. 591–592.

185. SIRIO, vol. 23, pp. 587–588.

186. Ibid., p. 186.

187. "Dostopamiatnyi razgovor Ekateriny Velikoi s kniazhnoi Dashkovoi," in *Russkii arkhiv*, vol. 2 (1884), p. 270.

188. P. P. "Platon Aleksandrovich Zubov," in *Russkaia starina*, vol. 17 (1876), pp. 453–454.

189. *Russkii arkhiv*, vol. 3 (1878), p. 7.

Index

Italicized page numbers indicate an illustration.

About the Author and the Translator

EVGENII V. ANISIMOV teaches at the Institute of History, St. Petersburg, Russia. He is the author of *The Reforms of Peter the Great* (1993).

KATHLEEN CARROLL is an American who has lived and taught in St. Petersburg, Russia.